Register for Free Membership to

solutions@syngress.com

Over the last few years, Syngress has published many best-selling and critically acclaimed books, including Tom Shinder's *Configuring ISA Server 2004*, Brian Caswell and Jay Beale's *Snort 2.1 Intrusion Detection*, and Angela Orebaugh and Gilbert Ramirez's *Ethereal Packet Sniffing*. One of the reasons for the success of these books has been our unique **solutions@syngress.com** program. Through this site, we've been able to provide readers a real time extension to the printed book.

As a registered owner of this book, you will qualify for free access to our members-only solutions@syngress.com program. Once you have registered, you will enjoy several benefits, including:

- Four downloadable e-booklets on topics related to the book. Each booklet is approximately 20-30 pages in Adobe PDF format. They have been selected by our editors from other best-selling Syngress books as providing topic coverage that is directly related to the coverage in this book.

- A comprehensive FAQ page that consolidates all of the key points of this book into an easy-to-search web page, providing you with the concise, easy-to-access data you need to perform your job.

- A "From the Author" Forum that allows the authors of this book to post timely updates and links to related sites, or additional topic coverage that may have been requested by readers.

Just visit us at **www.syngress.com/solutions** and follow the simple registration process. You will need to have this book with you when you register.

Thank you for giving us the opportunity to serve your needs. And be sure to let us know if there is anything else we can do to make your job easier.

SYNGRESS®

CONFIGURING
Check Point
NGX
VPN-1/FireWall-1

Robert Stephens

Barry J. Stiefel

Stephen Watkins

Simon Desmeules   Technical Editor

Eli Faskha   Assistant Technical Editor

FOREWORD BY
DAMEON D.
WELCH-ABERNATHY
A.K.A. PHONEBOY

KEY	SERIAL NUMBER
001	HJIRTCV764
002	PO9873D5FG
003	829KM8NJH2
004	JKBBBXZ349
005	CVPLQ6WQ23
006	VBP965T5T5
007	HJJJ863WD3E
008	2987GVTWMK
009	629MP5SDJT
010	IMWQ295T6T

PUBLISHED BY
Syngress Publishing, Inc.
800 Hingham Street
Rockland, MA 02370

Configuring Check Point NGX VPN-1/FireWall-1

Printed in Canada
    4 5 6 7 8 9 0
ISBN13: 978-1-59749-031-3
ISBN10: 1-59749-031-8

Publisher: Andrew Williams   Page Layout and Art: Patricia Lupien
Acquisitions Editor: Gary Byrne   Copy Editors: Adrienne Rebello and Judy Eby
Technical Editor: Simon Desmeules   Indexer: Odessa&Cie
Assistant Technical Editor: Eli Faskha   Cover Designer: Michael Kavish

Distributed by O'Reilly Media, Inc. in the United States and Canada.

For information on rights and translations, contact Matt Pedersen, Director of Sales and Rights, at Syngress Publishing; email matt@syngress.com or fax to 781-681-3585.

Acknowledgments

Syngress would like to acknowledge the following people for their kindness and support in making this book possible.

Syngress books are now distributed in the United States and Canada by O'Reilly Media, Inc. The enthusiasm and work ethic at O'Reilly are incredible, and we would like to thank everyone there for their time and efforts to bring Syngress books to market: Tim O'Reilly, Laura Baldwin, Mark Brokering, Mike Leonard, Donna Selenko, Bonnie Sheehan, Cindy Davis, Grant Kikkert, Opol Matsutaro, Steve Hazelwood, Mark Wilson, Rick Brown, Leslie Becker, Jill Lothrop, Tim Hinton, Kyle Hart, Sara Winge, C. J. Rayhill, Peter Pardo, Leslie Crandell, Regina Aggio, Pascal Honscher, Preston Paull, Susan Thompson, Bruce Stewart, Laura Schmier, Sue Willing, Mark Jacobsen, Betsy Waliszewski, Dawn Mann, Kathryn Barrett, John Chodacki, Rob Bullington, and Aileen Berg.

The incredibly hardworking team at Elsevier Science, including Jonathan Bunkell, Ian Seager, Duncan Enright, David Burton, Rosanna Ramacciotti, Robert Fairbrother, Miguel Sanchez, Klaus Beran, Emma Wyatt, Chris Hossack, Krista Leppiko, Marcel Koppes, Judy Chappell, Radek Janousek, and Chris Reinders for making certain that our vision remains worldwide in scope.

David Buckland, Marie Chieng, Lucy Chong, Leslie Lim, Audrey Gan, Pang Ai Hua, Joseph Chan, and Siti Zuraidah Ahmad of STP Distributors for the enthusiasm with which they receive our books.

David Scott, Tricia Wilden, Marilla Burgess, Annette Scott, Andrew Swaffer, Stephen O'Donoghue, Bec Lowe, Mark Langley, and Anyo Geddes of Woodslane for distributing our books throughout Australia, New Zealand, Papua New Guinea, Fiji, Tonga, Solomon Islands, and the Cook Islands.

Contributing Authors

Ralph Bonnell (CISSP, Linux LPIC-2, Check Point CCSI, Check Point CCSE+, Cisco CCNA, Microsoft MCSE: Security, RSA Security RSA/CSE, StoneSoft CSFE, Aladdin eSCE, CipherTrust PCIA, ArcSight ACIA, SurfControl STAR, McAfee MIPS-I, McAfee MIPS-E, Network Associates SCP, Blue Coat BSPE, Sygate SSEI, Sygate SSEP, Aventail ACP, Radware CRIE) is a Senior Information Security Consultant currently employed at SiegeWorks in Seattle, WA. Ralph has been working with Check Point products professionally since 1999. His primary responsibilities include the deployment of various network security products, network security product support, and product training. His specialties include Check Point and NetScreen deployments, Linux client and server deployments, Check Point training, firewall clustering, BASH scripting, and PHP Web programming. Ralph contributed to *Configuring Netscreen Firewalls* (Syngress Publishing, ISBN: 1-932266-39-9). Ralph also runs a Linux consulting firm called Linux Friendly. Ralph is married to his beautiful wife, Candace. In memory of Vincent Sage Bonnell.

Larry Chaffin (CISSP, PMP, JNCIE, MBCP, CWNP, NNCSE, NNCDE, CCNP, CCDP, CCNP-WAN, CCDP-WAN) is the CEO/Chairman of Pluto Networks and the Vice President of Advanced Network Technologies for Plannet Group. He is an accomplished author; he cowrote *Managing Cisco Network Security* (ISBN: 1-931836-56-6) and has also been a coauthor/ghost writer for 11 other technology books for VoIP, WLAN, security, and optical technologies. Larry has more than 29 vendor certifications such as the ones already listed, plus Cisco VoIP, Optical, Security, VPN, IDS, Unity and WLAN. He is also certified by Nortel in DMS Carrier Class Switches along with CS100'S, MCS5100, Call Pilot, and WLAN. Many other certifications come from vendors like

Microsoft, VMware, PeopleSoft, Avaya, IBM, and HP. Larry has been a Principal Architect around the world in 22 countries for many Fortune 100 companies designing VoIP, Security, WLAN, and optical networks. His next project is to write a book on Nortel VoIP and a new security architecture book he has designed for VoIP and WLAN networks.

Simon Coffey (CISSP, CCSE, CCSA) has eight years' experience working with Check Point products, providing support, training, and consultancy services. He is currently based in Reading, UK, working as a Support Consultant with Integralis, a security systems integrator. He is also a member of the Theale Volunteer Networking Group. Simon was a contributor to *Check Point NG VPN-1/FireWall-1 Advanced Configuration and Troubleshooting* (Syngress, ISBN: 1-931836-97-3) and coauthor of *Check Point NG VPN-1/FireWall-1 High Availability & Clustering* e-book (Syngress). More recently, he has been involved in testing of the early availability release of NGX.

Chris Geffel (CISSP) is a Manager of Operations at VigilantMinds, Inc., a national managed security services provider (MSSP), headquartered in Pittsburgh, PA. Chris is responsible for overseeing VigilantMinds' Secure Network Services, which include managed firewall and managed Cisco solutions. He has more than 10 years of professional experience in information systems, seven of which have been focused on information security.

Stephen Horvath (CISSP) is an Information Assurance Engineer for Booz Allen Hamilton in Linthicum, MD. He has been working with Check Point Firewalls for the last seven years, including Check Point 3.0b, 4.1, NG with Application Intelligence, and NGX. Steve was also a beta tester for Check Point's Edge SOHO devices prior to their release in early 2004. Steve's technical background is with computer and network forensics, firewalls, enterprise management, network and host IDS/IPS, incident response, UNIX system administration, and DNS management. He has extensive experience in network design with emphasis on high availability, security, and enterprise resilience.

Eric Seagren (CISA, CISSP-ISSAP, SCNP, CCNA, MCSE, CNE) has nine years of experience in the computer industry, with the last seven years spent in the financial services industry working for a Fortune 100 company. Eric started his computer career working on Novell servers and performing general network troubleshooting for a small Houston-based company. While Eric has been working in the financial services industry, his responsibilities have included server administration, disaster recovery, business continuity coordination, Y2K remediation, and network vulnerability assessment. He has spent the last several years as an IT architect and risk analyst, designing and evaluating secure, scalable, and redundant networks. Eric has also been the technical editor and coauthor of several other publications.

Robert Stephens (CISSP, CCSE+, NSA, NSA-IAM) was a contributor to *Check Point NG VPN-1/FireWall-1 Advanced Configuration and Troubleshooting* (Syngress, ISBN: 1-931836-97-3). Robert is a Senior Security Consultant at VigilantMinds Inc., a national managed security services provider (MSSP), headquartered in Pittsburgh, PA. Current work responsibilities focus on his firewall expertise. He has more than a decade of experience in network design, implementation, and security. Robert holds a bachelor's degree in Criminology from the University of Pittsburgh and a master's degree in Management Information Systems from Duquesne University.

Barry J. Stiefel ("Stee–ful") (CCSA/CCSE/CCSE+/CCSI, CISSP, NSA IAM, MCSE, CCNA, RCSA/RCSE/RCSI, FCSE) is the Founder and President of CPUG, The Check Point User Group (www.cpug.org). He's been a Check Point implementer, consultant, courseware developer, author, speaker, and instructor since 1997 and provides the only Check Point training course that includes earning the CCSA and CCSE certifications right in the classroom.

He is coauthor on *CCSA Next Generation Check Point Certified Security Administrator Study Guide* and *Check Point NG VPN-1/FireWall-1: Advanced Configuration and Troubleshooting*, both by Syngress Publishing. He is also the President of Information Engine, Inc. (www.InformationEngine.com), a consulting and technical services firm, and was previously the President of the Windows NT Engineering Association.

He holds a B.S. and MBA from the University of California. He lives and works in San Francisco. In his lab, he has more firewalls and routers than he needs, but not as many as he wants.

Stephen Watkins (CISSP) is an Information Security Professional with more than 10 years of relevant technology experience, devoting eight of these years to the security field. He currently serves as Information Assurance Analyst at Regent University in southeastern Virginia. Before coming to Regent, he led a team of security professionals providing in-depth analysis for a global-scale government network. Over the last eight years, he has cultivated his expertise with regard to perimeter security and multilevel security architecture. His Check Point experience dates back to 1998 with FireWall-1 version 3.0b. He has earned his B.S. in Computer Science from Old Dominion University and M.S. in Computer Science, with Concentration in Infosec, from James Madison University. He is nearly a lifelong resident of Virginia Beach, where he and his family remain active in their church and the local Little League.

Technical Editor

Simon Desmeules (CCSI, ISS, RSA, CCNA, CNA) is the
Technical Security Director of AVANCE Network Services, an
Assystem company with more than 8,500 employees worldwide.
AVANCE is located in Montreal, Canada. His responsibilities
include architectural design, technical consulting, and tactical emer-
gency support for perimeter security technologies for several
Fortune 500 companies in Canada, France, and the United States.
Simon has been delivering Check Point training for the past three
years throughout Canada. His background includes positions as a
firewall/intrusion security specialist for pioneer firms of Canadian
Security, Maxon Services, and SINC. He is an active member of the
FW-1, ISS, and Snort mailing lists where he discovers new problems
and consults with fellow security specialists. Simon has worked with
Syngress before while contributing to *Check Point Next Generation
Security Administration* (Syngress, ISBN: 1-928994-74-1) and *Check
Point Next Generation with Application Intelligence Security
Administration* (Syngress, ISBN: 1-932266-89-5).

He would like to thank all of the students who have passed
through his classroom and who have always brought new ideas and
challenges. Des remerciements particuliers aux étudiants du Québec.

Assistant Technical Editor

Eli Faskha (CCSI, CCSA, CCSE, CCSE+, CCAE, MCP). Based in Panama City, Panama, Eli is Founder and President of Soluciones Seguras, a company that specializes in network security and is the only Check Point Gold Partner in Central America and the only Nokia Internet Security partner in Panama. Eli is the most experienced Check Point Certified Security Instructor and Nokia Instructor in the region. He has taught participants from more than a dozen different countries. A 1993 graduate of the University of Pennsylvania's Wharton School and Moore School of Engineering, he also received an MBA from Georgetown University in 1995. He has more than seven years of Internet development and networking experience, starting with Web development of the largest Internet portal in Panama in 1999 and 2000, managing a Verisign affiliate in 2001, and running his own company since then. Eli has written several articles for the local media and has been recognized for his contributions to Internet development in Panama. He can be reached at eli@solucionesseguras.com.

Contents

Chapter 12 SecuRemote, SecureClient, and Integrity . 397

Foreword

Writing a book is hard. Writing a book about Check Point products is even harder. I should know; I did it twice. By myself. With a manual typewriter. In the snow. Barefoot. It was uphill both ways. And I liked it. Okay, maybe it didn't happen quite that way, but writing a book on Check Point is hard.

Why is it hard? Because the product contains so much information now, getting all the details down on paper is nearly impossible. Check Point's official documentation has grown more and more over the years, and it is now thousands of pages long. I remember the days when the product had one manual and even came on floppy disks!

I am the person behind a FireWall-1 FAQ page that used to exist on www.phoneboy.com. As of August 2005 the FireWall-1 FAQ page moved to www.cpug.org. It has been used by thousands of administrators over the years. I started the FireWall-1 FAQ page primarily because an obvious need emerged at the time for a public information source about FireWall-1. Check Point certainly wasn't providing it. The official documentation was abysmal.

Being a technical support engineer responsible for supporting the product at the time, I knew something about it. I could write in a way that people could understand, but what's more important, I was passionate about educating people about FireWall-1. My FireWall-1 FAQ page was born as PhoneBoy's FireWall-1 FAQs. My involvement with this Web site eventually led to the creation of a moderated mailing list and writing two books: one on FireWall-1 4.1 and another on VPN-1/FireWall-1 NG.

Because I have this kind of history, you might be wondering why I'm writing a foreword for a book on Check Point NGX instead of writing a book myself. Two important things happened in my life: My passion moved on to another product, and my job took me away from the day-to-day technical issues of Check Point products.

In the summer of 2004, I first became aware of Barry Stiefel and CPUG, the Check Point User Group (www.cpug.org). Meeting Barry ultimately led to two things: donating the bulk of my Check Point content to CPUG and writing this foreword.

When I began writing my first Check Point book, I was not the only person who had set out to write the book. However, I ended up being the only author remaining on the project, so it took much longer to complete the book than I initially had thought. Fortunately, one person could cover all the details about the 4.1 version of the product—barely.

When I set out to do a book on NG, I realized the product had grown quite a bit since 4.1. Because I was one person with limited time, and there were definitely a few parts of the product I didn't know as well as others, I know that I either ignored those parts of the product or didn't do the subjects justice.

I could not imagine tackling the NGX product on my own, even if I were still up-to-date on all the technical issues. Because NGX contains so many more features than previous releases, Chapter 2 of this book is dedicated to providing an overview of all of them.

I think Syngress Publishing has gathered a fine group of authors to write this book. After reading this book, you should have the information you'll need to get NGX up and running in your network.

—*Dameon D. Welch-Abernathy*
a.k.a. PhoneBoy
September 2005

Chapter 1

Introduction to Firewalls and VPN-1/FireWall-1

Solutions in this chapter:

- **History of Firewalls**
- **Firewall Innovations**
- **Packet Filters**
- **Application Layer Gateways**
- **Stateful Inspection**
- **Perimeter, Internal, and Web Security**
- **Inspect Script**
- **FireWall-1 Decision Making**

☑ **Summary**

☑ **Solutions Fast Track**

☑ **Frequently Asked Questions**

Introduction

Check Point FireWall-1 came out in 1994 and was an immediate success. It has been the market-leading firewall platform for over 10 years. It is no wonder the platform has done so well. The Check Point Graphical User Interface for managing firewall policies is extremely intuitive and easy to learn.

Check Point has come a long way since 1994. The first version of FireWall-1 ran only on the Sun Solaris operating system platform. Every year since then new features have been added to the product to keep up with emerging threats. In 1996 a Windows NT version was introduced. An alliance with Nokia, a network security hardware vendor, proved a perfect match and the hardware appliances are very popular. A Linux version arrived in 2002 and since then Check Point has released a hardened operating system specifically made for FireWall-1, and named it SecurePlatform.

Chapter 1 is a good starting point for new and existing VPN-1/FireWall-1 users alike. This chapter will discuss the various methods that are deployed among different firewall vendors and open source solutions. It is important to know the differences among firewall technologies to further comprehend the advantages of Check Point VPN-1/FireWall-1. This chapter will discuss the advantages and disadvantages of each technology with a strong focus on Stateful Inspection, which VPN-1/FireWall-1 utilizes.

History of Firewalls

In the beginning of the Internet there were no firewalls. Computers on the network were directly connected to the Internet and everything seemed to be fine—until November 2, 1998, that is. On that day the Morris worm, the first worm virus, hit the Internet. It was around that time network administrators started to take network security seriously.

Now the Internet is a very dangerous place to be in without protection. Popular operating system vendors are announcing patches for vulnerabilities on an almost daily basis. Fortunately, there are ways to protect servers and workstations from attacks before hackers exploit those vulnerabilities.

Why Firewalls Began

After several security-related Internet newsgroups started overflowing with posts, it became clear something had to be done to help secure networks. The first firewalls were implemented in routers between different segments of the network. These firewalls were basically ACLs (access control lists) in routers.

Slowly firewall technology started to evolve. Early firewall technology, known as packet filtering, was not enough to stop the constant attacks. The firewall had to be more intelligent and understand the different protocols.

Types of Firewalls

There are several different types of firewalls currently available on the market. The most basic type, the packet filter, is built into almost every router on the market today. A second generation of firewalls, called application layer gateway firewalls, or proxies, added yet another layer of security to networks. When Check Point announced Stateful Inspection it started a new era of firewall technology.

In addition to perimeter firewalls, client side firewalls are becoming more common. The latest version of Microsoft Windows XP, Service Pack 2, has a firewall built into the operating system. The Check Point SecureClient VPN software has extensive firewall capabilities built into it as well.

Notes from the Underground...

What Are We Protecting?

It is a fact that most intrusions into corporate networks come from inside the network. Employee theft of data happens often. Keep in mind a firewall can protect only data that goes through it. If a server contains critical data, it might be a good idea to put a firewall in front of that server or connect it to an unused interface on an existing firewall.

Most hackers attempt to bypass the firewall when they attack your network. They use an unsecured wireless access point or a modem connection that is directly connected to the outside world. When designing a security topology, keep in mind where the attacks come from and be one step ahead of the enemy.

Firewall Innovations

As firewall technology gets more and more advanced, hackers continue to figure out ways to get through them. The first types of firewalls, packet filters, looked only at the headers of the packets going through them. They failed to stop many attacks.

The second generation of firewalls, known as application layer gateways, improved security a great deal. They had a couple of problems, though: they were much slower than packet filters and supported only a few protocols.

Stateful Inspection was a good compromise as it allowed traffic to flow through the firewall without the need to buffer the traffic. Stateful Inspection also allowed the firewall to look at the entire connection.

Stateful Inspection helped, but application-level attacks still flowed though the firewall. Check Point added the ability to look for signatures in the data portion of the packets to combat these attacks. They called this technology Application Intelligence.

NOTE

Application Intelligence is built into Check Point firewalls starting with Check Point Next Generation Feature Pack 3.

As firewalls continue to advance, new features are added to help defend networks against the constant attacks that thrive on the Internet. Check Point can now detect attacks and dynamically modify the security policy to better defend the networks it is protecting.

Packet Filters

A packet filter is the simplest type of firewall. Almost every device with network capabilities has a packet filter built into it. Packet filters were the first type of firewall and they have a lot of limitations. These firewalls typically are installed on network routers.

How Packet Filters Work

Packet filters work by looking at the headers of the packet. Figure 1.1 shows the Open Systems Interconnection (OSI) stack and where the packet filter is in relation to it. Packet filter firewalls filter between layers 2 and 3. These filters work by looking at the headers of the packets and making a decision based on the contents. Most packet filters look at only the source IP address, destination IP address, and destination port. These filters either accept the packet and allow it to route or drop the packet.

Figure 1.1 The Packet Filter in Relation to the OSI Stack

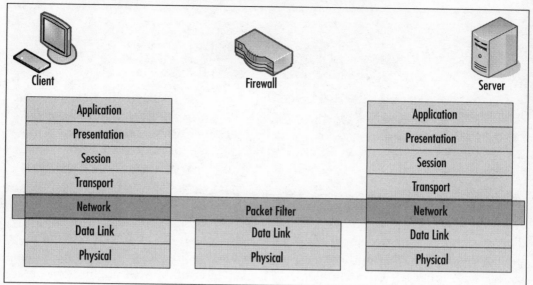

WARNING

Do *not* depend on packet-filtering routers for your firewall needs. Attacks can go straight through a packet filter and you will never know what hit you.

A good example of where a packet filter fails is with the FTP protocol. The FTP protocol requires a dynamic high TCP port opened back to the server. Since a packet filter does not understand protocols, it would have to have all TCP high ports opened back to the server to support the FTP protocol. Any protocol that uses dynamic ports would require all the ports opened through a packet-filtering firewall.

Tools & Traps…

Packet Filters Can Be Useful!

There are times when packet filters can be of great use in an enterprise environment. An external or internal router can drop traffic that should never reach the firewall. For example, if a network is blasting the firewall with ICMP (ping) packets, a simple drop on the router will save the firewall, and your log server, a lot of work.

Advantages

There are times when using packet filters makes sense. If the connections require high throughput or the protocol has proprietary technology that makes it not compatible with other firewall technologies, a packet-filtering firewall might be in order. Although packet filters have limitations, they also have the following advantages over other firewall technologies:

- **Compatibility** Packet filters do not modify the packet stream so they work with any protocol.

- **Performance** Packet filters are very fast since they look only at the headers.

- **Scalability** Since packet filters are simple, it is easy to scale the solution.

Disadvantages

You typically would not use a packet filter as your only security solution for your network. Packet filters have two major disadvantages:

- **Low security** Packet filters do not look at the data portion of the packets, so attacks can flow right through them.

- **No advanced protocol support** Since these filters do not keep track of connections, there is no way to support dynamic protocols.

Application Layer Gateways

An application layer firewall is also known as a proxy firewall. A proxy firewall is limited to protocols it can support. When using proxy firewalls, connections are terminated at the firewall and new connections are created. A direct connection through the firewall is not possible. Application layer gateways typically support only TCP connections. These types of firewalls often are considered the most secure type of firewall.

Check Point supports application layer functionality in order to do content inspection. Check Point's proxies are referred to as security servers.

Application gateways typically support only HTTP, SMTP, and FTP traffic. These proxies allow Check Point to send data to an external server for virus scanning or content scanning. They also allow Check Point to send the URL or IP address to an external server for URL matching. Check Point FireWall-1 has the ability to proxy CIFS (windows networking) and TCP (generic protocol support) as well.

> **TIP**
>
> Check Point has a proxy for generic TCP traffic. This proxy can be used to send the IP address of the server to a URL matching device for approval. This proxy also can be used to send any type of TCP traffic to a virus scanner server.

How Application Gateways Work

Application gateways run on layer 7 of the OSI stack. When a connection comes into an application gateway, the firewall completes the connection and creates a new connection from the firewall to the final destination. In a sense, a true proxy does not route network traffic. It buffers traffic, modifies the data if necessary, then sends the data to the destination (see Figure 1.2).

Figure 1.2 A Proxy Firewall

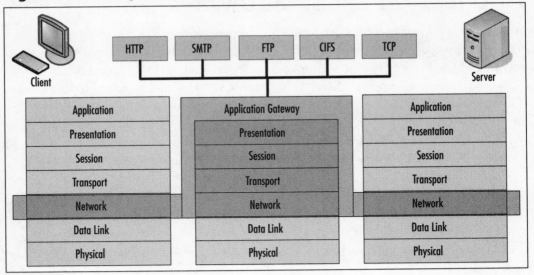

Advantages

Application gateways are known as the most secure type of firewall. Advantages of application layer gateways include the following:

- **Security** Since the proxy buffers the entire connection, it has the ability to do content filtering on the entire connection.

- **Application level awareness** Since the proxy fully understands the protocol, it makes sure all the data follow the standards.

Disadvantages

Although application layer gateways may appear to be the best solution in terms of security, there are a few disadvantages associated with them:

- **Performance** Since the entire connection is buffered, and there are two connections for every connection, proxy firewalls are the slowest type of firewalls.

- **Scalability** The Internet standards (RFCs) for TCP/IP state that communication occurs directly to and from the client and the server. This is referred to as the Client/Server model. Application layer firewalls break the Client/Server model, and this breaks some applications.

- **Application support** Application layer firewalls are specific to the protocol they are written for. Not all protocols are able to go through a proxy.

Stateful Inspection

Check Point's Stateful Inspection allows the best of both worlds. Stateful Inspection
allows the firewall to have complete application awareness without breaking the
client/server model. Incoming connections are added to a state table, which keeps
track of the connection and allows for session timeouts. Check Point's INSPECT
engine controls the flow of data through the firewall.

Stateful Inspection technology has the ability to utilize the following features:

- **Communication Information** Allows the filter to work with all software layers of the OSI stack.

- **Communication–Derived State** Allows the filter to handle dynamic
  protocols such as FTP.

- **Application–Derived State** Allows the filter to reference other applications. This would allow the firewall to authenticate a user and keep them
  authenticate for other authorized protocols and services.

- **Information Manipulation** Allows the filter to modify the packets as
  they pass through the firewall.

How Stateful Inspection Works

When a packet enters the firewall, a kernel level driver takes control of the packet at
the network layer, the lowest software OSI layer. A state table entry is made when a
TCP handshake is completed. Check Point also creates virtual state table entries for
the UDP and ICMP protocols to keep better track of them (see Figure 1.3).

Figure 1.3 Stateful Inspection

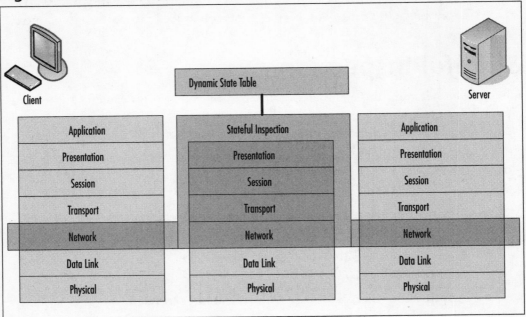

Since the INSPECT engine handles the entire packet, it has the ability to look at layer 7 data on the fly without needing to buffer the entire connection. Stateful Inspection looks at the data and determines if the protocol needs special attention. For example, if this was an FTP connection, the firewall would look for the dynamic return connection and allow the firewall to pass the high port through the firewall just for that specific connection.

Although Stateful Inspection has changed little since Check Point NG was released, the Application Intelligence version of Check Point (NG AI) introduced layer 7 scanning into the kernel. This means FireWall-1 can look for signatures in the data portion of the packets flowing through the firewall. This gives Check Point's Stateful Inspection some of the advantages of application layer gateways without the performance hit usually associated with proxies.

Advantages

Stateful Inspection has several advantages, which make it clearly the choice for a robust, secure network firewall. Reasons for using Stateful Inspection include:

- **High Performance** The Stateful Inspection engine is written into the kernel and is very fast.

- **Application awareness** The engine has the ability to support dynamic protocols.

- **Security** The entire packet is looked at when going through the gateway.

- **Transparency** Stateful Inspection does not modify the packets by default and is transparent to the client and server.

- **Extensibility** Additional components can be added to the Stateful Inspection engine adding functionality on the fly.

Perimeter, Internal, and Web Security

As the World's Most Intelligent Security Solution, Check Point offers a product line that can secure an enterprise network of any size. FireWall-1 and VPN-1 are just part of a complete security solution.

TIP

A complete security solution involves several security products and follows a written security policy. A properly secured network has a lengthy security policy and the products in the environment exist to enforce that policy.

Check Point's product line is split into three main areas. Perimeter security relates to security at the edge of your network. Internal security is for protecting data inside of your network. Web security is for locking down Web-based applications and encrypted tunnels into your network.

Perimeter

Check Point's solution for enforcing perimeter security includes FireWall-1/VPN-1 Pro, VPN-1 Edge, VPN-1 VSX, Web Intelligence, and SmartCenter. VPN-1 Pro enables secure, encrypted tunnels for data to pass through. VPN-1 Edge allows for remote offices to have firewall security and VPN end points at the Edge of your network. VPN-1 VSX allows for Virtual Security Gateways with VLAN security and multiple policies per gateway. Web Intelligence gives you the ability to inspect Web content and look for vulnerabilities. SmartCenter gives you the ability to tie it all together into a central management system.

The new Check Point NGX product line adds several new features. The SmartCenter NGX Management Server can now manage VPN-1, VPN-1 Edge, Connectra, and InterSpect gateways, all from a centralized management console. Significant enhancements have been made to the SmartDefense, Application Intelligence, and Web Intelligence engines. This includes enhanced peer-to-peer protection, Voice-over IP denial-of-service protection, and enhanced security servers. The VPN-1 Pro NGX product also adds the ability to run dynamic routing protocols on the firewall as well as enhanced VPN routing.

Internal

To enforce security inside your network, sometimes a bit more security is in order. Use FireWall-1 inside your network to secure internal segments. Check Point has two additional products to help secure the enterprise: InterSpect and Integrity.

InterSpect has the ability to stop the spread of worms through your network. InterSpect understands common internal protocols, such as Microsoft file sharing, and has the ability to block unwanted traffic using those protocols.

The Integrity product gives you the ability to enforce desktop security. Integrity has plug-ins for SecureClient or can run in stand-alone mode. The stand-alone version is based on the ZoneAlarm desktop firewall.

Web

Check Point has three products that are made specifically for Web traffic: Connectra, Web Intelligence, and the SSL Network Extender.

Connectra is Check Point's SSL VPN product. With Connectra, remote users can access your network through an SSL-encrypted Web browser.

Web Intelligence integrates with check Point's FireWall-1 gateway software and allows you to do application level scanning at wire speed. Web content can be inspected and Web-based vulnerabilities can be stopped at the gateway. Check Point NGX adds the ability to prevent directory listings, LDAP injection, and Web server error messages.

The SSL Network Extender is a Web-based plug-in that allows network level access through your Web browser. No need to worry about upgrading client side software because every time users access the firewall, they get a new client. The SSL Network Extender can be used with the Connectra product to provide a complete SSL VPN solution. Check Point NGX adds the ability to centralize management of the SSL Network Extender into the SmartDashboard console. NGX also adds enhanced SecurID features and ClusterXL functionality.

INSPECT Script

Check Point firewalls use the INSPECT engine to do Stateful Inspection. When a policy is pushed to a firewall, it is converted into INSPECT script. All of Check Point's advanced functionality is modifiable via INSPECT script. Even custom INSPECT script can be inserted automatically into policies before they are pushed to firewall gateways.

NOTE

Custom INSPECT code can be inserted into policies by editing files in the $FWDIR/lib directory.

Check Point has documentation available for custom INSPECT programming, but it is not very often needed as the SmartDashboard gives you the ability to create custom objects. The primary reason to write custom INSPECT code is to create a custom protocol for an application that Check Point does not yet support.

FireWall-1 Decision Making

When a packet reaches the FireWall-1 several things happen. First, Check Point goes through anti-spoofing rules to make sure the packet is coming in the correct interface. Then IP options and packet checksums are checked. Any errors and the packets silently get discarded. After the initial checks, the packet hits the FireWall-1 daemon.

Daemon Thought Process

Figure 1.4 shows what the Check Point INSPECT engine goes through with every packet. First the firewall looks at its rule base for a match. Rules are parsed from top to bottom, one rule at a time. Once a rule is matched, the connection is logged and the firewall makes a determination to Pass, Reject, or Drop the packet based on the policy. A Rejected packet sends a NACK (negative acknowledgment) packet to the server to close the connection. Normally you would not do this as it lets the hacker know something is rejecting packets. Reject typically is used when you want to avoid a timeout on a service your users use frequently.

Figure 1.4 The Check Point INSPECT Engine

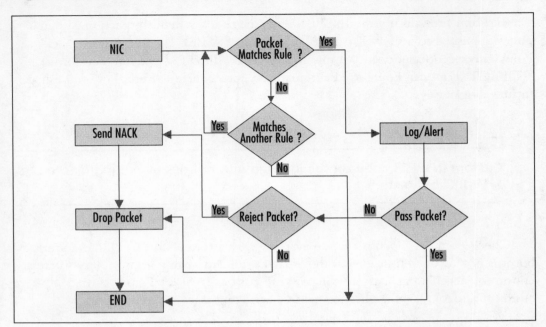

Summary

In this chapter we covered different firewall technologies and the differences between them. Early firewalls employed packet filtering in routers to allow or deny traffic to certain destinations.

Check Point offers a complete, comprehensive security solution for network environments of every size. Check Point pioneered Stateful Inspection, the standard to which firewalls are built today.

Packet-filtering firewalls run on the network layer of the OSI stack. They accept or deny traffic based on the headers of a packet. Packet-filtering firewalls do not look into the packet's layer 7 data portion.

Application layer gateways, also known as proxies, generate two connections for every connection. Application layer gateways support only a few protocols and require a service on the firewall for each protocol. These proxies give you full access to the data portion of the packets for anti-virus or content inspection.

Stateful Inspection runs on layers 3 through 7 of the OSI stack. Incoming connections generate state table entries, and the firewall has the ability to scan the data portion of the packets for signatures. Stateful Inspection allows for Communication Information, which allows the filter to work with all software layers of the OSI stack. Communication-Derived State allows the filter to handle dynamic protocols such as FTP. Application-Derived State allows the filter to reference other applications. This would allow the firewall to authenticate users and keep them authenticated for other authorized protocols and services. Information Manipulation allows the filter to modify the packets as they pass through the firewall.

PIW (Perimeter/Internal/Web) allows Check Point to provide a security rich solution. Perimeter security protects the network from the Internet. Internal security protects the internal network from internal attacks. Web security protects HTTP- and HTTPS-based connections.

The INSPECT engine is programmed by INSPECT script. The Check Point SmartDashboard generates INSPECT script, which is pushed down to the firewalls. Custom INSPECT script can be written and pushed to the firewalls along with a policy.

The INSPECT engine follows a process for handling network traffic. Rules are parsed from top to bottom, one at a time. Packets that do not match a rule are silently dropped. When a packet is Rejected a NACK is generated in order to properly close the connection.

Solutions Fast Track

History of Firewalls

- Early firewalls were just routers with access control lists.
- Check Point FireWall-1 came out in 1994.
- Check Point invented Stateful Inspection.

Firewall Innovations

- Desktop firewalls are getting more popular. Soon every device on the network will have firewall technology.
- Newer firewalls can actually defend the network against attacks by modifying policies in real time.

Packet Filters

- Packet filters exist between layer 2 and 3 of the OSI stack.
- They look only at the headers of the packets.
- They do not support dynamic protocols.

Application Later Gateways

- These gateways exist on layer 7 of the OSI stack.
- They can modify the data portion of the packets.
- They support only a few protocols: HTTP, SMTP, FTP, CIFS, and some TCP-based protocols.

Stateful Inspection

- Stateful Inspection exists on layers 3 through 7 of the OSI stack.
- Communication Information allows the filter to work with all software layers of the OSI stack.

- Communication-Derived State allows the filter to handle dynamic protocols such as FTP.

- Application-Derived State allows the filter to reference other applications. This would allow the firewall to authenticate users and keep them authenticated for other authorized protocols and services.

- Information Manipulation allows the filter to modify the packets as they pass through the firewall.

Perimeter, Internal, and Web Security

- Perimeter security protects the network from the Internet.

- Internal security protects the internal network from internal attacks.

- Web security protects HTTP- and HTTPS-based connections.

INSPECT Script

- Check Point FireWall-1 used INSPECT script to program the INSPECT engine.

- INSPECT script can be customized to extend Check Point's functionality and support additional protocols.

FireWall-1 Decision Making

- Anti-spoofing and IP options are checked before allowing a packet into the INSPECT engine.

- Packets that do not match a rule are Dropped without logging.

- A Reject is when a NACK is sent back to the client/server to officially close the connection.

Frequently Asked Questions

The following Frequently Asked Questions, answered by the authors of this book, are designed to both measure your understanding of the concepts presented in this chapter and to assist you with real-life implementation of these concepts. To have your questions about this chapter answered by the author, browse to **www.syngress.com/solutions** and click on the **"Ask the Author"** form.

Q: What types of firewall technology does Check Point support?

A: Check Point supports two different firewall technologies: Stateful Inspection and application layer gateways. The firewalls themselves use the Stateful Inspection engine for all traffic traversing it. Using Resources, Check Point has processes that act as application layer gateways that allow for modification of layer 7 data and other enhanced features.

Q: What application layer gateways does Check Point FireWall-1 support?

A: Check Point supports five security servers: HTTP, SMTP, FTP, CIFS, and generic TCP.

Q: What layer of the OSI stack is used for packet filtering?

A: Packet filtering is performed on layer 3 of the OSI stack, the Network layer. The packet filter looks only at the headers of the packets, and makes simple decisions such as allow or deny based on source, destination, or ports referenced in the header.

Q: What type of firewall is the slowest?

A: Application layer gateways have the biggest performance hit. They are considered the most secure type of firewall, but have limited protocol support and break some applications that require direct access between the client and the server.

Q: What does Reject do?

A: Using Reject in a policy rule sends a NACK packet to close a connection gracefully. This typically is done to keep a client from needing to timeout a connection, which can cause delays. Normally you would not use Reject because this would tell a hacker that some type of network security product may exist on the IP address the Reject comes from.

Q: What type of firewall supports Communication Information, Communication-Derived State, Application-Derived State, and Information Manipulation?

A: Stateful Inspection supports all these features. Communication Information means the filter can operate on all software layers of the OSI stack. Communication-Derived State refers to the ability to keep track of the connection and enforce timeouts. Application-Derived State means the filter can understand advanced protocols and disallow violations to the protocol. Information Manipulation means the filter has the ability to modify data in the packets.

Q: What type of firewall generates a state table?

A: Stateful Inspection. Stateful Inspection allows the firewall to have complete application awareness without breaking the client/server model. The state table also allows the filter to enforce timeouts based on the protocol.

Chapter 2

What's New in NGX

Solutions in this chapter:

- **SmartPortal**
- **SmartDefense/Web Intelligence**
- **Eventia Reporter**
- **VPN Functionality**
- **Dynamic Routing**
- **SecurePlatform**
- **VPN-1 Edge**
- **Network and Host Object Cloning**

☑ **Summary**

☑ **Solutions Fast Track**

☑ **Frequently Asked Questions**

Introduction

Every two or three years, Check Point releases a major upgrade to its main FireWall-1/VPN-1 product, now called VPN-1 Pro. Though the changes from versions 4.0/4.1 to NG (Next Generation) were significant, the changes from NG to NG with Application Intelligence (NG AI), and then from NG AI to NGX are both more moderate in scope.

This chapter discusses the significant changes between NG AI and NGX and partitions these changes into eight major categories. If you feel you're facile and competent with NG AI, a reading of this chapter will bring you most of the way toward preparing you for version NGX.

SmartPortal

The Check Point SmartConsole GUI clients have long been a significant competitive advantage for Check Point in the firewall space. Using SIC (Secure Internal Communications), these clients provide a common user interface and communicate with the SmartCenter Server over an encrypted, authenticated, private channel over any IP network, including the Internet.

However, when thinking about a "universal client" and considering the benefits of communicating over "an encrypted, authenticated, private channel over any IP network, including the Internet," most people's thoughts quickly turn to their Web browsers, particularly with HTTPS and SSL.

Until now, anyone who wanted access into the SmartCenter Server needed to install the GUI clients, a possible problem in organizations with strict configuration management policies or for administrators who can't always use their own laptops. SmartPortal is new to version NGX and allows the firewall administrator to extend read-only browser-based access to the SmartCenter Server to people outside the security team and to those on PCs without the GUI clients. It's essentially a secure Web interface into your SmartCenter Server that enables you to see the Security Policy and the Logs. The SmartPortal license is included in the SmartCenter Pro license; otherwise, it has to be purchased separately.

Browser Compatibility

SmartPortal is compatible with the following browsers:

- Internet Explorer 6.0
- Mozilla 1.7

- Firefox 1.0
- Netscape 7.1

The only other requirements are that you enable JavaScript and disable pop-up blockers.

Deploying SmartPortal

Configuring SmartPortal is actually fairly easy. Most of the complexity occurs behind the scenes. A key question at the start is whether to deploy on a dedicated server or on the SmartCenter Server itself.

Choosing Dedicated Server versus the SmartCenter Server

SmartPortal can be installed either on a dedicated server or on the SmartCenter Server. In most configurations, the SmartCenter Server itself doesn't create much processor load and thus doesn't require much in terms of resources other than in hosting it on very reliable hardware. The exception, of course, is in logging. Some organizations require logging of every connection, which can create a significant burden, but there's an easy solution in moving the logging server to a separate machine.

The same sort of thinking goes into deciding whether to host the SmartPortal on a separate, dedicated server, or hosting it on the SmartCenter Server. The amount of Web traffic to the SmartPortal server will probably be minor.

If you do decide to install SmartPortal on a dedicated machine, it will simply connect back to the SmartCenter Server using SIC and will relay data between the Web clients and the SmartCenter Server.

Limiting Access to Specific IP Addresses

Connecting to the SmartCenter Server with the GUI clients for the first time has always been somewhat problematic as you are required to not only have the correct username, password, and IP address of the SmartCenter Server, but you must first also configure the SmartCenter Server to accept Check Point Management Interface (CPMI, TCP port 18190) connections from your client PC.

This requirement adds a second *factor* in the authentication process (as it is now a *two-factor authentication*), ensuring you have both "something you know" (your password) as well as "something you are" (as in "coming from a prearranged IP address"). SmartPortal also allows limited access to specific IP addresses. This requires creating or editing the *hosts.allowed* file on the SmartPortal Server.

TIP

Be sure you think through the implications of your *hosts.allowed* file at the time of installation. Experienced Check Point administrators can tell you stories of hours of wasted time trying to figure out why someone can't connect with a management client, only to find the IP address hadn't been allowed on the access list.

Learning More about SmartPortal

A good resource for learning more about this functionality is the *SmartCenter* document, a PDF document issued by Check Point. You can find it under downloads at www.CheckPoint.com or at *\Docs\CheckPoint_Suite\SmartCenter.pdf* on the NGX CD2.

SmartDefense/Web Intelligence

Network attackers and firewall manufacturers have been in an arms race for years. This is good news, of course, for those of us who make our living on one side or the other of this arms race. If you're not on the side with the good guys (that would be us), then put down this book and go upstairs and help your mom finish washing the dishes.

One of the consequences of an arms race is that each side tends to get better with time, constantly improving attacks and defenses in response to and in anticipation of the actions of the other side. In the early days of firewalls, it was sufficient to inspect packets mostly at the Network layer (Layer 3) and Transport layer (Layer 4) and base filtering decisions on these simple identifiers. Within a couple of years, these battles were essentially over, with firewalls consistently winning the day. A well-configured firewall could stop just about all attacks directed at closed ports.

The problem now is that the battles are being waged through the open ports. If your firewall allows Web traffic to reach your Web server, or allows insiders to go out on most services, then all sorts of new attack opportunities are available to those who would do you harm.

SmartDefense/Web Intelligence is Check Point's way of providing an intelligent defense against attacks directed at open ports as well as a defense against other more sophisticated types of attacks. Though previous versions of FireWall-1/VPN-1 included early versions of SmartDefense/Web Intelligence, these defenses have been upgraded and improved in NGX.

Understanding the Capabilities of SmartDefense and Web Intelligence

SmartDefense and Web Intelligence have capabilities in three broad categories, and not every capability fits neatly into a single category. These categories are:

- Defenses against attacks
- Implicit defenses
- Abnormal-behavior analysis

Defenses against Attacks

SmartDefense provides defenses against these types of attacks:

- Denial-of-service attacks
- TCP/IP attacks
- Web and application vulnerabilities
- Network probing
- HTTP worms
- Microsoft Network-specific vulnerability
- Protocol vulnerability
- Buffer-overflow attacks

Implicit Defenses

These defenses include fingerprint spoofing and other tricks to reduce to ability of outside observers to reach conclusions about your internal network based upon information carried in packets leaving your network. The goal is to increase the difficulty your enemy will have in fingerprinting your network.

Abnormal-Behavior Analysis

SmartDefense can report on and analyze traffic patterns, alerting the administrator when certain criteria are met. Components include Successive Events detection, Port Scan detection, and Sweep Scan detection.

DNS Protocol Enforcement

DNS traffic usually gets special treatment in firewalls. Because it's easy to forget that UDP DNS resolutions need to pass through the firewall in order for many other services to work, administrators often create a rule simply allowing all DNS traffic (UDP and possibly even TCP) to traverse the firewall.

This is overly permissive and a security risk, and SmartDefense has a partial answer to the problem. By configuring the settings properly, SmartDefense can actually look inside each DNS packet and confirm they're genuine and unmodified, and block packets that appear as if someone is trying to tunnel other information through an otherwise open Port 53.

Configuring SmartDefense/Web Intelligence

SmartDefense and Web Intelligence have their own tabs in SmartDashboard, similar to the tabs you're already familiar with for **Security**, **Address Translation**, **VPN Manager**, and so on. By selecting the **SmartDefense** tab or the **Web Intelligence** tab, you may observe and change your configuration for these dozens of sophisticated and specialized filters.

Considering the SmartDefense Subscription Service

CheckPoint now also offers a subscription service called **SmartDefense Services**. This is an annual subscription program (separate from and in addition to your software subscription and support contract) that is licensed to each individual enforcement module. The goal is to provide ongoing and real-time updates and configuration advisories for defenses and security policies.

The price is currently $1,000 per gateway, and although it's frustrating that this is now a third annual support subscription paid to Check Point to keep your firewall current, the ability to get ongoing updates and enhancements is a significant benefit.

Understanding SmartDefense and Web Intelligence

By far the best way to understand SmartDefense and Web Intelligence is to click the **SmartDefense** and **Web Intelligence** tabs and jump in and explore. If you're a curious network engineer you'll be amazed at all the various nefarious possibilities they've considered and ways they found to defend against. The help system is generally useful.

If you're using FireWall-1/VPN-1 to protect Web servers, you'll be particularly interested in what's available to configure in Web Intelligence. The HTTP protocol has all sorts of risks involved and Web Intelligence offers a robust array of counter-measures. If you're a Web developer, exploring the options here is fascinating. You should note that Web Intelligence is a separate license that has to be purchased for the number of servers you want to protect.

In NGX you now have the added useful ability to configure individual filters and tests to monitor but not drop packets, which enables you to see the effect of implementation without actually causing unexpected network problems.

If you subscribe to the SmartDefense Services, new filters and options will be added dynamically to the lists through automatic updates.

TIP

It can be very useful when experimenting with the myriad settings in SmartDefense/Web Intelligence to enable the monitoring functionality first and then examining your logs to see how this filter is being applied.

Learning More about SmartDefense/Web Intelligence

A good resource for learning more about this functionality is the *Firewall and SmartDefense* document, a PDF document issued by Check Point. You can find it under downloads at www.CheckPoint.com or at *\Docs\CheckPoint_Suite\ Firewall_and_SmartDefense.pdf* on the NGX CD2.

Eventia Reporter

With the passage of Sarbanes-Oxley and the increased demand for auditing, the portion of firms requiring their firewall administrators to log all or essentially all traffic continues to grow. Anyone who's had much experience working with the FireWall-1/VPN-1 and SmartView Tracker knows how large and unwieldy the firewall logs can become if firewalls are misconfigured, particularly in organizations with large traffic flows or multiple gateways.

Eventia Reporter is a log analysis tool that provides fairly straightforward ways to audit and monitor network traffic. You can use it to create detailed or summary reports in a variety of formats (list, vertical bar, pie chart, and so on).

Choosing Stand-Alone versus Distributed Installation

Eventia Reporter can be installed in either a stand-alone or distributed installation. The choice depends largely upon hard drive and processor resources.

Choosing Stand-Alone Installation

In a stand-alone installation, the Eventia Reporter is installed right on the SmartCenter Server. Although this may offer some advantages in that you won't need a separate, dedicated server, there are issues to consider when it comes to processor and hard drive resources. The log files themselves can become quite large, and if the SmartCenter Server is both the logging server and the Eventia Reporter Server, you may face resource issues, particularly with hard drive capacity.

Choosing Distributed Installation

In the distributed installation, the Eventia Reporter Server is installed on its own dedicated server. This might be advantageous if you are expecting large amounts of log data. The Eventia Reporter Add-On must also be installed on the SmartCenter Server to facilitate communications with the Eventia Reporter Server.

Configuring a Consolidation Policy

Administrators create a Consolidation Policy to determine whether to store or ignore logging output from individual rules in the Security RuleBase. The Consolidation Policy contains consolidation rules that apply to this log data, rather than to the connections themselves.

The Log Consolidation process creates the Eventia Reporter Database, the database from which Standard Reports are generated.

Choosing Standard Reports versus Express Reports

There are two types of reports that can be created with Eventia Reporter: standard reports and express reports.

Standard reports are generated from information in the Log Consolidator logs. Express Reports are based on data collected by the SmartView Monitor History files and the Check Point system counters. The main benefit of Express Reports is that they can be generated more quickly than Standard Reports.

> **NOTE**
>
> Depending on the size of your logs, Log Consolidation can take a long time (perhaps even a day or more). A fast processor and fast hard drives can really help. Plan carefully and select only the rules you really need.

Learning More about Eventia Reporter

A good resource for learning more about this functionality is the *Eventia Reporter* document, a PDF document issued by Check Point. You can find it under downloads at www.CheckPoint.com or at *\Docs\CheckPoint_Suite\EventiaReporter.pdf* on the NGX CD2.

VPN Functionality

VPN technology has been an integral part of firewalls since the late 1990s. With the rise of the Internet in the early 1990s, most firms' first concerns were for a firewall allowing them safe connectivity between their internal networks and the Internet. Once organizations began to use the Internet to connect separate offices, it became obvious that providing VPN functionality was a natural fit for firewall manufacturers. The fact that NAT, IPSEC, and Anti-Spoof checking have complex interactions further drove the consolidation of these functionalities into a single perimeter device.

Although the VPN technology was initially a separate add-on to FireWall-1, it soon became part of the standard package and now with version NGX, the firewall product itself has been renamed VPN-1 Pro, for reasons that aren't entirely obvious, given the large mindshare and recognition of the name FireWall-1.

NGX offers several new updates and upgrades in VPN functionality.

Understanding the New VPN Options

Configuring VPNs in version NG AI was significantly easier than in versions such as 4.0/4.1 because of the concept of VPN Communities. Rather than creating individual encryption rules to handle the traffic between VPN terminator gateways, the user needed only create a VPN community and then specify the gateways and properties.

With version NGX, Check Point has preserved this useful simple mental model and added some additional functionality.

Allowing Directional VPN Rules

Enforcement of VPN rules by direction of connection is now possible. By going to the **Policy | Global Properties | VPN | Advanced** dialog box, you can check the box allowing directional specificity in the VPN element in the rule base. Whereas in NG AI, directionality in VPN communities was an all-or-nothing proposition, the ability to now specify directionality is useful.

Allowing Backup Links and On-Demand Links

A pair of VPN gateways can now have multiple links between them (say, through multiple ISPs), allowing more than one communication path between them. This allows the configuration of back-up links and on-demand links.

Allowing Wire Mode VPN Connectivity

VPN connections in NGX can now be labeled as wire mode, reflecting the fact that communications over the VPN are inherently trusted. By labeling a connection as wire mode, packets traversing this connection do not get inspected by Stateful Inspection, enabling these connections to successfully failover. In wire mode, dynamic routing protocols are available for VPN traffic.

Allowing Route-Based VPNs

NGX now supports OSPF/BGP for VPN traffic routing. Every tunnel is represented as a virtual adapter, allowing OSPF and BGP traffic to be encapsulated.

Allowing Always-on Tunnels

Always-on tunnels are "nailed up" connections. This permits more advanced monitoring of VPN traffic through these tunnels and prevents latency problems for applications sensitive to link setup delays.

Learning More about VPN Changes

A good resource for more details about this functionality is the *Virtual Private Networks* document, a PDF document issued by Check Point. You can find it under downloads at www.CheckPoint.com or at *\Docs\CheckPoint_Suite\VPN.pdf* on the NGX CD2.

Dynamic Routing

Check Point has added dynamic routing functionality in the Pro version of SecurePlatform (see the section on SecurePlatform). For some administrators, this is their long-awaited opportunity to further integrate their FireWall-1/VPN-1 gateways into their network infrastructure and provide additional redundancy. For others, primarily those in smaller organizations, its additional cost, risks, and complexities argue against implementation.

Considering the Security Implications in Choosing a Routing Protocol

It's generally considered a security risk to configure your firewall to accept any more information from external sources than is absolutely necessary. The more stealthy your firewall is, the better it can resist attacks. For this reason, it's generally considered a risk to use any sort of dynamic routing protocol in your gateway.

It often comes as a bit of a surprise to students new to firewalls that every firewall gateway is a router first and a border guard second. Except in unusual configurations, every firewall does, in fact, also act as a router. Static routes are best as they are hard-coded into the gateway's operating system and don't rely on or have to trust updates from any external source. It would be a particularly attractive attack vector if your enemy found out that simply by sending your gateway bogus dynamic routing updates he could redirect your traffic through one of his own routing nodes.

Static routes are also much easier to debug, and given that routing problems are a frequent underlying cause of "firewall" problems, keeping all your routes static is a great way to start the debugging process with at least some of the potential confusion eliminated.

However, it's also true that in many organizations there are somewhat separate teams managing networking and perimeter security, and for political or network management reasons you may be required to add dynamic routing protocols to your FireWall-1/VPN-1 gateways. The fact remains that some customers, particularly larger customers, request this functionality.

Notes from the Underground…

Dynamic Routing and Complexity Issues

Experienced firewall administrators will tell you that an awful lot of "firewall" problems are really routing problems in disguise. When packets don't flow like they're expected to, it is easy to make an initial hypothesis that they're being blocked in the firewall. Routing configuration errors may mean one or both directions in a connection don't make it to or through the firewall, making it very difficult to debug. Dynamic routing greatly adds to this complexity.

Think hard about all the possible hypotheses you'll have to consider if you have dynamic routing and you get a call that "the traffic's not getting through the firewall…."

Choosing a Dynamic Routing Protocol

SecurePlatform offers support for the following dynamic routing protocols:

- Border Gateway Protocol (BGP)
- Fast Open Shortest Path First (OSPF)
- Fast Open Shortest Path First Version 3 (OSPF)
- Routing Information Protocol (RIP)
- Routing Information Protocol Next Generation (RIPng)
- Distance Vector Multicast Routing Protocol (DVMRP)
- Internet Group Management Protocol (IGMP)
- Protocol Independent Multicast Dense Mode (PIM-DM)
- Protocol Independent Multicast Sparse Mode (PIM-SM)
- Virtual Routing Environment (VRE)

This is an impressive list, particularly given this is the first version of SecurePlatform to offer this functionality.

Configuring Dynamic Routing

Configuration is done through the command line, and offers command-line completion, context-sensitive help, and five distinct configuration modes:

- User Execution
- Privileged Execution
- Global Configuration
- Router Configuration
- Interface Configuration modes

Learning More about Dynamic Routing

A good resource for more details about this functionality is the *SecurePlatform Pro & Advanced Routing Command-Line Interface* document, a PDF document issued by Check Point. You can find it under downloads at www.CheckPoint.com or at *\Docs\CheckPoint_Suite\SecurePlatformPro_and_Advanced_Routing_Suite_CLI.pdf* on the NGX CD2.

SecurePlatform

SecurePlatform (known to most implementers as SPLAT) is Check Point's clever implementation of a combined operating system and the VPN-1 Pro software itself. The operating system is a proprietary, hardened, enhanced version of Linux that installs painlessly on most PCs. The creation of SecurePlatform gives users several significant advantages:

- Avoidance of licensing fees associated with Microsoft Windows
- Avoidance of security and maintenance problems inherent with Microsoft Windows
- Avoidance of the costs of a third-party appliance platform
- The benefits of a prehardened, purpose-built operating system
- The ability to take advantage of special Check Point-only enhancements, such as dynamic routing protocols
- The ability to automatically update the operating system when updating VPN-1 Pro

Understanding the New SecurePlatform Split Product Line

SecurePlatform is now a split product line in version NGX. In addition to "regular" SecurePlatform, there's also now a premium version called SecurePlatform Pro. The Pro version offers two distinct advantages:

- Dynamic Routing (see the section on Dynamic Routing)
- RADIUS Authentication for SecurePlatform administrators

SecurePlatform Pro requires a separate, additional license. This license must be installed on the SmartCenter Server managing the SecurePlatform module.

Notes from the Underground…

Choosing SecurePlatform versus SecurePlatform Pro

Unless your network management team insists your firewall support dynamic routing, there aren't many other reasons to pay for SecurePlatform Pro.

The only other advantage of SecurePlatform Pro is adding the ability for firewall administrators to authenticate with RADIUS, and this isn't a crucial benefit as it also adds some risk by configuring the firewall to authenticate to an external source. It would be more secure to have firewall administrators authenticate only to the SmartCenter Server itself, and leave the firewall password out of the hands of the other IT staff who manage passwords on the RADIUS server.

Understanding Other Improvements

SecurePlatform contains several other minor improvements in version NGX.

Configuring Speed/Duplex Settings

By using either the **eth_set** utility on the command line or the WebUI, you can configure the speed/duplex settings for each NIC. These settings are persistent and will survive rebooting.

Supporting SCP in the Patch Add Command

Applying occasional patches is regrettably still a reality with SecurePlatform. Fortunately, the **patch add** command now supports **scp**, permitting secure copying of patches.

Supporting Netscape 7.1 in the WebUI

The WebUI now supports Netscape 7.1, in addition to Internet Explorer, allowing non-Windows PCs to connect.

Learning More about SecurePlatform

A good resource for more details about this functionality is the *SecurePlatform SecurePlatform Pro* document, a PDF document issued by Check Point. You can find it under downloads at www.CheckPoint.com or at *\Docs\CheckPoint_Suite\ SecurePlatform&SecurePlatformPro.pdf* on the NGX CD2.

VPN-1 Edge

A full-blown installation of VPN-1 Pro can be a significant investment in licensing costs, hardware costs, and ongoing maintenance costs. For many organizations, home offices or branch offices need the protections of a firewall as well as VPN functionality, but a full VPN-1 Pro installation is too much.

In order to meet the needs of this market segment, and after several not-so-successful attempts, Check Point offers a line of hardware firewall appliances called VPN-1 Edge devices. They're small, they don't have hard drives, they boot a stripped down version of Linux, and they run FireWall-1/VPN-1 version NG.

These boxes are famously easy to spot because of their deep blue color.

Understanding the Product Line

VPN-1 Edge devices have a fairly useful standard set of features, including:

- 4 10-100 switched ports on the LAN side
- 10-100 WAN port
- WAN connectivity through static IP, DHCP, Cable modem, PPTP client, and so on
- DHCP Server
- DHCP Relay

- MAC Cloning

- Static NAT

- Static Routes

VPN-1 Edge devices all come with a WebUI interface, and all can be upgraded within their hardware product line. VPN-1 Edge devices come in two flavors, the S series and the X series.

Understanding the VPN-1 S Series

The VPN-1 Edge S series is less expensive and is intended for implementations requiring fewer features and less functionality. This series is intended primarily for telecommuters, offers firewall and remote access VPN functionality, and can protect up to eight internal IP addresses. It can also act as a VPN remote access server, allowing secure connectivity to internal devices protected by the device.

Understanding the VPN-1 X Series

The VPN-1 Edge X series offers all the functionality of the S series, and these additional features:

- Support for larger firewall and VPN bandwidth

- Dedicated hardware DMZ port

- Support for a dial-up modem

- Support for high availability by configuring a second X series device as failover

- Support for more efficient bandwidth usage through traffic shaping

There are three models in the X series line:

- X16: Supports 16 users

- X32: Support 32 users

- XU: There is no limit on the number of users

Be sure to think carefully about your future growth needs when purchasing a VPN-1 Edge box. The S Series is not upgradable to an X series.

Learning More about VPN-1 Edge

A good resource for more details about this functionality is the *Check Point VPN-1 Edge* document, a PDF document issued by Check Point. You can find it under downloads at www.CheckPoint.com or at *\Docs\VPN-1_edge_Getting_Started.pdf* on the NGX CD2.

Network and Host Object Cloning

For years the SmartDashboard user interface has been quietly gaining small bits of additional functionality that greatly enhance your ability to make the changes you need with a minimum of fuss. With NGX, you now have the ability to simply right-click any network or node object and create a clone with identical field values. This is enormously helpful when creating many objects that are identical except for, say, name and IP address, or something similar.

It's a minor improvement, but if you've been stubbing your toes on various quirks in the user interface over the years, your first use of this new feature will likely be an "Aha!" moment.

Before creating a large number of clones of a network or host object, think carefully about your naming convention. Now's your chance (before you start cloning) to make things as clear as possible for yourself and other administrators down the line.

Summary

Check Point releases a major upgrade to its core FireWall-1/VPN-1 product every two or three years, and version NGX is the latest in this line. The core product in the new version is called VPN-1 Pro. Although the upgrade from 4.0/4.1 to NG was a complete revamping of the product, the subsequent upgrades to versions NG AI and now to NGX are more modest in scope.

SmartPortal is a welcome addition, allowing administrators to extend browser-based connectivity to the SmartCenter Server. Users without the SmartConsole GUI clients and administrators not at their primary workstations can connect through HTTPS.

SmartDefense and Web Intelligence have received moderate upgrades in NGX. This is still a fascinating set of tools for the network security administrator to understand and configure against all sorts of higher-level attacks.

Eventia Reporter provides a way to tackle those large and growing log files and provide detailed, informative reports and traffic analysis.

VPN functionality has seen significant improvements and now delivers on the full promise of the enhanced community-based VPNs we saw in the previous version.

Dynamic Routing adds some risk and some complexity, and is now available to those larger organizations who wish to more fully integrate the underlying router in their Check Point firewalls into their existing dynamic routing configuration.

SecurePlatform continues to evolve and improve. The product line is now split, with the addition of SecurePlatform Pro, which offers Dynamic Routing and support for RADIUS authentication for firewall administrators.

VPN-1 Edge devices are simpler and cheaper than full-blown VPN-1 Pro installations and are best for telecommuters (by choosing the S series) and branch offices (by choosing the X series).

Network and Host Object Cloning is a small but useful enhancement to the SmartDashboard user interface. Although most administrators don't spend a lot of time creating new objects, for those of us setting up labs and classrooms to teach Check Point courses, it's a welcome addition.

Solutions Fast Track

SmartPortal

- ☑ Allows the firewall administrator to extend browser-based access to the SmartCenter Server to persons outside the security team and to those on PCs without the GUI clients.

- ☑ It's essentially a secure Web interface into your SmartCenter Server for viewing policies and logs.

- ☑ Can be installed either on a dedicated server or on the SmartCenter Server itself.

- ☑ You can limit access to specific IP addresses.

SmartDefense/Web Intelligence

- ☑ The "Hacker versus Firewall" arms race has moved up the stack to the higher levels.

- ☑ SmartDefense and Web Intelligence have capabilities in three broad categories: defense against attacks, implicit defenses, and abnormal-behavior analysis.

- ☑ The SmartDefense Service is an annual subscription service that provides ongoing and real-time updates and configuration advisories.

Eventia Reporter

- ☑ Eventia Reporter can be a big help in managing and understanding very large log files.

- ☑ Eventia Reporter can be installed on a dedicated server or right on the SmartCenter Server itself.

- ☑ The administrator can choose between standard reports (which are generated from information in the Log Consolidator logs) or Express Reports (generated from data collected by the SmartView Monitor History files and the Check Point system counters).

VPN Functionality

- ☑ Traffic between gateways in a VPN community can now be filtered based upon directionality.

- ☑ A pair of VPN gateways can now have multiple links between them, allowing for back-up links and on-demand links.

- ☑ Wire Mode connectivity allows the traffic between trusted gateways to skip Stateful Inspection and take advantage of dynamic routing.

- ☑ The introduction of always-on tunnels enables more advanced monitoring of VPN traffic and prevents latency problems for applications sensitive to link setup delays.

Dynamic Routing

- ☑ Dynamic Routing is available only in the Pro version of SecurePlatform.

- ☑ Be aware of the security and complexity risks in configuring your firewall gateway for dynamic routing.

- ☑ Dynamic Routing allows larger organizations to integrate the underlying router in their Check Point firewall into their larger dynamic routing configuration.

SecurePlatform

- ☑ SecurePlatform is now available in two separate versions, SecurePlatform and SecurePlatform Pro.

- ☑ SecurePlatform Pro offers the additional functionality of dynamic routing and enables support for RADIUS authentication for firewall administrators.

- ☑ Firewall administrators can now configure Ethernet speed and duplex settings and these settings are persistent and will survive rebooting.

VPN-1 Edge

- ☑ VPN-1 Edge devices are small hardware platforms for telecommuters and branch offices.

☑ The S series is for telecommuters and the X series offers more functionality and is for branch offices.

☑ VPN-1 Edge devices can be upgraded within their own hardware lines.

Network and Host Object Cloning

☑ To "clone" network or host objects in SmartDashboard, simply right-click and create a clone with identical field values.

☑ This is a fast way to create multiple copies of objects belonging to the same class.

☑ It's a small enhancement, but SmartDashboard keeps getting better through small enhancements.

Frequently Asked Questions

The following Frequently Asked Questions, answered by the authors of this book, are designed to both measure your understanding of the concepts presented in this chapter and to assist you with real-life implementation of these concepts. To have your questions about this chapter answered by the author, browse to **www.syngress.com/solutions** and click on the **"Ask the Author"** form.

Q: Limiting access to specific IP addresses was always an important part of two-factor security with the SmartConsole clients. Can I do that with SmartPortal?

A: Yes, limiting access to specific IP addresses is retained in the new interface. You can configure this by creating or editing the *hosts.allowed* file on the SmartPortal server.

Q: Where do I install the SmartPortal server?

A: SmartPortal can be installed either on a dedicated server or on the SmartCenter Server itself.

Q: Which Web browsers are compatible with SmartPortal?

A: SmartPortal is compatible with these browsers:

- Internet Explorer
- Mozilla
- Firefox
- Netscape

The only other requirements are that you enable JavaScript and disable pop-up blockers.

Q: Is a SmartDefense Services subscription required to use SmartDefense or Web Intelligence?

A: No. SmartDefense and Web Intelligence are built in to VPN-1 Pro. You need the subscription only to get real-time updates and configuration advisories.

Q: I don't see where in my rulebase I can select SmartDefense. Where is it?

A: SmartDefense and Web Intelligence are configured on their own tabs within SmartDashboard.

Q: What types of defenses does SmartDefense/Web Intelligence provide?

A: Defenses against attacks, implicit defenses, and abnormal-behavior analysis.

Q: Do I still have to use the old-style rulebase in order to specify directionality in VPN traffic filters?

A: No. With NGX, you can now configure your rulebase to allow you to specify directionality in VPN traffic filtering.

Q: Why would I want an always-on tunnel?

A: An always-on tunnel is like an old "nailed-up" telephone or ISDN connection in that the tunnel opens immediately and stays open. Some applications are particularly sensitive to the setup latency on connections and an always-on tunnel can eliminate this latency.

Q: Why would I want a wire mode VPN?

A: A wire mode VPN understands that all traffic between two trusted hosts can skip the Stateful Inspection and just be passed through the firewall. This allows gateways on SecurePlatform Pro to use dynamic routing.

Q: What's required to set up dynamic routing?

A: You must be running SecurePlatform Pro, which requires a separate, additional license.

Q: What are the risks of using dynamic routing?

A: There are security risks in that you're configuring your firewall to accept routing updates from external and possibly insecure sources, and there are complexity risks in that many "firewall" problems are actually routing problems in disguise.

Q: Why should I consider using dynamic routing?

A: You should probably consider using dynamic routing only if you're in a larger organization that wishes to integrate the underlying router in VPN-1 Pro into a larger dynamic routing configuration.

Q: What are the versions of SecurePlatform?

A: SecurePlatform now comes in two versions, SecurePlatform and SecurePlatform Pro.

Q: What enhanced functionality does SecurePlatform Pro offer?

A: SecurePlatform Pro offers two distinct functionality upgrades over SecurePlatform: dynamic routing and the ability to use RADIUS to authenticate firewall administrators.

Q: Do I need a separate license for SecurePlatform?

A: No. SecurePlatform (the regular version) is free. SecurePlatform Pro requires a separate, additional license.

Q: For what sort of configurations would a VPN-1 Edge appliance be best?

A: VPN-1 appliances work best for telecommuters and branch offices. They provide firewall and VPN functionality without the higher costs and maintenance requirements of a full VPN-1 Pro installation.

Q: What's the difference between the S Series and the X Series?

A: The S Series is for telecommuters and protects only up to eight internal IP addresses. The X Series is for branch offices, and offers support for higher traffic and VPN bandwidth and a dedicated DMZ port.

Q: The X Series appliances have specific limitations on the number of internal IP addresses. Can this be changed?

A: Yes, you can upgrade a VPN-1 Edge within the same hardware product line (S Series within the S Series and X Series within the X Series).

Q: What type of objects can be cloned?

A: Only network and host objects, but that's a good start.

Q: What sort of information gets copied with the cloning?

A: All field values come over as a perfect copy. Be sure to change the information in the relevant fields immediately in order to avoid having duplicate objects.

MZ15

Chapter 3

Installing Check Point NGX

Solutions in this chapter:

- **Preparing the Gateway**

- **Installing SecurePlatform**

- **SmartCenter Server Installation**

- **Putting It All Together**

☑ **Summary**

☑ **Solutions Fast Track**

☑ **Frequently Asked Questions**

Introduction

Check Point has worked hard to develop an easy-to-use interface for installing and configuring their product line. With the continuing development of SecurePlatform, installing FireWall-1/VPN-1 has become easier.

In this chapter we review what must be done prior to the actual installation and configuration of a Check Point environment. We then demonstrate how to install SecurePlatform and then install and configure the gateway and management server. Once communication between the different components is set up, we will install and configure the SmartConsole, which will be used to connect to the SmartCenter Server to configure the security policy.

Preparing the Gateway

Prior to installation of the gateway, Check Point recommends following a simple check list to ensure that your gateway is fully functional after installation. One of the most important steps to do in preparation for your gateway is to harden the underlying operating system (OS). You must ensure that your OS is not running any unnecessary services that may leave your gateway vulnerable and take up valuable processing time. For example, if you plan to run FireWall-1/VPN-1 on a Windows 2000 server, there may be many unwanted services that were installed during the installation of the OS. Take the time to review the services and remove or disable those you will not be using. Typical services include NETBIOS Extended User Interface (NetBEUI), File Transfer Protocol (FTP), and Web servers. If you harden the system from isolated networks, no one can access it.

Your gateway's prime function after inspecting packets is to forward those packets to their proper destination. Take time to review your complete architecture and make note of any special routes that have to be manually added. Perform communication tests prior to installation (e.g., ping the remote devices from the OS that will host your Check Point installation).

Gateways often have several interface cards, which can become confusing if they are not properly identified. Properly identify the interface cards on the hardware itself and tag the cables that connect to them at either end. Proper identification will make connecting your gateway to the network easier and less time consuming.

Installing SecurePlatform

This section walks you through an installation of Check Point NGX in a distributed environment, which is the recommended way to plan your installation of NGX. A distributed installation consists of separating the SmartCenter Server from the FireWall-1/VPN-1 Pro gateway. The SmartCenter Server, also known as the *management server*, contains all of the objects, security policies, user databases, time objects, logs, and so on that is required to push a security policy to a gateway. The gateway will contain an *inspect script* that it received from your SmartCenter Server. The gateway will then determine whether or not to pass the traffic according to the security policy it received. The second type of installation is called a *stand-alone* configuration, which consists of installing the gateway and SmartCenter Server on the same machine. The downside to a stand-alone configuration is that it requires a lot more time to rebuild in the case of disaster recovery.

SecurePlatform

SecurePlatform can be installed on Intel- or AMD-based systems with a CD-ROM, by using the Check Point-provided media kit. Simply insert the NGX CD1 and reboot the system. When the system reboots you will be prompted with the SecurePlatform Welcome Screen (assuming that your BIOS settings include the CD-ROM boot sequence). (See Figure 3.1.)

Figure 3.1 SPLAT Welcome Screen

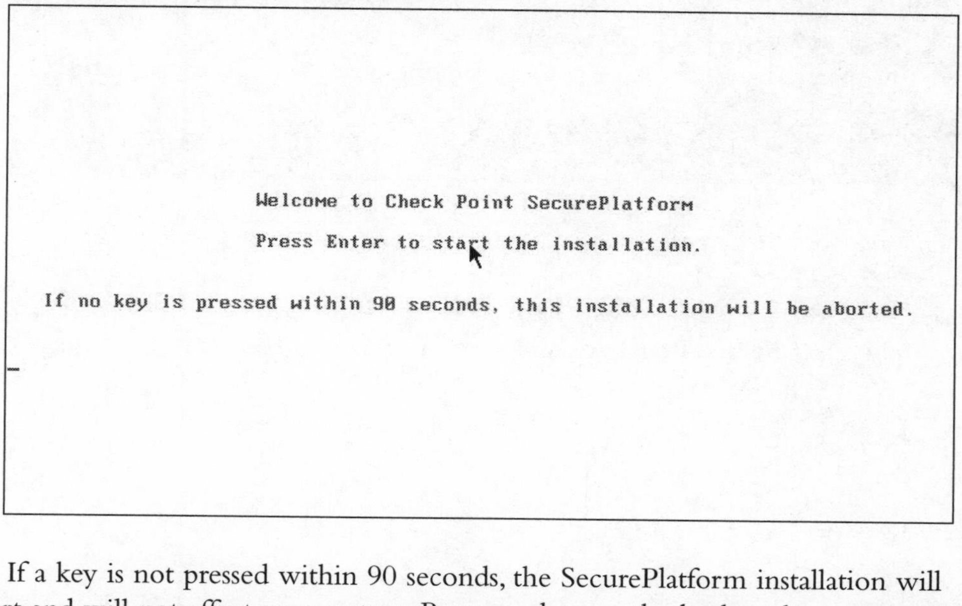

```
          Welcome to Check Point SecurePlatform

          Press Enter to start the installation.

 If no key is pressed within 90 seconds, this installation will be aborted.

 _
```

If a key is not pressed within 90 seconds, the SecurePlatform installation will abort and will not affect your system. Press any key on the keyboard to continue the installation. The Welcome Screen has several options. The Cancel option quits the installation process without affecting any data found on the OS. The Device List displays the devices that SecurePlatform has detected in terms of hardware. It is important that the operation of your gateway is compatible with all of your hardware, otherwise, it may cause problems later on. Check Point provides a Hardware Compatibility List (HCL) on its Web site, which should be consulted prior to purchasing a system to run SecurePlatform.

To add a hardware device to SecurePlatform, select **Add Driver**, which will prompt you for the path to the new driver (see Figure 3.2). Selecting **OK** assumes that you are ready for installation.

Figure 3.2 Options Shown in the SecurePlatform Welcome Screen

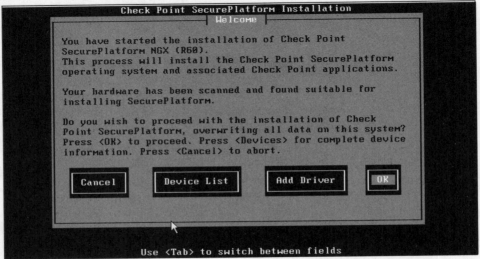

The next option provided is the "System Type." As discussed in the previous chapter, SecurePlatform Pro is a new addition to NGX, which also requires a license. If you do not plan to use the advanced routing capabilities in SecurePlatform Pro, simply select **SecurePlatform** and then press **OK** to continue (see Figure 3.3).

Figure 3.3 System Type

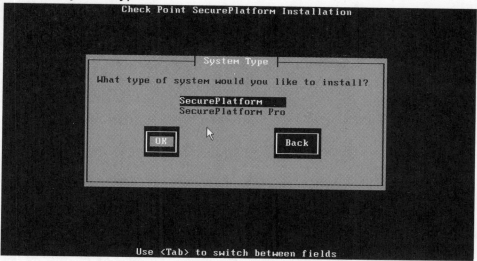

Depending on the region and the keyboard type that is attached to your gateway, you may have the ability to choose which keyboard type you want to use. For the purposes of this book, a U.S. keyboard is used and it is set at **default**. Click **OK** to continue (see Figure 3.4).

Figure 3.4 Keyboard Selection

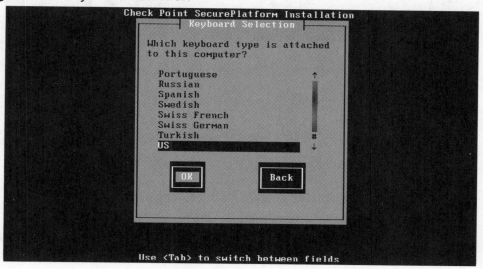

The next screen lists the Network Interface Cards (NIC) attached to the system. The screen also shows whether it detects a Link, No Link, or Unknown, if the interface doesn't support SecurePlatform's link detection protocol (see Figure 3.5).

When doing an initial installation of FireWall-1/VPN-1, it is recommended that it be installed on the interface that is facing the Internet. The installation process will determine that the installed interface is defined as external and will also be automatically listed in the operating system host's file. Select the external interface and then select **OK** to continue.

Figure 3.5 Network Device

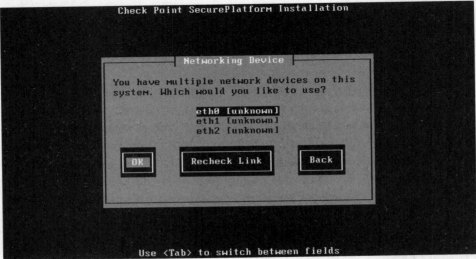

Configure the external interface on the following screen, as shown in Figure 3.6. For installation instruction purposes, we have chosen private addressing space as the external interface. In most NGX installations , you will use routable Internet Protocol (IP) addressing provided by your Internet service provider (ISP).

Figure 3.6 Network Interface Configuration

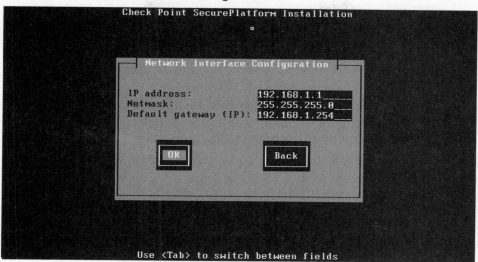

One of the best features of SecurePlatform is the ability to configure the OS from a Web-based browser such as Internet Explorer. Figure 3.7 displays the HTTPS Server Configuration screen, which prompts the user to decide whether or not to enable Web-based configuration and which port it should listen on. By default, it is enabled and most installations leave it enabled. However, it may be a good idea to change the default Hypertext Transfer Protocol Secure sockets (HTTPS) port 443 to another port. Once you have configured your options, select **OK** to continue.

Figure 3.7 HTTPS Server Configuration

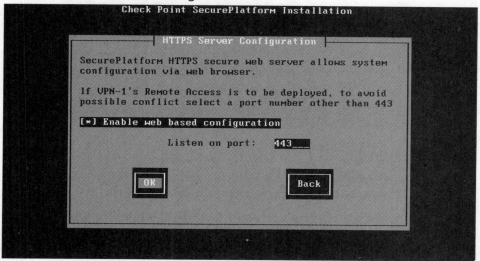

The next SecurePlatform installation screen is the confirmation screen (see Figure 3.8). This is the last step prior to the installation process, which will format and partition the disk. When you confirm your installation by selecting **OK**, the format process begins and Check Point SecurePlatform installs a pre-hardened OS within a couple of minutes.

NOTE

If you wish to obtain and verify the Linux kernel version on SecurePlatform at any time once it has rebooted, login to the SecurePlatform command line, either locally or in *SSH -> type "expert"* and enter *Expert mode password ->*. At the Expert mode prompt, enter the command *"uname -a"*. This will display the Linux kernel version; NGX SecurePlatform should display 2.4.21-20cp.

Figure 3.8 Confirmation

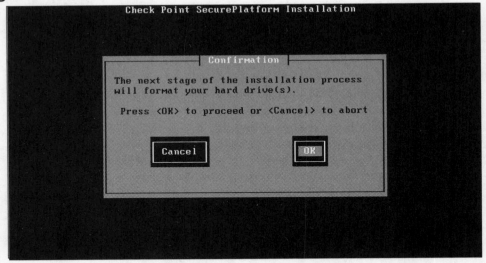

Once you select **OK** at the confirmation screen, you cannot stop the formatting process unless you physically power off your computer. Stopping the format process may cause unwanted and undefined consequences.

The installation process displays the progress of the installation. When you select **OK**, the system ejects the CD and reboots the OS. When the system is done rebooting, your login credentials by default are: username: admin and password: admin (see Figures 3.9 and 3.10):

Figure 3.9 Complete Check Point SecurePlatform Installation

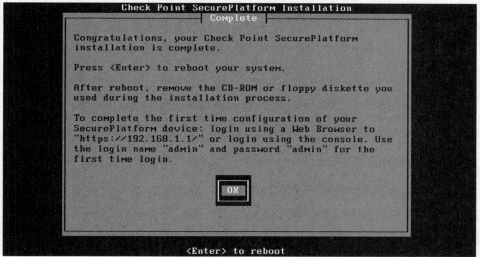

The login screen displays the current version of Check Point, and also indicates that you may connect to it with a Web browser in order to configure the OS and certain Check Point components via HTTPS.

Figure 3.10 Login Screen

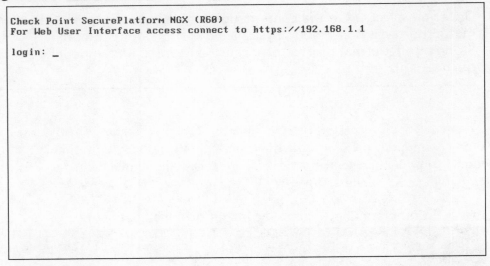

```
Check Point SecurePlatform NGX (R60)
For Web User Interface access connect to https://192.168.1.1

login: _
```

Once you are successfully connected, you will automatically be prompted to enter a new password and then given the option to change the username, "admin." When selecting a new password, SecurePlatform has a password-checking library (*cracklib-2.7-23cp*), which checks to ensure that your password "montreal" is not easily guessed. If you try using a password such as "montreal," you will be prompted to choose a different one because it is based in a dictionary file. If you choose a password that is too short, you will be prompted to enter a longer password since it wasn't long enough. These are some of the nice features that are built into SecurePlatform.

To configure your OS and install Check Point products, you can either log into SecurePlatform by HTTPS or by using the *sysconfig* utility (see Figure 3.11).

Figure 3.11 Welcome Wizard

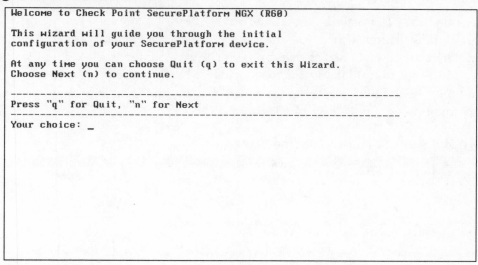

```
Welcome to Check Point SecurePlatform NGX (R60)

This wizard will guide you through the initial
configuration of your SecurePlatform device.

At any time you can choose Quit (q) to exit this Wizard.
Choose Next (n) to continue.

----------------------------------------------------------------
Press "q" for Quit, "n" for Next
----------------------------------------------------------------
Your choice: _
```

Selecting **n** for **Next** brings you to the various components that must be configured for your OS. Select all of the different components and go through the configuration screens. Ensure that you have properly configured all of the options;
especially routing. With incorrect routing, your gateway will not be able to communicate with other devices on distant networks (see Figure 3.12).

Figure 3.12 Initial Configuration

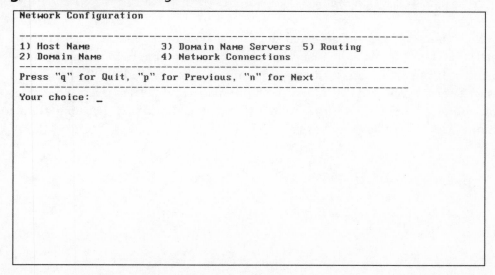

```
Network Configuration

----------------------------------------------------------------
1) Host Name        3) Domain Name Servers  5) Routing
2) Domain Name      4) Network Connections
----------------------------------------------------------------
Press "q" for Quit, "p" for Previous, "n" for Next
----------------------------------------------------------------
Your choice: _
```

FireWall-1/VPN-1 Installation

We are now ready to install the initial FireWall-1/VPN-1 gateway. When going through the installation wizard, you are prompted with the Check Point Welcome Screen. There are several choices that can be made at this point, such as installing the products in Evaluation mode or Purchased Mode. Selecting **Next** will suffice because the Check Point license can be installed at any time and by default we can evaluate the product for 15 days (see Figure 3.13).

Figure 3.13 Check Point Welcome Screen

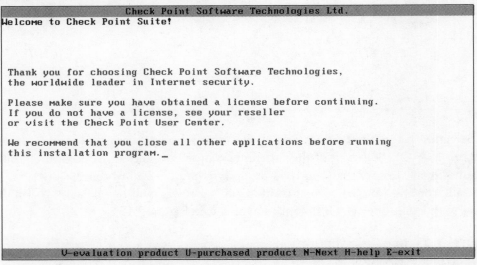

```
                    Check Point Software Technologies Ltd.
Welcome to Check Point Suite!




Thank you for choosing Check Point Software Technologies,
the worldwide leader in Internet security.

Please make sure you have obtained a license before continuing.
If you do not have a license, see your reseller
or visit the Check Point User Center.

We recommend that you close all other applications before running
this installation program. _




            U-evaluation product U-purchased product N-Next H-help E-exit
```

Once you have read and accepted the license agreement, you must select either "Enterprise" or "Express." The main difference between these two options is the number of IPs that an Express gateway can protect. The Check Point Express product targets small- and medium-sized businesses with 500 IPs or less. This installation will use the Enterprise/Pro product by selecting **1** and then selecting **Next** to continue with the installation (see Figure 3.14).

Figure 3.14 Enterprise/Express Selection

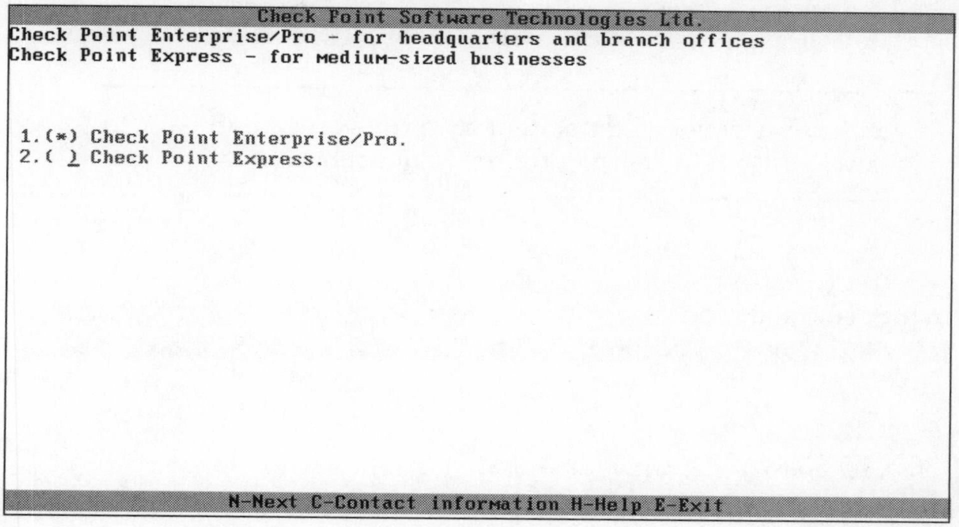

```
                 Check Point Software Technologies Ltd.
Check Point Enterprise/Pro - for headquarters and branch offices
Check Point Express - for medium-sized businesses



   1.(*) Check Point Enterprise/Pro.
   2.( ) Check Point Express.










                N-Next C-Contact information H-Help E-Exit
```

When selecting the Enterprise/Pro product feature, you are asked which products you want to install (See Figure 3.14.) As mentioned earlier, you want to install a distributed architecture; therefore, select option 1 VPN-1 Pro. Keep in mind that by selecting VPN-1 Pro, you are also installing FireWall-1 and VPN-1. Both products are now merged into one (see Figure 3.15).

Figure 3.15 Select Products

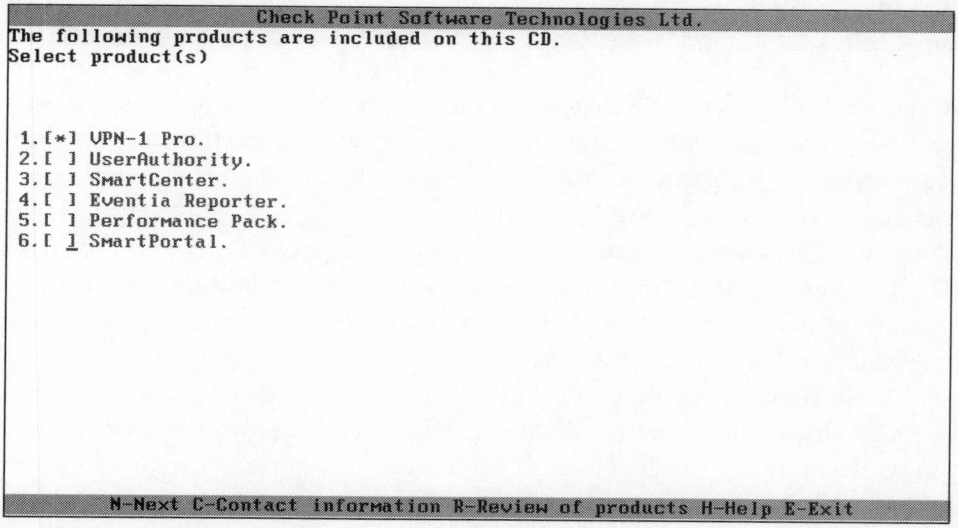

```
                 Check Point Software Technologies Ltd.
The following products are included on this CD.
Select product(s)


   1.[*] VPN-1 Pro.
   2.[ ] UserAuthority.
   3.[ ] SmartCenter.
   4.[ ] Eventia Reporter.
   5.[ ] Performance Pack.
   6.[ ] SmartPortal.








         N-Next C-Contact information R-Review of products H-Help E-Exit
```

The validation screen validates your choice of products (see Figure 3.16).

> **NOTE**
>
> If you have selected a component by error, you can go back to the previous screen to remove the product in question.

Figure 3.16 Validation

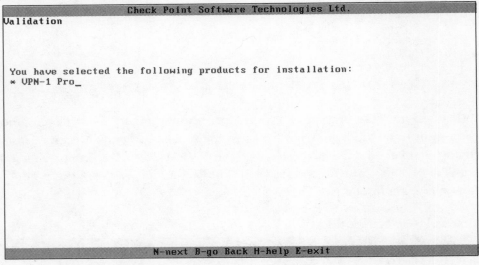

Once you have confirmed that you want to install VPN-1 Pro by selecting **Next**, Check Point will ask questions to help complete the installation. The series of questions asked at this point are configurable once the installation is complete and the machine has rebooted (see Figure 3.17).

The first question asks whether or not the gateway has a Dynamically Assigned IP (DAIP) address. Check Point supports the management of DAIPs and requires this information so that it can create a certificate to be sent to the SmartCenter Server for management, logging, and VPN purposes.

The next question regards clustering. If you installed a clustering product such as ClusterXL, which would create a highly available system between two or more gateways, you would select **yes**; however, this installation demonstration does not use a clustering product. SecurePlatform will then disable IP forwarding, harden the OS security, and generate the default filter for the gateway. The default filter, which is a "drop all" rule except for some Check Point communication protocols, are applied when the system reboots.

Figure 3.17 OS configuration

```
=================================================
Is this a Dynamically Assigned IP Address gateway installation ? (y/n) [n] ? n
Would you like to install a Check Point clustering product (CPHA, CPLS or State
Synchronization)? (y/n) [n] ? n
IP forwarding disabled
Hardening OS Security: IP forwarding will be disabled during boot.
Generating default filter
Default Filter installed
Hardening OS Security: Default Filter will be applied during boot.
This program will guide you through several steps where you
will define your Check Point products configuration.
At any later time, you can reconfigure these parameters by
running cpconfig


Configuring Licenses...
========================
Host            Expiration  Signature                        Features

Note: The recommended way of managing licenses is using SmartUpdate.
cpconfig can be used to manage local licenses only on this machine.

Do you want to add licenses (y/n) [y] ? _
```

Once the OS questions are done, you are prompted to configure the Check Point product that has been installed. Installing a license can be done at this time; however, it is easier to install through SmartUpdate.

One of the new features is the automatic collection of random data that is used for cryptographic operation. Prior to NGX, you would have to hit various keyboard values so that it could collect the random data (see Figure 3.18).

An important part to configure when doing a distributed installation is the SIC. The activation key is a one-time pass phrase that must be entered at any Check Point product that will be managed by a SmartCenter Server. In this case, enter a pass phrase to establish SIC from the SmartCenter, install the policies, and then send.

Figure 3.18 Product Configuration

```
===================================
Please specify group name [<RET> for super-user group]:

No group permissions will be granted. Is this ok (y/n) [y] ?


Configuring Random Pool...
============================
Automatically collecting random data to be used in
various cryptographic operations.

    [...................]

Automatic collection of random data is done.



Configuring Secure Internal Communication...
================================================
The Secure Internal Communication is used for authentication between
Check Point components

Trust State: Uninitialized
Enter Activation Key: _
```

Once you have established the activation key you will be prompted to reboot the server. You are now ready to incorporate your gateway with the SmartCenter Server.

SmartCenter Server Installation

Now that the installed the VPN-1 Pro server has been installed on a SecurePlatform OS, it is time to install the SmartCenter server. The SmartCenter Server installation guide is done on a SecurePlatform OS, as seen earlier in the chapter. Start the demonstration with the SecurePlatform wizard after the OS has been installed.

Using the *sysconfig* (system configuration) command and going all the way through the wizard, prompts you to the Check Point product selection. Select option 3 to install the SmartCenter Server (see Figure 3.19).

Figure 3.19 SmartCenter Server Product Selection

```
                    Check Point Software Technologies Ltd.
The following products are included on this CD.
Select product(s)


      1.[ ] VPN-1 Pro.
      2.[ ] UserAuthority.
      3.[*] SmartCenter.
      4.[ ] Eventia Reporter.
      5.[ ] Performance Pack.
      6.[ ] SmartPortal.







           N-Next C-Contact information R-Review of products H-Help E-Exit
```

Once you have selected the SmartCenter Server to be installed, the next option is to specify what type of SmartCenter Server installation you are conducting. Check Point has the ability to perform Management High Availability (HA). Management HA gives the security administrator the choice to have a secondary SmartCenter Server in case something happens to the first. This provides a robust solution for your SmartCenter Server. For this installation demonstration, choose selection number 1, Primary SmartCenter (see Figure 3.20).

Figure 3.20 Primary SmartCenter

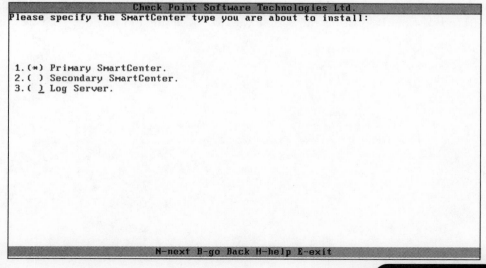

```
                    Check Point Software Technologies Ltd.
Please specify the SmartCenter type you are about to install:



      1.(*) Primary SmartCenter.
      2.( ) Secondary SmartCenter.
      3.( ) Log Server.










                    N-next B-go Back H-help E-exit
```

The validation screen shown in Figure 3.21 is standard prior to the installation process of the product. You can always go back a step and choose different options if you need to. Figure 3.22 shows the first SmartCenter Configuration screen. You may re-enter the Check Point configuration screen once the server reboots by typing the command **cpconfig** (Check Point Configuration).

Figure 3.21 SmartCenter Validation

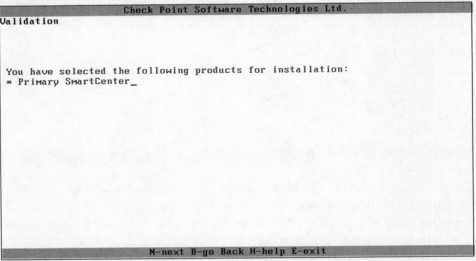

The first question is whether or not you want to configure the SmartCenter Server with a license. If you select **yes**, you can direct the configuration to the location of the license file *(*.lic)* or you can enter the different SKUs manually. The preferred method is to install it at a later time with the graphical user interface (GUI) SmartUpdate. SmartUpdate is the easiest way to configure and manage your licenses.

Figure 3.22 SmartCenter Configuration

```
Welcome to Check Point Configuration Program
=====================================================
This program will guide you through several steps where you
will define your VPN-1 configuration.
At any later time, you can reconfigure these parameters by
running cpconfig



Configuring Licenses...
=========================
Host             Expiration  Signature                      Features


Note: The recommended way of managing licenses is using SmartUpdate.
cpconfig can be used to manage local licenses only on this machine.

Do you want to add licenses (y/n) [y] ? n_
```

The next step is to define a SmartCenter Server administrator that will be used when connecting with one of the SmartConsole GUIs. You can only define a single administrator, which will have full permissions over all Check Point products. Once the administrator is defined, you must configure a GUI client (see Figure 3.23). A GUI client is the IP address of the machine from which the administrator will be connecting from. You may have several different GUI client IPs indicated here; however, they should be kept to a minimum. The administrators that will connect to the SmartCenter Server should have fixed IPs, which will make maintaining this list easier. You are not limited to a number of IPs. We have entered the IP addresses 192.168.2.10 and 172.30.30.10 that will be allowed to connect to the SmartCenter Server. You can always go back and configure more using the *cpconfig* command.

Figure 3.23 Configuring the SmartCenter Server

```
Read/Write Permission for all products with Permission to Manage Administrators

Configuring GUI Clients...
============================
GUI Clients are trusted hosts from which
Administrators are allowed to log on to this SmartCenter Server
using Windows/X-Motif GUI.

No GUI Clients defined
Do you want to add a GUI Client (y/n) [y] ? y

You can add GUI Clients using any of the following formats:
1.  IP address.
2.  Machine name.
3.  "Any" - Any IP without restriction.
4.  IP/Netmask - A range of addresses, for example 192.168.10.0/255.255.255.0
5.  A range of addresses - for example 192.168.10.8-192.168.10.16
6.  Wild cards (IP only) - for example 192.168.10.*

Please enter the list of hosts that will be GUI Clients.
Enter GUI Client one per line, terminating with CTRL-D or your EOF
character.
192.168.2.10
172.30.30.10Is this correct (y/n) [y] ? y_
```

The SmartCenter Server is also a certificate authority, which was introduced in NG and has continued to be successful in NGX (version 6.0). The Internal Certificate Authority (ICA) is initialized during installation and generates a certificate with the hostname and domain name (see Figure 3.24). It is important to have properly configured these options prior to configuring the ICA.

Once the ICA has been generated, you are prompted to save the certificate's fingerprint. The fingerprint can be used to validate that the ICA has not been tampered with. When first connecting with one of the SmartConsole GUIs, this same fingerprint will be displayed. It is good practice to validate the fingerprint with the one generated here. They should be identical; if they aren't, it means that somebody has tampered with your SmartCenter Server configuration and it should be looked into immediately.

Figure 3.24 Configuring the ICA for SmartCenter Server

```
Configuring Certificate Authority...
=======================================

The Internal CA will now be initialized
with the following name: mgmt-syngres.syngress.com

Initializing the Internal CA...(may take several minutes)
  Internal Certificate Authority created successfully
  Certificate was created successfully
Certificate Authority initialization ended successfully
Trying to contact Certificate Authority. It might take a while...
mgmt-syngres.syngress.com was successfully set to the Internal CA

Done


Configuring Certificate's Fingerprint...
=========================================
The following text is the fingerprint of this SmartCenter Server:
TOLD AM RACK RAN BERG SING MIRE CHUG QUIT ELI DAVY MANY

Do you want to save it to a file? (y/n) [n] ? _
```

The certificate's fingerprint is the last option before being asked to reboot the system. Now that you have completed your installation of the Primary SmartCenter Server, you must reboot with the reboot command. Once rebooted, you are ready to connect to the SmartCenter Server with one of the SmartConsole GUIs.

SmartConsole Installation

This section walks you through the installation of installing your SmartConsole, which should be installed on one of the GUI clients defined during your SmartCenter Server installation. If the SmartConsole will be installed on a new host that wasn't defined during the installation process, you can run **cpconfig** on the SmartCenter Server, which will allow you to reconfigure different aspects of the Check Point products installed, including the GUI list.

The Check Point SmartConsole can be installed on a Windows platform (demonstrated later). Check Point also has the motif GUI, which is licensed for Solaris operating systems.

To install the SmartConsole, either download the package from the Check Point Web site or download the package from the SecurePlatform HTTPS interface under **Product Configuration | Download SmartConsole**, or insert the NGX CD2 into the system. If you have enabled auto start on your CD-ROM, you will be prompted with Installation window (see Figure 3.25). Click **Next -> Accept the License agreement -> Choose Enterprise Pro -> New Installation** at which point you will select your SmartConsole options (see Figure 3.26).

Figure 3.25 NGX CD2 Auto Run

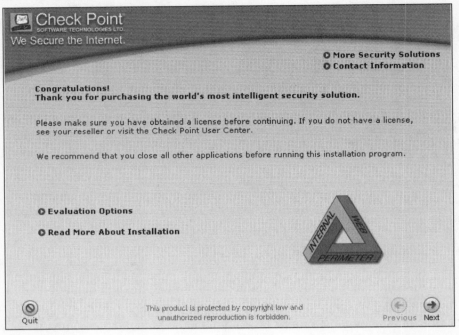

Figure 3.26 SmartConsole Options

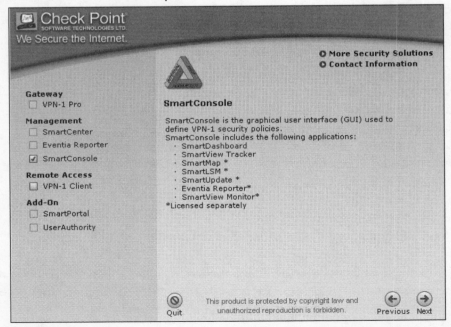

Select a SmartConsole product and leave your mouse over it to receive a brief description of what it consists of. Once you have selected the SmartConsole product to be installed, you will be prompted to select which products to install and what folder you want to install them to. By default, all options from SmartConsole are selected; however, if you did not purchase a particular product, you may want to remove them.

Putting It All Together

Now that you have installed your distributed configuration consisting of a VPN-1 Pro and a SmartCenter, you are ready to put it all together. Installing the SmartConsole consists of the Check Point framework called a *three-tier architecture*, which consists of the three different components communicating with each other. You will now see how to launch the SmartDashboard GUI and have it connect to the SmartCenter Server. Once connected, you will create and ensure that all components are able to communicate with each other.

SmartDashboard

Now you will connect your SmartDashboard to the SmartCenter Server to see if everything is working properly. First, you will launch the SmartDashboard GUI from GUI client 192.168.2.10, which was configured earlier in the SmartCenter Server. If you connected from another IP address, an error message would appear indicating that you are not authorized to connect from that IP.

Start the SmartDashboard application from its default installation directory from within Windows; **Start -> Programs -> Check Point SmartConsole R60 -> SmartDashboard**. When launching the SmartDashboard you will be prompted for the username, password, and SmartCenter Server IP address (see Figure 3.27).

Figure 3.27 SmartDashboard Connect

> **TIP**
>
> Check Point offers the choice of connecting using a certificate as credentials. To create a certificate, you must already be connected to the SmartCenter Server and create a Check Point Admin user that uses a certificate for authentication.

A fingerprint is presented, which must be accepted in order to continue. As mentioned earlier, when installing the SmartCenter Server, you have to verify the fingerprint shown against the one you exported. Accepting the certificate places a validation on the GUI client OS so that it doesn't have to check it every time. If for some reason the SmartCenter Server has changed its certificate, a new certificate will be presented during the first connection (see Figure 3.28).

Figure 3.28 Fingerprint

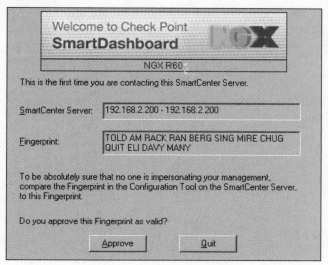

You must approve the certificate to continue, otherwise, the application will exit and you will have to double-check it to see why it has changed. When connected, the SmartCenter Server object is created automatically (see Figure 3.29). Because it is connecting to itself, it knows that there is a Check Point product installed and populates the objects database with itself.

Figure 3.29 Network Objects View

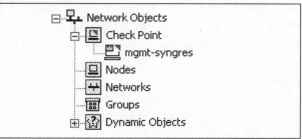

To complete the initial setup, you must define the VPN-1 Pro installed earlier. You can create new objects by expanding **Network Objects** and selecting **Check Point | New Check Point | VPN-1 Pro/Express Gateway**. If you have other Check Point objects to create, go to **Manage | Network Objects | New | Check Point | VPN-1 Pro/Express Gateway**. Both ways are valid. The latter method is the original way; however, the first method is the quickest.

There are two modes when creating a Check Point object. We demonstrate how to do it using the wizard (simple mode); however, you may opt to create a Check Point object using the classic mode. The result is the same, but the wizard mode has been greatly improved and very simple to use (see Figure 3.30).

Figure 3.30 VPN-1 Pro Object Creation

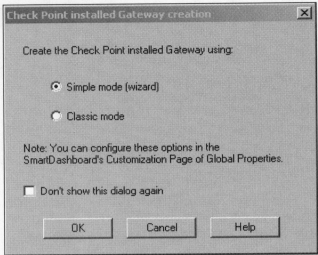

When choosing the wizard mode, it will prompt you to enter the gateway's name (see Figure 3.31). Earlier in the chapter, you installed the VPN-1 module with IP address 192.168.1.1. You also saw the different options within the sysconfig utility that give the OS its identity. To create the VPN-1 Pro object with its host name to take advantage of the option "Get address," you must first populate the SmartCenter Server hosts file.

NOTE

You can speed up the process of creating objects by populating the SmartCenter Server hosts file. When populated, it will enhance object creation.

Figure 3.31 Wizard Properties

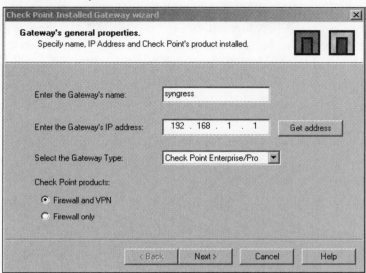

Once you have entered the gateway's name and fetched the IP address using **get address** you can choose the type of gateway that you want to install. The options are Enterprise/Pro or Express. Your installation of the gateway "syngress" was an Enterprise Pro. You must then select what products are licensed for the gateway. If you only have a FireWall-1 license, you can only select **Firewall only**; however, you can select "Firewall and VPN" if you are using the VPN functionalities. Once you have selected **next**, you are prompted to enter the Activation Key (see Figure 3.32).

Figure 3.32 SIC

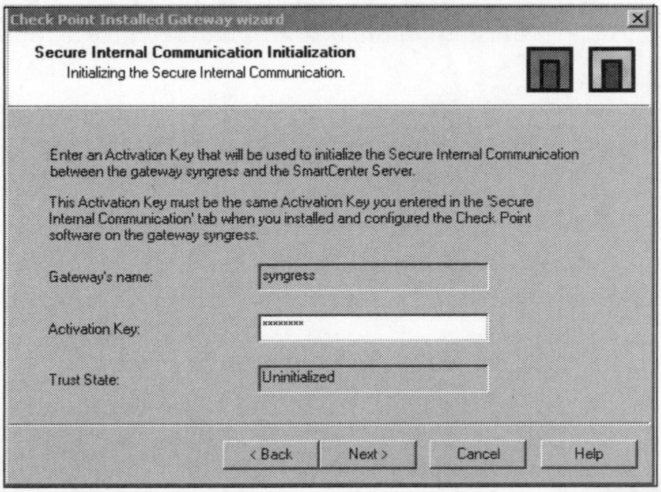

The activation key is the secure internal communication passphrase that you entered during the installation of the gateway. If you have forgotten the activation key, you can return to the module and enter **cpconfig** to re-activate a new passphrase. When you have entered the passphrase, select **Next** to test the communication status between the SmartCenter Server and the VPN-1 Pro gateway (see Figure 3.33).

Figure 3.33 Trust Established

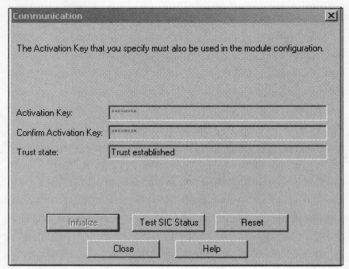

Once the trust has been established between the two Check Point products, the SmartCenter Server is able to configure and push security policies to the gateway taking control over it. By default, the gateway sends the log files to the SmartCenter Server when the trust has been established, assuming the correct routing and security rules are put in place.

After selecting **Close**, you can edit the newly created gateway's properties. The new object will be populated in the Objects tree under the Check Point heading. (see Figure 3.34).

Figure 3.34 Objects List with Newly Created Gateway

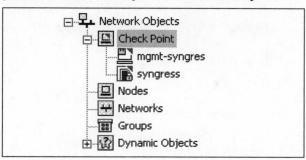

Now that you have successfully created your Check Point VPN-1 Pro gateway, you are on your way to creating your first security policy.

Installing on Microsoft, Sun, Red Hat, and Nokia

Although SecurePlatform is certainly one of the most popular options for installing Check Point NGX today, one of the strengths of Check Point is its OS portability. Check Point NGX can be installed on Microsoft Windows 2000 and 2003, Sun Solaris UltraSPARC 8 and 9, Red Hat Enterprise 3.0, and Nokia IPSO 3.9.

Among all UNIX-based operating systems (Solaris, Red Hat, Nokia), the installation is very similar to that on SecurePlatform. The Nokia IPSO platforms are the most popular dedicated appliances for running Check Point. Once you download the **IPSO_wrapper_R60.tgz** package to your IPSO platform, use the **newpkg** command to install NGX. On Solaris and Red Hat operating systems, insert the CD (CD1 for Linux, CD2 for Solaris), and run the **UnixInstallScript** on it. Once you follow the default options on each installation, you will eventually get to the Check Point Welcome Screen (as in Figure 3.13), and you can continue from the instructions at the beginning of the chapter.

Microsoft Windows is a convenient option for installing a SmartCenter Server, and it supports all options that SmartCenter or SecurePlatform does. However, we would not recommend installing your Security Gateway on it. To install NGX on Windows, insert the NGX CD2 into your machine, and the setup program will start. Follow the default options; just be sure to deselect the VPN-1 Pro option on the components to install screen. After the installation is complete, you will input the different configuration options (licenses, administrator, GUI clients, and the CA Fingerprint) using a graphical interface. Reboot and you're done.

System Requirements

Check Point is an extremely efficient firewall, and its hardware needs are small compared with other systems you have in your network. The minimum memory requirements are 256MB of RAM for Windows and 128MB of RAM for SecurePlatform, Solaris, Red Hat, and Linux. In terms of CPU, a Pentium II 300MHz is the minimum and at least a 6GB hard disk. Of course, the minimum requirements are just that, minimum. We recommend a machine with a Pentium IV 2GHz or similar processor, 512 MB of RAM, and a 40GB hard disk, which is a very standard configuration available today.

Summary

Check Point has put a lot of research and development into the creation of SecurePlatform and the new addition of SecurePlatform Pro with NGX. Providing a pre-hardened OS simplifies the task of preparing your host to run the Check Point suite.

With Check Point's extensive suite of Firewall products, ranging from the small, medium, and enterprise environments, there is a solution for every need.

The SmartCenter Server provides a centralized location to control and push out your security policies to your different environments. The SmartDashboard utilizes a GUI to quickly comprehend and build your security policy. Interconnecting Check Point devices has become easier with NGX, which corresponds to everybody's needs.

Solutions Fast Track

Preparing the Gateway

- ☑ Your gateway is the most important part of your security infrastructure. If your organization already has an Internet Usage guideline for employees, it may be helpful when creating adequate security policies.

- ☑ When initially installing your gateway, it automatically loads a default security filter named *Standard*. If you have communication problems at the start, you may want to unload the security policy by typing **fw unloadlocal** at the command prompt.

- ☑ Firewalls inspect a lot of traffic, so try to log traffic that will be useful to your organization. Your log files must be easy to sort through; unnecessary logging may take more time to filter out traffic.

Installing SecurePlatform

- ☑ Check Point allows you to install FireWall-1/VPN-1 software in either a distributed or stand-alone configuration.

- ☑ When considering hardware for your Check Point servers, keep in mind that not all hardware devices are compatible with SecurePlatform or other operating systems. Take the time to plan and view the HCL on their Web site.

☑ Make sure that you have all of your required licenses prior to installing your Check Point software.

☑ Take the time to plan your architecture with special emphasis on routing and documentation. A well-documented installation should ease the installation and any troubleshooting down the road.

SmartCenter Server Installation

☑ The SmartCenter Server contains all of your security policies, objects, users, logs, and almost all aspects of your Check Point infrastructure. You should back this server up frequently or have a secondary management server within your organization.

☑ The SmartCenter Server does not inspect any traffic; however, it contains all of the rules that will be installed on your gateways in the form of an *inspect* script.

☑ Connecting to the SmartCenter Server requires the server to have the list of allowed IPs that can connect to it. Populate the SmartCenter Server GUI list using the *cpconfig* utility on any OS.

Putting It All Together

☑ The HCL should be consulted prior to installing SecurePlatform. Make sure that your hardware will be supported and detected by SecurePlatform.

☑ If you choose the advanced capabilities of SecurePlatform Pro with its dynamic routing or for its centralized administrator management through RADIUS, an additional license is required.

☑ If you were not used to Linux or have decided to change operating systems, take the time to become familiar with SecurePlatform in a lab environment.

☑ NIC support has at times been a problem with SecurePlatform. NGX has provided almost every type of device driver possible; however, double-check the HCL.

Frequently Asked Questions

The following Frequently Asked Questions, answered by the authors of this book, are designed to both measure your understanding of the concepts presented in this chapter and to assist you with real-life implementation of these concepts. To have your questions about this chapter answered by the author, browse to **www.syngress.com/solutions** and click on the **"Ask the Author"** form.

Q: I want to install SecurePlatform but I don't understand Linux very well. What should I do?

A: Check Point SecurePlatform gives you all the necessary tools to configure the OS so you don't have to be an expert in Linux. You can configure all of the required aspects of the OS to run FireWall-1/VPN-1 by connecting to the SecurePlatform through HTTPS with a Web browser or by using the sysconfig utility.

Q: What's the difference between SecurePlatform and SecurePlatform Pro?

A: The main difference is that SecurePlatform Pro adds to the SecurePlatform framework by adding dynamic routing support for unicast and multicast protocols as well as centralized administrator management through RADIUS. SecurePlatform also requires a separate license.

Q: I would like to test Check Point FireWall-1 but I don't have a license. How can I get it to work?

A: By default, all Check Point products are provided with 15-day evaluation licenses. This gives you plenty of time to test it. If 15 days isn't enough, you can contact your local reseller or Check Point directly at *licensing@checkpoint.com*.

Q: What happens when a second person connects to the SmartCenter Server with a SmartConsole GUI?

A: Previous to version NGX, you would have to connect in "Read Only" mode. However, a new feature in NGX has the ability to disconnect the connected user to allow access to it. This shouldn't be done often, because it may corrupt the changes that other administrator are doing.

Q: My gateway rebooted last night and I want to be sure that it installed the latest policy. How can I check?

A: You may use the SmartView Monitor tool to view the current status of all of your gateways. It will also indicate what security policy is installed and at what time it was done. The second option is to run the **fw stat** command on the gateway itself.

Q: I'm can't install security policies anymore. What happened?

A: There could be several reasons for this; however, the most common problem is connectivity issues. Be sure that your routing hasn't changed, and double-check the Secure Internal Communication status.

Q: I currently have an NG/AI license. Will it work with NGX?

A: No. You must upgrade your NG/AI license to NGX within your User Center account. To upgrade the license, a valid software subscription license is required.

Q: How many gateways can a single SmartCenter Server handle?

A: There isn't a limit; however, you will require an unlimited Enterprise license to do so. When you start managing over 30 gateways from the same SmartCenter Server, you may want to have a secondary management server in case the primary fails.

Q: I currently have three NG/AI gateways in a distributed configuration. How do I upgrade only one NG/AI gateway to NGX to see how it handles the load and get accustomed to the new changes?

A: Start by upgrading your license to NGX. Once you have upgraded your SmartCenter Server and gateway licenses to NGX, upgrade your SmartCenter Server. Once the SmartCenter Server is upgraded, perform the NG/AI gateway upgrade to NGX. Once upgraded, double-check your Secure Internal Communication with all gateways and ensure that logging is operational.

Chapter 4

Upgrading to NGX

Solutions in this chapter:

- Backup
- Upgrade Order
- Minimal Downtime
- Rollback

☑ Summary

☑ Solutions Fast Track

☑ Frequently Asked Questions

Introduction

You have a current Check Point environment for managing security in your infrastructure. Version NGX is available with many enticing new features; the bells and whistles pique your interest. With NGX media in hand you are ready to invest the resources to forge ahead with the upgrade. The technologist inside you wants the green flag, but the pragmatist is looking for yellow.

This chapter will guide you through the necessary steps to perform the NGX upgrade. You need to ensure that you have the necessary tools and perform the appropriate tests prior to starting the actual upgrade. There are various paths, depending on uptime requirements and hardware availability. In all upgrade scenarios it is equally important to have proper rollback procedures in the event of failure.

Backup

It seems ironic that the first step of any upgrade procedure is to perform system backups. Consider this step as your insurance for the worst-case scenario. In the event of a failure it is important to be able to restore functionality in a timely fashion. The SmartCenter Server is the single most important piece of your Check Point environment. The databases on this system contain everything (keys, objects, services, rules, etc.) that is required to maintain your security configuration. Rebuilding everything from scratch is unacceptable and in some cases impossible. Gateways are easier to rebuild if necessary, although another undesirable alternative.

Ensure that you have a valid current backup if you are using some type of enterprise software. Use the Export function on the NGX CD to perform an export of your SmartCenter Server configuration. This export does not include operating system configuration parameters. On Nokia or SecurePlatform devices use the built-in system tools to perform the backup. The ideal situation is to perform these backups immediately prior to the upgrade process. Document the system parameters: hostname, IP address, ARP, and routing configuration.

Upgrade Order

Only NG versions can be upgraded to NGX. If your environment has any systems not currently at NG they must be upgraded before proceeding. NGX SmartCenter Servers are not capable of managing 4.x Gateways and NGX media will not perform the upgrade. The SmartCenter Server(s) must be upgraded first, followed by the Gateways. In a stand-alone environment both components are upgraded simultaneously. Before upgrading any software you should upgrade licenses, verify the existing configuration, and develop a clear strategy.

Licenses

Upgrading to NGX requires an upgrade of your NG licenses. Licenses can be upgraded in the Check Point User Center or by using the license_upgrade utility. Upgrading licenses in the User Center is a manual process per license. Using the license_upgrade utility requires you to copy the operating system–specific version of the utility from the CD to the SmartCenter Server. The license_upgrade utility is a menu-driven text-based tool. Running this tool brings up the following:

```
Running License_upgrade
- To upgrade to NGX R60, YOU MUST FIRST upgrade licenses for all NG
products.
- NGX R60 with licenses from previous versions WILL NOT FUNCTION.
- The license upgrade process gathers all the licenses from this machine,
sends
them in SSL encrypted format to the User Center, gets the upgraded licenses
and
installs them on the machine.
- The license upgrade process on the SmartCenter Server also handles gateway
licenses in the license repository.
- After the software upgrade, open SmartUpdate and attach the new NGX
licenses
to the gateways.
- For more details, see the License Upgrade chapter of the Upgrade Guide
  (located on the CD and at the Check Point Download site).


Current Machine Status: None of the 7 licenses on the machine are upgraded.


Please choose one of the following:


[L]  View the licenses installed on your machine.
[S]  Simulate the license upgrade.
[U]  Perform license upgrade now.
[O]  Perform license upgrade for an offline machine.
[C]  Check if currently installed licenses have been upgraded.
[Q]  Quit
```

> **WARNING**
>
> You must have a current Software Subscription to get updated licenses.
> Some license features changed between NG and NGX and others are no
> longer supported. Use the Simulation option to see if any of these
> changes apply to your environment. Resolve any license issues before
> continuing with the upgrade.

There are license features no longer supported in NGX. Additionally there are
changes in licensing components on the SmartCenter Server and Gateways. The
license_upgrade tool will inform you of any existing license changes if they are
applicable to your environment.

Pre_Upgrade_Verifier

Prior to proceeding you should run the pre_upgrade_verifier on the production
SmartCenter Server. This tool looks for configuration issues that are not compatible
with NGX. Using the pre_upgrade_verifier utility requires you to copy the operating system-specific version of the utility from the CD to the SmartCenter Server.
The pre_upgrade_verifier utility is a menu-driven text-based tool. The results are
displayed on the screen or they can be directed to a text file using the **–f** option.
Add the **–w** option to report to a Web format. Running the command with no
options displays the following:

```
C:\Temp\NGX>pre_upgrade_verifier

This is Check Point Pre-Upgrade Verifier Major Version 5, Feature Pack 9,
Service Pack 1 - Build 033.

Usage: pre_upgrade_verifier -p SmartCenterPath -c CurrentVersion -t
TargetVersion
[-f FileName] [-w]
   Or: pre_upgrade_verifier -p SmartCenterPath -c CurrentVersion -i
[-f FileName] [-w]

        -p Path of the installed SmartCenter Server (FWDIR).
        -c Currently installed version.
        -t Target version.
```

```
-i Check originality of Inspect files only.
-f Output in file.
-w Web format file.
```

where the Currently installed version is one of the following:
```
4.1
NG
NG_FP1
NG_FP2
NG_FP3
VSX_201
NG_AI
VSX_NG_AI
VSX_NGAI_R2
NG_AI_R55
GX_NG_25
NG_AI_R55W
NG_AI_R57
```

where the Target version is one of the following:
```
NG_FP1
NG_FP2
NG_FP3
VSX_201
NG_AI
VSX_NG_AI
VSX_NGAI_R2
NG_AI_R55
GX_NG_25
NG_AI_R55W
NG_AI_R57
NGX_R60
```

The report lists recommended actions for pre- and post-installation. There are two classes of actions, warnings, and errors. Warnings are informational for items to correct either before or after the actual upgrade. Errors are items that must be corrected before continuing. **Performing an upgrade with uncorrected errors will result in a failed upgrade.**

NOTE

Make sure that you review the hardware and software requirements for NGX. Ensure that your systems meet the requirements to facilitate a successful upgrade. Windows 2003 SP1 is not supported according to the Check Point Knowledge base. This is different from the minimum software requirements listed in the NGX Getting Started guide.

SmartCenter

There are two methods for upgrading the SmartCenter Server. You can perform an upgrade directly to your production server, the riskiest option. Alternatively, you can migrate to a new server. Migrating to a new server provides the opportunity to change platforms or upgrade the existing hardware. The next sections will walk through both upgrade scenarios on a Windows SmartCenter Server and the upgrade option on a SecurePlatform SmartCenter Server.

Windows

The first option we will perform is an upgrade on the production Windows SmartCenter Server. Insert CD2 of the NGX media kit into the drive. If auto-run is enabled for the drive, the install window will automatically open; otherwise run **Setup.exe** from the root of the CD. In the main screen click **Next** to open the license agreement. Check the radio button next to **I accept the terms of the license agreement** and click **Next** to open the upgrade options screen (see Figure 4.1).

Figure 4.1 Selecting the Upgrade Option

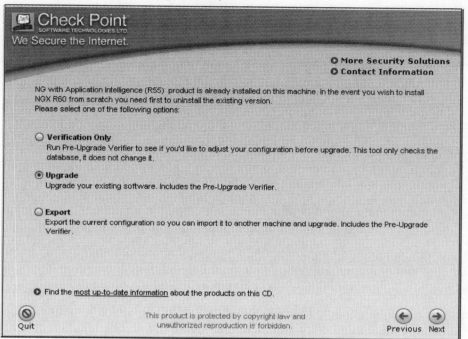

Select the **Upgrade** radio button and click **Next** to continue. A window opens, asking if you wish to upgrade licenses. Leaving the check on the **Upgrade Licenses during this installation process** will perform the license_upgrade function discussed earlier. Uncheck the Upgrade licenses box and click **Next** to get a strong recommendation to the upgrade licenses window and click **Next** again. This opens the upgrade utilities screen (see Figure 4.2). This screen recommends using the latest upgrade utilities and offers three choices: download the most updated utilities, use a local disk where the latest files have already been downloaded, or use the utilities on the current CD. At the time of this writing the utilities on the CD are the latest so the upgrade uses the files on the CD even if you select to download the most updated. Select the radio button for Use the upgrade utilities from the CD and click **Next**.

Figure 4.2 Upgrade Utility Options

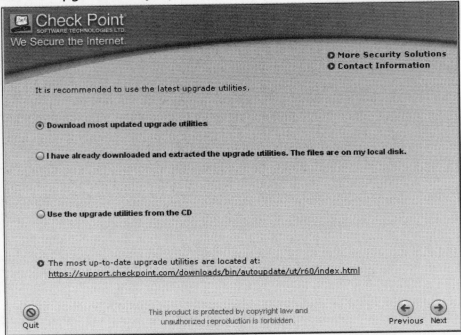

The Pre-Upgrade Verification screen opens to ask if you want to skip this test. Leave the Skip Pre-Upgrade Verification unchecked and click **Next**. The Pre-Upgrade Verification results opens, stating recommendations exist (see Figure 4.3). You can view these in HTML format by clicking **View Pre-Upgrade Verification results**. If there are no errors, select the **Continue anyway** radio button and click **Next**.

Figure 4.3 Pre-Upgrade Verification Results

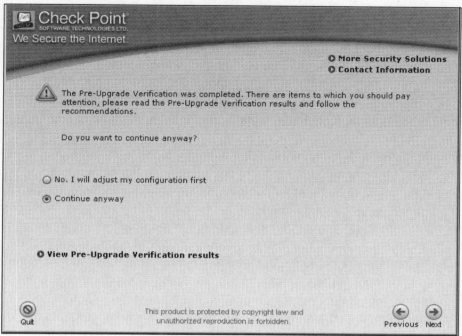

The next screen asks if you wish to add new products in addition to upgrading the existing software. Leave **Add new products checked** if you wish to add additional products, then click **Next** to open a window to select additional products. In this example uncheck the box and select **Next** to continue. The products that will be upgraded are displayed; click **Next** to continue. The installation begins and a question window opens, informing you a **cpstop** will be performed (see Figure 4.4). Click **Yes** to continue.

Figure 4.4 Upgrade Warning—cpstop

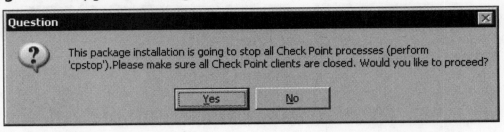

The installation will run and ask about copying log files automatically now or manually later. This can take time if there are a large number of log files. Select the preferred option and click **Next** to continue. If SmartConsole clients are installed on the SmartCenter Server you will be asked which clients to install and whether you want shortcuts on the desktop. After the installation wizard process completes, click **Finish** to return to a Thank You window and click **Finish** again. Now you are asked to reboot to activate the changes; click **Yes** to be asked to remove the CD from the drive. Click **OK** to eject the CD and reboot the system. The upgrade is complete.

The next option is the migration upgrade. For this option of upgrading we will plan on using the same IP and hostname as the original SmartCenter Server. There are additional steps if you plan on changing the IP address. Begin the process as described in the production upgrade section until the options screen appears. Select the **Export** radio button and click **Next** to open an upgrade utilities screen. Select the radio button for Use the upgrade utilities from the CD and click **Next**. The Pre-Upgrade Verification screen opens to ask if you want to perform this test. Leave the check to perform the Pre-Upgrade Verification and click **Next**. The Pre-Upgrade Verification results opens, stating recommendations exist. You can view these in HTML format by clicking **View Pre-Upgrade Verification results**. If there are no errors select the Continue anyway radio button and click **Next**. The next screen asks where to save the configuration file. You may change the directory or filename if you want; click **Next** to continue and create the export (see Figure 4.5). Click **OK** in this window followed by **Finish** to complete the export portion.

Figure 4.5 Export Completion

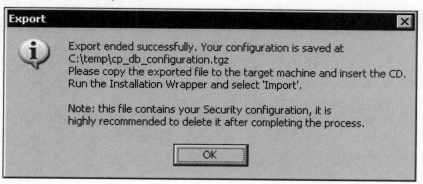

Transfer the configuration export file to the new SmartCenter Server. Insert the appropriate CD in the new SmartCenter Server. Proceed as earlier to accept the license agreement to open an options window, select the **Check Point Enterprise/Pro** radio button, and click **Next** to continue. A window opens offering installation options (see Figure 4.6). Select the **Installation Using Imported Configuration** radio button and click **Next**.

Figure 4.6 Selecting the Import Option

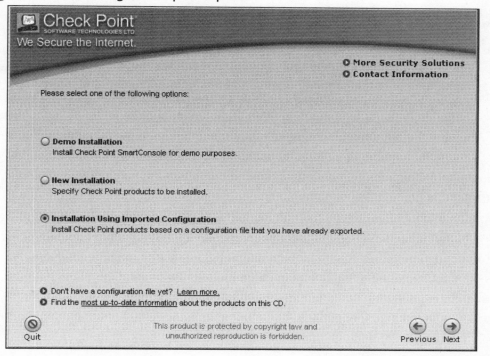

Type the location and name of the exported configuration file and click **Next**. You are again given the option to download the latest upgrade utilities. Select the **Use the upgrade utilities from the CD** radio button and click **Next**. After the upgrade licenses option opens, leave the option to upgrade during the installation unchecked and click **Next**. The next window lists products selected for installation; click **Next**. The licenses from the production SmartCenter Server are automatically transferred using this upgrade method.

The installation begins and you are asked to specify the installation directory; modify as desired and click **Next**. After the InstallShield Wizard window opens stating the installation is completed, click **OK**. A message advises that the database is being imported, followed by a Licenses screen where existing licenses are shown with an option to add new licenses if desired. Click **Next**. Existing administrators are shown with the option to edit the list; click **Next**. Existing GUI clients are shown with the option to add new clients; click **Next**. After the fingerprint is displayed, click **Finish**. You are now thanked for installing Check Point Software. Click **Finish**. Now you are asked to reboot to activate the changes; click **Yes** to be asked to remove the CD from the drive. Click **OK** to eject the CD and reboot the system. Disconnect the old SmartCenter Server from the production network and connect the Upgraded SmartCenter to complete the upgrade migration.

TIP

You are probably going to be really eager to connect to the new SmartCenter Server after the upgrade. The NGX SmartConsole clients are required for management. Install the NGX SmartConsole tools on the clients before upgrading the server. Multiple versions of SmartConsole software can be installed on the same computer.

SecurePlatform

The first option you will perform is an upgrade on the production SecurePlatform FP2, FP3, R54 or R55 SmartCenter Server. Insert CD1 from the NGX media kit into the CD drive on the system. If you are upgrading FP2 or FP3, enter expert mode and run the following commands to upgrade the patch command:

```
# mount /mnt/cdrom
# patch add /mnt/cdrom/SecurePlatform/patch/CPpatch_command_*.tgz
```

Once the commands execute, the upgrade process continues with the R54 and R55 upgrade process. Log in to the system as a user; you do not need to go into expert mode. The commands are typed as follows:

```
[smartctr-svr]# patch add cd
Choose a patch to install:


1) SecurePlatform NGX R60 Upgrade Package (CPspupgrade_R60.tgz)
2) Exit


Your choice:
 1


Calculating the MD5 checksum of the package.
The MD5 checksum is: 6a0b5bc83987830d571f8a2e0549e9f5
Is that right (Y/N)? Y
Extracting /mnt/cdrom/SecurePlatform/patch/CPspupgrade_R60.tgz package ..
Start Upgrading ..


Verifying ..
Extracting files ..
Extracting files completed successfully.
Upgrade program will now upgrade your system. This process may take several
minutes
```

After a welcome screen opens, type **N** for Next to continue and open the license agreement. Type **Y** to agree to the license agreement to open the Enterprise Options Screen.

```
Enterprise Suite Options


 1.( ) Export SmartCenter configuration.
 2.( ) Perform pre-upgrade verification only.
 3.(*) Upgrade.
```

Type **3** to highlight the Upgrade option and type **N** for Next to continue. This opens the license_upgrade utility screen; select **Q** to quit the license upgrade process and the system automatically performs a pre-upgrade verification test.

```
Pre-Upgrade Verification Results


The pre-upgrade verification process has completed.
```

```
See the Pre-upgrade verification results,
and follow the recommendations.
Select your choice and press Enter N-continue V-view the results E-exit: V
```

The pre-verification results are displayed by typing **V**; when done reviewing type **N** to continue. The next step asks if you want to create a snapshot image. If the upgrade terminates abnormally the system automatically will revert back to this snapshot; type **y** to create the snapshot.

```
Do you want to create a backup image for automatic revert (y/n)?: y
Creating the Snapshot Image. This can take up to 10 minutes...
Done
Upgrading the operating system.

Preparing to upgrade Check Point Products.

Existing Server/Gateway products have been detected.
Please specify one of the following upgrade options:
  1.( ) Upgrade installed products and install new products.
  2.(*) Upgrade installed products.
```

Type **2** to select Upgrade installed products, then type N for Next to continue and open a Validation screen.

```
Validation
 You have selected the following products for installation:
 * Primary SmartCenter
```

Type **N** to continue and the process will complete and return the following information.

```
Upgrade of Check Point products has been successfully completed.
Please wait while the upgrade process completes.
Installation finished successfully

Please remove Check Point CD from the CDROM drive.
Upgrade files completed successfully.
```

```
------------------------------------------------------------
In order to complete the upgrade process please reboot your system!
------------------------------------------------------------
Patch installed successfully.
[smartctr-svr]#
```

The upgrade is finished; remove the CD and type **reboot** to reboot the server to complete the upgrade.

WARNING

If you do not remove the CD and reboot, the system boots from the CD and begins a new installation of SecurePlatform. Accidentally pressing any key during this 90-second window will begin a fresh installation.

Solaris

Upgrading a Solaris SmartCenter is similar to the processes listed previously. Run the **UnixInstallScript** from the CD. The advanced upgrade option provides the capability to use the export and import functions to migrate to a new server. Before performing either upgrade verify that the correct packages and patches have been applied to the server.

Firewall Gateway

Upgrading Gateways presents a different challenge regarding network availability. SmartCenter upgrades create a period where administrative connectivity is unavailable. Gateway upgrades involve a potential network interruption where services are unavailable. In clustered environments where two or more gateways control connectivity there are options to minimize the interruption upgrading to NGX.

There are options for performing Gateway upgrades. You can use the same process to perform local upgrades like those used for the SmartCenter Server. Alternatively you can use the SmartUpdate client to perform Gateway upgrades from the SmartCenter Server. SmartUpdate is covered in Chapter 13.

Minimal Downtime

The primary motivation to upgrade is implementing the latest version and features into your environment. The primary concern is minimizing interruption while performing the upgrade. Developing the upgrade plan is the most influential component to limiting downtime. Consider resource availability and service level requirements when defining your strategy.

Migrating the SmartCenter Server to new hardware is the best way to minimize administrative interruption. Complete the upgrade on the new server then swap the two servers on the network. Remember to clear ARP entries from the old SmartCenter Server. Pre-installing the NGX SmartConsole client software allows for quick discovery of administrative issues.

Gateway upgrades involve an interruption to network connectivity. Migrating to a new server in a single gateway environment is the best way to minimize interruption. If you are running only a single gateway it is likely your budget makes this alternative unfeasible. In a cluster environment, upgrade the modules one at a time. Remove one gateway from the cluster and upgrade the software. Swap the upgraded gateway with the other module and upgrade. Remember to clear ARP entries from upstream and downstream routers and switches. In either scenario there is an interruption to established connections. It is not possible to perform state synchronization between NG and NGX gateways.

Future upgrades, from NGX and forward, will have a zero-downtime upgrade scenario where no connections are interrupted.

Rollback

All project plans must consider the worst-case scenario. You should be able to restore the previous configuration in the event of failure during the upgrade. The rollback options are directly linked to the chosen upgrade path. Restoring from a migration to new hardware is simple compared with restoring direct upgrades to production servers. The first step is to determine how far to roll back the changes.

If you are fortunate enough to have duplicate hardware to allow migration of functionality to new servers, reconnect the original servers and clear ARP entries as necessary. The procedures for removing upgrades from production systems are operating system-specific:

- **Windows** Remove the Check Point R55, R55W, and VPN-1 Edge compatibility programs followed by Check Point VPN-1 Pro NGX R60. Reboot the system.

- **IPSO** Disable then delete VPN-1 Pro NGX R60 package. Re-enable the previous packages and previous IPSO version. Reboot the system.

- **SecurePlatform** Revert to the snapshot image taken before performing the upgrade.

- **Solaris** Remove the CPfw1-R60 package and reboot the system.

The worst-case scenarios involve restoring a system from a backup or rebuilding a system. This is the reason that you should always have complete system backups, configuration documentation, and a project plan before beginning the upgrade. It is unlikely that you will need to endure this painful process if you perform the verification steps before upgrading.

Summary

There are different reasons for wanting to upgrade to Check Point NGX. Regardless of the motivation, develop a project plan for the upgrade using formal change control guidelines. Examine the components and determine the best strategy for your organization. Assemble the necessary resources and review your plan before implementation. Consider options for upgrading the components running your Check Point security infrastructure.

Proper planning includes precautionary measures for protection. Make sure you have current system backups available. Take the preliminary steps to upgrade licenses and verify configuration functionality. Make time to understand how new features in NGX will function in your environment. A successful upgrade requires attention to detail.

Solutions Fast Track

Backup

- ☑ The SmartCenter Server is the single most important component of your Check Point infrastructure.
- ☑ Ensure that current backups exist and know how the restoration process functions.
- ☑ Compile complete configuration documentation before performing the upgrade.

Upgrade Order

- ☑ Upgrade your current NG licensing ahead of time using the license_upgrade utility.
- ☑ Verify the compatibility of your configuration for using NGX.
- ☑ Validate that your systems meet software and hardware requirements.

Minimal Downtime

- ☑ Migrating the SmartCenter to a new system during the upgrade provides for easier recovery.

☑ Review service level agreements to resolve complications in a timely matter.

☑ Remember to clear ARP entries when upgrading hardware.

Rollback

☑ Know how to use the various methods for restoring to a previous configuration.

☑ Plan for the worst-case scenario to be properly prepared.

Frequently Asked Questions

The following Frequently Asked Questions, answered by the authors of this book, are designed to both measure your understanding of the concepts presented in this chapter and to assist you with real-life implementation of these concepts. To have your questions about this chapter answered by the author, browse to **www.syngress.com/solutions** and click on the **"Ask the Author"** form.

Q: When should I upgrade my NG environment to NGX?

A: There is no easy answer to this question. You should fully test your production requirements with NGX to ensure proper functionality before upgrading. Upgrading to an initial release of a major version without proper testing may create problems. There is a risk in running leading edge versions.

Q: What licenses are no longer valid in NGX?

A: VPN-1 Small Office and VPN-1 Net licenses are not available in NGX. These products are still supported in NG. If you are using these products you will need to convert them to upgrade to NGX.

Q: My SmartCenter does not have Internet access. Can I still use the license_upgrade utility?

A: Yes, the utility includes options for performing an offline upgrade. You need to run the utility to generate a license package file on your SmartCenter Server. Transfer this file and the license_upgrade utility to a machine with HTTPS Internet access. Run the license_upgrade utility from the online machine to generate a file containing the upgraded licenses. Transfer this file back to the SmartCenter Server and import the file using the license_upgrade utility.

Q: Does the export utility copy my network configuration?

A: No, the utility only exports the Check Point configuration.

Q: Why should I run the license upgrade and pre-verification tools before upgrading when the tools are part of the upgrade process?

A: There may be issues that need to be resolved prior to performing the actual upgrade. If you are missing required licenses, upgraded modules will not function properly. Verification errors will cause the upgrade to fail and you will be forced to roll back changes.

Q: If upgrading to a new windows SmartCenter Server using the Import option does it need to be connected to the network?

A: The interface needs to have a link but it does not need to have a connection to the production network. You can use a hub to provide a valid link on the interface to complete the upgrade. Once the upgrade is complete you can then disconnect the previous server and connect the upgraded server to the production network.

Q: Are there any updates to the documentation provided with the NGX media?

A: Yes, some documents have been updated; current documentation can be downloaded from www.checkpoint.com/support/technical/documents/docs_r60.html. You need to have a User Center account with the appropriate rights to access the documents.

Chapter 5

SmartDashboard and SmartPortal

Solutions in this chapter:

- **A Tour of the Dashboard**

- **New in SmartDashboard NGX**

- **Your First Security Policy**

- **Other Useful Controls on the Dashboard**

- **Managing Connectra and Interspect Gateways**

- **SmartPortal**

☑ **Summary**

☑ **Solutions Fast Track**

☑ **Frequently Asked Questions**

Introduction

In this chapter, we will take a tour of the interface used to configure your NGX installation: the SmartDashboard. Once we are done with the tour, new users of Check Point should know where to return in order to configure more advanced features of NGX; those familiar with Check Point NG will see where things have changed and what new features they can use to make management of their systems easier. We will then run through setting up a simple security policy and applying it to your NGX firewall gateway. The new SmartPortal management interface will be visited; we will look at how to install it and how it will help administrate your organization's Check Point systems.

A Tour of the Dashboard

Those unfamiliar with the Check Point NG interface may find the SmartDashboard interface a little daunting at first sight, what with so many different panes, views, and toolbars on one screen! Indeed, a large screen is a good place to start. Check Point recommends at least 800 x 600, but 1280 x 1024 over 19" is much more workable, and an excuse for the larger monitor you'd wanted for months.

The key to working with the interface is an understanding of what each area is for, and sticking to those you need. We will take a quick tour to help with this.

Logging In

First, we need to log in. Usually, you'd be connecting SmartDashboard to your SmartCenter, but there is also the option of Demo mode. This allows you to get familiar with the interface and take a look at some advanced configurations without risking doing any damage because the only configuration you are changing is the local Demo databases. You can choose a number of different Demo databases, varying in complexity from a firewall only, to advanced VPN scenarios. When you use Demo mode, SmartDashboard shows that it is connected to a SmartCenter named *local*—that's really just some static files. You can run SmartDashboard in Demo mode without any SmartCenter installed—choose a Demo Installation from your NGX CD.

For our tour, we will log in using Demo mode with the Basic Firewall+VPN database, as shown in Figure 5.1.

Figure 5.1 Logging in Using Demo Mode

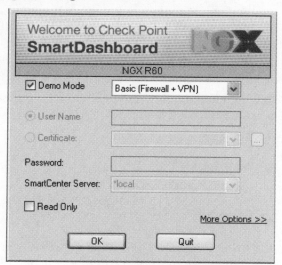

The SmartDashboard window includes a number of different panes. Our tour begins with the rulebases—those Check Point administrators who remember FireWall-1 v4 will recall when there was nothing more than the Security and Address Translation rulebases!

Tools & Traps...

Stuck on Solaris?

The vast majority of Check Point installations run SmartDashboard on Windows. However, SmartDashboard is also available for Solaris as a Motif application. If you really are not able or willing to run SmartDashboard on Windows, it is an option. However, be warned that the Motif version requires an additional license. In this chapter we will be looking at the Windows version only, but most here will apply to the Solaris version, too.

The Rulebase Pane

The tabs in Figure 5.2 are the default tabs we see in the Demo mode. Each tab configures a different product feature, the Security tab being the most commonly used—the firewall rulebase. Some of the tabs reflect a particular *policy*, where different policies can be loaded and applied to different gateways, whereas others apply *globally* across all the gateways managed by your SmartCenter. The combination of policies that you view at one time is called a *policy package*. Other tabs will appear if other product features are enabled.

Figure 5.2 Rulebase Pane Tabs

To get your first firewall policy up and running, you probably will make use of only the Security and perhaps Address Translation tabs, but here is the full list.

Security Tab

This tab is the policy-based definition of the firewall security policy. Rules here define what traffic is permitted through a firewall, whether to log the traffic, and whether the traffic requires encryption or authentication. The Security rulebase is part of the Security and Address Translation policy.

Address Translation Tab

These policy-based rules define what Network Address Translation (NAT) should be performed on traffic through a firewall. They are part of the Security and Address Translation policy.

SmartDefense Tab

This tab is the global configuration of the firewall's attack detection and prevention features. This includes everything from low-level IP packet sanity checks up to application layer controls for Instant Messengers and Voice-over IP (VoIP). The functionality here has expanded greatly since the introduction of SmartDefense back in NG FP2.

Web Intelligence Tab

This tab is the global configuration of Web (HTTP) –related SmartDefense features, including new features that were introduced in the R55W (Web Intelligence) version of NG.

VPN Manager Tab

This is the global configuration of VPN gateways when using VPN Communities. This method of VPN configuration applies only when a *Simplified Mode* Security and Address Translation policy is enforced on the gateways, so this tab is not present if a *Traditional Mode* Security and Address Translation policy is part of the current policy package. The difference between Simplified and Traditional Mode will be explained in Chapter 11.

QoS Tab

This policy controls the behavior of the Quality of Service (QoS) (Floodgate-1) gateway module where it has been enabled. It allows granular control of bandwidth usage per protocol and source and destination IP. This tab is not available in the Basic demo database.

Desktop Security Tab

This tab is the policy defining the desktop firewall rulebase that will be downloaded to SecureClient remote users when they connect. Check Point's SecureClient secure remote access solution consists of client software (SecureClient) installed on each remote user machine; the VPN-1 gateway, which acts as the endpoint for the VPN tunnel to the client; and the SecureClient Policy Server, which runs on the gateway. The Policy Server will supply the latest Desktop Security policy to clients when they connect.

Web Access Tab

This tab is the global configuration of UserAuthority WebAccess modules. UA WebAccess software can be installed on Web servers to provide URL level access control and single sign-on integration with gateways. This tab is disabled by default—if you are installing a WebAccess module, enable it in the **Global Properties, UserAuthority** page (see Figure 5.3).

Figure 5.3 Enabling the Web Access Tab

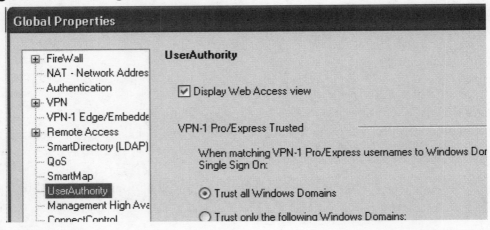

Consolidation Rules Tab

This policy controls the behavior of the Eventia Reporter Log Consolidator, if installed. To display this tab, use **View | Products | Reporter Log Consolidator**. Note that this removes all other tabs—to return to the previous view of tabs, use **View | Products | Standard**.

The Objects Tree Pane

To the left of the rulebases, you should see the Objects Tree, as shown in Figure 5.4.

Figure 5.4 The Objects Tree Pane

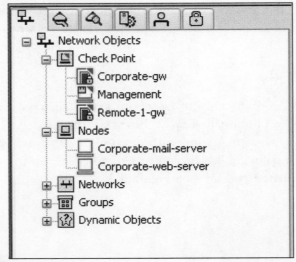

The tree is a convenient way to browse, edit, and create the objects that you need to define for your rulebases. Objects are needed to represent the SmartCenter, gateways, networks, and hosts you reference in policies, user accounts, and so on.

There are actually several trees of objects—use the tabs at the top of the pane to select the required tree.

To create new objects, simply right-click the top of the tree and choose **New**. To edit an object, double-click it.

Network Objects

This tree holds the objects that represent the hosts, gateways, networks, and address ranges that you reference in your policies. You can also create groups of network objects. There are a number of other special types of objects that can be defined here, representing DNS domains, external VPN peers, VoIP configuration, server load balancing controls, and routers managed by the Check Point OSE product.

By default, the Network Objects tree branches reflect each type of Network Object or can be sorted by color or name. Alternatively, a Group View will show each Network Object group as a branch, and its members within that branch—right-click the top of the tree to switch between **Arrange by Group** or **Classic View**.

Services

A wealth of objects resides here that define protocols that can be used in policies. The tree divides the objects by protocol type. The objects range from the obvious— like the telnet object that represents TCP port 23—to the obscure—such as SSL_v3, which represents an SSL connection, but enforces version 3 of the protocol.

Resources

Resource objects control the behavior of the firewall security servers—these are transparent proxy servers integrated into the firewall gateway. Security servers can be used for http, ftp, and smtp traffic. There is also a generic TCP proxy. A typical use of security servers is enabling redirection of web and mail traffic to third-party CVP or UFP servers that perform antivirus scanning or URL categorization. An additional type of resource object is the CIFS resource that can be used to control and audit use of Microsoft networking—allowing restriction of what server shares can be accessed. This CIFS enforcement is performed without the use of a security server.

Servers and OPSEC Applications

Check Point can integrate with a wide range of other servers and applications. Objects are defined here to represent applications that will be integrated. These include certificate authorities, authentication servers, LDAP servers, and content checking servers. There is one predefined object: the *internal_ca* Certificate Authority (CA) object. This represents the internal CA that is integrated into the SmartCenter Server.

Users and Administrators

To connect to the SmartCenter for the first time, an administrator account is used that was created as part of the installation process using the *cpconfig* utility. This account is visible in SmartDashboard in the object *cpconfig_administrators*. Once connected using this account, additional administrator accounts should be created here in SmartDashboard for each user that will require access to the SmartCenter. Each account can then have different access permissions as required.

In addition, nonadministrative user accounts can be created to make use of the firewall and VPN authentication features. These accounts can be defined with a fixed password, certificate, or authentication backed off to an external authentication server.

To avoid the overhead of user account management in SmartDashboard, the provision of the user database can be passed to an external server in two ways: first, External User Profiles can be created that back off all authentication requests that do not match a locally defined user. Second, it is possible to fully integrate with a LDAP directory server. This includes using the server for authentication plus the ability to manage user accounts on the LDAP server directly through SmartDashboard—once configured, the directory will become accessible in this object tree. Integration with LDAP for user authentication is a licensed feature—Check Point calls it SmartDirectory. If you have a SmartCenter Pro license, SmartDirectory should be included.

VPN Communities

This provides a tree view of community objects—the same as those displayed in the VPN Manager rulebase tab.

The Objects List Pane

This pane shows objects in a list format. The contents of the list is controlled by what is currently selected in the Objects Tree. For example, select the **Network Objects – Nodes** branch to see a list of all nodes.

The SmartMap Pane

SmartMap provides a visual representation of the network topology that can be gleaned from the network objects that have been defined. SmartMap can be disabled in **Global Properties, SmartMap** page. If you are not using SmartMap, disable it—this avoids the overhead of SmartDashboard calculating the visual topology.

Menus and Toolbars

Although most of the policy and object management can be performed via the panes we've looked at, there is plenty more than can be achieved via the drop-down menus or, for some of the most common actions, the toolbars.

Working with Policy Packages

To save changes to objects and the current policy package, create new policy packages, or open a different policy package, use the File menu. Remember that a policy package is all the policies you can see on the rulebase pane. If you wish to take a copy of just one of the policies—say the Desktop Policy—and save it in a new package, use the Copy Policy to Package option and specify a name for your new policy package.

Installing the Policy

Saving the Policy Package does not actually change the policy running on your gateways—it's just updating the SmartCenter database. To update your gateways, use the Policy menu, Install Policy option—or find the toolbar icon for Install Policies.

There are plenty more menu options to explore in your own time. The final option we will look at is the big daddy of all: Global Properties, from the Policy menu.

Tools & Traps…

One Policy for All?

If you have a number of different gateways, you should consider whether to keep a single policy package for all gateways, or instead, create new packages for each new gateway. The latter is usually the best option if there is very little overlap between the security policies of each gateway.

If you have a single policy for all, use the **Install On** column of your security rules to define which rules apply to which gateways.

If you go for different packages for each gateway, use the menu option **Policy | Policy Installation Targets** in order to define which gateway(s) a policy applies to.

Global Properties

The Global Properties window, as the name suggests, defines settings and fine-tuning of your Check Point systems that apply globally (rather than per policy or per gateway). To open the window, from the menus choose **Policy | Global Properties**, or from the toolbar, choose the icon that looks like a bulleted list (see Figure 5.5).

Figure 5.5 The Global Properties Window

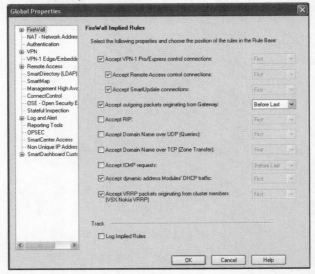

A detailed look at everything here easily could fill a whole book! We'll take a look at the more useful settings as well as new additions to NGX. Looking at new additions is fun since it's an NGX book. NG users will find this useful.

FireWall Page

The FireWall page shows Implied Rules settings. These "rules" are imposed over every security policy installed to your gateways. The idea is that they allow traffic that your gateways might need to function correctly—so you avoid pushing a policy that sends your gateway AWOL. There are obvious security implications here—to a degree, you are opening up "holes" in your security policy. Actually, as long as you are aware of what shape and size holes are involved, there is no need to panic. Fortunately, exactly this facility exists in SmartDashboard: with the Security rulebase displayed, use the View menu to choose View | Implied Rules. This will show the Implied Rules that are currently enabled by adding them to the view of your Security rulebase.

The tickbox for **VPN-1 Pro/Express Control Connections** enables a vast array of implied rules: the initial reaction may be to untick that box. However, on closer inspection, these rules are pretty specific—and in fact, if you disable these implied rules you will likely spend an awful lot of time recreating them as manual rules before you get back to a correctly functioning gateway. The decision is yours: the author's preference is to leave the option checked unless you are very confident you know what rules you will need to add manually. Are you sure you can avoid either a malfunctioning gateway or a bigger security hole than the implied rules may have left?

The option **Accept Outgoing packets originating from Gateway** is often left enabled, although we should consider whether we want to implicitly trust any and all connections from the gateway. Should the firewall gateway itself become in some way compromised, do we want to allow it unfettered access to the internal networks? It is preferable to investigate what outgoing traffic will be required from the gateway and accept only that in your rulebase. This is often just DNS queries to the configured DNS servers—remember that VPN-1 control connections (required to permit gateway to SmartCenter connections) are allowed elsewhere.

Of the other implied rules, most are undesirable. Consider the options for RIP and DNS: a sensible security policy would never allow these protocols without considering the source IP address. Those for Dynamic Address module DHCP traffic and Nokia VSX may be useful if relevant to your configurations, and are harmless enough. Note that the VSX VRRP setting does not apply for standard IPSO VRRP gateway clusters.

Finally, it is a good idea to enable **Log Implied Rules**. That way you can reassure yourself that you know exactly what connections are being allowed by the settings here, thanks to logging in SmartView Tracker. By default, Log Implied Rules is not enabled.

NAT—Network Address Translation Page

The default settings here are good for most configurations: be aware of the new option of **Merge manual proxy ARP configuration**. This allows the use of Automatic ARP when the old local.arp publishing method also is required on a Windows gateway. In gateway versions prior to NGX, if Automatic ARP configuration was enabled, the local.arp mechanism was disabled.

VPN Page

There are some global options here affecting site-to-site VPN gateways; however, most VPN configuration is performed in VPN community objects and VPN gateway objects.

VPN-1 Edge/Embedded Page

Where the SmartCenter is managing remote *VPN-1 Edge* or other similar Sofaware-based devices (e.g., *Nokia IP40*), this page controls some global behavior. This includes, new in NGX, the ability to inspect Web and mail content passing through these devices using central checking servers. Web traffic can be verified against a central UFP (URL filtering) server; SMTP and POP3 mail can be redirected via a central antivirus scanning CVP server.

Remote Access Page

On the Remote Access page and its subpages, there is a wide range of configuration settings—usually best left at their defaults unless a specific configuration requires otherwise. New in NGX is the ability to configure here: SSL Network Extender, SecureClient Hotspot, Office Mode IP reuse across gateways and SCV connection exceptions.

SmartDirectory (LDAP) Page

If you wish to use LDAP integration, don't forget to enable it here first!

Stateful Inspection Page

Fundamental to the operation of the firewall gateway is stateful inspection: that is, tracking the progress of a TCP connection (or other protocol sessions) to ensure that all traffic that arrives is consistent with the connection state. This page allows this behavior to be fine-tuned, or to a degree, disabled.

Dropping out-of-state TCP packets is sometimes disabled in scenarios where TCP connections remain idle for long periods, so the gateway will timeout the connection and then drop packets in the future. If at all possible, avoid this; first try extending the *TCP Timeout* on the object for the service affected. Extending the timeout globally may significantly increase the amount of stale data in the gateway state tables.

New in SmartDashboard NGX

For readers familiar with previous versions of SmartDashboard, this chapter may have yet to uncover much that is new for them.

For those readers in particular, we will now have a look at the improvements in NGX.

Security Policy Rule Names and Unique IDs

In previous versions, every rule had a number. At a stretch, the administrator may have bothered to scroll over to the far left column of the rule to add a comment. Neither helped clearly identify the purpose of each rule when browsing through the rulebase.

NGX introduces *rule names*: now the first column in every rule. Describing each rule in one or two words should make the rulebase far more readable. Figure 5.6 shows an example of annotating a rulebase in this way.

Figure 5.6 Naming Rules

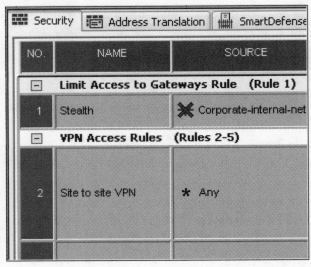

Also new are *Unique Rule IDs*. Every rule now has a hidden, unique ID that does not change throughout the rule's life span—unlike the visible rule number, which will change when rules above are added or removed. This feature comes into its own when viewing log entries in SmartView Tracker. Now it is possible to identify which rule triggered the log entry—whether or not the rule number has since changed. For good measure, the rule name is included in the log entry, too. An example of the logging you'll see is shown in Figure 5.7.

Figure 5.7 Logging with Rule IDs and Names

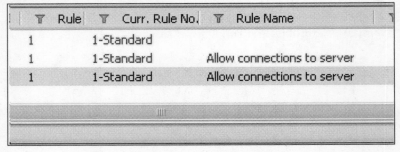

There is also an option in SmartDashboard to launch SmartView Tracker and view all logs relating to a rule. Right-click the rule to try this, as shown in Figure 5.8.

Figure 5.8 Launching SmartView Tracker for a Specific Rule

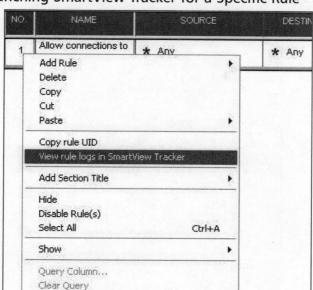

Group Object Convention

It is possible to specify a *convention* when defining a group. This consists of conditions based on object name, color, and IP, as shown in Figure 5.9.

Figure 5.9 Groups with Conventions

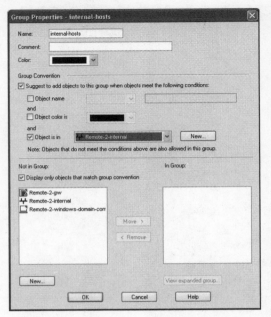

This can be used to assist when adding members to a group: a list of existing objects that meet the convention is provided. In addition, in the future when a new object is defined, SmartDashboard will check whether it meets a group convention. If so, you will be prompted to add the object to the relevant group.

Group Hierarchy

The Network Objects view in the Object Tree pane has been enhanced for Group objects to allow "drilling down" into groups. Right-click the **Groups branch** and choose **Show Groups Hierarchy**, as shown in Figure 5.10.

Figure 5.10 Enabling Group Hierarchy View

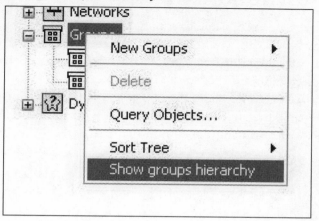

The tree will now show the members of groups, including subgroups. An example is shown in Figure 5.11.

Figure 5.11 Drilling into Groups

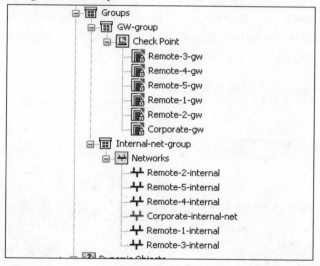

Clone Object

For those times when you need to create a large number of similar objects, **Clone Object** is here to help. Right–click any Node or Network object and you have the option to **Clone**. This creates a new object with the same properties. Just change the name and IP, and you are done.

Session Description

In previous versions, it was possible to supply a Session Description when logging in to SmartDashboard, and this would be written to the Audit Log. This provided a rudimentary way of tracking the reason for which administrators had logged into SmartDashboard, should they choose to supply one.

SmartDashboard NGX provides the ability to require a Session Description in order to log in: enable this in **Global Properties, SmartCenter Access**. However, as yet there is no way of forcing the administrator to enter something helpful.

Tooltips

In the rulebase, tooltips are provided for host and network objects—hover your mouse pointer over an object for a summary for example, for a network, its IP, subnet mask, and object comment (see Figure 5.12). This is particularly useful when analyzing a rulebase, allowing you to understand what the objects used in rules are representing. Of course, to make the tooltip really useful, you do need to have provided a helpful Comment in the object definition. This should be considered standard practice in order to make the effect of your rulebase clear. Losing track of what objects represent can easily lead to your defined security policy not providing the protection that you expected, or perhaps (in practice, more often) blocking legitimate traffic.

Figure 5.12 Tooltips Are Your Friend

We've now completed our SmartDashboard tour and highlighted the new features in NGX. With some luck you are now familiar enough with the interface in order to create a simple security policy.

Your First Security Policy

We will now run through the steps of configuring and installing your first security policy. In our example, SmartCenter Express has been installed on a Windows 2003 Server named "sleigh." You have a dedicated firewall gateway host running Nokia IPSO that has VPN-1 Express gateway installed, named "vixen."

Having installed the SmartCenter software successfully, you should be able to connect your SmartDashboard for the first time. If you have installed SmartCenter on a Windows platform, you will be able to run the SmartDashboard locally. Otherwise, you will need to install the SmartConsole package on a Windows host and connect to the SmartCenter over the network—make sure your *cpconfig* GUI clients settings allow the host to connect. Log in by specifying the administrator credentials that you configured in *cpconfig* and the hostname (or IP) of the SmartCenter, as shown in Figure 5.13.

Tools & Traps...

More Options?

You may have noticed the More Options link at the bottom of the SmartDashboard Log In dialog. Clicking this will allow you to tune how the SmartDashboard attempts its connection to the SmartCenter. The options are:

- **Change Certificate Password** If you are using a certificate to authenticate your connection, SmartDashboard allows you to change the password that protects the certificate.

- **Session Description** Specify a description that will be supplied to SmartCenter when connecting. As discussed earlier, this can now be enforced.

- **Use Compressed Connection** By default, the connection to the SmartCenter is compressed. If you wish, you can disable this—for a very large configuration database, doing this may help reduce load on the SmartCenter when a client connects.

- **Do not save recent connections information** By default, SmartDashboard will remember the last user ID and SmartCenter(s) to which connections were made. For more security and less convenience, check this option—no information will be remembered and prefilled.

Figure 5.13 Connecting to Your SmartCenter

> **NOTE**
>
> The first time you connect the SmartDashboard to the SmartCenter, you will be prompted to confirm the identity of the host to which you are connecting. This is achieved by verifying the fingerprint of the Internal CA. If you are at all concerned that the host you've connected to might not actually be your SmartCenter, you can compare the fingerprint with the one for your SmartCenter Internal CA: you can get that from the cpconfig utility on the SmartCenter. Once you have done this once, the host running SmartDashboard will trust that SmartCenter. Note that you will be warned again if the Internal CA on the SmartCenter is reset.

Once connected, you will notice in the Objects Tree that an object for the SmartCenter has been created automatically. Double-click the object to review the object settings: verify that the hostname, IP address, and OS are correct. If there are discrepancies, it might indicate a problem with the installation: double-check that the SmartCenter's host OS is configured correctly. The object for our SmartCenter *sleigh* is shown in Figure 5.14.

Figure 5.14 SmartCenter Object for *Sleigh*

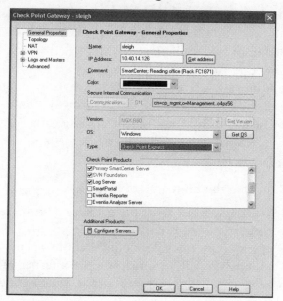

The Products Installed list indicates that *sleigh* is running a Primary SmartCenter, Log Server, and SVN Foundation (SVN is the base Check Point software module). In our example, no gateway is installed on *sleigh*, so Firewall, VPN, and QoS are all unchecked. We have provided a useful comment—here it identifies the location of the SmartCenter.

Creating Your Administrator Account

Your first job is to create an administrator's user account. Select the **Users** tab of the Objects Tree, right-click on **Administrators**, and choose **New Administrator**. Your user ID will be *clauss*. In order to configure your level of privileges, create a new **Permissions Profile** called *fulladmin*. You should select Read/Write Access, and the ability to Manage Administrators so that you can create further accounts for other admins, operators, and so on. Don't forget to choose an authentication method, too—in the object **Admin Auth** tab, you should select a Check Point password and set it. Note you can use stronger external mechanisms if you wish; for example, *RSA SecurID*. Additionally, you can create a certificate and use that to authenticate instead of a regular password.

Now, you have an administrator account; save your changes (**File | Save**) and then exit from SmartDashboard. Then, start SmartDashboard and log in again, this time using the new account.

Hooking Up to the Gateway

You are now ready to hook up the SmartCenter to your new VPN-1 gateway, *vixen*. As part of the installation of NGX on *vixen*, you specified a *SIC activation key*: you need that in order to define your object for the gateway.

To create your object, right-click on the **Network Objects** tree and choose **New | Check Point | VPN-1 Pro/Express Gateway**. You are prompted for the choice of a wizard or manual classic configuration. Unless you have a real aversion to wizards, the wizard is pretty reliable. We recommend that you use the wizard, supplying the following details:

- Gateway name: use the hostname of the gateway.

- IP Address : use the *external* IP of the gateway (also make sure that, on the gateway host itself, its own hostname resolves to this IP). Choosing the external IP is important for VPN configurations as clients or peers may use this IP for building the VPN tunnel, and the internal, private IPs are unlikely to be reachable. It is critical for the gateway's hostname to resolve correctly locally because the Check Point services on the gateway will use the resolved IP when locating the firewall object for that gateway. On UNIX platforms verify the hosts file is correct on the gateway. On Windows, it is not so straightforward: ping the gateways own hostname in order to determine which physical interface is considered the primary by Windows, then use that interface as the external interface.

- Gateway Type: Express or Pro (we are using Express). This depends on what license you have.

- Firewall or VPN: will you be using the VPN features of VPN-1? If not, only enable FireWall—this simplifies configuration. You can always switch on VPN later if needed. We'll have VPN from the start.

- SIC Activation Key: after supplying this key and clicking **Next**, the SmartCenter will attempt a connection to the gateway.

Hopefully the SIC connection is successful—if not, take a look at the sidebar, "Can't Communicate?"

Tools & Traps…

Can't Communicate?

What if SmartCenter can't connect to the remote gateway?

There are a number of reasons why the SmartCenter may fail to connect to the new gateway—you will get an error indicating that the SIC initialization process has failed. Common problems include:

- Routing from SmartCenter to the gateway external IP. Check routing tables—it may be that traffic is being routed to an existing Internet gateway. Configure routing so that traffic to the new external network range hits the new gateway.

- Routing from the gateway to the SmartCenter. Check gateway routing tables—ensure the gateway has the routing information required to reply to the SmartCenter.

- SIC initialization at the gateway. If there have been previous attempts to configure management of the new gateway, it may be that the gateway is no longer expecting a new SIC key. Use cpconfig on the gateway to reset SIC.

- Default policy on the gateway. If there have been previous policies loaded to the gateway, they may be blocking the connection from the SmartCenter. You can make sure that no policy is running by running the command **fw unloadlocal** on the gateway. Be warned that this will leave the gateway unprotected, so disconnect any live untrusted networks first!

The wizard will now ask you whether to automatically retrieve interfaces and topology from the gateway. This will fetch a list of interfaces and inspect the routing tables on the gateway in order to identify what subnets are connected to each interface of the gateway, creating any necessary objects for you—on complex networks this can save you a lot of time. It is also important that the interface list is defined accurately, so automatically fetching the list is highly recommended.

When the wizard completes, you can check the box to **Edit the Gateways Properties** to review the configuration of the new object. The hostname, IP address, OS, and Products Installed should all be as required.

Reviewing the Gateway Object

It's worth reviewing all the objects settings: first, to make sure the wizard got it right (they aren't perfect, you know), and second, so that you are aware of the available options to be configured if you need to later. The object for *vixen* is shown in Figure 5.15.

Figure 5.15 Gateway Object for *Vixen*

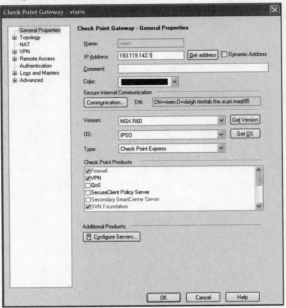

If you are satisfied that these general properties look good, move on to the Topology page for the object. Here you'll see a list of interfaces on the gateway and the IP addresses behind those interfaces, based on the routing tables. On your *vixen* gateway, the eth4c0 interface has an additional routed subnet behind that interface and SmartDashboard has created objects to reflect that. The topology is shown in Figure 5.16.

Figure 5.16 Gateway Topology

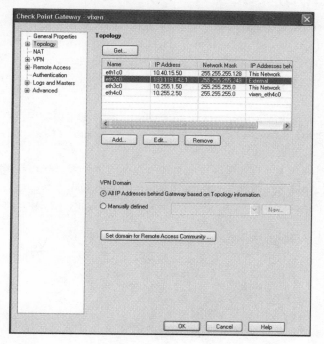

To edit the settings for each interface, just double-click the interface name. As well as the name and IP, the topology should be reviewed to ensure it correctly reflects what IP addresses lie behind that interface. Accurately configuring this allows Anti Spoofing protection to be enabled on the interface—essential in securing your networks against spoofed packets arriving at untrusted interfaces.

You may want to browse through the raft of other pages and settings available in the gateway object, but these are best left at their defaults for now.

TIP

SmartDashboard provides a handy shortcut for launching the Web interface to your SecurePlatform or IPSO gateways: right-click on the Check Point object and choose **Manage Device**. However, note that SmartDashboard will attempt to connect to the device using https on port 443, so if this isn't what your gateway listens on, this won't work for you.

Defining Your Security Policy

Before defining rules in your policy, you will likely need to define a few objects to represent internal hosts and networks. SmartDashboard automatically created objects for two of your internal networks when it fetched the gateway topology, so you can just change those object names to something more meaningful rather than creating new objects.

You will also create a group, *sleigh_internal*, which will include all your internal networks. To add the networks to the group, just drag and drop them into the group using the Objects Tree.

Figure 5.17 shows the Objects Tree with all our objects defined. You have objects for your networks plus an object for the Internet mail relay server on our DMZ. There is also a group that was automatically defined for use in the gateway topology.

Figure 5.17 The Objects Tree

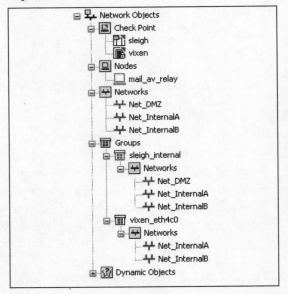

Policy Design

A firewall security policy should be designed with the principle of least privilege in mind: accept only the traffic that is required, drop anything else. When the firewall gateway implements the rulebase, each new connection is compared against the rulebase top down—when a rule is matched, that action is followed and no more rules are checked. Check Point helps you out with best practice by dropping any traffic

that is not accepted by either implied rules or a rule you have added to the p
in other words, there is an invisible rule at the bottom of rulebase: *drop anything*.

Two rules are usually explicitly added as part of every policy: the Stealth rule an
the Clean Up rule.

A *Stealth rule* is placed near the top of the policy and explicitly blocks access to
the firewall. It should be placed above other more general rules that would otherwise
allow access (maybe a rule allowing internal users access to the Internet—i.e., any
address—which would include the firewall itself). Don't forget to add a rule above
the Stealth rule to allow access for administrators—for example ssh to the gateway.

A *Clean Up rule* is placed at the bottom of the policy and explicitly drops and
logs all traffic that has not matched other rules. This traffic would have been dropped
by the gateway anyway because of the invisible drop-anything rule, but the Clean
Up rule ensures it gets logged.

In addition to the aforementioned rules, your security policy should be developed in order to reflect the formal network usage policies of your organization.

Creating Rules

Before we begin creating rules, it is a good idea to save the Policy Package using a
descriptive name. You will notice that the current policy name is "Standard." It is
good practice to use policy names that identify the date/time of the policy, or some
versioning reference. There are two reasons for this—first, it is easy to check what
revision of the policy package is installed on a gateway—SmartView Monitor will
show the current installed package name. Second, it makes it easy to roll back
changes to the policy (although be aware that saving the policy does not provide
version control over changes to objects—we'll discuss Change Management later in
this chapter). To save the policy under a new name, use **File | Save As**.

To add a rule to the rulebase, use the **Rules Toolbar**. This provides buttons for
adding rules at the top or bottom of the policy, and above or below the current
selected rule. Clicking one of these buttons adds a rule that by default, and will drop
all traffic. First you should give the rule a **Name**; then we can modify the rule
Source, **Destination**, and **Service** by dragging objects into the fields or right-
clicking and adding objects from a list. Then choose the **Action** you wish to take if
a connection matches this rule (right-click and choose from the list); to start with,
choose between Accept or Drop. Other options can be used to perform authentication or require encryption. The Reject option drops traffic but informs the client by
means of either a TCP Reset or ICMP destination unreachable message.

The full security rulebase for our example is shown in Figure 5.18.

Figure 5.18 A Full Example Rulebase

NO.	NAME	SOURCE	DESTINATION	VPN	SERVICE	ACTION	TRACK	IN
1	Manage vixen	admin_pc	vixen	*	TCP ssh_version_2 TCP https	accept	! Alert	
2	Manage sleigh	admin_pc	sleigh	*	TCP ms-rdesktop CIFS	accept	! Alert	
3	Stealth	* Any	vixen sleigh	*	* Any	drop	Log	
4	Mail in	* Any	mail_av_relay	*	TCP smtp	accept	Log	
5	Mail out	mail_av_relay	* Any	*	TCP smtp	accept	Log	
6	Web access	sleigh_internal	* Any	*	TCP http TCP https TCP ftp	accept	Log	
7	Clean Up	* Any	* Any	*	* Any	drop	Log	

Reviewing the rules, you have allowed our administrators PC access to the gateway and SmartCenter for the required protocols. You had to define a new Service object (right-click in the **Services** tab of Objects Tree) to represent the Microsoft Remote Desktop protocol (TCP port 3389). You ensure that ssh access to the gateway is using the more secure ssh version 2, not version 1, by using the special service *ssh_version_2*.

Once you have your policy defined, remember to review the implied rules that are enabled in Global Properties. The defaults in NGX are sensible, but make sure that you are aware what they are. In the example in this chapter, you have left Control Connections and Outgoing Packets from Gateway enabled. It is a good idea to enable Log Implied Rules so that it is clear what connections are being accepted and dropped.

Time Management

On the far right of your Security rules, you will see the column *Time*. This allows you to specify time periods during which a rule will be applied—from times of the day to days and months of the year. You achieve this by creating Time objects that represent a time period, and then add that to the rule. To define objects use the **Manage menu, Manage | Time**, and create a new Time type object. Note that Time objects are also used for scheduled events such as times at which a log server should start a new log file: these are Scheduled Event type Time objects.

Network Address Translation

To be allowed to access the Internet, and for your mail relay to receive incoming mail, you need to configure some address translation. Add Hide NAT to your internal networks (hiding behind the gateway itself) and Static NAT to your mail relay. The mail relay will be translated to an address supplied by our ISP, in the same range as our gateway external IP. This is simple to configure using Automatic NAT—edit the relevant objects and configure the NAT page. Figures 5.19 and 5.20 show the NAT configuration on an internal network object and the mail relay object.

Figure 5.19 Internal Network Hide NAT Configuration

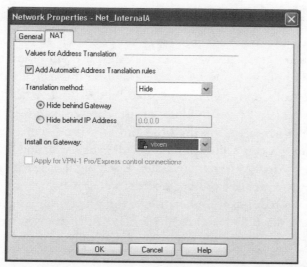

Figure 5.20 Host Object Static NAT Configuration

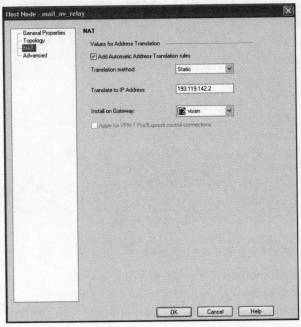

In the Network Address Translation rulebase tab, you can review the rules that have been created. You can add more rules to the rulebase manually if you need to—this is discussed further in the Network Address Translation chapter.

At last you are ready to test your policy!

Installing the Policy

To install the policy, use the Policy toolbar—the policy install button shows a rulebase with a downward arrow above it. SmartDashboard will prompt you to select which gateways the policy should be installed on—in this case, there is only one gateway to choose from, and it will be selected by default. If you later choose to enable the QoS or Policy Server modules on the gateway, you will also be able to select whether you wish to update the QoS and Desktop Security policies. Clicking OK to continue the process will show the Install Progress dialog box. This will indicate that the policy is first Verifying and then Installing. The Verify phase identifies any logical problems with your policy—for example, rules that "hide" later rules, making the later rule redundant. Installation is the process of connecting to the gateway, transferring the policy and database files to the gateway, instructing the gateway to update its policy, and waiting for a successful confirmation from the gateway. If all this succeeds, you will see a reassuring large green tick appear, as in Figure 5.21.

Figure 5.21 Success!

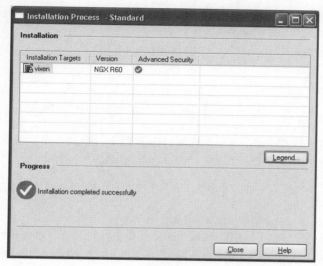

If you see anything else—red crosses, warnings, or the like—click the **Show Errors** button that will appear in order to view the reasons for this. This may not be critical in some cases—sometimes it is just a recommendation about your policy. Other times it will indicate the policy has not been installed, maybe due to connectivity to the gateway or some other serious error during the policy compilation process.

Before you make any further changes to the policy, you may want to save the current policy using a new name, indicating a new policy version.

Once you have your policy installed it is time to test whether connectivity is as expected: now is probably a good time to read the SmartView Tracker chapter so you can observe your connections being accepted, and the bad guys being dropped. Hopefully.

Other Useful Controls on the Dashboard

Once you are comfortable with the core features we've covered so far, you might want to explore some more SmartDashboard features. We'll quickly look at some of them now.

Working with Security Policy Rules

Rulebases tend to quickly become long and cumbersome—you might even end up with a few hundred rules. Keep in mind that the longer the rulebase, the more work the gateway needs to do per new connection. This can be reduced by making sure that the most common connections match rules early in the rulebase. The tools described in this section will help manage bigger rulebases.

Section Titles

As your rulebase gets larger you can use Section Titles to summarize the purpose of a group of rules, making the rulebase easier to read. To add a Section Title, right-click a rule number and choose **Add Section Title**. A section is the set of rules between two titles and it can be expanded or collapsed with a click.

Hiding Rules

Individual rules can be hidden (leaving a gray stripe instead) by right-clicking the rule number and choosing **Hide**. Once rules are hidden, you can store/restore the current list of hidden rules, unhide rules, and view hidden rules (without unhiding them!) using the menus—the **Rules | Hide** submenu.

Rule Queries

In order to locate rules that apply to a particular host or service (for example), use a *Rule Query*. These will hide all rules that don't match your query. To define queries, use the Search menu: **Search | Query Rules**.

Searching Rules

You can perform a simple text search through the Security Policy using the Search menu: **Search | Find in Rulebase**. This is useful as a quick way to locate an object in a rule, or, if you use the **Comments** field in a structured way, to locate some keyword or perhaps a change control reference.

Working with Objects

We'll take a look at a few useful tools we can use when we are working with Network Objects.

Object References

You can track all references to an object—right-click on any object and choose **Where Used?** This is very useful when you forgot why exactly you created that object all those months ago…

Who Broke That Object?

Curious who was the last person to edit an object? Right-click the object and choose **Last Modified**. You'll see when it was changed, by whom, and from where.

Object Queries

Under the Search menu, the **Query Network Objects** tool allows simple searching and filtering of Network Objects. You can also define a *Network Object group* based on your query.

Working with Policies

The policy you see in SmartDashboard is not automatically applied to the gateway—you have to install the policy (push it down to the gateway) first! If you are managing multiple gateways, this becomes more of an issue—are you sure you've installed the latest policy to all the gateways? Do you have different policies on each gateway? Which rules in your policy are relevant to a gateway?

What Would Be Installed?

If you are working with multiple gateways but a single policy, it is not always clear to see which rules would be applied to a particular gateway. You can use the Policy menu, **Policy | View Policy Of** tool in order to view selected gateway(s) rules. To return to the normal view, use the same tool and click **Clear**.

What's Really Installed?

You can check what Security policy is actually running on a gateway—rather than the one that you see in SmartDashboard, or the one that you think should be running. From the menus, choose **File | Installed Policies**.

No Security, Please

It is possible to request that the Security Policy be unloaded from remote gateways: from the menu, **Policy | Uninstall**. This is a bad idea, as it leaves your firewall gateway with no protection (although it will no longer forward traffic, so connections cannot be made through the firewall). Ironically, the only time you would want to remove a policy from a gateway is when you've accidentally pushed a policy that blocks the connections from the SmartCenter to the gateway—in which case, the SmartDashboard will not be able to request the policy unload anyway! For those times, you will need to run the command **fw unloadlocal** from the command line of the gateway itself—disconnect untrusted network interfaces first to avoid leaving the gateway open to attack.

For the Anoraks

You can view the underlying script that is generated by your security policy, should that sort of thing interest you. Use the menus: **Policy | View**. The script displayed corresponds to the *<policyname>.pf* file on the SmartCenter. This tool is rarely required.

Tools & Traps…

Why and What Is "Install Database"?

Under the Policy menu there is an option **Policy | Install Database**. In early versions of NG, this option was used to update the user database on gateways, without reinstalling the actual security policy rulebase. It is now prohibited to use **Install Database** to a gateway, because it can result in inconsistencies where the rulebase refers to objects that are no longer part of the user database. However, Install Database now has a different function: it is used to install the configuration database to hosts running nongateway Check Point software: for example, a dedicated Log Server. You can even install the database to the SmartCenter itself, although this happens anyway when you do a normal **Install Policy** to a remote gateway. Installing the database to the local SmartCenter might be used to modify the log management settings of the SmartCenter without having to perform a full **Policy Install** to a gateway.

Change Management

It is possible to take a snapshot of the whole configuration database: rulebases, users, and objects. To do so, use the **Database Revision Control** feature from the File menu. To take a snapshot, **Create** a new version. It is possible to review that snapshot at a later date and, if you need to, restore it. You can even choose to create a new version on every policy install—if you do this, make sure you manage the number of database versions you have created: each snapshot increases the size of the SmartCenter configuration directories, and you risk the stability of the SmartCenter if you have hundreds of versions. Note that each version is tied to the SmartCenter software revision, so if you upgrade your SmartCenter there is little point in maintaining the previous database revisions. Do not mistake Revision Control for a full system backup: if you badly corrupt your live database version, you may not be able to connect to SmartDashboard in order to restore an older database.

Tools & Traps…

Backing Up Your SmartCenter Configuration

A step further than Revision Control is a configuration database export. You can export the entire SmartCenter configuration database including rules, objects, and the internal CA using the *Upgrade Tools*. These utilities are designed primarily for exporting from one version of SmartCenter and importing into an upgraded installation, but can also be used to export and import on the same software revision.

The tools are found in the SmartCenter directory *$FWDIR/bin/upgrade_tools* (Windows: *%FWDIR%\bin\upgrade_tools*).

For example, to export your running configuration:
upgrade_export C:\temp\exported
To import this configuration archive:
upgrade_import C:\temp\exported
Warning: On Windows, before running the import, check that the file properties of *%CPDIR%\conf\dependencies.c* are not set to Read Only. If it is, set it to Read/Write before running the import.

Managing Connectra and Interspect Gateways

Check Point SmartDashboard NGX allows the definition of **Check Point objects** for *Connectra* and *Interspect* gateways. Check Point *Connectra* is a SSL VPN gateway product; Check Point *Interspect* is an internal network security gateway. However, configuration management of these devices from SmartDashboard is limited to launching a dedicated management client for the device: Interspect SmartDashboard or a Web browser session to the management port of a Connectra gateway.

Configuring Interspect or Connectra Integration

Right-click on **Network Objects** in the Objects Tree and choose **New | Check Point | Connectra Gateway** or **Interspect Gateway**.

Define the object's name and IP, then use the **Communication** button to initialize SIC keys. Configured objects are shown in Figures 5.22 and 5.23.

Figure 5.22 Check Point Connectra Object

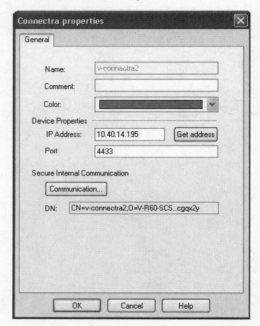

Figure 5.23 Check Point Interspect Object

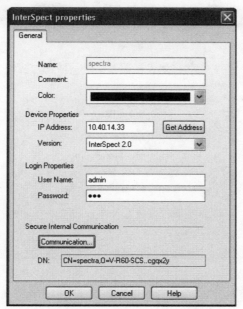

Once the object has been defined, you need to update the SmartCenter running configuration in order to allow connections from the device. To do this, use the SmartDashboard menus: **Policy | Install Database**. Then on the new object, you can right-click and choose **Manage Device** in order to launch the management client for the device.

In the Connectra or Interspect management interface, configure Central Management/Logging as per the device documentation. You will need to specify the SmartCenter name/IP and the object name that you have given to the new object.

After these changes have been made, the device logs should begin to appear in SmartView Tracker.

SmartDefense Updates

SmartDashboard also provides centralized SmartDefense Updates for Connectra and Interspect. If you have purchased a SmartDefense subscription for the device, you can update its SmartDefense features directly from the SmartDashboard rather than the management interface of the device: right-click on the object and choose **SmartDefense Service Update**. The latest SmartDefense database can then be downloaded to the SmartCenter and pushed out to internal Connectra and Interspect gateways, as shown in Figure 5.24.

Figure 5.24 Updating Connectra SmartDefense from SmartDashboard

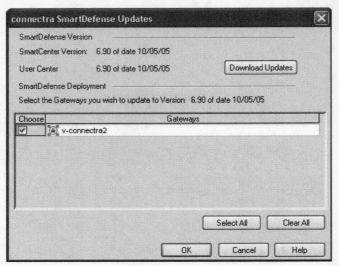

SmartPortal

The complexity and power of the Check Point management clients have a downside: the client software is a substantial suite of applications, not exactly lightweight. There are a number of situations when this is not ideal:

- There is often a requirement for operators to be able to view the logs or summary of status of the gateways, without any need for the full functionality of the SmartConsole suite.

- In a managed service environment, customers may want to view the logging from their sites' gateways, but not wish to install any software.

- Remote administrators may need to check on the status of the gateway, but are unable to install the software on the system they are using.

SmartPortal provides a browser-based alternative to the SmartConsole clients—ideal for these scenarios.

SmartPortal Functionality

The SmartPortal interface provides:

- **Status information** Similar information to the Gateway Status view of SmartView Monitor

- **Log viewer** Access to the traffic and audit logs, similar to SmartView Tracker

- **Policy and objects summary** A view of the *Security Policy* rulebase and object details

Installing SmartPortal

The SmartPortal server is available as an option when you first install NGX on the supported platforms: Windows, Solaris, Red Hat EL 3.0, and SecurePlatform.

Note that SmartPortal requires a license, although that license is included in most VPN-1 Pro and some extended VPN-1 Express licenses. To check yours, run *cplic check swp* on your SmartCenter.

If you didn't choose SmartPortal at install time, you can just run the wrapper again on Windows or Solaris—it should detect that NGX is already installed and give you the option to install additional products. Do this and choose SmartPortal. On SecurePlatform, you will need to install SmartPortal manually: enter Expert mode from a console session and run the command

```
rpm -i /sysimg/CPwrapper/linux/CPportal/CPportal-R60-00.i386.rpm
```

Usually you would install SmartPortal on the SmartCenter; however, it is possible to install it on other Check Point hosts or its own dedicated server. The SmartPortal server then makes an onward connection to the SmartCenter. A dedicated server would be advisable if there are likely to be many concurrent SmartPortal users.

Once the product is installed, ensure that the relevant object has **SmartPortal** checked in the **Check Point Products** list. Having done so, perform a database install to the SmartCenter (**Policy | Install Database**).

To access the portal, point your browser to **https://smartcenter-host:4433**.

Tip

SmartPortal officially supports a range of browsers: Internet Explorer, Mozilla Suite, Firefox, and Netscape. The latest versions of these browsers are recommended. However, with the NGX initial release code, Firefox 1.0.4 failed to connect, throwing a script error (Firefox 1.0.3 works just fine!). A change to the SmartPortal code to support Firefox 1.0.4 is expected in the first NGX hotfix release.

Tour of SmartPortal

At the welcome page (see Figure 5.25), supply your administrator credentials (this should be an account created in SmartDashboard) and the name (or IP) of the SmartCenter server.

Figure 5.25 Welcome to SmartPortal

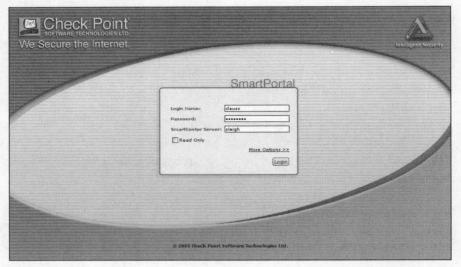

After a few seconds you should be connected to the SmartPortal front page, as shown in Figure 5.26. If the SmartPortal connection fails, check that you have correctly followed the installation steps and are using the correct SmartDashboard administrator credentials. Check that the SmartCenter Server name you supplied resolves successfully on the server running SmartPortal.

Figure 5.26 Logged In: SmartPortal Front Page

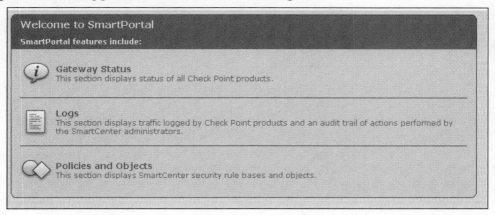

A sidebar allows selection of the different features.

The **Gateway Status** page will show a summary of status for each gateway and the SmartCenter itself (see Figure 5.27). To see more detailed status information, click the name of the gateway.

Figure 5.27 SmartPortal Gateway Status Page

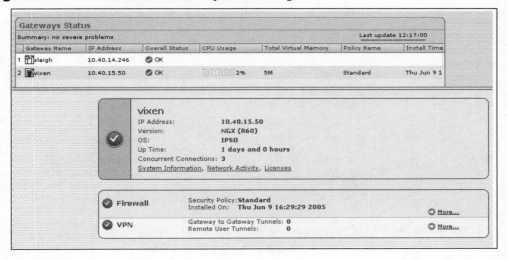

The **Logs** page can show either the **Traffic Log** or the **Audit Log**. The view is similar to SmartView Tracker but with a restricted set of columns shown. The Traffic Log is shown in Figure 5.28. Note the toolbar allowing navigation of the log, automatic scrolling, searching, filtering, and access to older log files. If the administrator has write access to the logs, it is possible to switch and purge logs. Clicking the record number will open a new window showing that log entry.

> ## Warning
>
> SmartPortal is entirely read-only with regard to policy and objects; however, the log page *does* allow purging and switching of logs. In a scenario where you wish to give users access to view configuration and logging only, make sure that you have restricted the user accounts to Read Only. You may need to define a new Administrator Permissions Profile with SmartPortal only and Read Only access and associate that with the user account.

Figure 5.28 SmartPortal Traffic Log Page

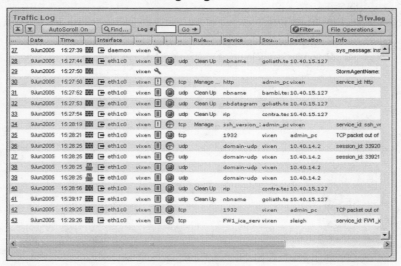

The **Policy and Objects** page provides a view of the *Security* rulebase. Figure 5.29 shows the SmartPortal view of the policy that was created in SmartDashboard.

Figure 5.29 SmartPortal Policy View

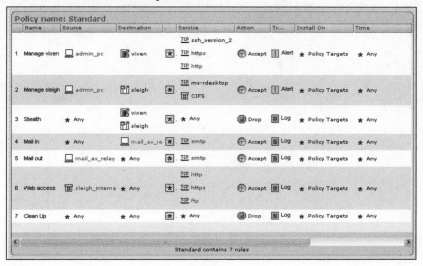

If you have multiple policy packages, you can view the security rulebase from these packages, too.

There are a number of pages for viewing objects: Network Objects, Services, Users, and Time objects. The views are equivalent to the Objects List view in SmartDashboard. A simple Filter on object name can be used to narrow down the list.

Tools & Traps…

Securing Access to the SmartPortal Server

Access to the SmartPortal server is not restricted by the GUI clients settings that apply to full SmartConsole access. By default, any client can connect to the SmartPortal. To restrict by client IP, create the file *hosts.allowed* in the SmartPortal *conf* directory:

   Windows: *C:\Program Files\CheckPoint\SmartPortal\R60\SmartPortal\conf\hosts.allowed*

   Linux/SecurePlatform/Solaris: */opt/CPportal-R60/portal/conf/hosts.allowed*
Add lines in the format

   ALL : <IP host address 1>
   ALL : <IP host address 2>

Continued

For each trusted host, or, for trusted networks:
ALL: <IP network address 1>/<subnet mask>

An example:
ALL: 10.40.6.0/255.255.254.0
ALL: 192.168.12.1

Summary

SmartDashboard provides an extremely powerful interface for configuring your Check Point installation—from the traditional firewall gateways, through VPN gateways, to the new Connectra and Interspect devices. It effectively provides a single management interface for your entire Check Point security infrastructure.

The interface, though complex, can be broken down into separate panes. Each provides different functionality and views of your configuration, and you can choose which panes are visible. This allows you to tailor the interface to suit the areas you need to work with and your preferred methods of accessing the settings.

The rulebase pane can be tailored to show just the policies and products you manage, again allowing simplification of the interface by hiding the functionality that you don't need to see. Conversely, when you have several different gateway products installed and therefore a number of different policies defined, these can be combined into a single policy package for the gateway.

The objects panes provide many different views onto your object database—with some experimentation you should be able to find a view ideal for your working style and requirements. Despite the ever-increasing range of object types available, these are broken down into different categories, and within each category, can be sorted and displayed so you see just the types that you are using.

The degree of fine-tuning allowed via the Global Properties windows increases in every software release, but the tree structure of the windows helps with navigation to the setting you need to adjust. The majority of the settings here can be left unchanged for most scenarios, so these pages can remain hidden away. We have outlined those that we do need to be aware of.

The NGX release introduces a range of new features to the interface that should be very helpful to administrators, making management and clear understanding of your configuration easier.

Your first security policy should be straightforward to define once you are familiar with the interface. Configuring a simple security rulebase and automatic NAT should have a typical Internet gateway up and running within minutes, or maybe an hour at the longest.

NGX begins to integrate management of Check Point Connectra and Interspect devices, continuing toward the goal of the SmartCenter being the single point of management for the whole network security infrastructure.

The new NGX SmartPortal Web interface provides a clientless management solution, enabling operator and managed customer access to view the status, logging, and configuration of a management server.

Solutions Fast Track

A Tour of the Dashboard

☑ Get familiar with SmartDashboard in Demo mode.

☑ Use the Objects Tree and Objects List to configure objects representing the network infrastructure.

☑ Use the rulebase pane to manage SmartDefense, Web Intelligence, and VPN communities.

☑ Define policy packages including security, NAT, QoS and Desktop policies.

New in SmartDashboard NGX

☑ Use rule names and UIDs to clearly identify which rule triggered a log entry.

☑ Group object convention can assist in defining groups and managing group membership.

☑ Drill down into defined groups by viewing the group hierarchy.

☑ Easily create similar objects with cloning technology.

☑ Requiring a Session Description might help with change tracking.

☑ Tooltips make it easier to see details of objects used in rules.

Your First Security Policy

☑ Define yourself an administrator account.

☑ Verify and configure the Check Point objects we need.

☑ Define objects we need to describe the network infrastructure.

☑ Define a simple rulebase.

☑ Configure NAT if needed.

☑ Install and test your new policy.

Other Useful Controls on the Dashboard

☑ Work better with rules using titles, hiding, searching, and query filters.

☑ Work better with objects by tracking references, making changes, and using queries.

☑ Work better with complex policies on multiple gateways.

☑ Full database change management using Revision Control.

Managing Connectra and Interspect Gateways

☑ Setting up connections to the devices to receive logging.

☑ Central SmartDefense management.

SmartPortal

☑ Installing or enabling SmartPortal.

☑ Status page shows state of Check Point hosts.

☑ Log page shows traffic and audit logs.

☑ Policy page shows Security policies.

☑ Objects pages show object lists.

Frequently Asked Questions

The following Frequently Asked Questions, answered by the authors of this book, are designed to both measure your understanding of the concepts presented in this chapter and to assist you with real-life implementation of these concepts. To have your questions about this chapter answered by the author, browse to **www.syngress.com/solutions** and click on the **"Ask the Author"** form.

Q: What software do I need to install in order to use the SmartDashboard in Demo Mode?

A: You only need the SmartDashboard software. The CD installer on Windows will present Demo as an install option. No SmartCenter is needed because the Demo database files are stored locally in the SmartConsole *PROGRAM\cpml_dir* directory.

Q: When I try to log into the SmartCenter, I get told that someone else is already logged in. I need to log in to make changes—Read Only access is no good for me. It gives me the option to disconnect them—should I do this?

A: Only one administrator can log into SmartDashboard in Read/Write mode at once. It is much better to get hold of the other administrator and ask him or her to cleanly log out of SmartDashboard, to avoid problems that could occur if they are in the process of making changes to the SmartCenter configuration. However, if his SmartDashboard or whole PC has crashed, or he can't be reached, you will need to force a disconnect.

Q: If I log in to SmartDashboard in Read Only mode, do I see any changes made by a SmartDashboard user in Read/Write mode?

A: Your SmartDashboard will be notified if another user has Saved changes, and when this happens the Toolbar Refresh icon is enabled: left-hand end of the toolbar, a circular arrow icon. Click the icon to load up the updated database. Note that this may take some time, so be patient!

Q: Why don't I see the VPN Manager tab?

A: You are using a Traditional Mode VPN policy—VPN Manager configures Communities, and these are used only with Simplified Mode VPN policies. The traditional policy will not include a VPN column; instead, Encrypt is available as an Action. To convert the policy to a Simplified Mode policy you can use the **Policy | Convert To** menu option. Be aware that conversion can not always preserve the exact functionality of the policy, so be prepared to review and troubleshoot the new policy. When creating New policies, the selection of Traditional or Simplified policy is implied by the setting in **Global Properties—VPN** page.

Q: I don't see a QoS rulebase tab; how can I add a QoS policy for my QoS (Floodgate-1) gateway?

A: Use the menu option **File | Add Policy to Package** and choose **QoS**.

Q: When I try to install a policy, it fails because one rules conflicts with another. What does that mean?

A: The rulebase works on a first-match basis—this means that the gateway compares connections to the rules from top down until it finds a match and follows that action. When you request a policy install, the SmartCenter verifies that the rulebase does not include rules that would never be matched—that is, there is a rule somewhere above it that will always catch the connection first. If this is the case, the error about conflicting rules is shown.

Q: Do I need to create network objects to represent every network and server protected by the firewall?

A: No, you only need objects for those hosts and networks you need to reference specifically in your configuration. This will include rules in your policies, objects used for NAT, and networks used in your gateway anti-spoofing settings. If you want to minimize the objects you require, you can create network objects that represent a large network range, rather than an object for an individual subnet. If you wish to represent a range of addresses that is not an exact subnet, use an Address Range object. Use large network objects and address ranges in rules (Security & NAT) where possible to make the rulebase clearer and more efficient.

Q: Is it possible to change a gateway's SmartDefense settings without installing the Security policy?

A: No, the SmartDefense and Web Intelligence settings are pushed to the gateway as part of the Security policy, so a policy install is required after a SmartDefense change or update.

Q: Tech Support has asked me to edit some settings using dbedit or Database Tool. What is this and why do I need to use it?

A: SmartDashboard allows you to manage the majority of possible settings in the configuration database; however, there are a number of settings that are not available in the main interface. Some are tucked away within **Global Properties**, **SmartDashboard Customization—Advanced Configuration—Configure**. However, some other settings are not available there either. Some are hidden because they are very rarely used, to keep the SmartDashboard interface tidier. Some are hidden and undocumented as they are not intended to be changed—perhaps they will be utilized in a future software release. The utility **dbedit** allows unrestricted access to the whole configuration database, in raw format—something like the Windows registry editor. Be warned that, like editing the Windows registry, trouble may follow if changes are made without a full understanding of what effect they may have—one wrong click can really ruin your day. The utility is available in two forms: a command-line version on the SmartCenter (**dbedit**), or a GUI included with SmartConsole: go to **\Program Files\CheckPoint\SmartConsole\R60\PROGRAM** and run **GuiDBEdit.exe**.

Q: Is it not possible to manage the configuration of Connectra and Interspect devices directly from SmartDashboard? And what about Integrity server?

A: At present the SmartDashboard interface does not include the functionality to configure the settings in Interspect and Connectra—there is little overlap between the existing settings and those needed for these devices so this would require significant extensions to the UI. The exception is the SmartDefense database: this can now be managed centrally in SmartDashboard. The same limitations apply to the Integrity server product. However, one of Check Point's priorities is centralizing security configuration, so it seems likely that all these devices will become increasingly integrated into SmartDashboard over the life of NGX.

Q: When I log in to SmartPortal there is a Read Only checkbox—but I thought all access via SmartPortal was read-only anyway?

A: The Read Only option prohibits the Log Switch and Log Purge options on the Traffic Log page.

Chapter 6

SmartView Tracker

Solutions in this chapter:

- **Tracker**
- **Log View**
- **Predefined Queries**
- **Custom Queries**
- **Active View**
- **Block Intruder**
- **Audit View**
- **Log Maintenance**

☑ **Summary**

☑ **Solutions Fast Track**

☑ **Frequently Asked Questions**

Introduction

Now that you have seen how to create your Check Point security infrastructure, it's time to see the traffic that is hitting your different components. SmartView Tracker enables the security administrator to visualize traffic that is passing by. What good is it to have a security policy if you are not able to see what is happening? The SmartView Tracker will be your daily friend—having the ability to parse through the logs is important to maintain and update your security policies.

Tracking users, connections, and administration through your logs is completely dependent on the gateway's configuration. To be able to audit rules, investigate misfeasors, or simply gather statistics, you need to enable logging for the items you care to examine. In some cases, you need minimal information about a particular connection. For example, if you are auditing a rule, you may need only to log it so that you can see the gateway's action for that connection. In other instances, you may desire more thorough data. If you need to audit HTTP requests, you need to not only log but also *Audit* the connections to receive more data.

In this chapter, we will discuss the need for tracking and walk through a few configuration examples. After reading this material, you should be able to parse through your firewall logs and easily find the data you are seeking.

Tracker

In your Check Point gateways, you, as an administrator, have a very robust tool that allows you to customize your product so that you are running an optimal configuration. In this light, you can review your output (logs) and verify that it is running how you think it is. Also, it never hurts for an administrator to review changes to the security policy. Moreover, it is not considered a bad practice to take in and just watch traffic every once in a while. SmartView Tracker allows you to have all these tools and more. As a result, SmartView Tracker enables you to do general oversight of your firewall, both over the administrative aspect as well as the security policy.

Depending on your configuration for SmartCenter or a Log Server, you can connect to one of them and have an immediate view of how your firewall is behaving. In larger networks, it may be helpful to use a distributed implementation that includes a separate log server. Also the quantity of traffic you are logging may have an impact on the configuration. You can also log locally to the firewall module. In any case, SmartView Tracker connects to either the Log Server or the SmartCenter Server in order to generate the views you use.

Once you open SmartView Tracker, you see that there are several frames to view and tabs from which to choose. The tabs let you choose between logged connection data, current connection data, and audit log data. The default view is the **Log** view. You will learn more about these views, how to navigate about SmartView Tracker, and how to generate custom views.

SmartView Tracker opens the current log file (*fw.log*) by default, but you can open an older saved log file if you want to parse through that to identify older connections. To do this, you click **File | Open** and choose the log file you want to examine. SmartView Tracker saves log files with a date/time format, so each file should be easily identifiable. Though this is the default naming convention, you can reconfigure this if so desired.

Log View

In the standard **Log** view, you see connection attempts that have reached your firewall. These attempts tell you many things about how the firewall is behaving. They may let you know that you are under attack if you see many similar attempts dropped or rejected. They may relay that you have routing problems or other networking issues if you see connection attempts that seem illogical. Also, these records may indicate a misconfiguration if you see traffic that either is passing but should not be permitted, or traffic that is not passing but should be allowed.

WARNING

SmartView Tracker will show only what you have configured your gateway to log. By default, the **TRACK** option on a rule in SmartDashboard is set to **None**. In order for your gateway to log connections, you must set the options to either **Log** or **Account**. Be sure that if you want to view connections in SmartView Tracker that you define the proper tracking options when defining a new rule.

In the **Log** view, you have three panes. Right away, you can see that your connection details are viewable on the right-hand side, the *Records* pane. A second pane on the right side is the *Query Properties* pane. To display this pane, click **View | Query Properties** from the menu. When you do this, the *Query Properties* are viewable above the records in the top-right pane (which is now split between the *Records* and *Query Properties* panes). These properties define what appears in the *Records* pane by inserting filter data or checking/unchecking the **Show** box. Third, on the left side of the **Log** view window, is the *Query Tree* pane.

As you can see within the *Query Tree* pane on the left-hand side there is one root level **Log Queries** tree and two branches, the **Predefined** and **Custom** branches. The leaves from these branches identify saved queries. When you activate a particular query, these queries change the parameters for the *Records* pane. SmartView Tracker prepopulates many predefined queries for you. However, you do not see any custom queries because you must define them yourself. A closer look at the prepopulated queries shows that many of them are labeled according to Check Point technology names. Later, you will leverage this set of queries to create custom queries.

When in **Log** view, SmartView Tracker presents you with a special toolbar containing many swift tools. This toolbar is directly over the *Query Properties* pane (see Figure 6.1).

Figure 6.1 SmartView Tracker Log Tab

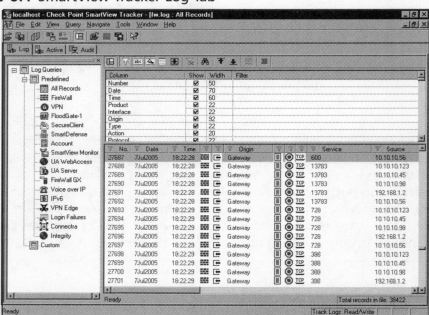

Here we briefly explain these buttons and their use. We will begin on the far left and make our way toward the right end.

- **Show or Hide Query Properties** Toggling this button simply displays or removes the *Query Properties* pane from the current view. It is not necessary to have this showing, though it is greatly helpful when defining a customized view.

- **Apply Filter** When enabled (default setting) a query is applied to the logs immediately. If you toggle this button, the query set is held in memory, but not applied to the current records. If this is off when you define a query, you simply click this button to apply the filter to the records.

- **Resolve IP** By default, SmartView Tracker will display records with hostnames if possible. As this takes time, you can disable this setting so that you see only IP addresses of the source and destination involved in each record. On the other hand, if you employ a filter and want to see hostnames to simplify reading your log data, you can toggle this button to do so.

- **Resolve Services** By default, SmartView Tracker will display records with any associated *Service* name such as *Telnet* for TCP port 23, *SMTP* for TCP port 25, and *Domain* for port UDP 53.

NOTE

If you have toggled the **Resolve Services** button and the log view still displays a port number instead of a name, check to verify that you have defined this protocol/port pair within the host or within the *Objects Database*. Each host has a *services* file where service names are matched with a protocol/port paring. In UNIX hosts, this file is generally found in the /etc directory. In Windows hosts, the file is normally located in Windows\System32\drivers\etc.

- **Show Null Matches** This button tells the SmartView Tracker to display records that do not have the opportunity to match the current filter; in other words, records that are not necessarily included or excluded by the current filter. For example, if you define a query to include only records where the **Action** is equal to **Drop**, control records are **Null** matches since they do not have an **Action** entry.

- **AutoScroll** Clicking this button tells the SmartView Tracker to continually update the view with the newest records. Essentially, it enables a pseudo-real-time view where you see the records as they reach the log server.

- **Clear All Filters** If you have applied a filter, you can click on this button to clear all the filters and return to viewing all records.

Tools & Traps…

Query versus Filter

It is important to understand how queries and filters differ in SmartView Tracker. Both are critical tools that allow you to manipulate the current log file so that you see only what you want to see. Think of a *Query* as a set of *Filters* and choice of columns that defines a view. Queries define your base view. Filters, on the other hand, further limit what you see after executing a query.

- **Find in All Columns** This button enables the standard string query against all the fields in each record.

- **Go to Top** Clicking this button takes your view to the very first log entry. Again, be mindful that it takes you to the first record in the current view, not the first record in the log file.

- **Go to Bottom** Clicking this button takes your view to the very last log entry. You don't see the very last record in the log file, but the last record in your current view.

- **Get Number of Filtered Records** Clicking this button will tell you the total number of records returned out of the total number of log records. This button is available only if you define a filter against the current query (view).

- **Abort** If there is a query or filter running and you want to end it prematurely, you can click this button to stop the action.

There are many other items in the **Log** tab view. We will cover these items more thoroughly in later sections of this chapter.

Active

The **Active** tab shows you the current open connections on the firewall. This allows you a bird's-eye view of all that is happening on a system. However, there is some performance cost, especially if you have a busy gateway. We will discuss some of the aspects of the **Active** windows and some of the operations you can execute from within this view.

Figure 6.2 displays the **Active** window with emphasis on some of the more important columns.

Figure 6.2 SmartView Tracker Active View

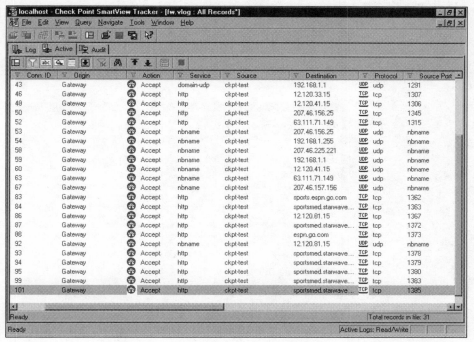

This window adds a **Connection ID** column to the view you don't normally see in the **Log** view. The other fields are also very similar to what you find in the **Log** tab of SmartView Tracker. In addition, the **Active** tab has the *Query Properties* and *Query Tree* panes. They are not shown in Figure 6.2 to maximize the view of the records. SmartView Tracker displays the *Query Tree* by default, though the *Query Properties* pane is hidden by default. Just as with the **Log** tab, you have the ability to filter the records and save the results as custom queries.

Audit

The **Audit** tab view allows you to see what has been happening with respect to administration on the firewall and modifications to the firewall's security policy. As shown in Figure 6.3, the visual representation is very similar to that of the **Log** and **Active** tabs. Though the SmartView Tracker does not display the *Query Properties* pane by default, it is possible to view this pane by clicking the **Show or Hide Query Properties** button on the toolbar.

Figure 6.3 SmartView Tracker Audit View

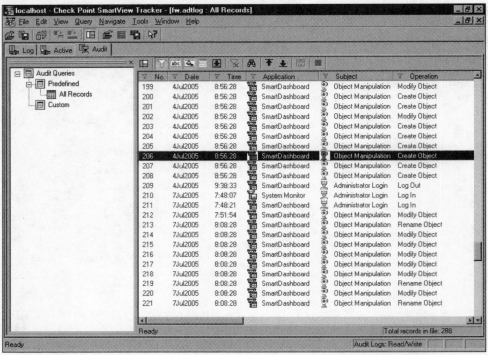

In the *Records* pane, you can see some of the entries that the system logs. In Figure 6.3, there are *Rename Object*, *Modify Object*, *Create Object*, *Log In*, and *Log Out* entries. These entries detail, to some degree, values administrators have changed in the security policy. And once more, you see that the toolbar is available for your use, but several of the buttons will not have an impact on some of the records.

Just as in the other tabs, you are able to create custom queries by modifying the predefined queries for your audit records. Consider if you want to know the last administrator to change the firewall policy and push it to the enforcement modules. This tab allows you the ability to filter the current records so that you can see only *Log In* operations. Also, you could filter to see the *Install Policy* records and correlate the two to identify who last pushed to policy. This activity allows you to collect details about a possible incident or just clarify why certain changes have been made to the policy.

Predefined Queries

As you have seen in the different tabs, SmartView Tracker has numerous *Predefined Queries* for your use. These queries, primarily in the **Log** tab, filter the record entries based on product type. To view the different queries, you can double-click on the name and then view the properties in the *Query Properties* pane. Let's take a look at the **Firewall** predefined query shown in Figure 6.4.

Figure 6.4 Firewall Predefined Query

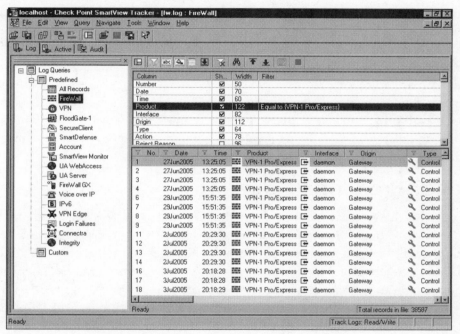

You need to take a careful look at the result of invoking the **Firewall** predefined query. For starters, you see in the *Query Properties* pane that the **Product** row has been automatically seeded with the **Filter** value *Equal to {VPN-1 Pro/Express}*. If desired, you are able to enter multiple values for each filter.

In addition, you see that several of the first columns have a check in the **Sh…** (Show) box. Each column with this setting enabled will appear in the *Records* pane. Further, note that the **Column** column defines the layout of the *Records* pane (the order of the columns from left to right).

To adjust column width SmartView Tracker provides you a few options. First, as with many products, you may click and drag the right edge of any column in the

Records or *Query Properties* pane and adjust the width as appropriate. The *Query Properties* pane gives you another means to adjust a column's width within the *Records* pane. All you need to do is modify the value in the **Width** column for each heading you want to adjust in the *Records* pane. For instance, if you want to modify the number of characters you wish to see in the **Product** column of the *Records* pane (as highlighted in Figure 6.4), then you simply change the current value of **122** to a number that better suits your needs.

Now let's focus on the **Product** column in the *Records* pane. You see that SmartView Tracker has colored green the filter image on the left of the text. This particular imagery indicates that you have applied a filter to this column. You can enable multiple filters at the same time on numerous columns. Each column you apply a filter to will also have a green filter image.

In looking at this one query, you can see that it just separates the records by product as covered before. So these predefined queries are not the end all to your needs. You cannot invoke one or two predefined queries and become satisfied in the results. If you look to invoke a query at all, there must be a set of records you are looking for. For this reason, these predefined queries are, in essence, a launching pad for further detailed custom queries, as you will learn later.

Use for Predefined Queries

Now that you have seen what a predefined query looks like, let's talk about what you use it for. Though these queries are not optimal for finding a needle in a haystack, it will separate the haystacks from one another and tell you where to look. If you have a SmartCenter Server that manages many different products, then these predefined queries become useful in an immediate manner. You don't need to try to query millions of records for what you want to see when you can invoke a predefined query and immediately and significantly reduce your query scope.

Using the previous example, you could invoke the **Firewall** predefined query if you wish to begin finding traffic that may match a rule number. In this manner, you immediately weed out all records that do not relate to the firewall security policy. From this point, you can further define filters that sift through a smaller set of records, which in turn delivers faster results.

Adding Custom Queries

Since you have invoked a predefined query you are now able to define and save a custom query that better suits your needs. Although you do not necessarily need to invoke any predefined query to save a custom query, choosing one of these queries offers you a great start.

NOTE

You are not able to change or modify SmartView Tracker's predefined queries in any manner. Each time you modify a predefined query, you must save it as a new custom query. All these new queries are saved under the **Custom** branch of the *Query Tree* pane.

When you create these custom queries, you will see them populate the **Custom** branch of the *Query Tree* pane. SmartView Tracker automatically populates this particular branch with your saved custom queries. As well, Check Point writes the custom queries to a file on the local drive of the PC hosting the management console. SmartView Tracker saves these files with an *##.vd* filename where *##* represents the next iteration in numerical order. For instance, if you already have a file named *19.vd*, then SmartView Tracker will save the next custom query as *20.vd*. You can find these files (in a default installation of SmartConsole) in the *\Program Files\CheckPoint\SmartConsole\R60\Program* directory.

It is important to note that these files exist only on the PC hosting the management console you use to view and save the queries. In order for you to use these queries on another machine, you must copy the *##.vd* files from one host to another. Another good bit of information is that SmartView Tracker automatically loads the file named *0.vd* when you first launch the application. So, if you want to change the default view in SmartView Tracker, all you need to do is save the current *0.vd* file to a backup copy and rename the desired default query to *0.vd*.

As you create and save your custom queries within SmartView Tracker, you will find this task both incredibly useful and less intimidating. Remember that a query is just a single filter or a set of compound filters. In this sense, all you need to do to define a custom query is apply different filters to the current *Records* pane, then save the query with a descriptive name.

Let's cover some simple steps that you can take to create a new custom query. First, open an existing query by following these steps:

- Double-click on a predefined (or existing custom query) query.
- Modify the filters as necessary.
- Save the new set of filters as a new custom query.

- Next, create a new query from the **All Records** (default) view. This query will enable you to do the following:
  - Modify the filters as desired.
  - Save the new set of filters as a new custom query.

Applying Filters

We've talked about filters and queries, but have yet to discuss how to implement a filter and save the settings as a query. Thanks to Check Point's easy-to-use GUI, you can effortlessly apply filters to the current records in SmartView Tracker. As usual, Check Point provides you with more than one way to easily implement such controls. As is always the case, both means deliver identical results.

The first way you are able to filter traffic is by utilizing the *Query Properties* pane. In this, you are able to right-click on the **Filter** column to bring up a menu. When you bring up the menu, the only option available (unless there are already filters applied to this attribute) is the **Edit Filter** option. Choose this and SmartView Tracker launches another window so that you can define the parameters for your filter. Figure 6.5 shows you what you see when you invoke a filter for the **Action** option.

Figure 6.5 Action Filter Options

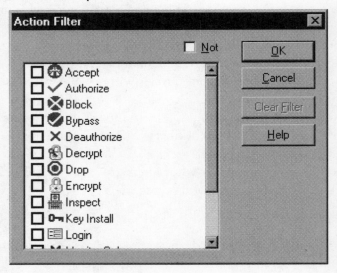

You can choose one or many filter options in this window and click **OK** to save the settings. This change will cause the settings you choose to show up in the *Query Properties* windows just as you saw with the **Firewall** predefined query.

The other method you use to implement filters is to right-click on any record (in the column you wish to filter) or the column header in the *Records* pane and choose **Edit Filter**. This action results in the same window, as shown in Figure 6.5. From here, again you can choose which parameters to filter and click **OK**.

Once more, you may add as many filters as you wish to as many columns (options) as necessary to achieve your desired result. Once you get to the point where your filters are optimal, you can save the set of filters as a custom query. To do so, all you need to do is click **Query | Save As...** from the File menu and type a name in the pop-up window. From there, you may need to expand the **Custom** queries tree to see your new entry, but you will be able to directly select this entry from this point forward to receive the current filtered view.

Notes from the Underground...

Outbound Filters

Though most firewall administrators are interested in seeing what's being blocked by their firewall as an indicator of what is going on, it is beneficial to sometimes filter for (allowed or denied/dropped) outbound traffic. Since outbound connections are less restricted than inbound connections, hosts infected with viruses, worms, or other malicious content may go undetected for some time since your security policy permits them to connect to the server they are trying to upload or download data to/from. Sometimes applying filters to block out well-known traffic produces a set of results containing generally lesser volume traffic. Such results may subsequently identify suspicious traffic. In no uncertain terms should you interpret this to mean all heavy traffic volumes are legitimate. The point here is that some attacks attempt to fly under the radar, and unless you look there from time to time, you won't see them.

Custom Queries

Now that you have a better feel for what a custom query is and how to create one, let's dive deeper into the subject. We will look at some of the options you have to track records and how to implement these options. Also, we will cover some nuances with how SmartView Tracker keeps tabs on rules.

Matching Rule Filter

In SmartView Tracker, Check Point has given you the ability to investigate desired traffic by filtering log entries based on a certain rule. In some sense, this is a bit misleading because there are two ways that SmartView Tracker identifies a rule and then filters the records to show the matching log entries. These two methods are filtering by *Current Rule Number* or filtering by *Rule UID*.

The *Current Rule Number* ties the rule to the active security policy and associates it with its place within that policy. This value is dynamic in that it may change from one policy to another or even within the same policy. In this sense, when you add or delete a rule from the security policy, all the rule numbers below the removed rule change. The *Current Rule Number* method will track those changes and filter for the records that are associated with the rule number you submit as a filtering parameter.

On the other hand, the *Rule UID* is a great tool that overcomes rule number changes. Unlike the dynamic nature of the *Current Rule Number*, the *Rule UID* is static and does not change across policies. Each rule has a unique UID, and as such, tracking by this field will return the records no matter what the current rule number is for the desired rule. This filter proves beneficial after a change has been made to the policy. Since a rule may have a different rule number, filtering for *Current Rule Number* may return only records logged since the last policy push. If you truly want to see all the records for this rule, you can use the *Rule UID* filter so that SmartView Tracker will ignore any policy changes.

To invoke either of these filters, right-click any rule and choose the appropriate option. To filter based on the *Current Rule Number,* choose **Follow rule number: <number>**. Otherwise, choose **Follow rule: <rule name>** to filter for *Rule UID*.

Viewing the Matching Rule

Now that you've filtered for a rule in your security policy, SmartView Tracker allows you to actually view the rule in context with the remainder of the security policy. If you right-click a record, you can choose **View rule in SmartDashboard** from the menu and SmartView Tracker will launch a read-only window for SmartDashboard and highlight the current rule. SmartDashboard will even open with the last revision this rule is in if you have revision control enabled.

NOTE

UID numbers are created only if the policy was generated via a Check Point NG with Application Intelligence R55 or later version module. If you are upgrading from a previous version, you must first save and install the policy from an R60 (NGX) SmartCenter Server in order to generate a UID for each rule. If you are not using revision control or do not yet have a *Rule UID* for your rules, the **View rule in SmartDashboard** option will appear grayed out.

Viewing Log Records from SmartDashboard

Just as you can go from SmartView Tracker to SmartDashboard, you can also invoke the converse transition. If you are in SmartDashboard, you can simply right-click the **NO** (rule number) column for any give rule. The menu will allow you to choose **View rule logs in SmartView Tracker**. Upon doing so, the *Log* tab will open and apply an automatic filter for this *Current Rule Number*.

Also, you are able to copy the *Rule UID* from the SmartDashboard and paste it into a filter yourself. In this manner you bypass any policy changes and pull all the records for this unique rule. You simply open SmartView Tracker and choose to edit the *Rule UID* **Filter** properties in the *Query Properties* pane.

Active View

With the **Active** view, SmartView Tracker enables you to examine open connections just as you would examine log records of connections. Essentially, if you are auto scrolling through the log records, you are just looking at these active records in a different manner. Each of these connections is also logging to the standard *fw.log* file.

Though there is a nice feature to **Active** mode **Block Intruder** (discussed later), there is also a performance penalty, as we mentioned earlier. Since the gateway must constantly update the table and forward the results to the SmartCenter Server, valuable resources are being used for this operation instead of being available for the firewall operations. However, utilizing the **Active** mode to catch or deter attackers may negate any penalty performance.

Live Connections

With this view, you see connections as they are formed and watch them disappear when they are torn down. The primary benefit here is that if you suspect an attack from a host or against an internal service, you can employ queries and filters to display only what you want to see. You can further examine these results to determine whether or not the attack is real.

If you conclude that an active attack is taking place, you can invoke a **Block Intruder** operation and block the source and destination or source, destination, and service triple. In essence, you want to block this connection and all identical subsequent requests. Although this command does not prevent the host/s from sending the message to the gateway, it does prevent the connection from being allowed and taking up extended resources on the gateway.

Custom Commands

SmartView Tracker allows you to use some utilities like *ping* and *nslookup* from within your views. You simply can right-click any of the records, and a list of commands appears at the bottom of the menu. You can choose any of these, and the gateway passes the appropriate parameters to complete the command.

To further make these tools usable, SmartView Tracker lets you define your own command-line tools. These tools are all run from the local machine (the one SmartView Tracker is running on), so it is imperative you consider path variables and platforms when configuring these commands. In other words, if you are going to add a custom command, be sure that all the administrators for this SmartCenter Server have the same executable file in the same absolute path on the host they use to connect. Otherwise, some of the tools you create may not work as thought, or they may cause undesirable results.

To configure a custom tool, just click the **Tools | Custom Commands** option from the File menu. From here, it is a few easy steps to complete the configuration of the command. Enter the values as defined in the **Add New Command** window and then click **OK**. There are limited options as far as automated parameters are concerned, but you can enter manual parameters if necessary. Also, you can use the current commands as a model to correctly configure your own custom command.

Following a Source or Destination

SmartView Tracker has a convenient method to extend a source or destination filter so that you can quickly parse the logs for the desired data. If you are examining the logs and see a suspect source or destination, you can select the record, right-click, and choose either **Follow source: <source name/ip>** or **Follow destination: <destination name/ip>**. In this way, you do not have to make a note of the source or destination address (if it is foreign to you). Instead, you can take advantage of this shortcut method and quickly see the records without much clicking or typing. For obvious reasons, this filter is available only in the **Log** and **Active** views.

Block Intruder

SmartView Tracker enables you to cease an active connection from a suspected intruder. You do so by identifying this suspect connection either in your **Log** *Records* pane or in the **Active** *Records* pane. To kill the connection you must utilize the **Active** tab. Once in the view, select the connection record and select **Tools | Block Intruder** from the File menu. This action causes the **Block Intruder** window to open (see Figure 6.6). From this point you need to configure some parameters that define your quarantine of the connection.

Figure 6.6 Block Intruder Window

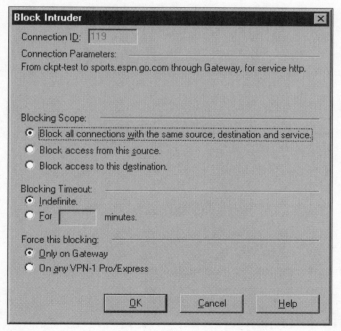

In the **Block Intruder** window shown in Figure 6.6, there are several fields. In the following list, we briefly describe each field and relate how each affects the gateway's behavior:

Blocking Scope

This field defines the type of connection you wish to block. You can block by connection profile, source, or destination.

Block All Connection with the Same Source, Destination and Service

This option tells your gateway to block only connections matching this particular connection profile (source, destination, and service). For instance, it will block an HTTP request from 192.168.1.50 to your server 10.10.1.10. However, it will not block an HTTP request from 192.168.1.50 to your other server 10.10.1.11.

Block Access from This Source

This option tells the firewall to deny any connection attempts from the source in this connection. In this way, any requests for any service to any destination inside your network coming from this one single source will not succeed.

Block Access to This Destination

Similar to the block source, but with the destination address. The gateway will drop any traffic requesting access to this destination, regardless of the source or service.

Blocking Timeout

This setting defines the period of time that you would like to block such connections. You can select indefinite or for minutes as options.

Indefinite

This setting will block access until you manually remove the blocking settings.

For...Minutes

This setting sets a time limit for blocking. The gateway will allow these blocked connections when the time period expires.

Force This Blocking

This option defines on which gateways you wish to block the defined connection. You are able to limit the action to one gateway or enable the action across all your gateways.

Only On…

This setting allows you to define which firewall module participates in the blocking action. In this way, you do not have to enforce the action on modules that will not see the connection attempts.

On any VPN-1 & FireWall-1 Module

This setting enforces blocking on all modules in your architecture. One important concept is that they must be defined within the SmartCenter Server. In cases where your Log Server is not the same as your SmartCenter Server, the block will occur on all modules known to your Log Server.

Once you enable blocking, you can disable blocking manually by choosing **Tools | Clear Blocking** from the File menu. In some cases where items are questionable and you block the connection prematurely, this option comes in very handy in order to quickly restore someone's connectivity.

When you utilize SmartView Tracker to block a connection, there are several actions the gateway invokes to protect you from the potential attack. In addition, there are several ways for you to monitor your blocking rules and modify them if you so choose.

For starters, each time you manually block an intruder in SmartView Tracker, the gateway adds an entry to its *sam_blocked_ips* database. You can view these entries with the *fw tab* command-line utility. As an example, let's say you have just blocked all connections from source 192.168.69.201 for an indefinite time period. Let's see what the Suspicious Activity Monitoring (SAM) database now looks like. We'll look at both the *sam_requests* table and the *sam_blocked_ips* table.

```
C:\>fw tab -t sam_requests
localhost:
-------- sam_requests --------
dynamic, id 8140, attributes: keep, expires never, limit 25000, hashsize
512, kb
uf 6
<c0a845c9, 00000000, c0a84597, 00000050, 00000006; 00000008, 00010001,
ffffffff,
 ffffffff, 0000001a, 00000000>
<c0a845c9, 00000000, 00000000, 00000000, 00000000; 00000008, 00010001,
ffffffff,
 00000000, 0000001d, 00000000>


C:\>fw tab -t sam_blocked_ips
```

```
localhost:
-------- sam_blocked_ips --------
dynamic, id 8141, attributes: keep, limit 25000, hashsize 512
<c0a84597; 00000000, 00000000, 00000000, 00000000, 00000000, 00000000,
00000000,
 00000001, 00000000>
<c0a845c9; 00000001, 00000000, 00000000, 00000000, 00000000, 00000000,
00000000,
 00000001, 00000000>
```

As usual, your gateway dumps the output in hex format. Once you convert some of the values to decimal, you can match it with the address you enforced via SmartView Tracker (192.168.69.201). In the *sam_requests* table, you see two entries. The first field shows the blocked IP address. Since you only cared about blocking all connections from this host, some of the other fields are all zeros (all zeros in the first five fields indicate ANY). The rest of the fields are as follows: blocked source port #; blocked destination IP; blocked destination port #; IP protocol; log option; action option; source netmask; destination netmask; filtered packets counter; time left/total time. So, now you can verify that your settings (as you enforced via the GUI) are correctly blocking the connections you want to reject. When you translate the entries to decimal, they look like this.

    <192.168.69.201; 0; 192.18.69.151; 80; 6; 8; inhibit or drop; 255.255.255.255; 255.255.255.255; 26; 0>
    <192.168.69.201; 0; 0; 0; 0; 8; inhibit or drop; 255.255.255.255; 0.0.0.0; 29; 0>

After converting to decimal, you easily understand that the first entry specifically blocks access from the intruder source to your Web server on port 80. The second rule follows blocking the source for all wildcard matches (ANY) for the destination/port pair. Now that you understand what your requests look like, you may be able to further understand what the *sam_blocked_ips* table shows you. Basically, this table tells you the number of requests for each block IP and its associated type of protocol filter. Knowing the hex conversion to decimal, you can now distinguish that the second entry says that there is one request to block the source IP 192.168.69.201.

To remove entries from the command line, all you need to do is invoke the *fw sam −D* command. This command removes all the current suspicious activity monitoring rules currently in the database. Of course, you may also remove single entries by applying additional parameters to the *fw sam* command (further discussion on this topic is not covered in this chapter).

Not only can these command-line utilities help you understand more about your blocking actions, but you can also use GUI tools. Using SmartView Monitor, you can view the currently applied blocking rules, delete them individually or all together, and receive alerts when one of your blocked intruders attempt to make a connection. To do this, you need to open SmartView Monitor (from within SmartView Tracker, click **Window | SmartView Monitor**). Once you are in the monitor GUI, you open **Tools | Suspicious Activity Rules** to view the entries. When the window opens, you may need to select your firewall from the **Show on:** drop-down list or select **Show on all VPN-1 & FireWall-1** radio button. Figure 6.7 shows you what you should see when you activate a blocking rule.

Figure 6.7 Enforced Suspicious Activity Rules Window

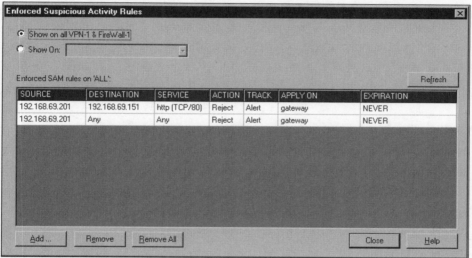

Right off the bat you notice that these rules resemble the output from the *fw tab −t sam_requests* command line utility. In order to remove any of the rules from the SAM database, all you need to do is highlight the rule and click the **Remove** button. As well, you may remove all the current rules by clicking **Remove All**. When you have SmartView Monitor open and an attacker attempts to bypass the firewall, the **Alerts** window pops up and notifies you about it and provides connection details. An example of such a screen is shown in Figure 6.8.

Figure 6.8 Alerts Window for Suspicious Activity Rule Violations

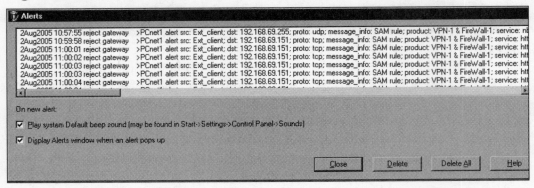

The entries in the **Alerts** windows look very similar to log messages. They provide information about the source, destination, protocol, services, and more. This window will appear only if you currently have the SmartView Monitor open and have not disabled the **Alerts** pop-ups. In this window, you are also able to remove individual messages or all the messages by clicking the appropriate button.

Audit View

What is most helpful in audit view is its accountability. All administrators have been in situations where they don't remember changing the policy and something is now being blocked. In this case, after you restore connectivity, you can review the **Audit** records to determine what happened and who did it.

WARNING

Unless you are a one-man show and the only one who even knows that there is a password on the firewall, you must ensure that each administrator has a unique username. If this is not currently the case, you should implement changes to allow for accountability within the firewall administrative interface. If "fwadmin" executes all the changes and there are several persons who know the "fwadmin" password, the **Audit** log will not provide sufficient information for you to determine who made the changes. If you desire such accountability, and all administrators should, then verify that these accountability controls are in place prior to setting your firewall into production.

Now let's take a peek in the **Audit** *Records* pane to see exactly what is there. When you double-click on an entry, you have a new window with the record's details. You can see these details after clicking on the **More Columns** option at the top right (see Figure 6.9).

Figure 6.9 Install Policy Record Details

Record Details	
△ Previous ▽ Next ▣ Copy ▦ Less Columns	
Number	257
Date	7Jul2005
Time	14:28:19
Origin	Gateway (192.168.99.1)
Application	SmartDashboard
Subject	Policy Installation
Operation	Install Policy
Status	✓ Success
Type	Log
Object Table	applications
Object Type	firewall_application
Performed On	Gateway
Changes	
Administrator	fwadmin
Client	ckpt-test
Uid	{A64D1947-6071-48FD-93B2-02A29E98B8DC}
Operation Number	7
General Information	Security Policy : Standard

Abort   Close

You can see that this record contains a significant amount of information. First, it tells you exactly when the administrator installed the policy on the gateway. Also of importance is the identity of this administrator, in this case "fwadmin." Further, the details include the host from which your administrator installed the policy. In this case, the SmartView Tracker resolves the hostname to "ckpt-test." If the address did not resolve, you would see an IP address. Also you could disable name resolution and receive the same effect. Just as SmartDashboard assigns a UID to each rule when you create it, SmartDashboard does the same assignment for your users. Any user defined within SmartCenter Server possesses a unique ID. In short, these details provide valuable information for you to follow up on if you are investigating particular changes or policy installations.

As well as policy modifications and installations, the **Audit** tab records many other operations. These options then have other filtering options, so you are able to drill down and reveal only those actions you wish to display. Just as in the **Log** records, you are able to create custom queries and store them for later use. These records provide an excellent means to recreate suspicious management events.

Log Maintenance

The volume of traffic your firewall processes necessitates your needs for log maintenance. If your organization hosts many public services or you have a ton of outbound traffic, you may need to pay closer attention to your logs than if you have a small office or home office network.

Check Point provides an array of tools so that you can manage your logs responsibly. It is imperative that you have a comprehensive rotation and archive plan in place, especially if your organizational policy defines log retention parameters. SmartView Tracker contains several options that let you contribute to automated log maintenance. However, some of your automated log management settings are configured using SmartDashboard.

One key point is that if you are utilizing log servers and the firewall module cannot communicate with the log server, the firewall module stores the logs locally. When the module restores communications with the log server, all new records are sent to the log server. However, the records that were stored locally remain on the module, and you must utilize SmartView Tracker's **Tools | Remote Files Management** tool in order to retrieve the records from the module.

Check Point's Eventia Reporter Server can automatically import logs for advanced reporting capability. However, if you want to use your own reporting applications, you can export log files into ASCII text format or a format compatible with Oracle databases.

If your log server or firewall module (if logging locally) does not possess significant disk space, you can employ cyclical logging that removes old logs when disk space is low. In this way, the logging facility never ceases. However, you may lose unrecoverable connection records and audit data depending on the disk space available and how often log files are removed.

Daily Maintenance

Log rotation is a key aspect of log management. For one, you do not want your log files to grow to a size where they become unmanageable. Check Point automatically rotates log files when they reach 2GB (by default). You can configure this setting and the rotation schedule via the gateway's object properties page in SmartDashboard. To do this, you simply double-click your gateway object and select **Logs and Masters** from the left-hand pane. You can reveal additional settings by clicking on the **+** to expand the **Logs and Masters** subproperties.

There, you can define an automated log rotation schedule and a log file size limitation (other than the default 2GB). There are other options on this page, as shown in Figure 6.10, but you reserve these details for another section in this book.

Figure 6.10 Gateway Log File Settings

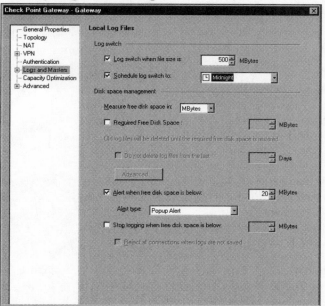

When you consider a rotation schedule, you need to mull over file size limitations as well. If you want to keep your log files under a specific size, you may incur this action prior to, say, a nightly log switch. This action results in having multiple log files for one single day of activity, as well as having multiple day entries within one single log file. However, if you want to keep only one day's log entries within one single log file you need to increase the log file size limitation so that the gateway does not truncate the log prematurely and start a new log file. This activity results in a separate log file for each day. In the event that your log file exceeds the prior maximum defined size and you have a scheduled nightly log rotation, SmartView Tracker still executes the log switch at the predetermined time. The end result here is that you may have multiple log files for a single day, but you maintain your log day segregation since scheduled log rotations execute regardless of the current log file size (one file may be very larger while the other is significantly smaller).

To enable the rotation schedule and file size limitations, you need to place checks in the appropriate boxes under the gateway's object properties. For nightly rotation, place a check in the **Schedule log switch to:** and select **Midnight** from the drop-down box. To modify the file size, place a check in the **Log switch when file size is:** box and enter a value in MB for the file size. Remember that the default size is 2GB (2000MB).

After setting these options, you must audit your configuration following the first log rotation and possibly several subsequent log rotations. Getting the right setting may take a few days and include several configuration changes to the value of the log size. However, establishing a baseline for such procedures often requires a bit of tweaking. Once the process is defined and each of the values is set to your liking, there is really little to no further modification necessary.

Log Switch

In addition to an automated log rotation schedule, FireWall-1 gives you the ability to manually invoke a log change through SmartView Tracker. If you so desire, you simply click **File | Switch Active File**. This action saves the current log file (*fw.log*) with a default date/time filename format or a name you provide. After this, the gateway begins writing to a new *fw.log* file. You may invoke the manual log switch at any time and as often as you wish. For example, if you want to capture a defined time frame within one log file, you can execute a manual log switch at the beginning of the time period, then again at the end of the time period. As long as your desired capture period either does not exceed your file size limitations or incur a nightly log rotation, all the traffic within the capture timeframe will exist in a single log file. In this sense, you may isolate suspect traffic into a single log file and perform further analysis without having to parse through a regular (dependent on your environment) size log file.

Summary

SmartView Tracker is a tool that helps you collect information about your traffic profiles, about your management changes, and shows you a glimpse of what is currently happening on your firewall. SmartView Tracker also lets you parse the log data by providing baseline queries, executing your custom queries, and applying your filter settings.

The most utilized tab in SmartView Tracker is the **Log** tab. Here you can invoke predefined queries or custom queries to quickly reveal records you are looking for. These records may be pseudo-real-time or latent records you are searching through for connection information.

The **Active** tab gives you insight into what connections currently exist on the firewall. One great aspect of this tool is that you can block intruders and deny the connections based on several options. The downside of this tab is that it carries a potential performance hit, but in the case of an active attack, it can prove invaluable.

The **Audit** tab reveals important accounting information regarding the management of your firewall. You can use this tool to investigate management incidents or audit your processes to verify you are meeting organizational policy guidelines and/or goals.

As a firewall administrator, you need to realize the value of logs. In this sense, you need to learn how to configure your tools to produce meaningful data and then to massage these resultant logs to quickly divulge the information that you seek. You have now seen that SmartView Tracker is a comprehensive tool that not only displays your log files in an easily understood format but also provides to you sufficient tools to further manipulate the information into productive views.

Solutions Fast Track

Tracker

- ☑ SmartView Tracker provides numerous tools for you to exercise proper oversight of your firewall's security policy and the management events within your firewall.

- ☑ Tracker uses distinct views to segregate normal log events, active connections, and audit log events. In addition, these views are all easily manipulated using toggles to shape the view into the most beneficial representation of the current record profile.

☑ Not only does SmartView Tracker allow you to investigate current activities within your firewalls, but it also permits you to revisit older log files to review specific connections.

☑ Remember, SmartView Tracker logs only what you tell it to. Proper *Rules* configuration in your security policy is a crucial aspect to log review. If you are not logging specific connections, you will not see these records in SmartView Tracker.

Log View

☑ The **Log** tab reveals to you all the connection records contained in the current *fw.log* file. This includes the most recent log entry and the first log entry from the current collection period.

☑ When you apply filters within the **Log** tab's Records pane, you focus the output on traffic you specifically want to view. These filters can be simple, or they can be compound filters that you later define and save as a query.

☑ Log view gives you sufficient flexibility with respect to the configuration of the output. In this way, you can rearrange the record columns so that the details provide maximum benefit. In addition, you can modify the value of the fields by toggling different options on the toolbar.

Predefined Queries

☑ These queries serve as baseline filters and provide great launching points for creating custom queries. In other words, if you want to see a particular type of connection, invoking a predefined query will not reduce the scope enough to single out that connection profile. However, it will narrow the range of records you must further filter.

☑ In no way are you able to modify predefined queries. You must save all changes to the predefined set of filters from these queries under a new name (written to the *Custom* queries branch).

Custom Queries

☑ Beyond the predefined queries, SmartView Tracker allows you to define your own set of filters in a custom query. These filters will quickly reduce the record set to what you truly want to see.

☑ You can create custom queries to follow a rule by its *Rule Number* or its *Rule UID* (its unique identifier that SmartDashboard assigns when the rule is first created).

☑ Custom queries are saved locally on each management station; the SmartView Tracker interface does not write them to the SmartCenter Server for all management clients to use.

Active View

☑ The **Active** log shows you connections that your firewall is currently handling and gives you the ability to block connections on-the-fly.

☑ **Active** view may allow you to identify a rogue client. You can filter based on source address and possibly identify a single source having excessive connections open.

☑ In **Active** view, SmartView Tracker provides custom commands so that you can quickly determine specific items from your current connection. Check Point provides *ping* and *nslookup* by default.

☑ Another tool in **Active** view helpful to you is the follow source or destination utility. Right-clicking on a record and choosing the proper option instantiates a set of filters to follow the current source or destination. This utility allows you to focus on the task at hand instead of writing filters.

Block Intruder

☑ Block Intruder allows you to single out connections based on source, service, and destination. You can then decide to block these connections from the firewall.

☑ Your decision to block connections can last for a predetermined amount of time, or until you manually remove the block.

☑ Blocking connections is a useful way to intervene with suspected intruders or virus/worm activity.

Audit View

- ☑ If you need to verify management changes to our security policy, you can peruse the **Audit** log to see detailed records of the events

- ☑ These **Audit** records are invaluable as they reveal which user installed the latest policy and when it was applied.

- ☑ The **Audit** records also reveal details regarding changes to objects within the firewall security policy.

Log Maintenance

- ☑ FireWall-1 gives you the ability to schedule log rotation by the file size, a daily schedule, or both.

- ☑ Through SmartView Tracker, you can manually invoke a log switch so that your current records are saved to a file and the gateway begins a new log file.

- ☑ The policies within your organization should drive your log rotation and retention. FireWall-1 provides a flexible environment with which to meet your organization's goals.

Frequently Asked Questions

The following Frequently Asked Questions, answered by the authors of this book, are designed to both measure your understanding of the concepts presented in this chapter and to assist you with real-life implementation of these concepts. To have your questions about this chapter answered by the author, browse to **www.syngress.com/solutions** and click on the **"Ask the Author"** form.

Q: Why can't I save changes to the any of the predefined queries?

A: Changes to SmartView Tracker's set of predefined queries cannot be saved. You may save these changes as a new custom query, but not as the current query.

Q: I'm trying to filter using the *Rule UID* but something isn't working right. What's the problem?

A: Remember that versions prior to R55 did not assign *Rule UID* to rules. You must first save and install your policy using your R60 SmartCenter Server.

Q: When I try to filter by *Rule Number*, I do not get any results, but I should get tons of records. What's going on?

A: Keep in mind that filtering by *Rule Number* most often pulls only the results using the current revision of the security policy. Instead, try filtering with the *Rule UID* to get records based on the rule, regardless of its association with the current security policy.

Q: Sometimes my log view appears to hang. Could this have something to do with resolving names?

A: Since the log server is doing a name lookup for each record, it could decrease performance a bit. Toggling the **resolve IP** toolbar button will disable these name lookups.

Q: How often does my firewall module send the records to the log server?

A: By default, the firewall module will send records as they are written. You can configure your module to log locally and automatically send the files to the log server on a defined schedule.

Q: Why doesn't rule X show up in my logs?

A: Be sure that each rule you want to log actually has the **Log** option selected in the **TRACK** field of the rule. Otherwise, the connections for this rule will not appear in the log files.

Q: My log server crashed and now is back online. What happened to my log files while the log server was down?

A: When a module cannot communicate with the log server, it will begin logging locally. When the log server is back online, the module begins forwarding records to it. However, you must recover the records that were logged locally using the **Remote Files Management** tool.

Q: I don't need all these empty columns in my *Records* pane. How can I get rid of them?

A: You can right-click on the column header or any cell in the column and select **Hide Column**. You can also remove the check from the check box for that column in the *Query Properties* pane.

Chapter 7

SmartDefense and Web Intelligence

Solutions in this chapter:

- Network Security
- Application Intelligence
- Malicious Code
- Protocol Inspection
- DShield Storm Center

☑ Summary

☑ Solutions Fast Track

☑ Frequently Asked Questions

Introduction

Since the release of NG Feature Pack 2, Check Point has added a new component that can verify packet integrity up to and including layer 7 from the Open Systems Interconnection (OSI) model. To further concentrate on Web attacks, Check Point has separated Web Intelligence from SmartDefense and has made Web Intelligence a component of NG AI (R55W). SmartDefense and Web Intelligence are two distinct products that are licensed separately. SmartDefense is licensed as an annual maintenance fee per number of VPN-1 Pro Gateways that your SmartCenter Server manages. Having the proper SmartDefense license within the Check Point UserCenter enables you to download new SmartDefense and Web Intelligence signatures from the Check Point Web site.

SmartDefense and Web Intelligence combine to provide network, application, and Web server protection for your architecture. This chapter discusses both basic and advanced concepts for network security and reveal how Check Point's technologies supply relief for current threats. In addition, we walk through specific exercises to block particular threats.

Network Security

It is your job to provide administrative guidance over your network's perimeter, which means that you have control over your organization's gateway to the Internet. Let's begin by discussing some of the finer protections a NGX gateway offers and why it is recommended that you employ such protections.

In the most obvious sense, gateways (firewalls) are often the single device in your network path that handles every packet to and from the Internet. If the entire world were compliant and played by the rules, this would not be such a big deal. However, it has become commonplace for attackers to launch exploits remotely. In this sense, you now have become much more important in the grand scheme of protecting your information systems assets. After all, you manage the one device that handles all of the traffic. Congratulations, you have now graduated from firewall administrator to network security administrator. Check Point VPN-1 Pro Gateway (NGX) provides multiple technologies to protect your organization's assets in such a hostile environment.

Because most attackers seem to prefer to not be physically present while compromising your assets, you must consider how to introduce NGX's security controls to your network in such a manner that they will identify, prevent, notify, and possibly react to specific (or not) threats. We will refer to this group of actions as network security. In other words, exercising what it takes to reduce risk associated with permitting at least one host the ability to communicate with other hosts via some physical medium. Not to say that all communications through your gateway must interact with the Internet. There are certainly circumstances that do not call for Internet connectivity. Does the absence of the Internet make your network safer? Well, you could postulate that it certainly reduces risk in some sense. However, all risks are not associated with Internet hosts, so you cannot rest on the fact that your private network has no connectivity to the Internet. If you employ a VPN-1 Pro Gateway, there is obviously some reason you want to segregate one network (user population) from another. Your choosing to deploy this device is, in and of itself, risk mitigation for network security issues.

As we will cover later in this chapter, network security involves risk reduction for intercommunications between hosts (at several levels). This could be legitimate traffic between two good hosts, or legitimate traffic between a bad host and a good host, or any combination of good and bad hosts for that matter. The key here is that you either know what you are looking for or hope that something (bad) sticks out like a sore thumb. Network security may or may not be a legitimate science, but it is definitely an exercise in trial and error. The bad guys are turning out new threats faster than the good guys are protecting themselves against the known threats. Unfortunately, this fact implies that networks remain vulnerable to the unknown threats since most technologies rely on signature-based detection. The fact that worms and viruses continue to propagate through networks seems to adequately confirm this assertion.

NOTE

Some administrators spend a lot of time patching vulnerable systems and applications to protect against known threats. While this practice is obviously necessary, it doesn't provide for threats that are not yet public knowledge. Keep in mind that highly skilled attackers with unethical motives may not necessarily want to reveal something they have found. Not all hackers are "security researchers" seeking credit for finding vulnerability X. Deploying an NGX gateway and enabling appropriate security controls allows you to increase an attacker's work factor when they are trying to successfully exploit vulnerabilities. Such controls may even prevent an attack from taking place. At the very least, a properly configured NGX gateway broadens the possibility that an attack will be noticed immediately.

To further define the scope of network security relevant to your VPN-1 Pro Gateway, you must consider the procedural aspect of sending information from one host to another over some type of network medium. This includes each host's network interfaces; hubs and/or switches, routers, firewalls, proxy servers, and any other device that helps packets get to their destination. Network security also encompasses devices that do not necessarily contribute to packet transfer (passive devices), but monitor the traffic on the network. A good example of this type of device is an Intrusion Detection System (IDS). Engaging security controls on any of theses devices will help reduce the possibility of a successful attack. An IDS is installed on your network to help you become aware of possible attacks. Moreover, your NGX gateway can intervene during an active attack. It can deny a connection, send reset packets to both hosts, or apply other means to halt the conversation. As you can see, network security comprises a broad spectrum of services, devices, and processes to provide protective measures.

In short, network security introduces solutions into your architecture that reduce the opportunity for successful attacks, notify you of active attacks (successful or not), and diminish the effects of a successful attack. An NGX solution aims to prevent or reduce the harm done by attacks against confidentiality, integrity, and availability associated with your hosts and the services they offer. With one product, you can license many Check Point technologies to provide a wide range of network protections. Not only does your Check Point gateway possess access control capability, it can detect and prevent network attacks trying to traverse your gateway.

Threats

In today's technologically advanced society, there are many threats you must deal with when your duties include protecting your network. Although there may be more than one definition of a threat, we will use this term to convey the possibility that an attacker will successfully carry out an exploit against one of your assets. So how do you go about identifying threats and enacting measures to mitigate them, or in some cases accept them? The answer to this question is risk management; a simple term (though not the most simple process) that relates to procedures identifying risk, applying cost factors for these risks to your assets, and finally accepting the risk or introducing a solution to reduce the risk.

In recent history, attackers have predominantly shifted the focus of their attacks from network attacks to application layer exploits (more on the network model later). More to the point, miscreants often target a few application groups because of the global accessibility of these services. Two of these services—Hypertext Transfer Protocol (HTTP [default port 80]) and Structured Query Language (SQL) [default port 1521])—are widely deployed together to facilitate dynamic Web content.

Because of the proliferation of servers available, and the lack of administration in some cases, attackers smell blood with regard to these services and attack when they discover a victim.

What kinds of threats exist? The answer to this question differs for each network. However, there are specific classes of threats that everyone must deal with. The following sections discuss some threat vectors and how you can configure your NGX gateway to prevent them. This will help you understand what to look for and how to utilize your Check Point technologies to locate it.

Structured Threats

Although the term may seem sophisticated, a *structured threat* is simply a threat an attacker targets to a certain asset because of a specific interest the attacker has in successfully exploiting that asset. In other words, some script-kiddie blindly launching a "sploit" to a range of addresses does not exactly embody the essence of this category. For example, professional criminal hackers carefully and meticulously plan and execute events so as to minimize the possibility of being caught, but maximize the probability of success. This is no suggestion that only professional criminal hackers are capable of posing a structured threat. What it does imply is that a deviant plans and targets an attack on an asset for a specific reason. For instance, say that an E-commerce Web site has an online database that houses credit card information for customer convenience. A miscreant may plan to attack the database in order to steal the credit card numbers so that he or she can sell them on the black market. The attacker in this case does reconnaissance to find out which database software is running, researches which vulnerabilities apply to this version of software, and carry out the exploit against the application. This chain of events demonstrates the backbone of a structured threat.

Sometimes it is the case that we often find out about these threats after an author/discoverer has already successfully exploited victims. For instance, earlier this year (2005) a Linux kernel exploit became public knowledge. The author of the exploit later recounted that he or she had already *owned* a significant amount of servers anyway, so it didn't bother him or her that it was then public. On the other hand, it is often the case that large public disclosures result from known vulnerabilities: ones in which vendors have already issued patches. If the vulnerability is significant and the result of the exploit is great gain, then it is likely that an attacker will try to launch the exploit against servers running the vulnerable application. Again, this is a structured threat; an attacker targets specific systems (possibly anything running application *X*) as intended victims of a specific exploit. Except in this case, an attacker does not have to be a professional criminal hacker, but just willing to perform reconnaissance and execution.

You can reduce the likelihood of these threats by understanding how to configure your NGX gateway to prevent them.

Denial of Service

A structured denial-of-service (DOS) attack usually involves the deliberate interruption of service by one individual to one victim. Sometimes, flooding a machine with requests is enough to deny service to legitimate customers. Some of these attacks may be unintentional, but most are usually the result of a deliberate attack. In some cases, attackers compromise other hosts and have them contribute to the DOS attack, which is called a distributed denial of service (DDOS). These attacks cause resources to be unavailable to customers (users), which can result in lost productivity and lost sales, and cause you to have to spend large amounts of money in recovery.

Three such DOS attacks are the *Teardrop*, *Ping of Death*, and *LAND* attacks (described in later sections). Your NGX gateway has the ability to recognize and block such attempts against hosts within your protected zones. In addition, NGX can block non-Transmission Control Protocol (TCP)-based flooding attempts by limiting the percentage of the state table that non-TCP connections can occupy (see Figure 7.1).

Figure 7.1 Denial-of-Service Configuration Settings

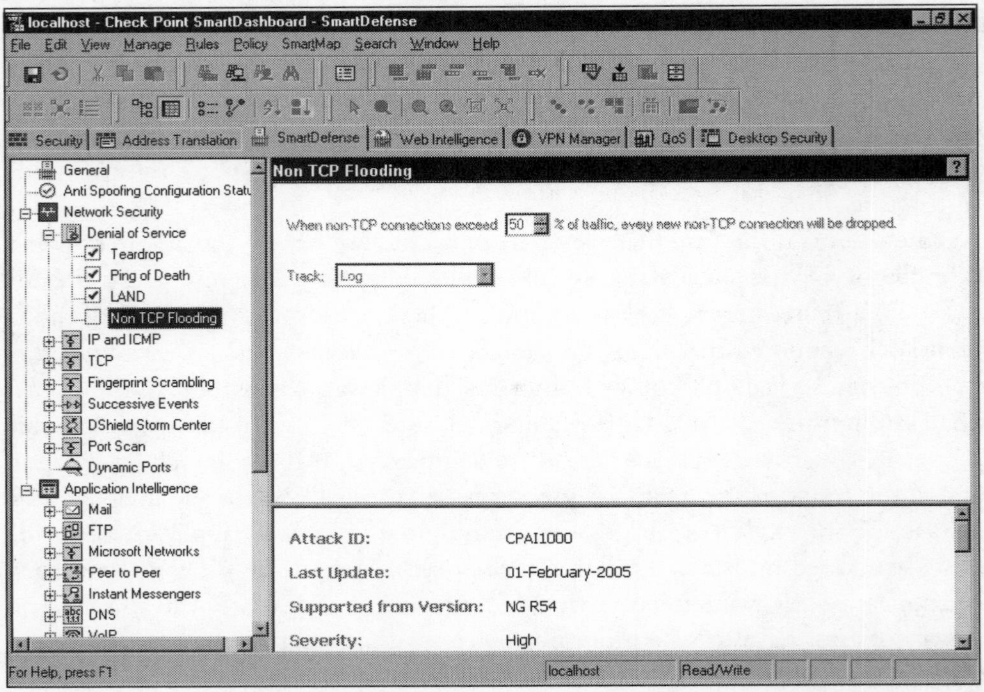

You can see in Figure 7.1 that all the Non-TCP Flooding leaves are default-enabled. To disable any of these protections, delete the checkmark. For the first three leaves, the only options are to monitor or change the tracking method. For the Non-TCP Flooding settings, you can define a percentage value that defines when to trigger the blocking action. Be careful when enabling this prevention; NGX will drop all non-TCP connections if the threshold is met. This may be undesirable if you have legitimate non-TCP traffic traversing your gateway.

External Threats

Here is where we combine all threats that originate from outside of your network. In this case it could be anything or anyone perpetrating the act. What it boils down to is that you have vulnerable services or hosts; you permit external sources to initiate connections with these items, so now you have a threat on your hands. This, unfortunately, is very commonplace for most administrators.

Consider a fairly standard network architecture consisting of a single VPN-1 Pro Gateway with a Demilitarized Zone (DMZ) interface, an external interface, and an internal protected interface. Also consider the loose rule base that allows the protected network to go anywhere; permits the DMZ hosts to talk back to private hosts for database or other lookup information; and then allows some HTTP, Hypertext Transfer Protocol Secure sockets (HTTPS), and File Transfer Protocol (FTP) to go from anywhere to a few DMZ hosts. This is where network administrators experience port scans, exploit attempts, and DOS attacks. A fair majority of the noise network administrators see on their networks comes from the outside. It could be college computer science students (or high school students) experimenting with scripts. The fact is it could be anyone doing a number of things to your network. Attackers on the outside are capable of defeating confidentiality, integrity, and availability even though they may not be inside your network.

Let's expand on that thought for a moment. External attacks are just that, external. They originate from a host on another network somewhere and attempt to compromise the security policy of one of your hosts. If the attack succeeds, what does that mean for your network now? Does this still pose an external threat? You must consider all possible scenarios when configuring your NGX gateway, securing your hosts, and protecting your network against attacks. Protecting your infrastructure from external threats is critical. What is even more critical is preventing a successful (external) attacker from being able to use your public hosts as stepping stones to reach your internal hosts. So ask yourself, "If I were an attacker, how could I use box X to get to the inside?" Remember, your VPN-1 Pro security policy allows outsiders into your DMZ. However, it does not permit them to initiate communications with your internal hosts. Since your devices are not smart enough to know who is initiating connections from which server (attacker or administrator), you must be more savvy than the attacker and consider the domino effect of a successful external attack.

TIP

To reduce the possibility that these and other external threats could propel an attacker to compromise one of your internal private hosts, you should become familiar with the advanced configuration options on your NGX gateway and subscribe to the multilevel security theory. Providing security controls at multiple levels throughout your network increases the work factor for an attacker that tries to compromise one of your hosts. Even though having a VPN-1 Pro Gateway at your perimeter is a great start, it does not in and of itself provide depth. Consider instituting an architectural "firewall sandwich." In this configuration, DMZ hosts are segregated from internal hosts in a hierarchical manner. In essence, you have a VPN-1 Pro Gateway in front of your DMZ and another gateway behind your DMZ that protects your internal (private) networks. Further, you configure your internal firewall so that no host on the DMZ (or from the Internet) may initiate a connection to a host within your private networks. This way, if an attacker compromises one of your DMZ hosts, the internal gateway's access control policy, combined with the advanced protections NGX offers, would continue to deny unauthorized access and detect and prevent attacks determined to compromise your internal (private) hosts (from one of your DMZ hosts or an Internet host). Remember that your Check Point gateways not only do access control, but they supply many functions that contribute to a comprehensive network security approach. Also understand that no security control or combination of controls absolutely prevents attacks. However, you should not retreat from implementing security controls that increase an attacker's work factor.

Welchia Internet Control Message Protocol

During 2003, an attack known as the *Welchia* worm broke out across the Internet. This attack targeted systems running vulnerable versions of Microsoft's Distributed Component Object Model (DCOM) Remote Procedure Call (RPC) service. Once a system was compromised, the worm tried to spread itself using that service. One of the ways it did this was to scan the local network for other active hosts by sending out a specifically crafted Internet Control Message Protocol (ICMP) Echo Request message. Imagine that you have a large network and none of your workstations were patched against this vulnerability. The result was chaos. The reality for many organizations was unwanted down time. To prevent this from happening, all you need to do is configure your NGX gateway to block attacks from traversing the firewall. Go to **SmartDefense | Network Security | IP and ICMP** and place a check in the box next to **Block Welchia ICMP**. Again, there aren't many options as far as configuration goes. You can enable the "monitor only" option and change the tracking, but for the most part, it's on or off for this attack prevention mechanism.

Network Quota

In addition to the Welchia preventative measures, you can also configure your NGX gateway to limit the amount of connections that one (external or internal) host may have open to your protected hosts at any given time. A single Internet Protocol (IP) address could be passing a network-wide port scan or port sweep through your gateway. In this case, your NGX protections will block an offending machine from traversing the firewall if the gateway detects abuse. This setting applies to all source addresses. However, the advanced settings can be configured with a list of "exception" objects. In this case, you can allow your internal hosts to have as many connections open as necessary.

To enable this setting, go to **SmartDefense | Network Security | Network Quota**. When there, you will be able to set the number of connections and then click the **Advanced** button to change these settings. Other than the exclusion list, you can set a period of time to drop connections for the offending host. The Check Point default settings are 100 connections per host and a drop time of 60 seconds following an infraction.

Internal Threats

Internal threats are similar to external threats in that this category encompasses many attack vectors. However, internal threats now come with supplementary risk in that (some) attackers may possess privileged information. That is the key to internal threats. Whereas an external threat must overcome layers (you hope) of defense mechanisms, an internal threat may not be seen by any of your security devices.

It is often difficult to convince uninformed management folk that you need to protect your assets from internal threats. Time after time we see that statistics show most compromises come from employees of some kind. As mentioned before, what makes these threats so real is the inherent ease (in comparison to external attacks) with which the attacker executes an attack and the stealth-like manner in which he or she does it. For all you know, when your coworker exports the list of credit card numbers from the database, he or she could have disabled auditing, sanitized (removing suspicious events) the logs, or just plain removed the logs. When insiders launch attacks, it's not only the effects that arise from the breach that cause damage, but the fact that it may take a long time to realize there has been a breach. Further, there are times when an employee (commonly known as "disgruntled") is aware that the ax is coming down on him or her and he or she plants a time-delayed attack in the system. In this way, after the insider is gone, the attack shuts down some services, or worse, the entire network.

Not all internal threats stem from administrators gone bad. It could be as simple as an open campus-type network providing connectivity on an internal (private) network to any host that connects to the network—perhaps something similar to the way a university provides an open campus. When a student (or not) attaches to the network, he or she is not all of a sudden granted administrative privileges, but most often, internal connectivity implies less access control or other security controls. Sure, everyone has a network operating system (OS) that users must authenticate with in order to receive network services, but you aren't facing someone looking for service; rather, you are protecting your network against an attacker with malfeasance in mind.

As such, you should continue to deploy a defense-in-depth strategy to protect against internal threats. Further, you might concentrate on segregating your networks so that user populations must traverse access control devices, IDS/IPS devices, or other security control devices in order to reach your protected assets. In the case that you cannot provide such segregation, you should focus your security on the valued hosts. Enable sufficient auditing and logging so that events are discernable. Also, introduce separation of duty controls so that your organization doesn't have a one-man-show for any of your valuable assets. In this way, the admin who is about to be fired does not have sufficient privileges to disable all of the logging and auditing on the database server so he or she can implement an attack script.

! **W**ARNING

All internal threats are not the product of angry employees, contractors, or visitors. Have you stopped to think about the threats you pose as an administrator of the network? What if you are loading the configuration on the router and have a typo in the upload file? Does this pose a threat to your network? Yes, the result of this unintended attack may be a DOS for your organization. Keep in mind that proper configuration control and change management procedures are also risk mitigation techniques for internal threats. Changing configurations on systems always poses a threat to system availability. Be sure to include such controls so that you mitigate the risk of administrative mishap.

Reconnaissance (Port Scans and Sweeps)

Though attackers may execute reconnaissance from external points on your network, an internal scan or sweep may result in a more telling result. Again, it is common for many organizations to allow any traffic originating from their internal networks to pass through their security rule base. For this reason, you should enable NGX's **Port Scan** configuration options. While it will not stop a port scan or port sweep against a resident network scan, it can be configured along with the *sam_alert* command to prevent scans against hosts that reside on different interfaces of your VPN-1 Pro Gateway.

To enable these protections, go to **SmartDefense | Network Security | Port Scan**. Figure 7.2 shows what you can expect to see when configuring a **Host Port Scan**. Note that when you make a change to a SmartDefense setting, or when a new protection is added when you make an online update, the setting turns to boldface and will have an asterisk after it until you install the policy.

Figure 7.2 Host Port Scan Configuration Options

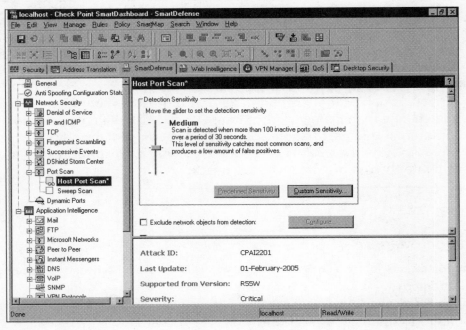

Note that the **Detections Sensitivity** can be changed to predetermined settings of High, Medium, or Low to allow you to configure the detection of less obvious scans (high), or to only react to blatant port scanning attempts. Note that the descriptions mention that it will trigger on inactive ports. Since port scans are looking for any open ports on one or more hosts, you must consider these options. If you do not like the predefined levels, you can set your own **Custom Sensitivity...** levels by clicking this button and entering values for the number of ports and the time period. Also note that you can configure an exception list using your defined objects. If you have some test servers or you have your settings set to detect even the most minute scan and one host keeps popping up (for legitimate traffic), you can set your protections to omit this particular server using the exclusion list.

It is also important to understand how a port sweep is different from a port scan. A port scan runs a range of ports over one host (too see which ones are open). A port sweep is when an attacker looks for a specific service running on multiple servers. Therefore, instead of hitting one or more hosts with a range of ports, he may scan many hosts for a single port to see which servers respond. The configuration settings for the **Sweep Scan** are similar to those in the port scan. Remember, you may find that what you think is okay will still set off an alarm when there isn't a true attack (false positive). In this case, you must tune your NGX protections so that it fits the characteristics of your network.

Tools & Traps...

Port Scanners and Banner-Grabbing

How do attackers know which servers to hit? Some of them launch a script against a large range of IP addresses and wait for the results. Some attackers perform reconnaissance (port scanning, banner grabbing, and so forth) to focus their attacks against a set of known vulnerable servers. The Internet offers many tools to scan ports, grab banners, and report a list of possible victims back to the attacker. This action results in a list of servers that are likely vulnerable to a specific attack. Now the attacker can remotely execute the exploit against only possible victims instead of a wide range of addresses that may or may not be vulnerable to the attack. To defend this technique, NGX has three distinct capabilities. In addition to the port scan and port sweep mechanisms you just learned of, Web Intelligence lets you configure "Header Spoofing" (you will incur performance penalties) that will prevent banner disclosure to attackers. Basically, you define a regular expression that your gateway looks for and either replaces or strips out the response. Though these protections certainly increase an attacker's work factor, they do not necessarily thwart an attack. NGX's network- and application-level components complement these measures along with a secure host configuration to prevent unwanted attacks.

The OSI Model

All persons holding a (network) security-related job must be familiar with the OSI model. Not only does the model help you understand how packets go from one host to the other, it gives you perspective on how attackers exploit vulnerabilities in each layer in order to compromise your security policy. There are seven layers to the OSI model (see Figure 7.3).

Figure 7.3 The OSI Model

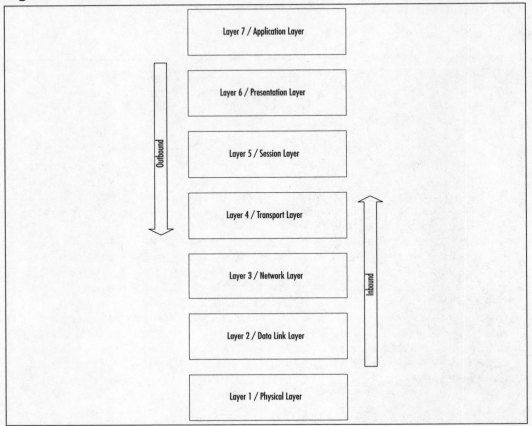

Notice in Figure 7.3 that layer 1 is on the bottom. This is because the diagram represents the flow of packets from one host to another (in a two-host communication). Consider that host A sends a packet to host B. The first thing that happens is the application layer creates the data. The flow then proceeds down the model to the physical layer where the packet travels to the other host. Once at the destination host, the packet travels up the model to layer 7 where the application processes the data.

To help you understand how your NGX gateway protections work, the following sections concentrate on three of these layers: the network layer, the transport layer, and the application layer, which represent the place where a majority of all remote attacks occur.

Layer 3: The Network Layer

IP and ICMP reside within this layer. As such, there are many attacks available against these protocols. For example, the *Ping of Death* attack targets ICMP (ping), and if it reaches a vulnerable host, it will crash, causing a DOS. Though other protocols exist within this layer (ARP, RARP, RIP, OSPF), SmartDefense only provides protections against IP and ICMP attacks. Protecting your network not only includes protection for applications, but also the protocols that carry application data. Check Point's SmartDefense technology provides sufficient coverage of these attacks and more.

To configure your VPN-1 Pro Gateway to detect and/or prevent these attacks, go to **SmartDefense | Network Security | IP and ICMP**, where you will find protections against such attacks as the aforementioned *Ping of Death* as well as other IP and ICMP protections. For instance, you can enable protections against an attack aimed at Cisco IOS. By turning these protections on, your gateway will block any attempts to attack devices with the **SWIPE**, **IP Mobility**, **SUN-ND**, or **PIM** protocols. Again, there are options that enable you to block other attacks against IP and ICMP; you should investigate which options will best protect your organization's network. Enabling these is straightforward. If you come across a setting or option that is unclear, Check Point's "help" files are an informative aid to help you determine how to set an option.

Layer 4: The Transport Layer

Devices process the Transport Control Protocol (TCP) and the User Datagram Protocol (UDP) in the transport layer. Recall that many of today's applications utilize one of these two transport layer protocols for data transfer. Again, there are vulnerabilities within implementations of these protocols, so that attackers can exploit them if you have vulnerable hosts. One such example is a synchronized (SYN) attack. In this attack, one (or more) hosts send an overload of SYN packets to the victim. As this single packet itself is not illegal, it does not complete the three-way handshake TCP connections are looking for. The attacker is hoping that the victim will allocate a connection for each of the SYN requests and wait for the handshake to complete. Subsequently, the victim host will run out of connections, resulting in a DOS for legitimate clients. Your NGX gateway, with a proper SmartDefense SYN Attack configuration, will detect this attack and protect your host from such a DOS. There are also numerous other attacks at the transport layer that your gateway will fend off.

To detect SYN attacks and protect against them, NGX offers a two-fold approach. First, it passively monitors all incomplete three-way-handshake attempts and only forwards the connections to the destination server after receiving an

Acknowledgment (ACK) from the originating client. In doing so, the gateway enforces a shorter time-out period than the destination server. If a gateway considers a host to be under attack, it activates the second defense mechanism, "SYN Relay defense." This protection waits for the completion of the three-way-handshake prior to handing off the connection to the destination server. This prevents the destination server from receiving SYN packets that have no intention of being part of a valid connection. This counters the attack by not allowing the destination host to fill its connection buffer with bogus requests. Thus, the queue will not fill up with connection requests that have not completed the three-way-handshake (invalid attempts) and deny valid requests for new connections

To enable this protection, go to **SmartDefense | Network Security | TCP | SYN Attack Configuration**. There is an option to set the timeout period that your gateways will enforce when deciding whether or not a SYN packet is part of an attack. You can also define whether or not to enforce this protection only on external interfaces (defined in your anti-spoofing settings), or on all interfaces. In addition, you can define how many packets will invoke SYN Relay defense. The last options to set are logging and tracking options.

Layer 7: The Application Layer

As mentioned before, all kinds of organizations are making their applications available via the Internet. As such, there are many attackers that seek to compromise these hosts and harvest data from them to sell to others. Moreover, a greater number of organizations have Web servers (HTTP/HTTPS), FTP servers, and remote access ability (Telnet, SSH, RDP) to servers available to hosts on the Internet. Although many of these organizations have installed an access control device for some of these services, the other services such as HTTP and FTP are meant to be available to anyone from anywhere. This is where NGX does more than just access control. NGX provides application-level protections in both SmartDefense and Web Intelligence.

What this means is that you must understand that thee are plenty of attacks for these services. Attackers have progressed from simple attempts against application configuration mistakes that lead to information disclosure (directory information, and so forth) to attacks that exploit the code-level vulnerabilities that lead to greater information disclosure (credit card data, trade secrets, intellectual property, and so forth). To protect your organization against such attacks, you must have a device that is capable of inspecting the data at the application layer. When you enable the associated options embedded within SmartDefense and Web Intelligence on your NGX VPN-1 Pro Gateway, you gain protection from application layer attacks. Keep in mind that the technologies involved with Web Intelligence not only operate based on attack signatures, but also possess built-in logic to detect unknown attacks.

One such SmartDefense control within the application layer lets you manage how your organization handles instant messaging (IM) traffic. SmartDefense lets you configure your gateway for four IM products: MSN Messenger, Skype, Yahoo! Messenger, and ICQ. While the MSN settings allow you to get more granular, the other settings allow you to block proprietary protocols on all ports. Some of your staff may not realize that each message passes plaintext through an Internet-based server prior to reaching the other participant. For this reason, they may think that it is okay to discuss confidential dealings via IM applications. This NGX security control gives you the ability to reduce information disclosure.

NGX gets more specific for MSN Messenger. There are two settings for MSN, one for the Session Initiation Protocol (SIP) and one for the MSN Messenger Service (MSNMS). The controls for these two settings are similar (see Figure 7.4).

Figure 7.4 MSN Messenger over SIP Configuration Settings

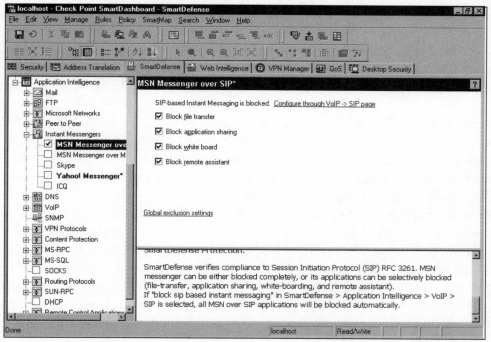

Note that you can configure SIP-based blocking through more than this option. If you have SIP blocking enabled on the VOIP settings, it will block MSN Messenger over SIP. Instead of blocking the whole application, you can configure

NGX to block specific parts of the application. If you don't want anyone to invoke the remote assistant, you can place a check in this box. These settings can be changed to fit your network and the services you wish to offer your users. For the MSN Messenger over MSNMS settings, you have the additional ability to block multimedia (audio and video).

Though there are weaknesses in these applications, which may lead to attacks against your network, these NGX controls allow you to stop inadvertent information disclosure. This is not all that NGX offers the application layer. As mentioned previously, AI offers configuration options for many different services and protections against a variety of attacks.

The Need for Granular Inspection

Begin by considering what the term *granular* means in this context. You may understand it to communicate the idea that something is so dense with cohesive components that it must be broken down to fully evaluate the contents of the entity. That is precisely what you need to do in order to protect your applications and servers from attacks. You know that packets come across the wire in a standard format (headers, data, and so forth). Unfortunately, there are many ways in which attackers violate these standards in order to facilitate an attack. For this reason, it is necessary to employ solutions that sustain the ability to inspect each packet with respect to its individual components. In addition, these devices must assess the communication as a whole. To do this, your solutions must reassemble packets in order to restore the context of the request. In this manner, your device thoroughly examines each packet and also evaluates each request (as a whole).

In a previous section, you learned that attackers have migrated (for the most part) from localized attacks to network-based attacks. In this sense, remote attacks focus on violating internetworking standards and (application) protocol standards. Network packets have a structure that allows devices to determine the destination of the packet. The packet also contains the *data* portion of the communication between the hosts. If the request is small enough to fit into one packet, the *data* field inspection is both a granular examination and a contextual evaluation for this communication. However, some requests span multiple packets. In this manner, the originating host (or device in between) may fragment the request into *n* packets to conform to the network packet size limitations between hosts. Security devices are still able to inspect the *data* fields in each packet as they come across the wire. However, these devices must store and reassemble each *fragment* in order to evaluate the context of the request. These processes expose the network to vulnerability.

Attackers may tweak one of many bits within a transmission to alter the processing of a packet. There are several examples of attacks that violate the intended function of networking. For example, the *Teardrop* attack targets improper fragment reassembly. If two successive packets are sent with fragments, the second packet contains the first (within its offset). This attack exploits the lack of a proper fragment handling procedure; however, the NGX protections are intuitive enough to detect and block this attack. Other attacks exist that alter packet fields to induce chaos on devices. In some cases, creating a synchronization request (SYN) packet with the same source/destination (a LAND attack) and port pairings will crash the host. Again, this packet does not represent the intended use of networking, and exploits the fact that there is insufficient packet handling controls in place on a victim.

Besides network attacks, misfeasors often modify the data field of a packet in order to exploit an application vulnerability. If devices in the path of communication do not properly detect these attempts, the attack may succeed. For example, some post office protocol (POP) servers are vulnerable to long username or password parameters when authenticating users. To exploit this fault, an attacker may write a section of code that will populate the packet with a parameter that will violate the program and induce the desired result. As mentioned earlier in this chapter, this parameter can be included in one packet or spread across multiple packets. In either case, an undetected attack may result in server/service compromise. NGX has protections against this very weakness. The **Application Intelligence | Mail | POP3/IMAP Security** settings can be set to prevent binary data in the parameters, or place a limit on the number of characters for usernames and passwords. In addition, there are a couple of DOS settings that can be enabled for this application that increase protection.

Because of the proliferation of the Internet, there is widespread availability of scripts and programs that furnish semi-skilled users with the ability to craft packets containing invalid options, create corrupt data fields, or apply improperly attributed fragments. Because these programs make attacks easy to execute, you must defend your network, applications, and servers with robust security architecture. Check Point VPN-1 Pro NGX gateways provide such security.

Application Intelligence

To help you combat these types of threats (and more) and enable you to employ a more comprehensive perimeter defense, Check Point introduced its Application Intelligence (AI) technology a few versions ago. Since then, Check Point has split this advancement into two distinct technologies. The first is SmartDefense. This offering—the original product, which was all inclusive—concentrates on several layers of the OSI model. Although the concept is to protect and ensure data (and application) confidentiality, availability, and integrity, some of these attacks reside outside of the applications layer. The second offering is Web Intelligence, which focuses on protecting Web servers and Web-based applications. Both Web Intelligence and SmartDefense operate with the knowledge of known attacks, and also possess the capability to recognize potential risk even if it does not fit an established attack profile.

The following sections examine why these two technologies are pertinent to securing your network. Further discussion reveals the classes or protections for each of these technologies. In addition, these sections cover the options that SmartDefense and Web Intelligence offer. We also walk through examples of how to block *peer-to-peer* communications and how to prevent *SQL Injection* attacks.

The remainder of this chapter stands to dispense specific details about how you can utilize your NGX gateway to protect your network, standard applications (FTP, SMTP, etc.), and Web-based applications. As you have learned throughout the course of this text, Check Point demonstrates a keen understanding of ease-of-use by designing simple, logical GUIs. You will again experience this truth as we walk through these tasks, because the procedures remain quick and easy.

Configuring Hosts and Nodes for AI

To utilize some of the protections that NGX offers you must first properly configure your nodes. The Web-based protections only relate to defined Web servers and other protections only apply to certain servers. Let's walk through configuring a simple Web server and then enable some of the many protections that NGX offers.

To begin, go to **Security** in the SmartDashboard. Under **Objects Tree**, right-click **Network Objects | Nodes** and select **New Node | Host**. After entering the host name and IP address, click the **Configure Servers** button, which will give you the option of configuring your server for Web, Mail, or Domain Name Service (DNS). Choosing one of these options will generate a new branch in the left side or your host properties window. Place a check in the box next to **Web Server** and click **OK**. Now, if you expand the **Web Server** branch in the left pane, you see the protection options for this type of server (Web server). On the primary configuration page, you can define the OS and applications your web server uses. In addition, you can select which ports the server listens on. The **Protections** leaf lets you configure precise security controls that you want to enable or disable for this server. Once you are done configuring the options, click **OK** to save your new Web server. Not only does configuring a Web server object provide additional security, it also allows you to define further protections in Web Intelligence since it is a Web server object. Once you select any node as a Web server, you must have a Web Intelligence license in the SmartCenter or the policy will not install.

SmartDefense Technology

Check Point introduced SmartDefense technology as a means to protect your network and your applications from attackers. These protections not only span the three layers identified earlier in the OSI model (the Network Layer, the Transport Layer, and the Application Layer), but also protect layers 5 and 6 (Session Layer and Presentation Layer). SmartDefense accomplishes these protections by offering two separate means to detect attacks.

The first is via signature detection. As discussed earlier, your NGX gateway inspects packets as they come across the wire, and if one is found that matches a signature, your gateway invokes a predefined action, possibly blocking the connection. In addition, *SmartDefense* has the ability to detect anomalous network behavior. However, some anomaly detection actually occurs on the SmartCenter Server instead of the enforcement module. This happens for several reasons. Consider an environment where you may have a clustered gateway architecture. Since connections may pass through all your active firewalls, one firewall may not see the connections profile as a whole. Further, each of the gateways sends log information to the SmartCenter Server. For these reasons, it makes sense that the anomalous behavior detection happen on the SmartCenter Server as opposed to each individual enforcement point. If the server detects an anomaly, it too can invoke several actions depending on the current configuration. In any case, SmartDefense offers you advanced protection for both your network and your hosts.

Figure 7.5 shows what the **SmartDefense** tab looks like in the Check Point GUI.

Figure 7.5 The SmartDefense Tab

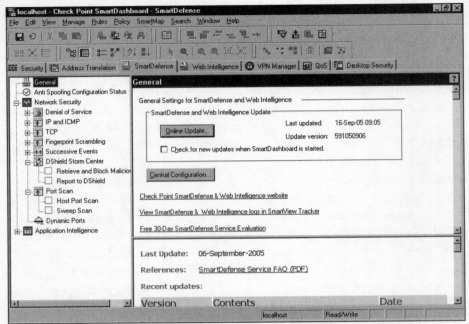

This view omits the Objects Tree in order to maximize the **SmartDefense** tab. You can see that the left-hand pane displays the different protections that SmartDefense offers. As you now know, there are both **Network Security** and **Application Intelligence** controls in this tab. You can expand each item with a **+** next to it to reveal further configuration capability. In later examples, you will see just how to utilize these controls to block attacks.

SmartDefense can be broken down into three class-like categories: defense against attacks, information disclosure protections, and abnormal behavior analysis. The following sections discuss these particular classes as well as how to configure the central options for SmartDefense, what the SmartDefense Web site can do for you, and how to update SmartDefense.

Central Configuration and the SmartDefense Web Site

Figure 7.5 demonstrates that you can click the **Central Configuration** button to configure these options. When you do this, you will receive a simple window instead of a page full of checkboxes and drop-down menus (see Figure 7.6).

Figure 7.6 SmartDefense Central Configuration Settings

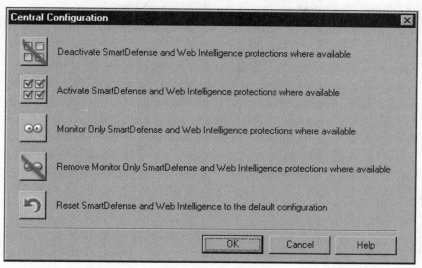

You now have five choices for configuring your SmartDefense and Web Intelligence options. The first option disables all settings except some default protections that are always on (FTP Bounce) and others that require more specific configuration. Next, you can enable everything so that your NGX gateway is a full IPS, but there will be performance implications. Also, the specific configuration protections exemption applies to the "enable all" settings. The next two involve "monitor only" settings. The first enables monitoring on all possible protections, and the second setting disables monitoring on the same protections. Keep in mind that not all protections have a "monitor only" option; therefore, these changes will not affect all of your configuration options. Lastly is the option to return to the default configuration of SmartDefense and Web Intelligence. Click this button and any changes you made to the protections are wiped out and the configuration returns to the install configuration. In any case, the changes do not occur until you select one option and click **OK**. In some cases, you will receive a window informing you about the side effects of your choice or seeking confirmation that you want to do what you have selected.

Check Point has also created a SmartDefense Web site to assist you with understanding threats and to receive pointers on how to combat these threats. If you already have a SmartDefense license, you can login using your UserCenter credentials. If you don't have a SmartDefense license, Check Point allows you to test drive the site for 30 days using your UserCenter credentials. Either way, you will find a lot of information on this site. Go to *http://www.checkpoint.com/defense* to see detailed explanations of current risks (vulnerabilities) and how to utilize your SmartDefense or Web Intelligence protections to defend the vulnerability.

Updating SmartDefense

Another **General** option is to update your protections for SmartDefense. When you click on the **Online Update** button, SmartDefense goes to the Check Point site to check for and download any updates to your SmartDefense and Web Intelligence protections. You must enter your UserCenter credentials in order to receive these updates. You can also configure automatic updates when you open SmartDashboard. If you save your credentials, you will only notice a slight delay in response when the update is occurring. Otherwise, you will be prompted every time a new update has to be downloaded to your SmartCenter server. Check Point offers frequent updates as new attacks become known or variants to current attacks pop up.

Defense against Attacks

The first SmartDefense class teaches attack detection and prevention; it also covers known and unknown attacks. SmartDefense has some capabilities that rely on the characteristics of an attack, not attack signatures. SmartDefense also has "always-on" protection from the FTP Bounce attack, which may allow an attacker to open a port on a non-originating client. In this case, your NGX gateway will not allow the attempt to compromise the host. Since NGX knows the true source of the connection, it has the ability to verify destination with respect to the open port command. If the destination does not fit the original client profile, NGX denies the connection before it arrives at your host.

Peer to Peer

Another example of non-signature based prevention is peer-to-peer protections. There are many peer-to-peer applications (protocols) that permit file sharing from one host to another. Doing this allows one host to download (or upload) files from another host's directory. An unsuspecting victim may accidentally download a file with malicious code meant to compromise the victim's host and/or extend the virus to other users. In any case, most organizations do not permit their protected hosts to run peer-to-peer applications (protocols).

Check Point NGX with SmartDefense enables you to block several popular file-sharing (peer-to-peer) protocols through a quick and easy process. Just like Instant Messaging client options, NGX allows you to state whether or not to block these applications over proprietary protocols, block them if they tunnel over port 80

(HTTP), or both. Additionally, you can configure an exception list that allows one or more of your objects to bypass this protection.

> ## WARNING
>
> When you configure exclusions for peer-to-peer protections, your gateway applies them to all of the protocols, not just one single protocol. These global exceptions allow you to configure an exception for either a service or an object. If you'd like to block all but a specific service, you can include the service object in the exclusion list. Likewise, if you want to allow a certain object access to run these protocols, include it in the exclusion list. Do this by clicking on the **Global exclusion settings** link under the peer-to-peer branch.

To configure peer-to-peer blocking first, open SmartDashboard and click the **SmartDefense** tab. In the left-hand pane, expand the **Application Intelligence** tree by clicking the +. Next, expand the **Peer-to-Peer** branch by clicking the +. You will see six protocols listed: **Kazaa**, **Gnutella**, **eMule**, **Bit Torrent**, **Soulseek**, and **IRC**. Place a check in the box next to each protocol you wish to block (see Figure 7.7). The last step is to save the configuration and install the policy on the enforcement module.

Figure 7.7 Peer-to-Peer Blocking

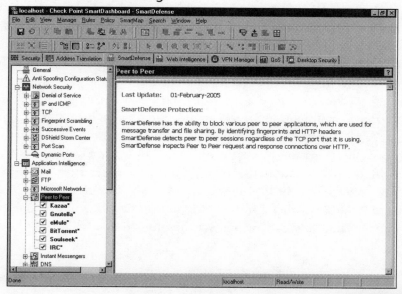

In Figure 7.7, you will see that each of the peer-to-peer protocol has a check in the box next to it. The result of this configuration is that the gateway will now block all these protocols from passing either way (inbound/outbound) through the firewall.

Preventing Information Disclosure

The next class of protections is aimed to prevent information disclosure. You've already read about how NGX offers some information disclosure protections either directly or indirectly. Now consider the possibility that your hosts' behavior will reveal either its OS platform or which application software it is running. There are a few specific protections in SmartDefense that guard against information protection, such as **ISN Spoofing**, **IP Identifier (ID)**, and Time-to-Live (**TTL**). These protections reside under the **Network Security | Fingerprint Scrambling** branch of the SmartDefense settings. Be aware that activating these protections will disable any acceleration features like SecureXL or IPSO Flows.

Fingerprint Scrambling

In each of these scenarios, your host will probably respond to an attacker and inadvertently divulge some information regarding its OS or software. One such attack is against the Initial Sequence Number (ISN) of a host. For the most part, the ISN is supposed to be somewhat unique for each connection. However, the algorithm for selecting such number displays a weakness in that it has a degree of predictability. In this sense, attackers guess the ISN and if the victim responds, the attacker knows which OS the victim host is running. To further introduce uniqueness, some operating systems introduced pseudo-random number generators (some people like to call them random number generators). However, these also have shown repeatability.

To further complicate matters, different OS platforms use different sequencing algorithms. Merely establishing connections with such hosts and studying the ISN for each connection may reveal an identifiable pattern for the ISN. Thus this reveals the OS to the attacker. To defend against this and the other attacks (TTL and IP ID) your NGX gateway will replace the value from the host with one from a more unique number producing algorithm (inherent to NGX). In the least, there are numerous connections passing through so if an attacker tried to establish connections and study the ISN relation, there would not be a discernable pattern. Turning on these protections is as easy as placing a check in the box next to the desired setting. There are minimal further configuration options for each attack, but it is not difficult to understand how each will affect the protection.

Abnormal Behavior Analysis

Similar to the way that we understand when a person is acting out of character by observing his or her behavior, network traces (logs) reveal abnormal connection profiles. Thus, NGX can identify questionable connections and actions based on these traces. In this chapter, you have seen an example with clustered enforcement modules and how the SmartCenter Server carries out the anomalous behavior detection. This is apparent in port scan and port sweep attacks. To further expound on the cluster example and NGX's ability to detect port scans, consider that the attacker's packets are split among three enforcement points. If your configuration settings trigger at a higher level of packets than each of your members is receiving, the attack may go unnoticed. However, since your SmartCenter Server receives the logs from each of these gateways, it will see all of the connection requests and can then detect the scan or sweep and invoke the proper response to alert an administrator or even to block the requests (with a user-defined alert and the **sam_alert** command).

A significant dependency for network anomaly detection exists in the fact that you must first know what "normal" is. In the same manner that you've come to understand normal human behavior, you must familiarize yourself with normal traffic patterns on your network. It will take time, but there are different NGX abilities to help you do this. However, Check Point's reporting server (Eventia Reporter), along with comprehensive logging, can provide you with a similar understanding of your traffic patterns. Once you have a basic understanding of what normal network traffic is, you can begin to identify suspect operations. Thus, you can provide even more specific configuration settings to your NGX protections to identify or drop anomalous connections you have identified. Check Point also offers Eventia Analyzer, which in real time can correlate security events from different sources (firewalls, IPS, switches, routers, and so forth) and generate alerts immediately.

TIP

Every administrator should be able to spot a lion in a crowd of geese. However, to be able to find the needle in a haystack you must thoroughly understand your normal network behavior. If you are able to turn on extended logging on some devices for a little while, you can learn more about your environment. Even though your NGX gateway logs tell you a lot about your network, don't solely rely on them to tell you what your organization's normal traffic patterns are. Use logs from routers, switches, application proxy servers, application servers, and so forth. Though sometimes a bit cryptic, log entries can reveal a plethora of information to help you define better security policies.

Abnormal behavior conveys one single implication: you must know what is normal to be able to label something abnormal. If you don't know what your connections profile resembles, then trying to find a single suspicious connection may take forever. However, if you have a general idea of what your network traffic looks like, you should be able to identify a connection that does not seem logical, or in the least, seems uncharacteristic.

Web Intelligence Technology

Check Point originally included Web Intelligence within the SmartDefense product, but the company broke Web Intelligence into its own entity to focus more energy on protecting your Web-based applications and your Web servers. This offering is what Check Point refers to as *Malicious Code Protector*, *Active Streaming*, and *Application Intelligence* technologies. These technologies work on signature recognition and anomaly. Since its primary focus is Web applications and Web servers, it has the ability to identify harmful code while it still resides in the data stream. It also has the capability to determine whether a user's submission (passed code) has ill-mannered intent. If so, your NGX gateway reacts with predetermined responses, either blocking the connection, or by alerting an administrator (or both). In any event, this technology applies what Check Point created in Application Intelligence and has cultivated a better product that focuses on a significant point of attack. Thus, Web Intelligence provides to you a security control that targets attacks aimed at your public applications and servers.

Malicious Code Protector

This patent-pending Check Point technology has the ability to recognize malicious code without having specific knowledge of the signature. This kernel-level function protects your Web servers and Web-based applications by inspecting all communications for their applications. If executable code is found within the data, it will then check to see if its intent is malicious. Should your NGX gateway determine yes, it will block the connection and execute the appropriate (defined) tracking option.

Active Streaming

This protection also resides at the kernel level of your gateway and protects your Web servers and Web-based applications by evaluating the context of the communication. There are several key aspects that active streaming applies to the connection in order to determine if there is harmful content. First, this is where fragment reassembly happens. As mentioned before, fragments don't embody the essence of the context, so diligent protection mechanisms must have the ability to reassemble the packets and evaluate the context. Next, if an attacker tries to encode worms or other harmful URLs, this technology will decode it so that it can be evaluated appropriately. Another function of active streaming is to initiate new sessions. If there is a protection in place that will send a new Hypertext Markup Language (HTML) page as the response to an identified attack, active streaming is where this response occurs. Lastly, active streaming possesses the ability to rewrite headers or strip out specific data. This response is useful in header spoofing attempts.

Application Intelligence

Application Intelligence technology aims to prevent attacks by knowing which communications have "bad" intentions. This collection of attack signatures and inappropriate command sequences lets you weed out some of the more harmful traffic from your network. Specifically, Check Point geared Application Intelligence to ensure compliance with protocols and application standards, to identify inappropriate usage of these protocols and standards, to block known attack signatures, and to prevent dangerous commands that some applications allow.

Looking at Figure 7.8, you see a similar screenshot as with the SmartDefense product. Again, this view omits the Objects Tree to increase recognition.

Figure 7.8 The Web Intelligence Tab

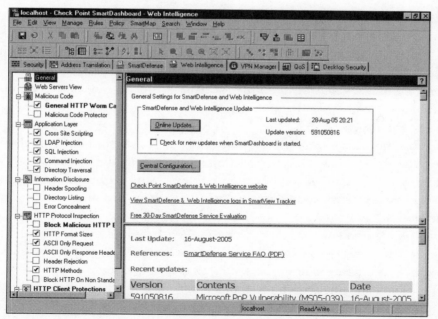

Again, in the left-hand pane you see an array of options to choose from regarding Web-based attacks. This time, in the right-hand pane, you see that there exists the ability to update the signatures and other settings associated with both SmartDefense and Web Intelligence. In the coming sections, you will dig deeper into these settings as you configure custom Web blocking for your firewall through a configuration example.

Web Application Layer

NGX offers specific protections for Web application layer detection. Specifically, it prevents an attacker from entering code into a Web page or other medium that will introduce harmful effects on the backend of the server. This acts in a similar manner to the malicious code detector. The biggest difference is that these protections are mostly based on known commands and other strings that may invoke harmful results.

As an example, you will learn how to configure your NGX gateway to block an SQL Injection attack. This attack embodies the essence of the protection in that an attacker tries to substitute commands or other strings in a data field to provoke the server into revealing alternative information. In the same sense, someone could try to place harmful tags or other malicious characters in a Web site that one of your users may visit. Let's look at how you can apply settings to your VPN-1 Pro Gateway in order to block such an attack.

SQL Injection

SQL injection attacks are meant to inject an SQL command into a place meant for data input only. An attacker visits a Web form, and instead of putting only his or her name into the "Last Name" field on the form, he or she puts in some code to execute on the back-end server. In any case, the result is not what the designers intended to produce.

Since you now have an NGX gateway in place, Check Point Web Intelligence gives you the ability to block SQL Injection attacks. Again, this is a very simple procedure, but you will see that additional options exist with regard to where you enforce the configuration and how you wish your gateway to react to a positive identification.

First, open SmartDashboard and click the **Web Intelligence** tab. Expand the Application Layer tree by clicking the **+**. Then select **SQL Injection** by clicking it. Place a check in the box next to the setting to enable the option.

In the top-right pane within the Protection Scope block, you have the option to **Apply to all HTTP traffic** or **Apply to selected web servers** (default). Choose an option based on whether you want to affect all traffic by this setting or limit the inspection to a select group of predefined Web servers.

In the top–right pane within the Action block, choose the action you want your gateway to enforce. Choosing no options in this box means you want the default action to block the connections. If you only wish to monitor the connections, choose the **Monitor only – no protection** option. Choose the **Send error page** option if you want to respond to the attacker with a custom Web page. You also need to define these properties by clicking the **Configure** button (enabled only when you check the box). Choose a Track option by selecting one of the options from the drop–down menu.

Lastly, under the **Advanced Configuration** heading, you can configure specific SQL commands to trigger the action for when the gateway detects them. When completed, your configuration may look similar to Figure 7.9.

Figure 7.9 SQL Injection Blocking

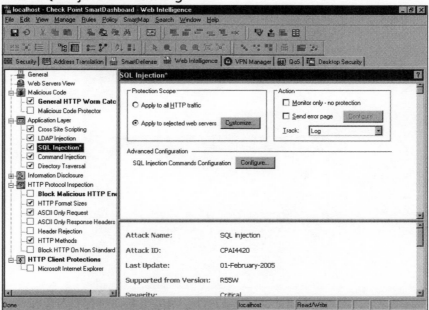

As seen in Figure 7.9, the Action block does not define one of the selections. For this reason, the gateway enforces the default action to block the connections. Again, when you experiment with these settings on your own network, you will identify what works best for you. In the beginning, with all of the options enabled, you may find that the gateway is blocking legitimate connections (false positives). If you do want to block this type of attack, you must approach this process as an opportunity to learn which settings will reduce the false positive rate and which commands your servers need to run to satisfy your business requirements.

Custom Web Blocking

As you have seen in the Web Intelligence interface, Check Point enables you to apply single settings to one, many, or all Web servers. Since you define your Web servers and applications, you should rest easy that security settings can be applied to whichever server you want; nothing less, nothing more. In this sense, you have a very customizable product that provides you with a security environment that best fits your organization. For instance, take the SQL settings you saw during the configuration example. The selection of commands in Figure 7.10 shows you that if you had one specific command that was legitimate for your environment but all the rest indicated a possible attack, you could simply remove the check from this one box and carry on. It's that simple (see Figure 7.10).

Figure 7.10 Custom SQL Commands

With this ease of use, Check Point has granted you the power to build a robust security perimeter with one device. Not only will your gateway perform advanced access control, but it will also deliver a high-performance security inspection technology implemented (by you) specifically for your organization's security concerns.

Preventing Information Disclosure

In previous sections, you learned that attackers sometimes perform reconnaissance to gain information to help them adapt an attack to a specific host's configuration. To do this, the attacker may send specific requests to the host in order to have it reveal information about the OS version, software application name and version, or other configuration information. When your server responds to these requests with information, it results in disclosure and gives the attacker information that will provide him leverage to further attack your host. To detect these requests and responses, NGX uses a set of regular expressions combined with known response codes and values. NGX lets you configure three specific attack detection profiles within the Web Intelligence tab: *Header Spoofing*, *Directory Listing*, and *Error Concealment*. The former embodies an attacker's attempt to gain information by deliberately sending the server a bad request. The response to the attacking client may reveal information about internal properties of the server and therefore lead to future structured attacks.

Header Spoofing

Though this is not a complicated attack, it can lead to a more direct attack. Specifically, reply headers usually contain the version of the Web server you are running. NGX allows you to configure this protection to identify these replies and substitute different text for the one you do not want the attacker to receive (see Figure 7.11).

Figure 7.11 Header Spoofing Configuration

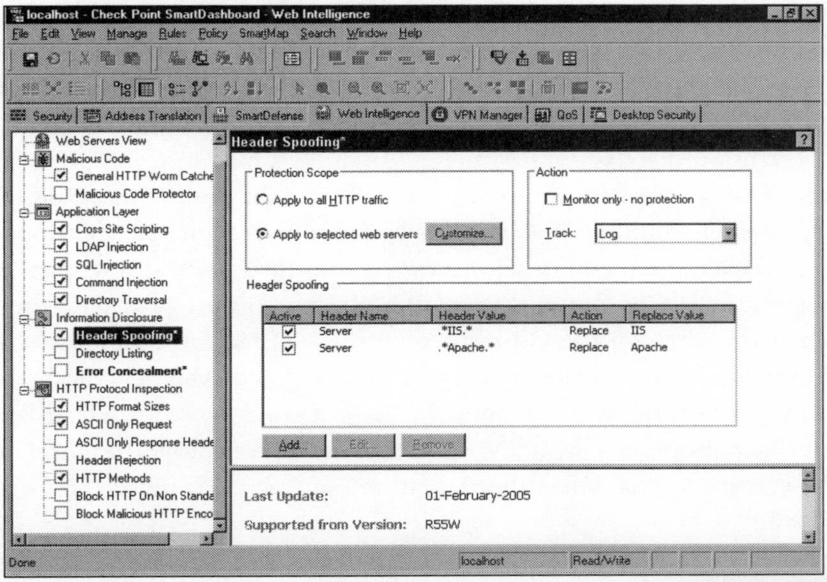

If the gateway sees that one of your Web servers is replying to a client with the text value ".*IIS.*", it will remove that value and substitute the value "IIS" in its place. This removes any versioning information from the header and reduces the attacker's information scope regarding your Web server. To add new strings in the detection, click **Add** and input the appropriate regular expressions; one for the header name and the other for the value you are looking for. In addition, if you want to replace the value with another one, you must input a text string for the replacement value. Once you've done that, click **OK** and you're done. Your new search string will show up in the window shown in Figure 7.11.

> **NOTE**
>
> There is a performance penalty associated with this setting. You should receive a warning dialog box when you enable the **Header Spoofing** protection.

Directory Listing

Some Web servers list the contents of the current directory if there is no default page present (and the file permissions comply with the listing). In this case, one of your Web servers may give away too much information in script files or configuration files. When this happens, it usually means that there has been some kind of misconfiguration or mistake somewhere along the line. To configure this protection, you must identify your Web servers individually. In other words, once you enable the protection by placing a check in the box, you must click on the **Customize** button in the **Protection Scope** box to apply the settings for each server.

This prevention mechanism has three settings: low, medium, and high. The low setting only looks at suspicious responses and triggers on three indications of directory listing. The medium and high settings both look at suspicious and nonsuspicious responses. However, the medium setting triggers on three indications, whereas the high setting requires only one indication of a directory listing to trigger the NGX action. When you click on the **Configure** button you receive a window where you must add the servers individually and where your defined Web Servers show up. To configure each server, highlight the one you wish to change and select **Edit**. You are now in the "host properties" window with the Web server properties displayed. To change the current setting, select the **Advanced** button adjacent to the **Directory Listing** heading.

Malicious Code

A hot topic over the past few years, malicious code can cause your organization great harm. In recent years, you are sure to know that malicious code has caused billions of dollars of total damage to small and large firms alike. Since your Check Point VPN-1 Pro Gateway includes the ability to reduce the risk of massive damage from harmful code, let's take this opportunity to go over the finer points of what constitutes malicious code and what it may look like.

Definition

NGX interprets malicious code as anything that, when executed, violates the security policy of or compromises the integrity of one of your Web servers or Web clients. In other words, anything that when executed will bring harm to your environment (server or client).

Consider the normal scenario of your typical Web session. When you open a Uniform Resource Locator (URL), you expect to download the text, images, or multimedia that you desire to see. What happens if there is code in the executable that will remove files from your hard drive or install a worm, virus, or other spyware utility on your computer? You did not intend for this to happen, you expected a completely different result from launching the site. You may not even know that your computer has been compromised. This is another reason to have an NGX gateway protect your network. Even though you may think that something is normal, there could be unexpected results. NGX protects your servers and clients from these undesirable results using its Malicious Code Protector technology.

Though this is a simple explanation for malicious code, it is clearly understandable. Now, translate that to one of your Web forms that accepts user input. What if a vulnerability exists in your form processing software, allowing an attacker to insert commands into the submission field. The result of this action will be that the system processes the command and returns a result (success, failure, list of data). In any case, the malicious code has compromised the system via information disclosure in that it produced an unintended result for the attacker.

WARNING

Harmful code does not have to come from an attacker to be considered malicious. What if you have a department that runs reports against the production database and they write the code for their own reports? As you are aware, reports tend to induce high utilization as they comb through tons of data. What is the result if an employee introduces improper logic into a report and hangs the job? Even with Check Point's comprehensive security measures, you must consider additional controls in order to provide an all-encompassing security architecture for your organization. Though this employee is not deliberately trying to induce undesirable results, he or she has essentially DOS'd your entire population of database users by hanging the job (via poor logic). Always consider the consequences of (unintended) harmful code in your security controls. Check Point's NGX will catch the stuff that is intentionally bad for your hosts, but you still must be diligent to protect your network from all possible scenarios.

Different Types of Malicious Code

It is incredible the number of worms, viruses, Trojans, or other exploits that magazine columnists write about these days. These different types of malicious code take advantage of poorly written application code or other weaknesses in hosts in order to compromise or wreak havoc on organizations. Malicious code can come through e-mail messages, IM clients, peer-to-peer file sharing, Web sites, and so forth.

The NGX gateway comes with signatures that identify harmful code as well as general detection capabilities that don't rely on a signature. When you enable the **Malicious Code | Malicious Code Protector** option in the Web Intelligence tab, you'll see that there really isn't much to configure. Other than the options to change the tracking and monitor settings, you only have an advanced configuration **Configure** button. When you click this button, you will see that there isn't much to this either. You actually define only two trade-offs: one between memory consumption and speed and the other between a more secure search or a faster search. When you are done selecting these options, click **OK** and then install the policy on the enforcement points. Let's look at further protections that your NGX gateway provides in order to defend your hosts from malicious content.

General HTTP Worm Catcher

Because worms have the inherent ability to self-replicate, they are more dangerous than most attacks because they don't require human intervention. There is a significant amount of worms that use the Web to replicate to new hosts. To protect your organization from this, enable this setting. You'll see that there are 13 predefined worms that NGX checks for. This mechanism works solely on the regular expression patterns that you define within the configuration utility, and those added via an online update. In addition, you can configure this setting per server. Let's take a look at the configuration settings for the worm catcher (see Figure 7.12).

Figure 7.12 General HTTP Worm Catcher Configuration

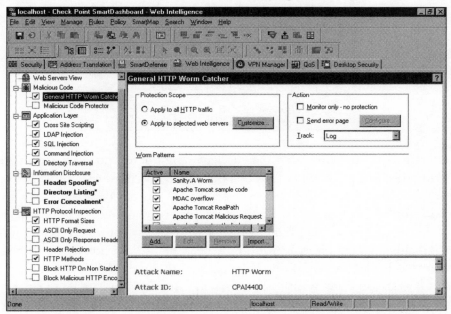

The setting mentioned earlier is in most of the Web Intelligence attack profiles. You can change the servers that receive the protection and how NGX enforces the protection (monitor only, send error page, or the default block). In addition, you can add regular expression patterns so that your gateway will detect specific threats. Let's look further into the patterns for the "Sanity.A" worm. Highlight the entry and click the **Edit** button (see Figure 7.13).

Figure 7.13 Worm Pattern Settings

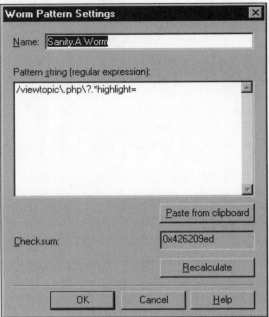

Notice that you must be fairly specific regarding the text string that you are looking for. Also notice that if you read about a new worm online (or anywhere else) and have copied the pattern to your clipboard, you can click the **Paste from clipboard** button to place that string into the pattern window. Sometimes it proves more accurate to copy a string rather than try to retype it yourself. You can also import individual worm patterns from the Check Point Web site. If you do this, you may want to calculate the checksum to make sure that the value is the same as the original value. If you don't want to do this, you can simply update all of the protections together. When SmartDefense or Web Intelligence updates are sought, they include new worm patterns. When you have entered the correct string and verified its checksum (if needed), click **OK** to save the new pattern to the profile.

Egress Filtering

If you believe that one of your hosts is owned, but you cannot find anything indicative on the host, you may be able to utilize Worm Pattern Strings to identify if the affected host is sending out a specific request to any Web sites. When investigating incidents, you must think like the attacker and try to find ways to identify clues. Event though your NGX security controls are helpful in keeping the bad guys out, you can manipulate the options and settings to help you identify whether the attacker is already in and trying to get out to do further damage. This is just one example of how to use a tool to help you identify suspect traffic.

Protocol Inspection

You may be asking what the difference is between all that you've learned to this point and Protocol Inspection. Well, in this section, you may discover some things about applications and protocols that don't necessarily jibe with the way things should be. As the name implies, a protocol, regardless of the context, is a set of rules or ways to do things. This layman's definition also applies to the protocols that you consider in terms of networking and applications. What you may not be aware of is the fact that often there are applications that do not conform to protocols as the designers intended. This nonconformity may be a mistake, or it could be an attempt to attack the protocol and produce undesirable results. Let's discuss more about protocol conformity and see how our Check Point gateway helps us enforce the intentions of the designers.

Conformity

As briefly mentioned earlier in this chapter, there are a considerable amount of applications whose aim is to comply with protocols. However, a subset of applications exists that, for whatever reason, simply do not conform to protocol X. Though this does not normally cause issues with the application, it does present problems for you if your firewall or other security device forces applications to conform to the protocol as the designer intended and as documented in the RFC. Because attackers know that some legitimate applications may not conform to protocol specifications, they may create malicious code with similar nonconformity that will violate your application or host. So this poses a threat to your network's security and the security of your applications and hosts.

> **NOTE**
>
> It is not unheard of for vendors or service providers to alter the listening port of Web-based applications to fit the outgoing rule base of your organization's firewall policy. What does this mean to you? For starters, it means that you may have a custom (probably non-HTTP compliant) application passing traffic over outbound TCP port 80. However, since you installed a VPN-1 Pro Gateway on your network, you are now enforcing HTTP protocol standards. NGX employs some protections by default when Web Intelligence is enabled. Look at the **HTTP Protocol Inspection** branch within Web Intelligence to see what is enabled. If you need to disable any of these settings because they may block your non-compliant application, all you need to do is remove the check from the box or modify the configuration options appropriately. Don't forget to install the policy to the enforcement modules after making changes.

Before you enable protocol standard enforcement on your firewall, you should be certain that you will not disable any critical applications. You may even learn of an application that is pertinent to the operation of your organization that does not fully comply with the RFC. In this case, you may or may not be able to continue enforcement, depending on the impact to your business. Let's review how NGX provides protocol enforcement for the DNS protocol.

DNS Enforcement

When an attacker wants to use DNS packets to exploit a host, he changes the pay-load in the packet and sends it on to the victim. NGX inspects these packets for both TCP and UDP queries (and other communications) to verify that they are in accordance with the DNS protocol. If they are not, the gateway blocks the packet from progressing. NGX allows you to enable this option for TCP only, UDP only, or both TCP and UDP packets. You also have the option to monitor illegal packets without blocking them. However, the most pressing issue here is volume. Since most applications want a fully qualified host name versus an IP address to identify the other party in the connection, they must query their local DNS server to translate the name into an IP address. This protection has the ability to severely reduce the performance of your gateway.

HTTP Inspection

Check Point's Web Intelligence provides enforcement of the HTTP protocol. When you view the settings in SmartDashboard, you will see that there are many different options from which to choose. Each of these settings either enforces strict adherence to the HTTP protocol, or enforces limitations with the intent to reduce risk associated with a threat model. In either case, these options permit you to define how granular you wish to lock down one, many, or all of your Web servers and applications.

In addition, this option provides you with the ability to block HTTP over non-standard ports. Though not all servers running on ports other than 80 are mischievous in nature, servers do exist that provide no good purpose running on such ports. In practice, this may prove a difficult option to enable as many legitimate services run HTTP services over nonstandard ports. However, if you are certain that your organization does not need any such services, this option may come in very handy. Being able to block access to servers running on these ports will unarguably reduce your organization's risk. Figure 7.14 shows the **HTTP Protocol Inspection** tree in the SmartDashboard interface.

Figure 7.14 HTTP Protocol Inspection

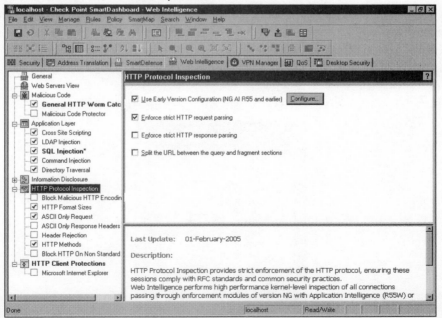

In any case, it is an easily configurable setting. If you sense an immediate or imminent threat, you can enable this setting for the duration and disable it to restore service to your organization. Just like many options within SmartDefense and Web Intelligence, this one is useful in either a short-term or a long-term role.

Default Configuration

When a Web server is defined, it inherits a set of default protections from NGX. With regard to protocol inspection, NGX performs three inspections: *HTTP Format Sizes*, *ASCII Only Request*, and *HTTP Methods*. These settings protect your server from buffer overflow attempts in the case of the format sizes. There isn't really a limit to the size of a URL; sometimes attackers try to submit an extremely long URL to attack a Web server. In addition, you can set limits on the length for headers and the number of headers. Further, NGX blocks all non-American Standard Code for Information Interchange (ASCII) HTTP requests, as well as non–ASCII values for form fields. This setting prevents an attacker from submitting a worm or other harmful values in binary formats.

NGX also offers protections against HTTP methods that most servers don't need (and most administrators don't disable). For example, the *trace* and *track* methods will probably always show up in a vulnerability scan if you do not disable them after turning on your Web server. NGX separates these methods into three categories: *standard safe*, *standard unsafe*, and *WebDAV*. As a baseline, NGX blocks all methods except for those in the standard safe group. To disable blocking for a specific method (or enable blocking) all you have to do is highlight the **HTTP Protocol Inspection | HTTP Methods** leaf in the left pane and click the **Configure** button (see Figure 7.15).

Figure 7.15 Select Blocked HTTP Methods Configuration

You can see the category that each method is in (far right column). To select or deselect a method, click in the box to place or remove the check mark. When you have modified the list to meet your needs, click **OK** and the SmartCenter Server saves the changes to the profile. Don't forget that you must push the policy to the enforcement modules in order to apply the settings.

Remember, when you define a new host and configure it as a *Web Server*, the host inherits the default settings within the protection profiles. Some settings have the option to change the default level of protections, like we saw in the *Directory Listing* configuration options. Therefore, keep these protections in mind when you add a new server. You don't want to waste a lot of time trying to troubleshoot an issue when it could be an aggressive protection setting on your NGX gateway preventing the successful communication.

DShield Storm Center

As organizations become more security conscious, they begin to understand that they are not alone with regard to the threats they face. In addition, these organizations learn that the intrusion attempts they are seeing are not isolated to them. What you may discover is that organizations all over the world battle similar attacks. For this reason, Check Point integrated the ability to share your log information with the DShield Storm Center (www.dshield.org). In addition, the storm center can send information about current threats and your firewall may invoke blocking lists based on this communication.

With the common threat model that everyone faces, professionals in all aspects of information security have begun to push for broad information sharing among organizations (corporate and government alike). In 2000, Euclidian consulting launched the DShield Storm Center to begin correlating worldwide traffic profiles to detect attacks. Soon thereafter, SANS (www.sans.org) joined the fray and began contributing to DShield Storm Center. As such, this engine is now the basis for the SANS Internet Storm Center. The aim of this effort is to combine network traffic that organizations see for the sake of consolidating these individual traffic models into one large model. From this point, automated systems discern similar traffic patterns and determine whether they are malicious in nature. In simplest terms, DShield Storm Center is a global correlation engine, which relies on you, other organizations, and its own population of collection engines for data. Everyone gains from sharing this type of information. The more information there is to evaluate, the more likely the system will find commonalities.

Some organizations may be somewhat hesitant to send their log files to a third party. After all, when you configure your firewall to submit logs to the storm center, it will include the source and destination IP addresses, source and destination ports, and the IP protocol of the connection. You may utilize private addresses within your protected networks, and disclosing that information, even to an organization that aims to help the cause, results in information disclosure. For this reason, Check Point has made certain that you have options concerning the data you select to send to DShield. The first option is that you can define a **TRACK** option in your security rule base and send only these (identified) specific log records to the storm center. Also, your gateway has the ability to sanitize your log files so as not to reveal your internal IP address scheme. You provide a bit mask that directs your gateway to change to 0 the number of bits you want. So instead of sending log entries to the storm center with 192.168.1.50 as the source of the connection, your 8-bit mask instead will cause the gateway to change the address to 0.0.0.50 (the number of mask bits tells how many bits to reveal; a zero mask reveals nothing and a 32-bit mask reveals all). In light of these configuration options, it makes sense that an organization should (properly) configure its firewall to share information with the storm center.

Essentially, DShield is an online correlation engine. Instead of having only one organization's logs to review and evaluate, the storm center accepts logs from any organization, inserts them into their database, and then looks for trends. In essence, the storm center provides free services to you if you so choose to utilize them. The service that you receive from DShield is invaluable. Consider that information sharing provides a platform for quick response in the face of a worldwide threat. For example, imagine that a new attack broke out and it was concentrated from a set of specific source IP addresses. Properly configured firewalls all over the world would experience this attack and as they submit their logs to the storm center, the correlation engine would recognize the threat. Automated evaluation of the logs ensues, and the system draws the attention of some administrators at the center who then publish reports on their Web site. In addition, the storm center updates their block list with the offending IP addresses. When your gateway downloads the block list again, you will have protected your network without really doing anything. Imagine this happening over a weekend, or while you are on vacation. Enabling this service is beneficial to you in many ways, especially with regard to convenience (convenience does not always result in the best policy, but you must determine this on your own). Not only that, but your information sharing efforts prove beneficial to other organizations as well.

Retrieving Blocklist

The configuration options you will work with are located in the SmartDefense tab. Let's walk through configuring the gateway to retrieve a blocklist from DShield Storm Center.

First, open SmartDashboard and choose the **SmartDefense** tab. Expand the **Network Security** tree by clicking the **+** and expand the **DShield Storm Center** branch by clicking the **+**. Place a check in the box next to **Retrieve and Block Malicious IPs**. In the upper right-hand pane, select whether you want to invoke this action for all of your gateways, or just a specific group of them. Your configuration should look similar to Figure 7.16.

Figure 7.16 Retrieving the Blocklist from DShield

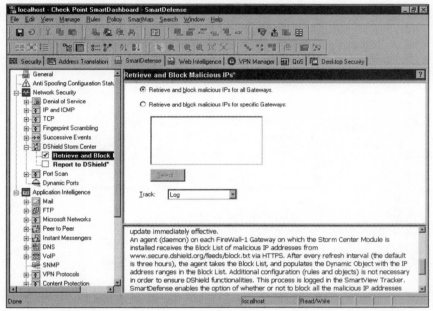

Submitting Logs

Now let's take a quick look at how to configure your gateway to send logs to DShield. Again, you have several options, as you will see, that you need to consider in order to safely and properly configure this setting. Note that you need to enter a password associated with an e-mail account in order to submit logs to DShield. You may create such an account by going to DShield's Web site and registering at *http://secure.dshield.org/cp/signup.php*. Enter the proper information and you will receive verification regarding your DShield account shortly.

Open SmartDashboard and choose the **SmartDefense** tab. Expand the **Network Security** tree by clicking **+**. Next, expand the **DShield Storm Center** branch by clicking **+**. Place a check in the box next to **Report to DShield***. In the upper-right pane's **Storm Center Login** block, enter *userid@domain.com* (your account's email address) for the **E-mail:** field. Then enter *xxxxxx* (your password) in the **Password:**

field. Select the type of logs you want to submit and the frequency you want to send them to DShield. Now, select the mask you want to invoke to protect your internal addresses Remember that your mask tells the gateway how many bits to reveal (see Figure 7.17).

Figure 7.17 Submitting Logs to DShield

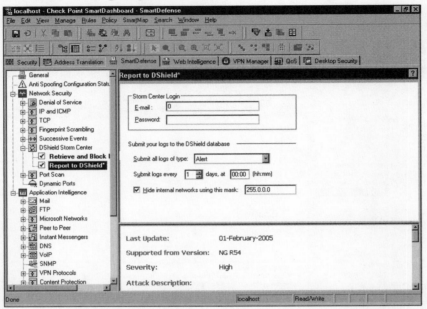

Summary

You should now have a good understanding of how a Check Point VPN-1 Pro Gateway (NGX) administrator has evolved into a network security administrator. The powerful options that Check Point NGX gateways offer help protect your network from internal and external threats. You will also appreciate the fact that some threats are arbitrary, but that some attackers target their exploits for specific applications or servers. Either way, NGX provides sufficient detection and prevention for such threats.

Throughout this chapter, you learned about specific examples of threats, peer-to-peer and SQL, and some ways to mitigate the risk associated with these threats. Deploying an NGX gateway properly takes more consideration than just implementing a typical security policy. You must consider where protections will provide you the most "bang for your buck." Check Point designed a comprehensive security product that you can leverage to protect your organization at the perimeter. NGX not only provides access control, but it allows you to employ solutions that detect, prevent, or block attacks targeting your protected hosts. You've seen some specific configuration examples and how easy it is to apply these protections. At this time, your understanding should be clearer about existing threats and ways to reduce the risk of successful compromise using your NGX gateway. While you apply these protections to your environment, keep in mind that securing your network is a continuous process. Strive to stay ahead of the curve by utilizing the tools that NGX provides to help you perform your duties. Check Point's NGX version of its VPN-1 Pro Gateway is an exceptional way to begin securing your network because it provides a multitude of protective and preventative tools to aid in the task of securing your environment.

Solutions Fast Track

Network Security

☑ Firewalls have evolved into more security conscious devices, providing multiple services to thwart attacks at the perimeter. Because of this, yesterday's firewall administrators have become today's network security administrators. Keep this in mind as you deploy your VPN-1 Pro Gateways; remember that it may include more capability than just access control.

☑ Not all networks require similar protections. Structured threats such as DOS attacks can prevent your legitimate customers from reaching your services. While you may need such protection on an external gateway, you may not need it on an internal device. NGX provides the flexibility to administer controls not only on specific enforcement points, but also for specific servers and services (where appropriate).

☑ As the Internet has provided a platform for remote exploits, network security has come to the forefront of the battle. Providing sufficient security to detect these attacks has become a vital aspect of network security. Consider which NGX controls you will implement and where they best fit into your current or proposed architecture.

☑ An increase in Web-based applications and publicly available servers has catapulted awareness of both network vulnerability and the ramifications of compromise. In this sense, organizations have begun to focus on network security in order to protect their assets. To stay abreast of this ever-changing pace, Check Point provides an update service and Web site to help you stay on top of security threats.

Application Intelligence

☑ Once you configure your hosts as Web servers, FTP servers, or mail servers, you begin to receive protections for these hosts. Check Point introduced Application Intelligence as a means to combat known threats and anomalous behavior. Your gateway will detect and react (as you have configured it to) to these threats as they try to traverse your NGX gateway.

☑ Application Intelligence provides protections in multiple layers of the OSI model. Since many attacks try to exploit weaknesses in the Application Layer, the Transport Layer, and the Network Layer, NGX provides many attack protections relevant to these layers of the OSI model.

☑ Application Intelligence includes two distinct offerings in the NGX product. The first is SmartDefense. This defense offers protections for network and application threats. The second, Web Intelligence, focuses on providing advanced protections for Web-based applications and Web servers.

Malicious Code

- ☑ Check Point's patent-pending Malicious Code Protector technology runs at the kernel level to detect known and unknown malicious code. It works to identify executable code, and then verifies that it has malicious intent. Once it does this, it blocks the code from reaching your protected host.

- ☑ Malicious code is any code segment that deliberately causes harm to the entity that executes it. Checkpoint detects and prevents both known and unknown attacks with its comprehensive malicious code prevention measures.

- ☑ The worm catcher ability lets you define regular expressions to help weed out possible threats to your clients and servers. You can also import signatures into the worm catcher or let the automatic (or invoked) updates keep you on top of current threats.

Protocol Inspection

- ☑ RFCs define protocol standards as the designers intended. Though many applications adhere to these standards, some attackers attempt to violate these standards to compromise your servers. Enabling NGX's protocol enforcement properties protects your hosts against such attacks.

- ☑ NGX has the capability to inspect numerous protocols at multiple layers of the OSI model. It can enforce strict adherence or just notify you (monitor only) of any deviation from the norm. In addition, you can define custom signatures so that NGX will perform a reactive action against matching packets.

- ☑ Some applications do not conform to protocol standards. This makes difficult the job of enforcing these standards. The intention here is not to violate the protocol, but to take advantage of known open ports in most firewalls. Some organizations will not budge on opening outbound ports, so some vendors/providers offer nonstandard applications over commonly open ports (HTTP/port 80). Check Point's granularity allows you to define which servers will receive these protections and in some cases, also lets you create exclusion lists.

DShield Storm Center

- ☑ With DShield, your organization can contribute firewall log files to a global correlation engine. In this manner, continuous analysis will be able to detect current attacks, corroborate source IP addresses, and dispense a list of offenders.

- ☑ You can configure your firewall to download a list of source IP addresses that the DShield engines label as an offender. In this manner, you receive protection against recent threats even before other device vendors publish signatures for the attack.

- ☑ Check Point's flexible configuration controls allow you to sanitize your protected information prior to sending your logs to DShield. This prevents information disclosure by releasing your protected internal address information.

Frequently Asked Questions

The following Frequently Asked Questions, answered by the authors of this book, are designed to both measure your understanding of the concepts presented in this chapter and to assist you with real-life implementation of these concepts. To have your questions about this chapter answered by the author, browse to **www.syngress.com/solutions** and click on the **"Ask the Author"** form.

Q: What's the difference between SmartDefense and Web Intelligence? Don't both of them provide application protection?

A: Yes. Whereas SmartDefense encompasses network threats and application threats, Web Intelligence focuses only on Web-based applications and Web servers. Both of them provide significant protections for their respective domains, but each of them serves a different purpose.

Q: If I enable all of the defense mechanisms, will I provide my organization maximum protection?

A: Since each organization is different and requires its own set of protections, this approach will probably not suffice. First, you must consider the performance impact of running everything. In addition, you should become familiar with your network so that you can optimize NGX's security controls to maximize the benefit. In addition, you may inadvertently disable some traffic if you enable everything. Though it may help you understand your network somewhat, the process probably won't be enjoyable because of your unhappy users.

Q: I'm sending my logs to DShield and I do not want to reveal my internal IP addresses. What can I do to protect them from disclosure?

A: The Check Point GUI gives you the option to set a bit mask when enabling this option. When you define the mask, you are instructing the gateway to reveal that number of bits. If you configure the gateway to reveal 16 bits (255.255.0.0), then your 192.168.1.1 address will appear as 0.0.1.1 in the sanitized logs your gateway sends to DShield.

Q: I'm trying to discern what is happening on my network by looking at my firewall's logs. How do I know what's normal and what's not?

A: There isn't really a yes/no answer to this question. The only way to really understand what may be abnormal traffic on your network is to understand what normal traffic is on your network. NGX has built-in technology to aid in this in that it checks the run-time behavior of code to see if it has malicious intent. Also, NGX has the ability to block (or monitor only) communications that do not comply with the documented protocol specifications. Both of these functions can help you identify irregular traffic within your network. Otherwise, you need to become more familiar with the traffic patterns that traverse your firewall in order to spot suspicious events.

Q: Does Application Intelligence inspect packets for only Application Layer (Layer 7) attacks?

A: No. Application Intelligence inspects packets at multiple layers of the OSI model. SmartDefense can detect network attacks at the Network and Transport Layers (3 and 4), and Application Layer attacks at layer 7 (Application Layer). Since Web Intelligence focuses on Web-based traffic it operates primarily in layer 7 (Application Layer). Keep in mind that as a stateful packet inspection engine, your NGX gateway also provides security at layers 5 and 6 (Session Layer and Presentation Layer).

Q: What does it mean when something says it does Granular Inspection?

A: Granular inspection implies that the device looks into the packet's individual components as well as evaluates the communication as a whole. One request can span multiple packets, so NGX's inspection engine (Active Streaming) often examines each packet in order to detect malformed fields, illegal flag combinations, and known attack signatures in the data field. Also, NGX reassemble packets (if other devices have fragmented them) so that the engine can scrutinize the context of the communication. In some cases, this reassembly inspection detects an attack that survived single packet inspection.

Q: I've deployed a defense-in-depth architecture and have a single SmartCenter Server with multiple NGX enforcement modules. How can I enable application protections for only a certain set of servers?

A: What is great about the extensibility of AI is that you can enforce protective measures for specific servers. If your defined servers are accessible via multiple enforcement modules, then each module will provide the protections. However, if your enforcement module does not provide access to that particular server, then the module will not apply these protections unnecessarily.

Q: Do most threats really come from insiders? How can my VPN-1 Pro Gateway defend against such attacks?

A: Statistics tend to show that this is true. Whether or not these results are from a lack of reported external compromises or lack of knowledge of external compromise is unknown. In any case, if you have the resources to segregate your servers from your user populations (private or public), you can enforce NGX's powerful security profiles. If you cannot do this, you must rely more heavily on host-based protections and other security controls such as separation of duty controls, sound policy and procedures, and an extraordinary monitoring program.

Chapter 8

Network Address Translation

Solutions in this chapter:

- **Global Properties**
- **Configuring Dynamic Hide Mode NAT**
- **Configuring Static Mode NAT**
- **Configuring Automatic NAT**
- **Configuring Port Translation**

☑ Summary

☑ Solutions Fast Track

☑ Frequently Asked Questions

Introduction

This chapter will allow you to enable or disable Network Address Translation (NAT) for a single host, for a range of addresses, or for an entire network. There are two different ways to employ NAT. In this chapter we will demonstrate and explain both methods in detail. In the first method, you configure a single address or a range of addresses to hide protected addresses; this is *Dynamic (Hide) mode NAT*. When you use the second method, *Static mode NAT*, you define a single address that allows a protected host to participate in two-way communications with hosts outside of the protected network.

To understand more about the impact NAT configuration changes have on the gateway, you first need to review a few fundamental concepts. As is easily conveyed by the term itself, Network Address Translation provides a means to convert the source address, destination address, source port, or destination port within a packet. The dominant use of NAT allows internal hosts with nonroutable IP addresses to successfully navigate to the Internet. Since many firewall administrators work with networks that have a limited number of public (routable) IP addresses, their internal private networks utilize private IP address ranges as defined in RFC 1918. For these hosts to be able to access public hosts and services on the Internet, they require a process that translates their private source address into a public, routable source address. NAT provides this very service. When the packet destined for the Internet reaches the gateway, NAT effectively changes the source address so that the destination host may reply to a routable address. When the gateway receives reply packets from the destination server, the NAT process executes a change from the public address to the private address. In doing so, the gateway may now forward the packet to the appropriate internal host. In this manner NAT provides the additional benefit of concealing the internal network topology from external entities.

There are two ways that you administer NAT behavior within the gateway. The easiest way is to define translation automatically within object properties. You will see that the gateway creates the necessary rules for translation in the Nat Rule Base (this topic is addressed later in this chapter). You have the option to automatically configure nodes, networks, and address ranges for automatic address translation. The other way you manage address translation is through manual configuration of the NAT Rule Base. In this way, you will possess greater manageability regarding how translation occurs. Manual NAT configuration also increases your ability to manipulate NAT rules for optimal benefit.

The NAT Rule Base is very similar to the Security Rule Base. Both rule bases process rules in sequential order and cease when a match is found. When you configure automatic NAT for objects, the rules are seamlessly created and placed into the rule base. Note that automatic NAT has a defined order for placing rules into the rule base. The gateway installs Static NAT rules first, then Hide NAT rules. Within Static and NAT rules, Node objects are first, then Address Ranges, and finally, Networks. On the contrary, you may create manual rules wherever you see fit. Again, this action is similar to adding a rule to the Security Rule Base where you create new NAT rules above or below an existing rule. Figure 8.1 shows the view you see when looking at the NAT Rule Base. The **Original Packet** and **Translated Packet** sections both have the same structure in that each contains a **Source**, **Destination**, and **Service**. We will later discuss how to configure NAT rules in order to satisfy your networking requirements.

Figure 8.1 The Address Translation Tab

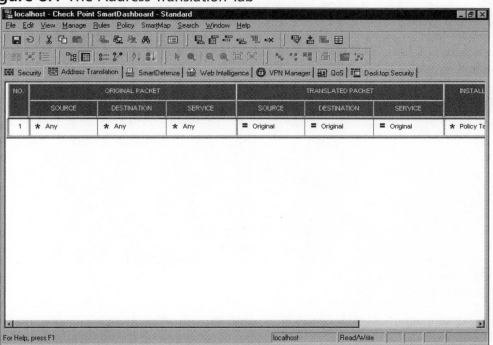

In the remainder of this chapter, we will cover what global settings exist and how each may affect the behavior of your gateway. Further, we will walk through configuring address translation in various ways. We will discuss manually configuring Static and Hide mode NAT, as well as using the automatic NAT features inherent to your FireWall-1 NGX gateway.

Global Properties

In Check Point NGX, you need to consider the **Global Properties** that affect NAT. You find these settings in SmartDashboard by clicking **Policy | Global Properties**, then choosing the **NAT – Network Address Translation** option in the left window. Figure 8.2 displays the settings we will review.

Figure 8.2 NAT Global Properties

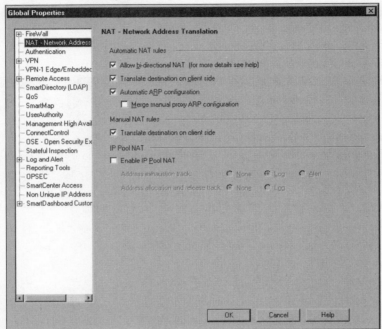

WARNING

At this point, it is imperative to note that pre-NG versions of the product behave differently with respect to some of these settings. For instance, older versions may not provide **Automatic ARP** for the gateway. In this case, you will need to define all the required ARP settings in the *local.arp* file.

Network Address Translation

The **Allow bidirectional NAT** setting permits two hosts to communicate even though they are both hidden behind address translation. These subjects can be any single host, network address, or address range with an automatic NAT definition. When these two hosts communicate with one another, the gateway applies bidirectional NAT to successfully facilitate communication between the hosts. In essence, the bidirectional NAT lets a connection match two NAT rules. Normally the NAT Rule Base only permits one match and then subsequently exits the process. In the case of bidirectional NAT, if the source match is an automatic rule, the gateway continues to traverse the NAT rules to identify if there is a destination rule match. If the gateway finds a second match, it applies both NAT rules to the connection so that the packet is routed properly between source and destination. The gateway executes this translation in both ways, allowing either host to initiate communication with the other if the security policy permits.

Tools & Traps…

Bidirectional NAT

It is imperative that you properly consider rule processing when you employ manual NAT rules. More to the point, you need to understand the consequences of the rule placement prior to pushing the policy. If bidirectional NAT is enabled, improperly placed manual rules may negate such connections. If a manual NAT matches a connection, it will exit the NAT Rule Base immediately. Only when the first match is an Automatic NAT does the gateway continue to inspect the remainder of the rule base for a subsequent match.

The **Translate destination on client side** option, a gateway default setting, tells the gateway to translate destination addresses on the client side of the connection. This setting helps to remedy anti-spoofing and routing implications in previous versions of Check Point. In older versions of Check Point FireWall-1, address translation occurred on the server side and static routes were necessary to forward packets to the correct destination. This setting allows backward compatibility within NGX if you have upgraded from a version without this functionality.

When enabled, **Automatic ARP configuration** instructs the gateway to automatically provide configuration changes to the ARP table in order to advertise for any automatically configured NAT addresses. Keep in mind that this is only for *Automatic* rules, not *Manually* created rules. In previous versions of Check Point, manual ARP entries were necessary for all NAT addresses. This enhancement removes the necessity to create a manual ARP entry for automatic NAT configurations.

The **Merge manual proxy ARP configuration** setting is new for Check Point NGX. What this option does is attempt to centralize ARP configuration to one single process. Since automatic NAT uses automatic ARP and manual NAT requires manual proxy-ARP entries, you can enable this setting to merge the two repositories into one single action. When Automatic ARP configuration is enabled, this setting (enabled) will merge the manual proxy-ARP configuration (in the local.arp) file with the automatic ARP entries (based on automatic NAT objects). In the case of address conflict, the gateway disregards the automatic ARP entry and instead publishes the manual proxy-ARP entry found in the local.arp file. If Automatic ARP configuration is enabled and this setting is not enabled, the gateway will disregard all manual ARP entries in the local.arp file.

In one manner, this setting could eliminate an unintentional duplication. Consider a case where you may accidentally configure automatic NAT for an address for which you have already defined a manual proxy-ARP entry in the local.arp file. Should this happen, you now know that the gateway will resolve the duplication issue by ignoring the automatic ARP entry and publishing the manual proxy-ARP entry. Although this inherent resolution may benefit you if the proxy-ARP entry is correct, it may induce undesirable results on your gateway, and possibly some undue stress on you, if the proxy-ARP entry is old and does not accurately reflect the desired configuration. So if you utilize this option, you must execute due diligence and audit your manual proxy-ARP entries to ensure that you do not have any duplicate entries, and that all your current entries are accurate.

Under the Manual NAT rules, the **Translate destination on client side** setting causes the same action as the same setting for automatic NAT rules. Again, older versions of the product translated the connection on the server side causing additional route configuration in order to facilitate a successful connection. Check Point recognized the growing need to resolve this and delivered this feature in its Check Point NG version.

Within the **IP Pool NAT** configuration settings, the **Enable IP NAT Pool** option primarily focuses on Secure Client/Secure Remote connections where there is an IP tunnel involved. Since the true address of the client may not be routable to hosts protected by the gateway, the IP NAT pool serves to create a range of addresses for such clients to utilize. In this manner, your gateway will translate a tunneled connection to a (internally) routable address for proper communications.

You may also configure the **Address exhaustion track:** and **Address allocation and release track:** options if you want to enable tracking for NAT pooling actions. If you have a need to troubleshoot an issue with routing to remote clients, then you can enable one or both of these options to the appropriate setting in order to populate your logs with usable information. In that way, you will see if you are running out of addresses to translate to, or you will simply be able to track which assignments are given to specific clients. In a sense, the tracking of allocation provides you with a small bit of an audit trail in that it accounts for the distribution of IP addresses to each requesting client.

Configuring Dynamic Hide Mode NAT

One of the most practical ways you employ address translation on your gateways is with *Dynamic Hide mode*. In this way, you protect internal hosts and preserve valuable routable IP addresses. In this chapter we will explore how to set up NAT rules so that an internal host, address range, or network is hidden behind a single public IP address.

Dynamic NAT Defined

When we speak of *Dynamic* NAT, we should simply consider this term the same as *Hide* NAT. Throughout this chapter, we will use the two expressions interchangeably. With that said, we will show you how to hide a single node, an address range, or an entire network behind a *Hide* NAT.

In the most simplistic configuration, you hide all the internal addresses behind the gateway's external interface address. If you want to use another routable address, you can define one, and then hide nodes behind it.

With *Hide* NAT you allow only outbound (one-way) communication from your internal hosts. This method does not permit external hosts to initiate connections with any of your protected hosts. In short, *Hide* NAT allows you either to translate private addresses so that your hosts can communicate with public addresses or to conceal the true addresses of your internal hosts so that you do not disclose confidential network topology.

Because *Hide* mode has the potential to conceal many connections behind a single address, the gateway has a unique way of handling connections. When your firewall receives a request for *Hide* NAT, it modifies not only the source address but also the source port. When the packet returns to the gateway, the firewall consults its tables to reveal which true client to send the packet to based primarily on the source port of the connection. If you think about the number of connections your gateway could potentially translate at any given time, up to 50,000 per server, you then understand why your gateway modifies the source port.

In most cases, the firewall uses high ephemeral ports when translating the source port. There are actually two port ranges from which your gateway chooses a translation source port. The first pool of ports ranges from 600 to 1023. In reality, your gateway only utilizes this range of ports for specific services matching more specific connection information. For instance, if you have an *rlogin*, *rshell*, or *rexec* connection request that is also using a source port less than 1024, the gateway will utilize this range of ports to choose the translated source port. On the other hand, the gateway assigns all other translation connections a port from the range of 10,000 to 60,000.

Although you are able to customize both ranges for translation ports, you must consider your environment prior to doing so. Keep in mind that the gateway is able to handle only up to 50,000 concurrent connections per server, hence the 10,000 to 60,000 port range. So, if you do modify the port ranges, you must ensure that your configuration satisfies this capability by providing no less than 50,000 source ports to choose from. For most environments, the default settings provide adequate coverage. For most of us, if you have more than 50,000 connections to one server, you are most likely experiencing a misconfiguration or some type of attack (possibly self induced).

To change these settings, you need to use the *dbedit* command-line utility. Essentially, you are changing the settings in the *objects_5_0.C* file on your firewall module. The valid range for the minimum high port is 1,025–60,000, and the valid range for the maximum high port is 10,003–60,000. When you execute the *dbedit* utility from the command line, you must supply administrative credentials in order to make changes to the database. Once you provide sufficient credentials, the firewall presents you with a *dbedit* command prompt. The following directives instruct the firewall to set the minimum high port to 15,000 and the maximum high port to 59,000.

```
C:\>dbedit -s localhost -u fwadmin -p password


Please enter a command, -h for help or -q to quit:
dbedit> modify properties firewall_properties hide_min_high_port 15000


dbedit> modify properties firewall_properties hide_max_high_port 59000


dbedit> update_all
```

```
properties::firewall_properties Updated Successfully


dbedit> quit
```

As you can see in the previous code snippet, there are several items you must know in order to actually execute the proper commands. In the *dbedit* command prompt, you can call the *–h* parameter to display usage guidelines. In this command, you want to *modify* from the *properties* table the *firewall_properties* object, and lastly the *hide_min_high_port* and *hide_max_high_port* fields. To save the changes you made, you must invoke the *update_all* directive. Then, you can *quit* the *dbedit* utility. To validate that your changes were made, you open the *objects_5_0.C* file on your enforcement module and search for the settings (*hide_min* should suffice as a search string). When you come upon the entry, you should see both settings, one after another, with the modified values.

As previously mentioned, there isn't necessarily a need to modify these settings. Doing so without considerable reason and advanced understanding of the changes may invoke undesirable results on your firewall and may impede connectivity. As such, you may actually carry out a denial-of-service attack on yourself if you are not careful.

Advanced Understanding of NAT

Now that you somewhat understand how your firewall provides address translation, let's lift the hood and try to see what is really happening inside. In the firewall kernel, there are four distinct inspection points that move packets in one interface and out another. These four points are referred to as *i I o O*. They each provide a service so as to help the successful verification and routing of packets while they are being transferred through the firewall.

To begin, a packet must enter your firewall's external interface (we use an inbound connection to a private server using NAT as an example). We refer to this action as the inbound (i) packet arriving at the kernel. Next, the gateway submits the packet to the Security Rule Base. If the security policy permits the connection, the kernel offers the packet to the NAT Rule Base for translation of the destination address. The resultant packet is the (I) packet that the gateway has accepted and translated for appropriate internal routing. Then the kernel sends the packet through the TCP/IP stack and to the appropriate firewall interface for outbound (o) processing. Again, the kernel matches the packet against the NAT Rule Base, this time for source address translation. This is so that when your internal server receives the packet, it will have the correct address that the host can route a reply packet to. Lastly, the kernel passes the packet out (O) the internal interface to your server to complete the connection.

On the return packet, you see a similar process as the packet enters the firewall's internal interface. This time the packet goes through the NAT Rule Base and translates the destination (original packet's source) to the true address. Next, the kernel passes the packet up the TCP/IP stack. Once more, the packet goes through the NAT Rule Base to translate the source (original destination) to its routable address. Finally, the packet moves through the firewall's external interface to the upstream router. It is important to note that this return packet does not pass through the firewall security policy. As the firewall accepts original request packets, it creates an entry in the connections table. When packets arrive at the firewall and are party to an existing connection (within the connections table) the firewall allows the packet to bypass the firewall's security policy inspection process. However, the packets continue to traverse the NAT Rule Base in order to satisfy any binding translation requirements.

As you may expect, Check Point provides you with a few tools to inspect translation tables and troubleshoot problems if necessary. One of these tools is the *fw monitor* command. If you are familiar with packet capture utilities, then you should not have any problems with this tool. Even if you are not familiar with such tools, the output from this command is understandable after some familiarization. When you use this tool with the *fw tab –t connections* command, you will see how the firewall maintains the connections with respect to both the Security Rule Base and the NAT Rule Base. The following example includes captures of these commands to illustrate the firewall's behavior.

```
1     C:\>fw tab -t connections

2     localhost:

3     -------- connections --------

4     dynamic, id 8158, attributes: keep, sync, expires 25, refresh, limit
      25000, hash size 32768, kbuf 16 17 18 19 20 21 22 23 24 25 26 27 28
      29 30, free function f6c

5     2c210 0, post sync handler f6c2d6f0

6     <00000000, c0a845c9, 00000476, c0a86301, 00000050, 00000006> ->
      <00000000, c0a845c9, 00000476, c0a84597, 00000050, 00000006>
      (00000011)

7     <00000001, c0a86301, 00000050, c0a845c9, 00000476, 00000006> ->
      <00000000, c0a845c9, 00000476, c0a84597, 00000050, 00000006>
      (00000005)


1     C:\>fw monitor -m iIoO

2      monitor: getting filter (from command line)

3      monitor: compiling
```

```
4       Warning: COMPILER_DIR undefined, using FWDIR instead
5       : No error
6       monitorfilter:
7       Compiled OK.
8        monitor: loading
9        monitor: monitoring (control-C to stop)
10      PCnet1:i[48]: 192.168.69.201 -> 192.168.69.151 (TCP) len=48 id=6031
11      TCP: 1142 -> 80 .S.... seq=ca49b9f4 ack=00000000
12      PCnet1:I[48]: 192.168.69.201 -> 192.168.99.1 (TCP) len=48 id=6031
13      TCP: 1142 -> 80 .S.... seq=ca49b9f4 ack=00000000
14      PCnet1:o[48]: 192.168.99.1 -> 192.168.69.201 (TCP) len=48 id=28998
15      TCP: 80 -> 1142 .S..A. seq=4d96287f ack=ca49b9f5
16      PCnet1:O[48]: 192.168.69.151 -> 192.168.69.201 (TCP) len=48 id=28998
17      TCP: 80 -> 1142 .S..A. seq=4d96287f ack=ca49b9f5
18      PCnet1:i[40]: 192.168.69.201 -> 192.168.69.151 (TCP) len=40 id=6032
19      TCP: 1142 -> 80 ....A. seq=ca49b9f5 ack=4d962880
20      PCnet1:I[40]: 192.168.69.201 -> 192.168.99.1 (TCP) len=40 id=6032
21      TCP: 1142 -> 80 ....A. seq=ca49b9f5 ack=4d962880
```

As you see in the *fw tab –t connections* results, the firewall sends hex data to standard out. If you sift through the damage, you can identify the source and destination original and translated addresses. For instance, the original client in our example is 192.168.69.201. After translating the decimal to hex, you end up with *c0a845c9*. You can see in the results that this value exists in the sixth and seventh lines of the output. In addition, the NAT destination address, 192.168.69.151 (*c0a84597*), exists in the same connection. You then see the following connection entry in line 7 has a similar structure to the request connection in line 6.

To further simplify the hex output, let's take a look at the same lines compared with decimal format representation.

HEX <00000000, c0a845c9, 00000476, c0a86301, 00000050, 00000006> -> <00000000,
c0a845c9, 00000476, c0a84597, 00000050, 00000006> (00000011)

DEC <0, 192.168.69.201, 1142, 192.168.99.1, 80, 6> -> <0, 192.168.69.201, 1142, 192.168.69.151, 80, 6> (17)

All right. Now you can see the resemblance of a connection. From left to right, you see the connection id, source, source port, destination, destination port, and pro-

tocol. The firewall associates this translated packet with the packet following the ->
symbol. In this light you see that the firewall substitutes the NAT destination address
(192.168.69.151) with the server's real address (192.168.99.1). Looking at line 7, you
see the firewall executes a similar translation for the reply packet.

Now if you take a look at the *fw monitor* output, you can see that there are several connections going on, but that they meet what you expect to see after looking
at the firewall's connections table. These captures show that the firewall is properly
executing address translation. For instance, the first two captures beginning in lines
10 and 12 show that the source remains the same, but the destination address is different. Also, you can see reply packets in this output. You see that the gateway translates the reply packet in the manner you studied earlier. The packet comes into the
interface (first capture line 14), and then it is translated if applicable (second capture
line 16).

Several items to note in this particular set of output: First, the firewall left the
source port for the connection unchanged during translation. Remember that only
in *Dynamic* (Hide) mode does the firewall change the source port of the connection.
Also, you see that you have a crude interpretation of the rule base. Recalling that
there are four inspection points, you can combine that knowledge with this output
and troubleshoot any problems with packets not being able to get through the firewall. Since you know that a packet first comes into an interface and then is sent to
the Security Rule Base and NAT Rule Base, you may identify problems if the
output does not reflect addresses translation (if applicable). In other words, if you see
a packet come into the firewall, but do not see the translated packet bound for the
destination host, you may safely presume that the connection did not satisfy your
Security Rule Base. Lastly, if you have other packet capture utilities, you may use
them in conjunction with any one or both of these tools to aid in troubleshooting
issues or to just to learn more about your firewall's internal behavior.

When to Use It

Since Internet service providers (ISPs) and the Internet Assigned Numbers Authority
(IANA) do not liberally allocate IP addresses to their customers, NAT allows you to
preserve your limited allowance of public IP addresses. As such, the majority of your
internal networks employ private address schemes. Creating this topology gives you
the flexibility you need to populate your networks with all the appropriate servers,
workstations, and other hosts you need without running into IP address limitations.
Because of this, you need to employ NAT in order to route communication with
hosts residing outside the scope of your network address space. The primary purpose
in this sense is for packets bound for public address space; in essence, the Internet.

However, you are also able to employ NAT when you simply do not want to expose your network topology to another party. In this manner, you may actually NAT from one private address to another or from a public address to a private address. This method is flexible in that it allows translation from any category address (public or private) to an identical range of addresses. Another way you configure NAT helps you to preserve address space.

Let's look at how you manually add a *Hide* NAT to your gateway so that your internal protected hosts are able to communicate with Internet hosts. For this example, consider that the internal network address is 192.168.90.0/24. Therefore, your gateway address (the default next hop for internal hosts) has an address of 192.168.90.1, and your internal hosts will use an address range from 192.168.90.2 to 254 (either using static or dynamic assignment via DHCP).

Now you need to open your NAT Rule Base by clicking the **Address Translation** tab in the SmartDashboard utility. You need to understand that there are going to be several objects that you will use to create this NAT rule. The first is the address range that you want to hide: the network object **Local_Net**. The other object, **Gateway**, will hide the internal addresses. As discussed earlier, you can hide behind other addresses, but you would need to create a separate object for such an address. Don't forget that routing and ARP issues may accompany this kind of NAT.

Begin by adding a rule to the rule base so that you can add your objects to it. From the menu, click **Rules | Add Rule | Bottom**. This action adds a rule to the rule base, as shown previously in Figure 8.1. Now, add your **Local_Net** object as the **Source** in the **Original Packet** section of the new rule. Since you want this rule to translate to any destination using any services, both the **Destination** and **Service** in the **Original Packet** section will remain **Any**.

Now determine how you want the translated packet to appear to outside hosts. In the **Source** section of the **Translated Packet** section, add your **Gateway** object selecting **Add (Hide)** from the pull-down menu when prompted. This tells your gateway to translate all packets from internal hosts using the IP defined for the gateway in the SmartDashboard object database. Since you are applying this to all packets, you do not change the value of **Destination** or **Service**. Both of these values should remain **Original**.

The **Install On** field defines which gateways will receive this policy. If you have defined policy targets, leave this value unchanged, reading **Policy Targets**. As for the **Comment** section, you just add a brief description of the rule "Hide NAT for Internal Network" to explain the rule's purpose. Figure 8.3 shows the completed NAT rule.

Figure 8.3 The Completed NAT Rule

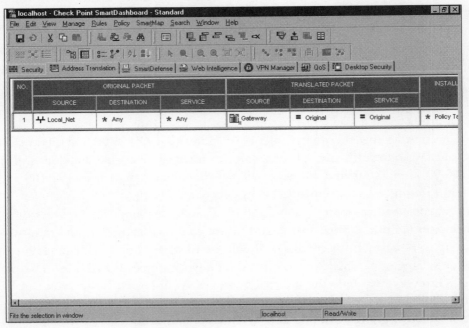

Again, your NAT rule does not permit your internal hosts to communicate; it just translates the packets in order to facilitate the connection. You need to be sure that there is a rule in your security policy that allows your internal hosts this communication. Figure 8.4 shows the characteristics of this rule.

Figure 8.4 The Rule to Allow Outbound Traffic

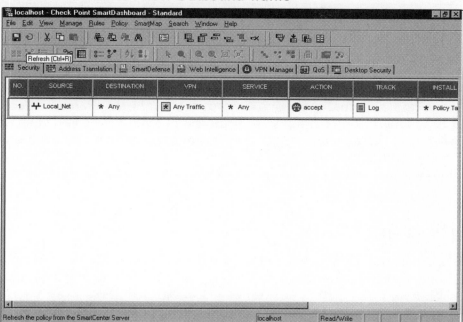

This rule has **Local_Net** as the source, destination and service remain **Any**, and the **Action** is **Accept**. This allows all traffic from your internal network, 192.168.90.0/24, to initiate connects to any destination. As desired, your NAT rule will translate outbound packets for proper routing and to conceal your private topology.

There are some instances where you may have a single host on your protected network that needs to communicate with an external server for one particular reason or another. Further, you may not desire any of your other protected hosts to share the ability to complete such connections. On the other end, your connection partner may also employ access control. For this reason, you need to inform them of the sole IP address that will request the connection. In this case, you can employ a one-to-one *Hide* NAT. This is where it may be easier for us to use the term *Hide* NAT. You are not configuring this rule for *Static* NAT, as discussed later in this chapter, but you must single out this one connection based on your requirements. In this way, the gateway will use one single NAT address for only this protected host.

NOTE

Although configuring a one-to-one *Dynamic* NAT makes sense in some cases, you must be careful to manage the rule base in such instances. Your gateway allows you to configure *Hide* NAT for either an IP address or its external interface address. For this reason, you are capable of configuring multiple objects with the same *Hide* NAT address. For the previous case, this configuration does not meet your requirements because it is a many-to-one relationship. A thorough audit of the NAT Rule Base will reveal these inconsistencies, so it is imperative that you have such configuration controls in place.

Routing and ARP

Without delving too far into specifics, we shall consider basic routing with regard to NAT. To this end, let's agree that proper routing facilitates the successful transmission of a packet from source host to destination host. In simplest terms, a host forwards a packet to its appropriate next hop as defined in its local routing table. Each router or gateway in the communication path then sends the packet on to the next hop as determined in its own local routing table until the destination host's router receives the packet. Since this router belongs to the same local network as the intended destination, it delivers the packet to the destination host. In most cases, you don't NAT outside of your allocated public IP space. Since your upstream provider already routes this range to your perimeter router, you need not worry about making arrangements for new routes to your NAT address. However, if you utilize an address that your upstream provider does not currently route to your router, then you must request that your provider add the necessary routes to accommodate your NAT.

The Address Resolution Protocol (ARP) aids routing in that it translates an IP address to a physical hardware address (MAC address). Where routing tells a host which IP address to send the packet to next (next hop), ARP queries the current network to resolve which hardware address corresponds to that IP address. It is only following an ARP query and response that a router determines which host (router or gateway) is the next hop and transmits a packet to the host that owns the hardware address that the ARP query returned. Any device, including your Check Point gateway, that does NAT must have ARP entries for each address it translates. If it didn't, the gateway would not respond to an ARP query telling the originator it is the next recipient of the packet. As a consequence of the nature of ARP, your gateway's ARP behavior is no different for *Dynamic* or *Static* NAT.

Adding ARP Entries

Because Check Point is compatible with a host of operating systems, there are different ways to add ARP entries in order for them to survive a reboot. In this section, we touch on several platforms and how to achieve the desired result. In each case, you need to associate the address you are NATing to (the virtual address) to the MAC address of the gateway's interface the traffic will be exiting from. You can see the interface's MAC address with the **ipconfig /all** command in Windows or the **ifconfig –a command** in Unix.

Secure Platform

To add ARP entries using Secure Platform, follow these steps:

- Create the */etc/ethers* file.
- Add a line to include your ARP entry:
  00:02:B1:C0:D7:78 192.168.1.100
- Add the following line to the */etc/rc.local* file:
  arp –f /etc/ethers

Solaris

To add ARP entries using Solaris, follow these steps:

- Create the file /etc/rc2.d/S99arp.
- Add a line to include your ARP entry:
  arp –a 192.168.1.100 00:02:B1:C0:D7:78 pub
- Change the file permissions to make it executable:
  chmod 744 S99arp

Windows

To add ARP entries using Windows, follow these steps:

- Create a *local.arp* file in the $FWDIR\conf directory.
- Add a line to include your ARP entry:
  192.168.1.100 00:02:B1:C0:D7:78
- Save the changes to the *local.arp* file.

IPSO

To add ARP entries using IPSO, follow these steps:

- Log into the *Voyager* administrative interface.

- Click the **Config** button.

- Under the **System Configuration** heading, click **ARP**.

- Scroll down to the **Proxy ARP Entries** section.

- In the **Add a new Proxy ARP entry:,** add the appropriate address to the **IP address:** field.

- Click **Apply**, then enter the appropriate MAC address in the field for this ARP entry.

- Click **Save**.

Although these guidelines may provide you with a successful persistent ARP entry, there are certainly other ways to negotiate ARP entries, especially with the flexibility of Linux and Solaris. You may be more comfortable doing things your way. The key point here is that your ARP entries survive a system restart. As the old saying goes; there is more than one way to skin a cat.

Tools & Traps…

Determining ARP Entries

Configuring automatic and manual NAT rules may generate conflicting ARP entries. One troubleshooting method you can use to see exactly what your gateway is ARP'ing for is the command:

fw ctl arp

This command dumps the ARP table to standard out so that you may investigate any ARP configuration issues. Also, both Windows and UNIX hosts execute the command

arp –a

to display the hosts ARP table.

When you use *Hide* NAT, you may or may not run into routing and ARP issues. If you simply hide your internal objects behind the external gateway address, you shouldn't encounter any issues with either of these technologies. Because your upstream providers should be routing to the gateway's external address already, you are not required to modify any configuration settings to receive proper address translation. However, if you utilize a separate address for hiding your objects, one other than the gateway's external interface address, you must modify the ARP table to include this new address. In this way, the gateway responds to an ARP query for the NAT address with its external hardware address. As such, the upstream router forwards the packet to your gateway. Again, recall that you must notify your upstream provider of any NAT address you use if it is not within the current network that they route to you. In this case, your provider may need to modify its routing tables accordingly. Later in this chapter, we will configure ARP manually and automatically.

Configuring Static Mode NAT

The single most obvious use for Static NAT is when you configure a protected host for public use. Again, if you have a limited IP address allocation, you may utilize private IP space within your DMZ network(s). In such cases, you must apply Static NAT to your servers that host your Web, mail, and other public services. In this chapter, we will examine configuring protected hosts with Static NAT.

Static NAT Defined

Similar to *Hide* NAT, *Static* NAT conceals a host's true address. Whereas most implementations of *Dynamic* NAT exhibit a many-to-one ratio, you are able to configure your gateway with a one-to one Static relationship if you have such a need. The primary difference between the two modes is *Static* NAT's ability to allow an external host to initiate inbound connections. Instead of hiding your protected hosts, you are in some way announcing their addresses to the external networks. In contrast to Hide mode, Static rules must utilize the same object type for translation.

You have numerous options when it comes to configuring Static NAT. In this section we will further discuss these options, and later we describe how to configure a gateway for Static NAT.

When to Use It

To let servers and other service-oriented hosts communicate with the outside world, you need to uniquely identify them via NAT. Your DMZ hosts in this case utilize private addresses, and your gateway must convert them to public routable addresses when leaving your protected network. Similar to *Hide* NAT, you create a *Static Source* rule so that the gateway conceals your server's real address during outbound connections when the packet reaches your firewall.

To configure this translation, add a rule to the NAT Rule Base above your hide rule. In addition, you will need to add an object that represents your **Web_Server** with internal address 192.168.90.10. Further, configure a **Web_Server_Valid** object that represents the routable address of your server, 198.53.145.2, as seen in Figure 8.5.

Figure 8.5 The Web Server External Object

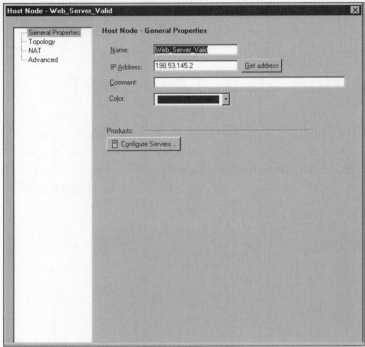

Now that you have your objects defined, move on to create the NAT rule. You need to **Add Rule | Above** your current *Hide* rule. You define the **Web_Server** object as the **Source** in the **Original Packet** section. The **Destination** and **Service** remain **Any**. On the **Translated Packet** side, set the **Source** to **Web_Server_Valid**. Again, the **Destination** and **Service** remain unchanged. Figure 8.6 shows the new rule base with the previous *Hide* rule and the new *Manual Static Source* rule.

Figure 8.6 The Static Source NAT Rule

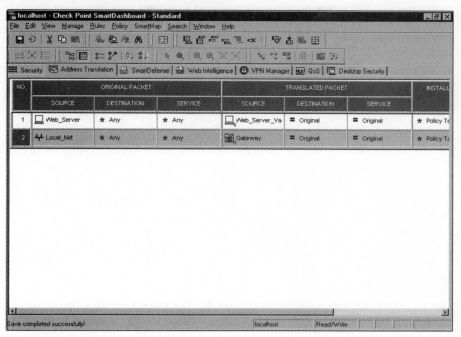

Once the gateway receives the packet, it translates the packet so that the external client can route the packet back to your gateway. This again is very similar to *Hide* NAT, except that you now see why *Static* NAT requires a one-to-one relationship for proper routing or packet forwarding to your public servers.

Lastly, verify that your security policy permits the **Web_Server** object to initiate connections outbound. If your Web server is in your internal network, the current rule would cover this traffic. However, if the server is in your DMZ, create rule 1, as seen in Figure 8.7.

Figure 8.7 The Outbound Rule for the Web Server

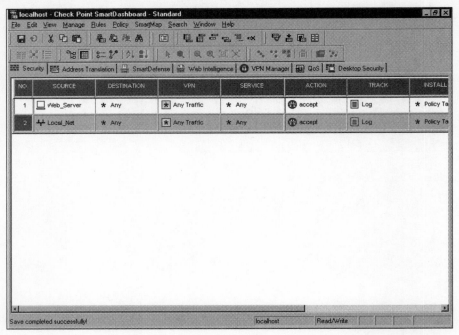

You also utilize *Static* NAT if you need to differentiate between your outgoing clients. Since *Hide* NAT converts many clients behind the same address, you need to use *Static* NAT to individually identify single clients. In this case, it is not necessary to add two NAT rules because inbound connectivity may not be necessary. Additionally, since *Hide* NAT modifies the source port, you must employ *Static* NAT if you use protocols that cannot survive such modifications.

NOTE

Static NAT configuration requires you to generate two rules in the NAT Rule Base: one for *Static Source*, and the other for *Static Destination*. If you use automatic configuration, the gateway will complete this action for you. When you manually configure *Static* NAT, you must be sure that you add both rules to the rule base.

Inbound Connections

We've already mentioned that you employ *Static* NAT when you want to let external hosts connect to your DMZ servers. In essence, you refer to this translation as *Static Destination*. In contrast to *Hide* NAT, this action doesn't translate the source of the packet, but translates the destination. So when an external host's connection request reaches your gateway (via a routable address), the gateway converts the destination address to an internal protected address and then forwards it to the corresponding server.

To create this translation rule, choose **Add Rule | Below** from the menu to create it below your *Static Source* rule. In the **Original Packet** section, change the **Destination** to **Web_Server_Valid** and leave the **Source** and **Service** as **Any**. In the **Translated Packet** section, the **Destination** is **Web_Server** and the **Source** and **Service** remains **Original**. Figure 8.8 shows the completed NAT rule.

Figure 8.8 The Static Destination Rule

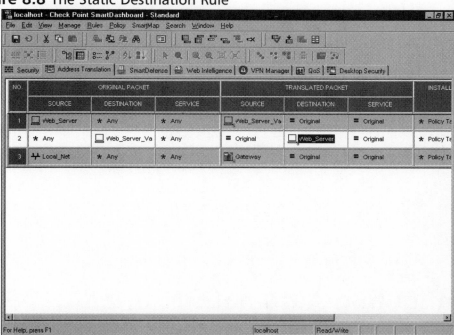

As is always the case, you need to verify that your security policy permits your desired traffic. In this case, you need to add a rule to allow any host to your **Web_Server_Valid** address. Since you want to allow only http to this host, set the **Source** to **Any**, the **Destination** to **Web_Server_Valid**, and the **Service** to **http**. Figure 8.9 displays the completed rule 2.

Figure 8.9 The Rule for Incoming Traffic to the Web Server

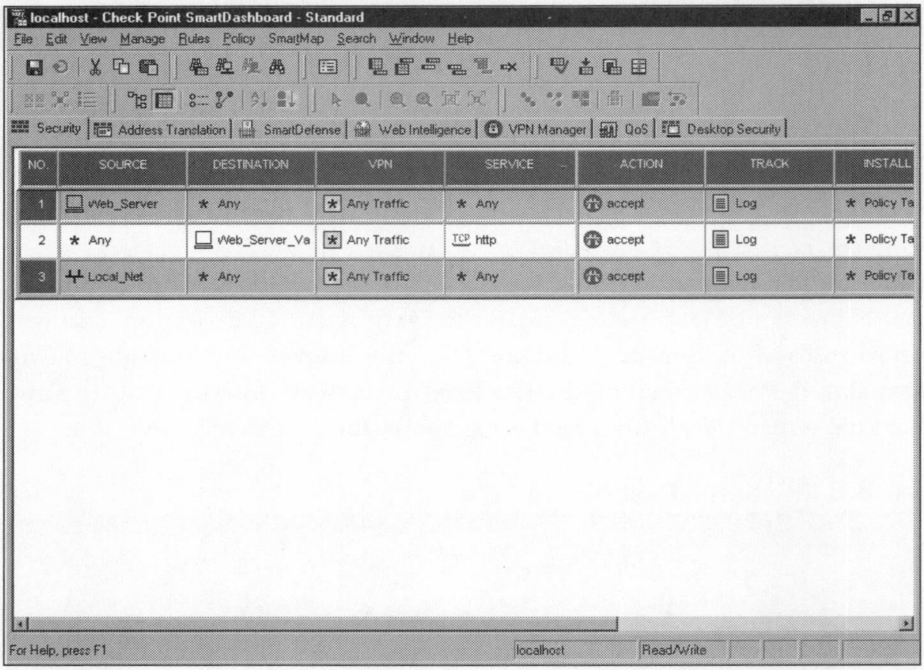

You must remember that your gateway not only performs NAT but also provides access control. When you want to employ Static NAT to let external clients initiate connections to your protected servers, you must configure Security rules as well. If you configure NAT without adding a Security rule, the gateway will not permit the client's request to communicate with the server. If you use Check Point's Automatic NAT feature, the Security rule's destination can be the internal host object. However, if you deploy a *Static* NAT rule manually, you need to define a second node object with the routable (translated) address. Then, you create the Security rule with your new public object as the destination.

Configuring Automatic NAT

Though you are able to create all the rules you need manually (as we have already discussed), Check Point's automatic NAT configuration capability also suits your needs. This method is generally easier to configure, decreases error rates, and also takes considerably less time.

When to Use It

Just as with manual configuration, you can configure *Hide* or *Static* NAT automatically. Under the same circumstances as your manual configuration, you can modify existing or new objects to do the translation automatically. Figure 8.10 shows the object with an automatic NAT configuration.

Figure 8.10 The NAT Tab of the Network Object

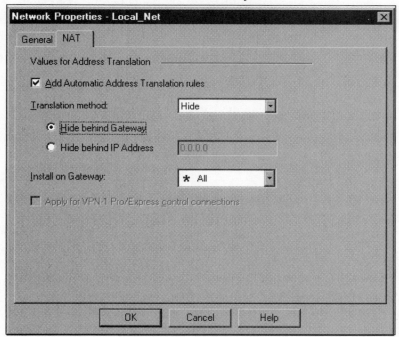

For *Hide* mode on your internal private network, all you need to do is modify the **Local_Net** object's properties. In SmartDashboard choose **Manage | Network Objects** from the File menu, then select **Local_Net** and click **Edit**. Select the **NAT** tab at the top and check the box for **Add Automatic Translation rules**. For **Translation Method** accept the default **Hide**. You also should not change the default setting of **Hide behind Gateway**. In the **Install on** box, select your gateway, or leave it the default setting **All**.

When you enable this setting, you essentially tell the entire outside world that your connection source from all your internal clients is your firewall's external interface. Though you are able to easily configure this setting, there are some items you need to consider before making this decision.

Hiding all your internal addresses behind your gateway's address allows you to save IP address space. We've covered this topic before, so we won't expound on it again here. Another great benefit is that it minimizes your management of NAT within your firewall. Since all the internal IP space is hidden behind one IP address, you should introduce minimal configuration changes to your firewall. In addition, you need to provide only a single IP address to connection partners for access control on their end.

On the other hand, hiding all your internal clients behind your firewall's external address can attract undesirable attention. For instance, if you use an alternative IP address to hide all your internal clients behind, you are then able to shield your gateway address from the Internet (possibly adding an ACL to the upstream perimeter router). In this sense, your firewall maintains a low connection profile and provides a very limited footprint across the public wire. Though this configuration requires you to add an object to define the internal clients and configure NAT for this object, you still minimize the changes to a manageable level.

TIP

Also, you may define a range of addresses to hide behind. In this case, an address range with a similar quantity of hosts would correlate almost one to one with a NAT range. For instance, if the address range is 10.1.1.100-110 and the NAT range is 192.168.1.10-20, then the address 10.1.1.102 would be hidden behind the address 192.168.1.12.

In the case where you require *Static* NAT (like our Web server example), you simply make a small adjustment to the same steps as *Hide* mode. Again, open SmartDashboard and choose **Manage | Network Objects** from the file menu, then select **Web_Server** and click **Edit**. Select the **NAT** tab from the left menu pane and check the box for **Add Automatic Translation rules**. For **Translation Method** choose **Static** from the pull-down menu. In the **Translate to IP Address** box, enter **198.52.145.2** (your routable address). Figure 8.11 shows the *Static* NAT configuration for the Web server.

Figure 8.11 The NAT Tab of the Web Server

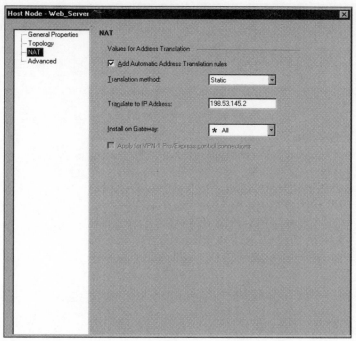

NAT Rule Base

Now let's take a look at the NAT Rule Base after you successfully configure your *Static* and *Hide* translations automatically. Figure 8.12 shows the new NAT Rule Base, and you can see that two automatic configurations have resulted in the gateway creating four rules.

Figure 8.12 Generated Address Translation Rules

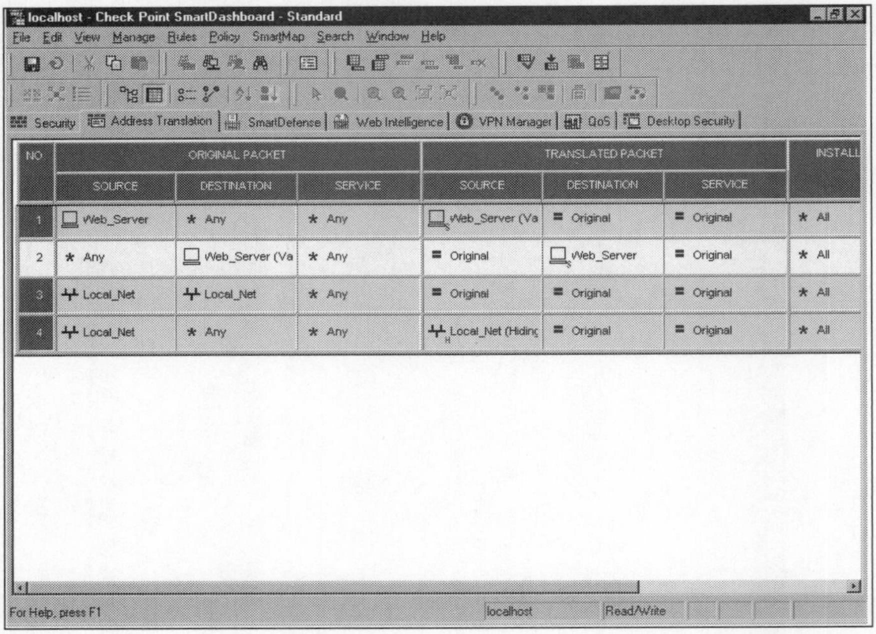

The first rule translates the **Web_Server** private address to the valid address you defined in the object's properties for outbound connections. The second rule translates the valid address for **Web_Server** into the private address for incoming connections. Both of these rules equate to your two *Static* rules you created manually: one for *Static Source* and another for *Static Destination*.

Likewise, rules 3 and 4 correspond to your *Hide* NAT rules you created manually. However, when you create *Hide* NAT automatically, the gateway generates a rule that does not translate packets from **Local_Net** hosts to other **Local_Net** hosts. This rule ensures that translation is not done internally and that routing from within **Local_Net** does not become complicated.

TIP _____

It is possible for you to automatically configure all your internal networks for *Hide* NAT via the gateway object's properties. In this manner, the gateway hides all the networks defined as internal within your gateway's topology. However, if you have other automatic or manual NAT rules in place, these take precedence over this particular option. Figure 8.13 shows this configuration setting.

_____

Figure 8.13 Gateway NAT Properties

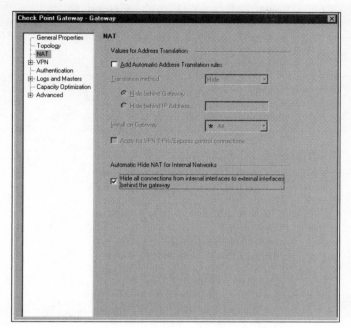

Access Control Settings

Just as with your other NAT rules, you need to configure proper access control via your security policy to ensure that you are permitting traffic as desired. One difference in the case of automatic configuration is that you are not required to define a separate object for the valid address of your Web server. The gateway intelligently handles all outside communications to your Web server with the valid address and any internal communications via the private protected address. Take a look at Figure 8.14 to see the difference between manual and automatic translations' effect on the security policy.

Figure 8.14 The Security Policy for Automatic NAT

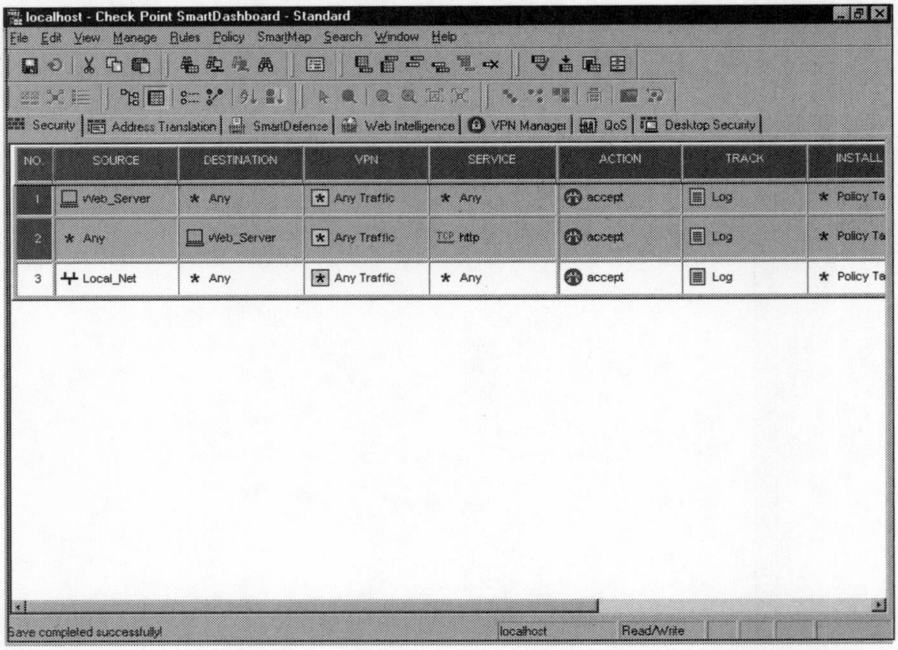

Configuring Port Translation

Essentially, we have already covered how to manually configure NAT, both in *Hide* mode and *Static* mode. In this section we discuss a different aspect of manual NAT, port translation. In this sense, you can further save IP address space if you have numerous servers that provide different services.

When to Use It

Consider three servers: an SMTP server, an HTTP server, and an FTP server. If you are considerably strained by having only a few public routable IP addresses, you may configure your gateway so that these requests could go to one single IP address. The gateway handles all the translation and, from the rules you create, will designate traffic to the appropriate internal application server.

You can even implement this technique when you have a service running on a nonstandard port and want to conceal the true port from external users. If you are running an HTTP server on port 8080, but want to respond to port 80 (standard HTTP port) requests from the outside, you can configure the gateway to translate the incoming request so that the client talks to the server on port 8080 without realizing it. In truth, the gateway translates destination port 80 to port 8080.

NAT Rule Base

As you configure manual NAT entries, your primary consideration concerning the NAT Rule Base is that you properly compose translation rules to intercept inbound and outbound packets.

For instance, let's say that your three servers are hiding behind the gateway's external address and that you are using port translation to redirect services. Figure 8.15 shows this configuration using the **DMZ_NET** and the corresponding NAT rules. In all, the gateway accepts connections to its external address for three separate internal servers, each one hosting a single application. When a client makes a connection request to the gateway for, say, FTP (rule 5 in Figure 8.15), the gateway translates the packet so that the destination is the **Ftp_Server** object's internal IP address. When the **Ftp_Server** replies to the client, the gateway then translates the packet's source to its own external IP address. In this manner, the requesting client and **Ftp_Server** continue a normal conversation as if both of them were talking directly to one another. The client in this case is unaware that the gateway is performing the translation.

Figure 8.15 Port Translation Rules

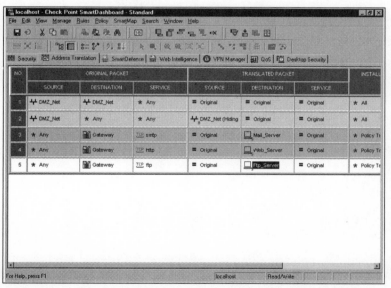

Security Policy Implications

Using port translation, you benefit from defining a set of NAT rules that makes one single IP address appear to host many services. To accompany these rules, you need access control rules that permit external hosts to talk to your servers. Since your server addresses are private and not routable from external sources, your rules must reflect a destination that matches the NAT rule. Similar to manual *Static* NAT from earlier, your security policy rule must use the routable object, not the true internal object as you used in automatic NAT. Figure 8.16 shows the security policy reflecting appropriate access control rules for port translation rules. Notice that you do not need to define rules explicitly permitting external clients access to your application servers. The gateway will accept the connections to its external address and apply the necessary NAT rules in order to facilitate a successful connection.

Figure 8.16 The Security Policy for Port Translation

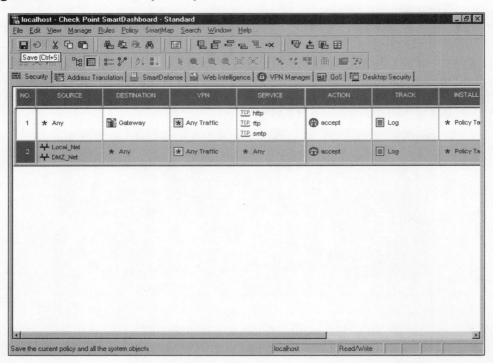

Summary

Network Address Translation gives you flexibility and protection within your architectures. It allows you to conserve valuable IP address space and prevents your production servers from full exposure to Internet threats.

Check Point provides two primary methods for deploying NAT: *Hide* mode and *Static* mode. Having said that, you are capable of manually configuring your rules or are able to take advantage of Check Point's intuitive automatic configuration utilities. Either method delivers the same end result.

Hide mode allows you to configure your gateway to translate outbound traffic so that your internal hosts may access the Internet (or other external hosts) without revealing your private topology. In addition, *Hide* NAT provides the necessary address change that is needed for proper routing on public networks.

Static mode provides similar address hiding, but permits you to offer services on your internal or DMZ servers. This option places a one-to-one relationship between two hosts and the gateway redirects all transactions bound for the public address to the coordinating internal address.

Not only does the gateway handle basic address translation needs, it also has the capacity to conduct advanced port translation so that you make optimal use of your minimal IP address allocation. Port translation provides the necessary means to utilize a single address for multiple services hosted on one or more servers.

Now that you have learned to configure NAT with FireWall-1, you will be able to deliver advanced security for your networks. The tools you use for NAT help you to protect your networks from disclosure and minimize your hosts from exposure to the outside world. NAT is a key instrument in supplying a sound, optimal security policy.

Solutions Fast Track

Global Properties

☑ The **Global Properties** setting tab allows you to configure the options that affect the gateway as a whole. Since version NG, the gateway now translates addresses on the client side by default. To retain compatibility with older versions (in the case of an upgrade), uncheck the **Translate destination on client side** boxes.

☑ A new setting in NGX allows you to **Merge manual proxy ARP configuration** entries with any automatic ARP configuration within your gateway. If you leave this box unchecked, then the gateway will ignore all of your manual proxy-ARP entries.

☑ Enabling the **Allow bidirectional NAT** option in the **Global Properties** lets us have connections where the gateway translates both the source address and the destination address.

Configuring Dynamic Hide Mode NAT

☑ *Dynamic (Hide)* mode conceals one or more protected host addresses behind one single routable IP address. You can hide all your protected hosts behind the gateway's external IP address or an alternative IP address.

☑ *Hide* mode allows your internal protected hosts to initiate outbound connections without exposing them to inbound connection requests.

☑ When using addresses other than your gateway's external interface address, you must consider any ARP and/or routing issues. Sometimes, it may be necessary to contact your upstream vendor and have them add routes to assist with proper connectivity.

Configuring Static Mode NAT

☑ Use *Static* NAT to enable external clients to initiate connections with your internal protected hosts. In addition, you can use *Static* NAT to individually identify outbound connections by allotting a one-to-one NAT for an internal host.

☑ Unlike *Hide* mode NAT, *Static* NAT does not modify the source port and has a one-to-one ratio of translation.

☑ Take into consideration routing and ARP issues when using *Static* NAT. You may have to manually add proxy-ARP entries and/or modify routing tables on the gateway or other network devices.

Configuring Automatic NAT

☑ FireWall-1 allows you to create NAT rules by modifying an object's properties. You are able to configure *Static* or *Hide* NAT for several types of objects in your firewall.

☑ Automatic NAT simplifies the creation of NAT rules. It also allows you to understand an object's full configuration by viewing its properties.

☑ Using automatic NAT saves you the trouble of adding ARP entries (when global properties are enabled). As is normally the case, NAT rules may induce routing and ARP issues so this benefit reduces the configuration steps you need to complete in order to successfully set up NAT.

Configuring Port Translation

☑ Utilizing port translation allows you to advertise many services while only having a single routable IP address. This is useful if you have a small network, or if you just want to minimize exposure to your internal servers.

☑ Just as you do with all inbound NAT rules, you need to associate a rule from your Security rule base to allow the inbound traffic to the internal servers (with private IP addresses). With port translation, you have to configure the Security rule for connections inbound to the NAT (publicly routable) address instead of the host's real (private internal) address.

Frequently Asked Questions

The following Frequently Asked Questions, answered by the authors of this book, are designed to both measure your understanding of the concepts presented in this chapter and to assist you with real-life implementation of these concepts. To have your questions about this chapter answered by the author, browse to **www.syngress.com/solutions** and click on the **"Ask the Author"** form.

Q: When I configure NAT rules, should I do it manually, or use the object's properties to generate them automatically?

A: Since the result of either method is similar, you should choose whichever method you feel more comfortable with. Remember that manual NAT gives you more control over how and when NAT occurs. Automatic NAT populates the rule base itself, but is easy to use.

Q: How do I know whether I should use *Hide* mode or *Static* mode?

A: Remember, the primary use for *Static* mode is to allow external clients to initiate connections to your protected hosts. If you just need to give internal protected clients the ability to establish outbound connections (to the Internet), then *Hide* mode satisfies your needs without exposing your hosts.

Q: When does the firewall create an ARP entry for me, and when do I need to manually create proxy-ARP entries?

A: If you are configuring NAT via an object's properties (host, network, address range), the firewall will automatically generate an ARP entry for your NAT address, providing the proper global properties are enabled (automatic ARP). If you are creating NAT rules manually, then you must modify the *local.arp* file to include a proxy-ARP entry for your NAT address.

Q: Does routing really affect my NAT configuration?

A: When you use NAT addresses that exceed your defined subnet it may be necessary to modify routing tables to properly reach these hosts. Like any address (real or NAT), other hosts must know how to get to it via an entry in its routing table. In most cases, clients use a default route (next hop router). It is usually these devices that have dynamic or static routes to external devices. If your router is not advertising a route to your NAT address, you must modify your tables to include this new NAT address.

Q: I have many NAT rules, and it takes some time to compile them. What can I do to speed things up?

A: You can start by taking advantage of the gateway's ability to hide all internal clients behind its external address. If you have individual rules that hide several networks, address ranges, and other objects behind the gateway's address, you can eliminate them by taking advantage of this option. All *Static* entries will still apply, and you reduce the total number of entries for the rule base. Also, you can combine consecutive subnets into a larger subnet or an address range.

Q: My management console is managing several firewalls, and our internal 10.x.x.x address space spans several local and remote sites. How can I keep my NAT Rule Base simple?

A: Either use the gateway properties to hide all internal addresses or create an object for the entire 10.0.0.0/8 network and hide it behind 0.0.0.0. This accomplishes the same thing in that all hosts will be hidden behind each gateway's external address.

Q: I'm having issues when connecting to my gateway over our virtual private network (VPN) because the firewall is hiding our internal networks. What can I do to solve this?

A: Sometimes you need to create manual NAT rules that instruct the gateway to not translate your internal addresses when speaking to certain addresses. In this case, you create a NAT rule where the Original Packet fields match the VPN packets and the Translated Packet section maintains all three columns (Source, Destination, and Service) as **Original**. You can also edit the VPN community's Advanced VPN Properties in the Advanced settings, and select **Disable NAT inside the VPN community**.

Q: Why can't I get to any of my DMZ servers after I rebooted my firewall?

A: Two words: routing and ARP. Check to make sure that your gateway is answering for all NAT addresses by examining its ARP entries. Also, go through your routing table to make sure that your gateway knows how to get to your hosts. It may be the case that a route you added was not configured correctly and was lost on the reboot. In Windows, use the −p option to survive a reboot. In *nix servers, place the static route entry into a startup file. With Nokia, use Voyager to make your changes and be sure to click **Apply** then **Save** before exiting.

Q: How can I troubleshoot my NAT configuration?

A: Here is a list of steps that you can follow to start investigating NAT issues. If you are having issues using ping, open SmartView Tracker to examine your log entries for dropped or rejected packets:

1. Verify internal connectivity by pinging the host's true address from the firewall. If this is unsuccessful, check your physical connection through the cable or a switch configuration.

2. Verify external connectivity by pinging the host's routable address from the firewall. If this is unsuccessful, look at the routing on your firewall. If all seems correct there, review the NAT rules to make sure that they are correct.

3. From the host, verify that you have connectivity by pinging the firewall's internal address. If not, then check the cabling or switch configuration.

4. From the host, verify that you have connectivity by pinging the firewall's external address. If you cannot, make sure that your default route is correct on this host and any in-between routing devices.

5. From the host, verify outbound connectivity by pinging the firewall's next hop router address. If unsuccessful, check that NAT is taking place as expected and that the firewall is ARP'ing for the NAT address.

Chapter 9

Authentication

Solutions in this chapter:

- **Authentication Overview**
- **Users and Administrators**
- **User Authentication**
- **Session Authentication**
- **Client Authentication**

☑ **Summary**

☑ **Solutions Fast Track**

☑ **Frequently Asked Questions**

Introduction

Using Check Point NGX, you can control the traffic coming into or going out of your networks. A good definition of your networks, hosts, gateways, and services allows you to have granular control of traffic through the Security Gateway. However, there are times when you will need or want to authenticate specific users who are accessing your resources.

For example, an administrator might have to download privileged files using a restricted user's workstation, and would need to be granted special privileges for a specific amount of time. Networks that use DHCP with different classes of users in the same network would need to authenticate privileged users to grant them access to the resources they need. Enterprises might have a need for registering in the log the specific user accessing a specific Web site.

With authentication, Check Point NGX's features are greatly expanded and complement already strong security with the ability to implement security on a per user basis. Once you understand how NGX Authentication works, you will probably find many uses for it in your environment.

Authentication Overview

Check Point NGX works based on the information it has to permit or deny a connection. The firewall has no knowledge of which user is logged into a Microsoft Active Directory, or if a user is moving among different machines. To be able to authenticate a particular user that is crossing the firewall, it needs additional information to match the user and the connection. The main topic of this chapter addresses the best way to authenticate users so they can access privileged resources. There have not been many changes between how authentication works in NG with Application Intelligence and how it works in NGX, and we list the major changes in this chapter.

We will first address the issue of which users can authenticate. Check Point NGX is flexible enough to authenticate users created in various sources, databases, or external directory servers. We will then examine the different types of authentication that NGX allows, which are called User, Session, and Client Authentication. These authentication schemes are for unencrypted authentication.

Using Authentication in Your Environment

Using Authentication involves additional configuration of the firewall and planning an environment that allows users to access the resources they need. Some of the environments that can benefit from authentication include the following.

- You use DHCP without IP reservations in your network, but you need to give a few of your users access to special resources.

- Your CIO wants strict logging of the traffic habits of your users, and so you need your log to contain the username of every connection from your internal networks.

- A support technician needs to download drivers and antivirus programs from the Internet, on machines in a restricted segment that are not allowed to access the Internet.

- You have an extranet site and want to add an additional layer of password security via your firewall.

Users and Administrators

Think of a user as an entity: Bob, Peter, and so forth. To recognize (or authenticate) a user, the user either needs to know something (a password) or have something (a digital certificate). This chapter focuses on passwords, since Digital Certificates are for VPNs only. Most companies already have some sort of user database (MS Active Directory, a RADIUS server, etc.), and would like to integrate this database with their firewall, through the use of an Authentication Scheme.

Managing Users and Administrators

Before you can authenticate users, you need to define them and place them in groups. Check Point NGX is very flexible in this sense. You can use NGX's built-in user database, as well as external user directories. Let's first focus on the built-in database, which you'll probably use the most or at least have to interact with most often.

There are two ways you can access and edit the user database. You can access the *Manage Users and Administrators* dialog from the **Manage | Users and Administrators** menu (look at Figure 9.1). This dialog includes a listing of all user-related objects: users, groups, templates, administrators, external users groups, LDAP, and so on.

Figure 9.1 Manage Users and Administrators Dialog

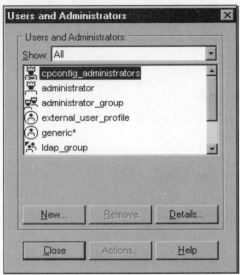

You can also select the *Users* tab in the Object Tree, and then expand the different entity classes to edit their objects (as in Figure 9.2). You can right-click on any entity class to add new objects.

Figure 9.2 Object Tree Listing of User Entities and Their Icons

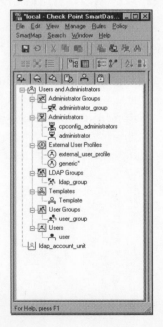

The first item you will see in the Manage Administrators dialog box will be a yellow icon named *cpconfig_administrators*. It represents the administrators configured by the *cpconfig* utility in the SmartCenter server. In NGX, you can define only one administrator via cpconfig (in the cpconfig menu, it now says Administrator instead of previous versions' Administrators). If you have upgraded from NG, you can migrate the existing cpconfig administrators to the SmartDashboard by using the **cp_admin_convert** command in the SmartCenter server (you need to use expert mode in SecurePlatform).

Each entity that you can create in the Users and Administrators dialog box is represented by a different icon. Administrators have crowns over them, groups are represented by two users, templates are outlines, and external users have a circle around them. Look at Figure 9.2 to identify the different icons.

Permission Profiles

Before you create an administrator, you need to create a *Permissions Profile*. Go to the **Manage | Permission Profiles** dialog, and select **New.. | Permissions Profile...** (see Figure 9.3).

Figure 9.3 The Permissions Profiles Dialog

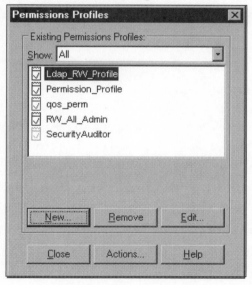

In the *General* tab, you can name the profile, select a color and enter a comment. In the *Permissions* tab, you allow access via two methods:

- **SmartPortal and Console Applications** Administrators can use SmartDashboard, and all the Smart management applications, as well as the SmartPortal web interface.

- **SmartPortal only** Administrators can access only the SmartPortal web interface, which is read-only and designed for auditors and restricted administrators.

In the *Permissions* tab, you also can choose the following profiles (see Figure 9.4):

- **None** Use this to disable an administrator's permissions.

- **Read/Write All** Allows full access to all NGX management applications. A Read/Write All profile can also select Manage Administrators, which will allow the administrator to create, modify, and delete other administrators from the SmartDashboard. It will also grant access to the Permission to Install setting for objects.

- **Read-Only All** Administrators will be able to read every configuration, but won't be able to change anything.

- **Customized** Here you can create a personalized profile for administrators with very specific functions. The permissions for each option can be None (disable the option with the Check Box next to the item), Read Only, and Read/Write.

You can select the following specific functions for a customized profile:

- **SmartUpdate** Administrators can use SmartUpdate for managing product updates and assigning licenses. An administrator with Read/Write SmartUpdate access will automatically have Read/Write access to the Objects, LDAP and Users databases, the Security and QoS policies, and the Log Consolidator, Eventia Reporter, and UserAuthority Web Access.

- **Objects Database** Working with the networks objects and services in the SmartDashboard interface.

- **Check Point Users Database** Working with the internal user database.

- **LDAP Users Database** Working with an external LDAP database using the SmartDirectory functionality (which requires a separate license).

- **Security Policy** Working with the Security and Address Translation rules and installing a policy (with Read/Write access).

- **QoS Policy** Working with the QoS rules and installing a policy (with Read/Write access).

- **Log Consolidator** Working with the Consolidation Policy. Eventia Reporter uses that policy for compiling information from the logs.

- **Eventia Reporter** Working with the Eventia Reporter tables.

- **Monitoring** Access to the SmartView Monitor database for statuses.

- **UserAuthority Web Access** Working with the UserAuthority Web Access product.

- **ROBO Gateways Database** Working with Remote Office/Branch Office Gateways, using the SmartLSM (Large Scale Manager) application.

- **Events Database** Working with the Eventia Analyzer database.

- **Event Correlation Policy** Working with the Eventia Analyzer Events database.

- **Track Logs** Accessing the Traffic Log and Active sessions in the SmartView Tracker. Users with Read/Write permissions can purge and switch the logs, and to Block Intruders from the Active Sessions page.

- **Audit Logs** Accessing the Active sessions and Audit Logs in the SmartView Tracker. Users with Read/Write permissions can purge and switch the logs, and block intruders from the Active Sessions page.

Figure 9.4 The Permissions Tab of the Permissions Profile

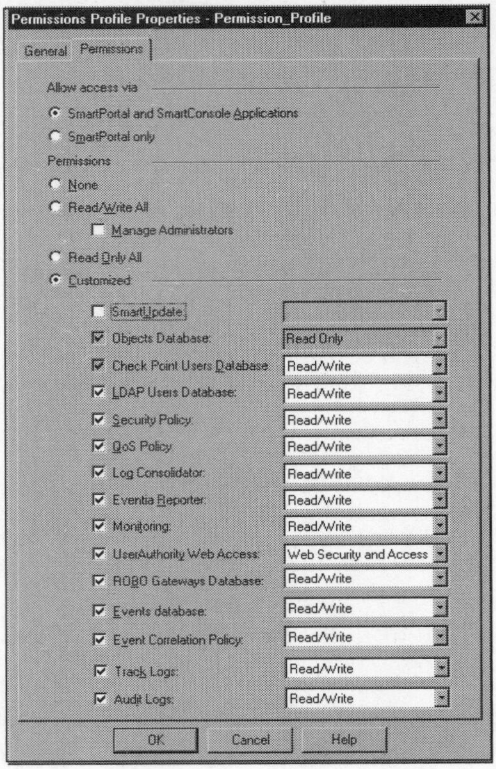

Administrators

The administrators are the users who have access to the configuration of the firewall. Depending on the Permissions Profile assigned to the administrators, they may or may not have permission to read and write to different parts of the security policy. Once you create or edit an administrator, you'll see the following tabs.

General Tab

In the **General** tab of the Administrator you can give a name to the administrator and select a previously created Permissions Profile. You can also click **New...** and directly create a new profile. **View Permissions Profile** allows you to view and edit existing profiles. Look at Figure 9.5.

Figure 9.5 Creating a New Administrator

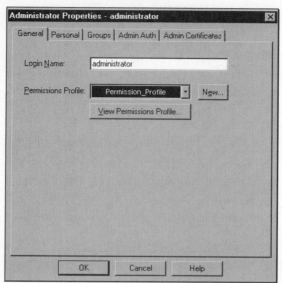

Personal Tab

You will find a **Personal** tab for both administrators and users. The **Expiration Date** field (in dd–mm–yyyy format) is used to set a valid time period for an administrator. For example, you can use an administrator with a set expiration date for an auditor that needs to review your policies during the next month. By default in NGX, the expiration date is December 31, 2008.

Enter a Comment for the Administrator and select a Color for the display of its icon. These fields are for informational use only.

Groups

You can select which Administrators Groups this administrator belongs to. You can **Add** and **Remove** from the **Available Groups** and the **Belongs to Groups** boxes.

Admin Auth

Here you can select what **Authentication Scheme** will be used for administrators, basically what you check the password against. The options are Undefined, SecurID, Check Point Password, OS Password, RADIUS, and TACACS. If you select Undefined, then the administrator will not be able to authenticate using a password, only a digital certificate.

Admin Certificates

One of the advantages of using SmartDashboard administrators is that you can implement authentication via digital certificates generated by the Internal Certificate Authority (ICA). In this tab, you will see the certificate **State** (there is no certificate for this object, or Object has a certificate), and the Distinguished Name if it has a certificate, as in Figure 9.6.

Figure 9.6 The Certificates Tab

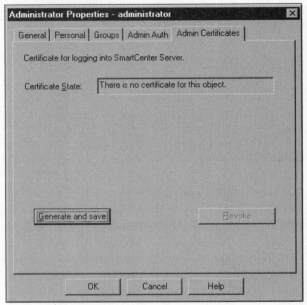

If there is no certificate for the administrator, you can click **Generate and Save**. You will see a prompt warning that the generation cannot be undone unless revoking the certificate, and then you can enter and verify the password for the certificate. Finally, you will select where to save the .P12 file in your hard drive. This file you can distribute to the appropriate administrators, save on a USB device, and so on. Once the administrator has a certificate, you use View… to see its details, or Revoke to eliminate the certificate.

Administrator Groups

You can create Administrator Groups and place administrators in them. You can use Administrator Groups by editing a Check Point Gateway, using the **Advanced | Permissions to Install** tab (see Figure 9.7). Here you can **Remove** the **Any** group from the selected groups and add the specific Administrator Groups you want to grant install access to. Only administrators with Manage Administrators permission can modify these properties.

Figure 9.7 The Permissions to Install Tab

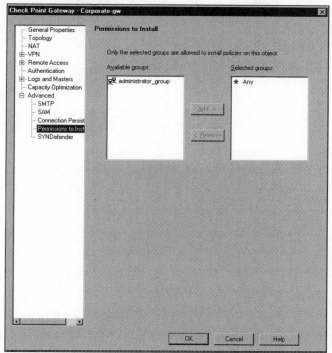

User Templates

Before you create users, you have to understand templates. Since there are many options to configure on users, templates save you time by preconfiguring options at the time of user creation. If you change an option on a template, it does not affect users already created from that template, only future users. The Standard template is preconfigured for quickly adding a user if you don't want to go into details. Let's look at the different Tabs you see once you select **New... | Template...**.

General

Select the **Name** the template will have. This is the name you will use when selecting **New... | User from Template...**.

Personal

The **Expiration Date** field (in dd-mm-yyyy format) is used to set a valid time period for users. For example, you can use a template for a group of temporary employees that will leave the company at a specific date. By default in NGX, the expiration date is December 31, 2008.

Enter a **Comment** for the Template and select a **Color** for the display of its icon. These fields are for informational use only.

Groups

You can select which User Groups the users will belong to. You can **Add** and **Remove** from the **Available Groups** and the **Belongs to Groups** boxes.

Authentication

Here you can select what form of **Authentication Scheme** will be used for these users. The options are Undefined, SecurID, Check Point Password, OS Password, RADIUS, and TACACS. If you select Undefined, then the user will not be able to authenticate using a password, only a digital certificate. You will only be able to select the Authentication Scheme, but won't be able to enter a Password for the Template, for security reasons.

Location

Location refers to the users' allowed sources and destinations. You will be able to select **Network Objects** and move them to either the **Source** or **Destination** boxes, or leave them as **Any**, as in Figure 9.8. The location then becomes a restriction as to where the users can connect from (i.e., IT_Users restricted to IT_Networks source location), and where the users can connect to (i.e., Extranet_Users restricted to Extranet_Servers destination). This field can give you flexibility in having few authentication rules that behave differently for specific users and groups. It's a bit complex to keep track of, but if you need it, it's very useful. When you configure an authentication rule, you can decide whether the rule has to intersect with the location of the users, or it can ignore it (we'll look at that later).

Figure 9.8 The Location Tab

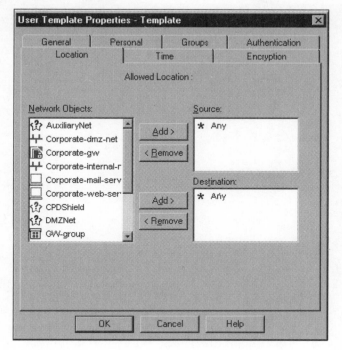

Time

You can select what day of the week and range of time **User may connect at**. Although you can select several **Day in week options**, you are limited to a single range for **Time of Day**.

Encryption

Encryption is used for VPN Remote Access, and will be covered in Chapter 12, "SecuRemote, SecureClient, and Integrity." If you select **IKE** for **Client Encryption**, the user will be able to participate in the Remote Access community.

User Groups

You can create User Groups and place users in them. You can select a **Name**, **Comment**, and **Color** for the group, and **Add** and **Remove** from the **Not in Group** to the **In Group** boxes, as in Figure 9.9.

Figure 9.9 Creating a User Group

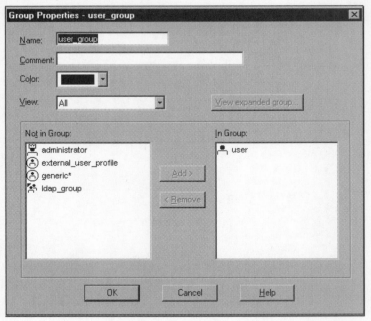

User Groups can also contain other groups in a nested fashion. When you add a group to another group, NGX will ask **Would you like to add each member of the group separately?** and each group would be expanded in the new group. With nested groups, if you change a group the change will be reflected in the parent group, but that will not happen if you expand the group.

Check Point NGX does not reference individual users directly in rules or object properties, so if you have a user, you will want to place them in the appropriate group. If they're not in any group, they're still part of the *All Users* group.

Users

When you want to create a user, you have to work based on an existing template. Once you select **New… | User from Template…** (see Figure 9.10), you can select the initial template you want and then you will see a dialog box with many tabs. Let's look at them.

Figure 9.10 Creating a User from a Template

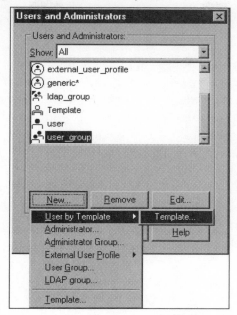

General

Select the **Login Name** for the users. It can have special characters in it, as well as spaces and periods, and long names.

Personal

The **Expiration Date** field (in dd-mm-yyyy format) is used to set a valid time period for a user. By default in NGX, the expiration date is December 31, 2008. Enter a **Comment** and select a **Color** for the display of its icon. These fields will be prepopulated with information from the Template.

Groups

You can select which User Groups the user belongs to. You can **Add** and **Remove** from the **Available Groups** and the **Belongs to Groups** boxes. The tab will be prepopulated according to the Template.

Authentication

Here you can select which **Authentication Scheme** the user will have. The options are Undefined, SecurID, Check Point Password, OS Password, RADIUS, and

TACACS. If you select Undefined, then the user will not be able to authenticate using a password, only a digital certificate. If you select RADIUS or TACACS, you can select which server to use for verification.

If you select Check Point Password, you can click **Enter Password** to assign and verify it. The passwords should be four to eight characters in length. Check Point stores a hash for these passwords in the internal database. A hash function is an irreversible, one-way, highly-sensitive-to-change function, specifically the UNIX *crypt* function, which can use only eight characters with DES-based encryption. There is virtually no probability that two strings will have the same hash value, even if they differ by only a letter. When a user inputs a password, the gateway compares the hash of the password with the hash stored in the user database to authenticate the user. For those technically inclined, when a user's password is modified, Check Point creates a random salt, which is then returned in the first two characters of the hashed result. You could programmatically create a file that uses the crypt function to create a large list of users and password that can then be imported with the *fwm dbimport* command.

Location

Here you can select specific **Source** and **Destination** locations for the users. The fields will be prepopulated from the template. Remember that when you configure an authentication rule, you can decide whether the rule has to intersect with the location of the users, or it can ignore it.

Time

You can select what day of the week and range of time **User may connect at**. Although you can select several **Day in week options**, you are limited to a single range for **Time of Day**. The fields will be prepopulated from the template.

Certificates

In this tab, you will see the **Certificate State** (the message can be *There is no certificate for this object*, *The certificate is pending for the* user, or *Object has a certificate*), and the **Distinguished Name** if a certificate exists. Digital Certificates for users apply only for Remote Access VPNs, and will be covered in the SecuRemote/SecureClient chapter.

Encryption

Encryption is used for VPN Remote Access, and will be covered in Chapter 12. If you select IKE, the user will be able to participate in the Remote Access community.

External User Profiles

If you're working with external directory servers (RADIUS, TACACS, OS Password, SecurID), you would still need to define each user that exists in the external directory server, and select the appropriate authentication method for the user. This can be a tedious and error-prone process. By creating *External User Profiles*, you can deal with users who are not defined in the Check Point user database. If users are recognized by an external directory server, they will be granted permissions based on the appropriate External User Profile.

Match by Domain

This profile allows you to selectively query an external user database base on the Domain that the user enters. The important properties are in the General Tab.

　　If you use Distinguished Name (DN) format, you can select a specific organizational unit, organization, or country to authorize. Or, you can use Free Format, where the domain will be separated from the username by a character like @ or \ (for Microsoft), either before or after the username. In Free Format you can choose Any Domain as Acceptable, or a specific Domain Name you select. Finally, select whether to omit the domain name when requesting authorization at the external directory server. See Figure 9.11 for details.

Figure 9.11 External User Profiles | Match by Domain

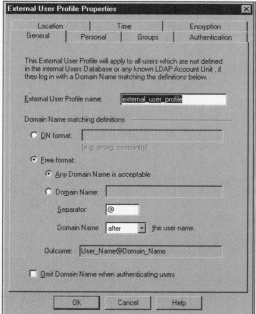

The other tabs in the External User Profile (Personal, Groups, Authentication, Location, Time, Encryption) function as they do in the normal user entity. Remember that in this scenario, you're leaving authentication and authorization decisions to an external entity.

Match All Users

If you don't need to be selective of a domain users have to log with, you can use the *Match All Users External Profile*. It is named *generic*★ and will match any user recognized by the external directory server. Remember that in this scenario, you're leaving authentication and authorization decisions to an external entity.

The other tabs in the External User Profile (Personal, Groups, Authentication, Location, Time, Encryption) function as they do in a normal user entity.

LDAP Group

If you are using SmartDirectory LDAP integration, you can create LDAP groups. You will give a name to the group, a comment and a color, and the Account Unit that the LDAP Group belongs to. You should have created the LDAP Account Unit from the Manage Servers and OPSEC Applications dialog box.

In the Group's Scope, you can select to recognize all the Account-Unit users, or only those in a certain subtree, branch, and prefix, or only a group in a branch, with a DN prefix. You can also apply a filter to create a dynamic group (for example, all users in ou=Access).

Understanding Authentication Schemes

Check Point NGX is flexible enough to work with several external directory servers, where a user entity can be defined in the Internal Check Point database, but the password is verified from different sources. Check Point refers to these as Authentication Schemes.

Undefined

The Undefined Authentication Scheme is used for disabling the user's ability to enter a password. This will force users to employ strong authentication with a digital certificate.

SecurID

Selecting SecurID as the Authentication Scheme will enable Check Point NGX to become an ACE/Agent for RSA's SecurID Tokens. This integration will require use of a special *sdconf.rec* generated by the ACE server, and will allow you to enter new PIN numbers and reauthenticate often to secure servers. However, it's a lot more difficult to configure than through SecurID's RADIUS interface.

Check Point Password

If you select Check Point Password (called VPN-1 & FireWall-1 Password previously), you will enter the user's password directly into NGX's internal database. Passwords are four to eight characters in length. Be aware that the only way to assign or change passwords is through the SmartDashboard interface.

RADIUS

The *Remote Authentication Dial-In User Service* (RADIUS) is a standard protocol that can authenticate users with a RADIUS server that holds a database. The RADIUS protocol is very flexible and relatively secure. It uses a specific secret key for securing the authentication and only authorized clients can request authentication from the server. You can also set up backup servers in case one of them is out of service.

To configure RADIUS Authentication, first create a RADIUS Server from the **Manage | Servers and OPSEC Applications...** dialog as in Figure 9.12. Select **New... | RADIUS...** to create the server. Input the appropriate data in the **Name**, **Comment**, and **Color.** For **Host**, select the physical server that is running the RADIUS server. If you don't have the server created, use the **New...** button to create a new node. Select the **Service** to use, either NEW-RADIUS (the official port number) or RADIUS (the most common port number used). The **Shared Secret** is a password used to secure the information sent between the Check Point Gateways and the RADIUS server(s). You can select the **Version** to use, either version 1.0 or 2.0. Also select a **Priority**, to know which server to use first if there is more than one available. You can also create **RADIUS groups** for high availability and load sharing. Figure 9.13 shows the dialog box for creating a RADIUS server.

Figure 9.12 The Manage Servers and OPSEC Applications Dialog

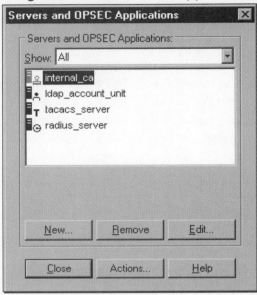

Figure 9.13 Creating a RADIUS Server

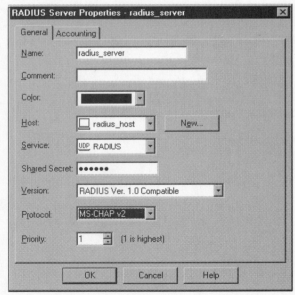

TIP

New for RADIUS support in NGX is being able to select a RADIUS **Protocol**, either PAP or MS-CHAP v2, for improved Microsoft compatibility. Also new is support for RADIUS' accounting features. If you enable **IP Pool Management** (used in VPN environments), the RADIUS server can assign IPs to users.

TACACS

The *Terminal Access Controller Access Control System* is a standard protocol that can authenticate users with an external user database. To configure TACACS Authentication, first create a TACACS Server from the **Manage | Servers and OPSEC Applications...** dialog. Select **New... | TACACS...** and input the appropriate data in the **Name**, **Comment** and **Color,** as in Figure 9.14. For **Host**, select the physical server that is running the TACACS server. If you don't have the server created, use the **New...** button to create a new Node. Select the **Type** of server used, either TACACS or TACACS+, which is more secure. If selecting TACACS+ you can also enter a **Secret Key** for encryption. Finally select the **Service** to use (UDP TACACS or TCP TACACSPLUS).

Figure 9.14 Creating a TACACS Server

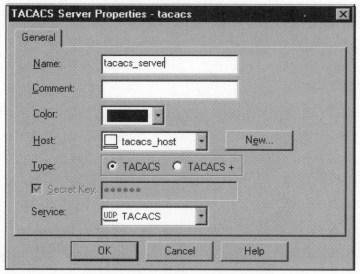

Tools & Traps…

Using Microsoft Internet Authentication Service (IAS)

Microsoft Windows Servers (NT, 2000, and 2003) have a built-in component called the Internet Authentication Service (IAS). It is basically a RADIUS service integrated into the NT Domain or the Active Directory. RADIUS authentication does not require a Check Point SmartDirectory license. To make the connection between IAS and NGX:

1. Create the appropriate RADIUS Server in the SmartDashboard. In the **Start | Programs | Administrative Tools | Internet Authentication Service** management console, add a new **RADIUS client**. The IP address should be the firewall gateway's IP facing the RADIUS server. If you have a cluster, add a client for each cluster member. Input the same **Shared Secret** you defined when creating the RADIUS server in the SmartDashboard.

2. In the Remote Access Policies, edit one of the policies listed (in NT and 2000 you'll see only one, in 2003 select the one for Connections to other access servers). **Edit the Profile** and go to the **Authentication** tab. Select either Unencrypted Authentication or Microsoft Encrypted Authentication version 2, which is more secure. In the **Advanced** tab of the profile, eliminate all attributes.

3. Modify the Active Directory users to allow connections. Go to **Start | Settings | Control Panel | Administrative tools | Active Directory Users and Computers**, edit the properties of the user you want to authenticate using RADIUS. In the **Dial-In** tab, select **Allow Access** and **Apply**.

4. In the SmartDashboard, create a generic* user (an external user profile that matches all users) with RADIUS authentication. Include the generic* user in User Groups you insert in the rulebase.

5. You can differentiate among RADIUS users by setting the *add_radius_groups* property with the GUIdbEdit application, and then configuring the RADIUS server to send a Class attribute for different user groups. In SmartDashboard create groups named *RAD_<ClassAttribute>* and integrate them in the rulebase.

User Authentication

User Authentication allows privileged use of some common Internet protocols, with little change to the user experience. It works by intercepting connections that are passing through the firewall (Check Point calls this "folding" the connection), and modifying the traffic in such a way that the firewall asks users to identify themselves before allowing the connection to pass through. Since the users request a connection to their final destinations, User Authentication is a type of *Transparent* authentication; in other words, the user doesn't need to go through an intermediate process. Also be aware that this type of authentication is very demanding on the firewall, if it needs to fold a large number of connections.

Because NGX needs to modify the traffic itself, it can do so only with four specific services that it can understand well: HTTP, FTP, Telnet, and RLOGIN. These services belong to the *Authenticated* group in the predefined Check Point services. When one of these services is used to access a restricted resource, and there's a rule configured to allow User Auth for that connection, the traffic is modified so the user can enter a password to enable the traffic. For Telnet, FTP, and RLOGIN, the user sees an intermediary prompt from the firewall, and once the user authenticates, a new connection to the final destination is made. In the case of HTTP traffic, the firewall instructs the user's browser to display an authentication dialog.

User Authentication is performed on each connection so that if a machine is being shared by different users (for example, in a client/server or thin client environment) each user will authenticate his or her connection only, which is safe. Because the firewall needs to examine the traffic of these authenticated services, it requires more processing power from the firewall than Session and Client authentication.

Configuring User Authentication in the Rulebase

To allow user authentication, create a new rule. In the source field, select **Add User Access**, and add the user groups that will be able to authenticate using that rule. You can also select a restriction for the origin of the user connections. Add the appropriate **Destination** to that rule (if you want to authenticate all traffic to the Internet, leave it as **Any)**, select which **Services** you'll authenticate (remember, only HTTP, FTP, Telnet, or RLOGIN—if you enter any additional services, the policy will have compilation errors), select **User Auth** as the Action, and add appropriate **Track**, **Time**, and **Comment** configurations. See Figure 9.15 for a User Authentication Rule.

Figure 9.15 Create a User Authentication Rule

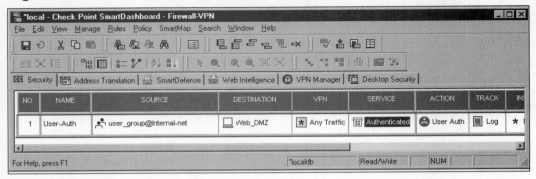

You should edit or verify the properties of the Action field in the User Authentication rule, as in Figure 9.16.

Figure 9.16 Properties of the User Authentication Action

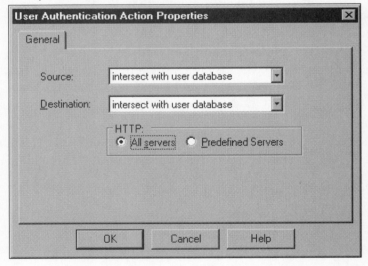

UserAuth | Edit Properties | General | Source

Source is used to control whether the Restrict To location in the source of the rule has to intersect the configured location of the user in the database, or if it can ignore the location. Select **Ignore** to override the user database.

UserAuth | Edit Properties | General | Destination

Destination is similar to Source, in which you can choose to ignore the user database so that if a user has a configured destination location, and that location does not intersect the destination of the rule, the authentication will still take place.

UserAuth | Edit Properties | General | HTTP

Here you can select whether you want to allow authentication to a restricted number of servers, or to any accessible machines. The default is **Predefined Server**. When Predefined Servers is selected, users will be able to access only the list of servers that can be defined in the **Policy | Global Properties | FireWall-1 | Security Servers** dialog. To be able to authenticate traffic to any destination on the Internet, you need to select **All Servers** in the properties of the User Auth action.

Interacting with User Authentication

Depending on the service you will authenticate (HTTP, FTP, Telnet, or RLOGIN), the way your users will authenticate is different. Remember that if users need to resolve Web addresses (e.g., www.checkpoint.com), they will need to have access for domain-udp requests through the firewall, or to an internal DNS server. Let's see what the user experience is for these services.

Telnet and RLOGIN

User Authentication for Telnet and RLOGIN is easy for the end user to understand. When a user tries a command like **telnet 172.29.109.1**, the firewall will intercept this command and present its own Telnet prompts, as in Figure 9.17. Once the user correctly authenticates, he or she will see the prompts from the original destination and can proceed accordingly.

Figure 9.17 Telnet User Authentication

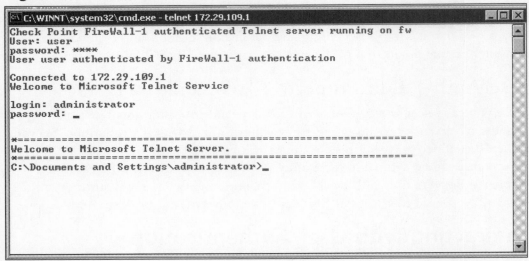

FTP

User Authentication for FTP is a bit more complex to understand. The user will still use the command **ftp 172.29.109.1**, which will be intercepted by the firewall's FTP security server, but the username will have to reflect the user that is authenticating at the FTP server (i.e., administrator), the user that is authenticating at the firewall (i.e., user), and the final destination of the FTP connection (even though it was used in the original ftp command). For example, in this case the username will be **administrator@user@172.29.109.1**, and the password will be the passwords of the FTP user separated by an @ sign from the password of the firewall user—**ftppassword@fwpassword**. Then a connection to the FTP server will be established. Look at Figure 9.18 for details.

Figure 9.18 FTP User Authentication

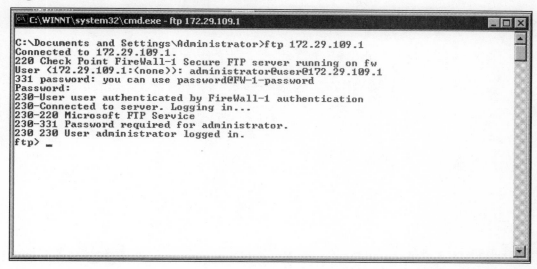

```
C:\WINNT\system32\cmd.exe - ftp 172.29.109.1

C:\Documents and Settings\Administrator>ftp 172.29.109.1
Connected to 172.29.109.1.
220 Check Point FireWall-1 Secure FTP server running on fw
User (172.29.109.1:(none)): administrator@user@172.29.109.1
331 password: you can use password@FW-1-password
Password:
230-User user authenticated by FireWall-1 authentication
230-Connected to server. Logging in...
230-220 Microsoft FTP Service
230-331 Password required for administrator.
230 230 User administrator logged in.
ftp> _
```

HTTP

User authentication for HTTP is simple for users to use. When activated, an HTTP connection that should be authenticated is modified by the firewall in such a way that the user's browser displays an authentication dialog box or prompt, using HTTP's authentication mechanism. The prompt says FW-1: No user. Once the user authenticates with this prompt, the requested site is displayed in the browser. Look at Figures 9.19 and 9.20 for examples using Microsoft Internet Explorer and Mozilla Firefox.

WARNING

Selecting User Authentication for HTTP traffic to the Internet will mean that a user might need to authenticate as much as 10 times before seeing a single web page, since current web pages usually reference images or code from other sites, and the browsers need to reauthenticate for each different site.

Figure 9.19 HTTP User Authentication with Microsoft Internet Explorer

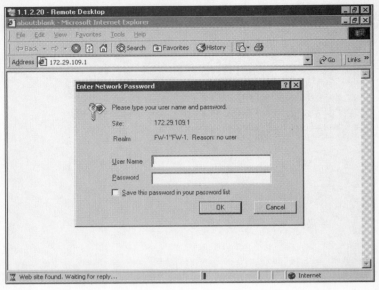

Figure 9.20 HTTP User Authentication with Mozilla Firefox

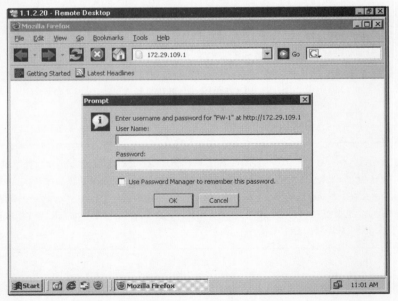

In Figure 9.21 you can look at the entry in the SmartView Tracker generated from the authenticated HTTP access.

Figure 9.21 SmartView Tracker Entry for HTTP User Authentication

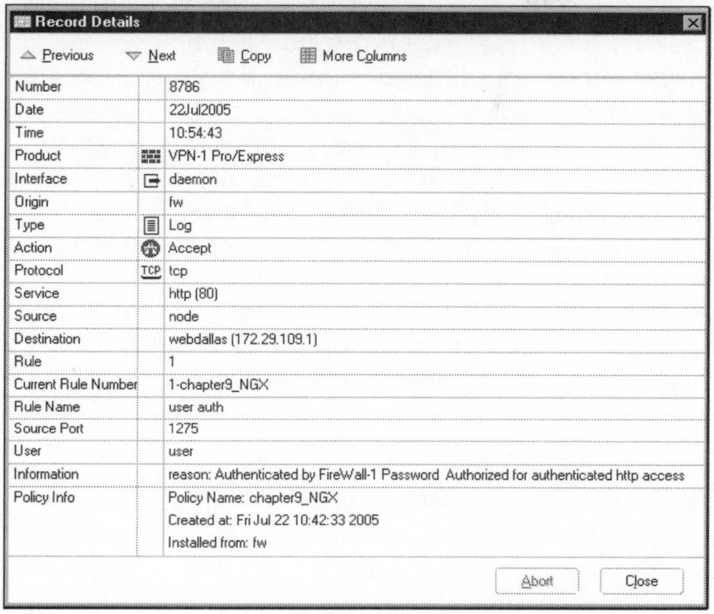

Record Details	
Number	8786
Date	22Jul2005
Time	10:54:43
Product	VPN-1 Pro/Express
Interface	daemon
Origin	fw
Type	Log
Action	Accept
Protocol	TCP tcp
Service	http (80)
Source	node
Destination	webdallas (172.29.109.1)
Rule	1
Current Rule Number	1-chapter9_NGX
Rule Name	user auth
Source Port	1275
User	user
Information	reason: Authenticated by FireWall-1 Password Authorized for authenticated http access
Policy Info	Policy Name: chapter9_NGX
	Created at: Fri Jul 22 10:42:33 2005
	Installed from: fw

Abort   Close

TIP

If the requested site itself requests a password, users can enter the list of usernames and passwords in reverse order, separated by an @ sign (or even @@ if you're crossing multiple authentication daemons). You might need to use this for Outlook Web Access.

Placing Authentication Rules

Check Point rules are sequential, which means that once a rule can be applied to traffic passing through the firewall, that rule is applied and the next packet is processed. However, there is one exception. If there is a rule that allows traffic to a destination, even if there is a rule that would require authentication before that rule, the traffic will pass through without the need for users to authenticate. The reason for this is that an authentication rule does not deny traffic that fails to authenticate.

TIP

The best scenario for User Authentication is when you need to grant authenticated access to a limited number of servers you control (i.e., your intranet or servers you host in a data center). The reason for this is that you can control the HTML code of those servers so that they do not refer sites different from their own. Your users will have an easy-to-understand experience and will authenticate only once. Remember that if your code refers to external servers, each connection will prompt the user to authenticate again.

 User Authentication for Telnet is also easy to understand and implement, as your users receive simple prompts to authenticate first to the firewall and then to their final destinations.

For example, look at Figure 9.22. If a machine in Net_Internal tries to access Web_DMZ, you would think that NGX would require the user to authenticate. If the user successfully authenticates, the traffic will be allowed. However, if the user doesn't successfully authenticate, NGX would continue processing rules and would find the Any to Web_DMZ rule, and would allow the traffic nevertheless. Therefore, NGX will not ask for authentication.

Figure 9.22 Placing User Authentication in the Rulebase

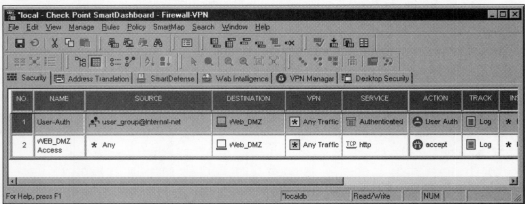

You could still require users in Net_Internal to authenticate before accessing Web_DMZ by creating a rule that will block the http traffic before it is allowed, as in Figure 9.23. This would force Check Point NGX to authenticate the users.

Figure 9.23 Forcing Users to Authenticate

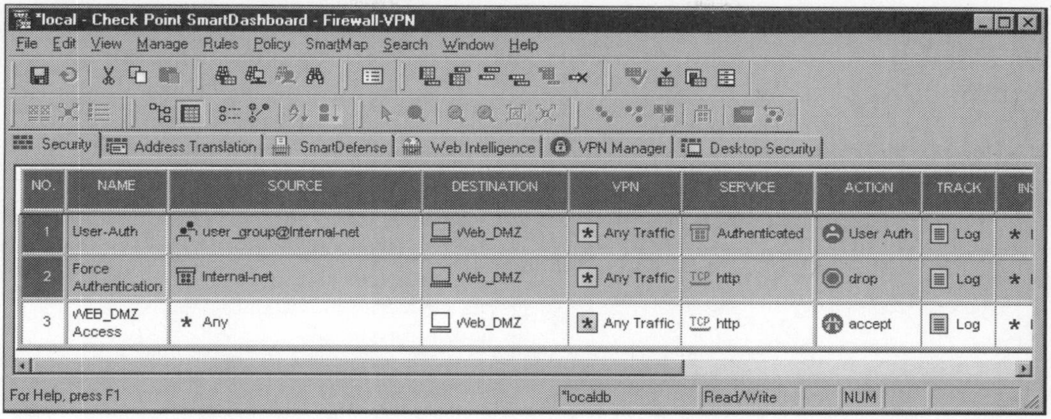

NO.	NAME	SOURCE	DESTINATION	VPN	SERVICE	ACTION	TRACK	INS
1	User-Auth	user_group@internal-net	Web_DMZ	Any Traffic	Authenticated	User Auth	Log	*
2	Force Authentication	Internal-net	Web_DMZ	Any Traffic	TCP http	drop	Log	*
3	WEB_DMZ Access	Any	Web_DMZ	Any Traffic	TCP http	accept	Log	*

Advanced Topics

User Authentication is a useful and convenient way to add an extra layer of verification to your users' connections. However, many times you will find that the default configuration breaks some connections or isn't secure enough for your needs. There are a myriad of configurations that you can make to User Authentication, and here we cover some of the most frequently requested ones.

Eliminating the Default Authentication Banner

You should always try to avoid disclosing unnecessary information. Check Point's default banners (the initial identification) for the FTP, Telnet, and RLOGIN security servers identify your firewall as a Check Point Firewall. You can avoid this by setting the *undo_msg* property to *true* in the dbedit *firewall_properties*, using the *dbedit* utility. From a command prompt (or in SecurePlatform's expert mode), run **dbedit,** log in with a username and password, and type **modify properties firewall_properties undo_msg true** and then **update properties firewall_properties**. After installing a policy, you will no longer see the default prompt. Be aware that some FTP clients need a banner for them to connect. In the following topic you can set your own banner.

Changing the Banner

Traffic that is intercepted by the firewall, be it FTP, Telnet, RLOGIN, or HTTP, displays a message from Check Point NGX requesting authentication. It is advisable to change this default message to a generic one that doesn't broadcast the firewall's identity, and that can include additional information for users. You can select a file to be presented instead of the regular banner for FTP, Telnet, and RLOGIN (not for HTTP), in the SmartDashboard's **Global Properties | Firewall | Security Servers** dialog box, as in Figure 9.24.

Figure 9.24 Changing the Security Server Banners

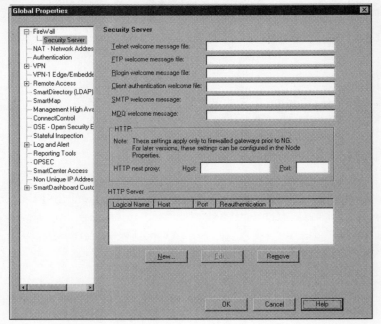

Use Host Header as Destination

If you are making HTTP connections, once the connection is authenticated, the firewall needs to redirect the original query to the intended destination. It does so by looking at the original URL's IP address and redirecting the user's browser to that IP. However, if the firewall resolves the destination URL to a nonroutable IP (i.e., the non-NAT'ed IP), or if the web server is configured to need the Host Header for access (i.e., a web hosting service that shares one IP with multiple web pages), then the connection will fail. To solve this, enable the setting *http_use_host_h_as_dst* using **Policy | Global Properties | SmartDashboard Customization | Configure | FireWall-1 | Web Security | HTTP Protocol**, as in Figure 9.25.

Figure 9.25 Changing Advanced Properties with SmartDashboard Customization

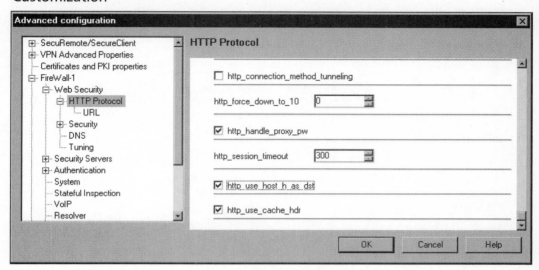

Tools & Traps…

User Authentication and Webmail Sites

When you activate user authentication, the firewall needs to process and modify the traffic going through it, using the Security Servers (which are better explained in the Content Security chapter). In HTTP's case in particular, having the traffic pass through the Security Server also means that the verifications that the firewall makes on HTTP traffic will be made on all authenticated traffic. These verifications might break some connections that your users regularly make. In particular, accessing sites like Hotmail and downloading attachments can be affected and should be thought of when activating this.

    Two changes you will need to make are enabling *http_allow_content_disposition* and *enable_propfind_method* settings in the **Policy | Global Properties | SmartDashboard Customization | Configure | FireWall-1 | Web Security | Security** section, as in Figure 9.26.

Figure 9.26 Allowing Webmail Sites through Security Servers

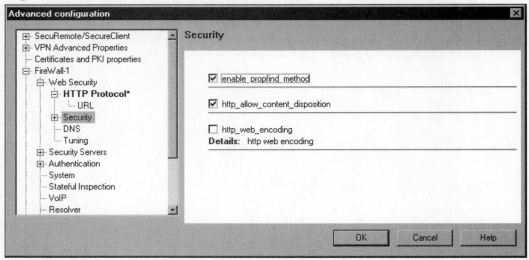

Session Authentication

Another method available for authentication in Check Point NGX is Session Authentication. This method uses a client program, called the Session Authentication Agent, which usually is installed on each machine that will be used for authentication. The Session Authentication Agent can be used for any service, and authenticates a particular session by the user. When the firewall encounters a rule with Session Authentication, it tries to query the appropriate machine using the FW1_snauth service on port 261. The Agent will then automatically present the user with an authentication dialog. Session Authentication combines User and Client Authentication, since it can authenticate per session for any service.

However, you need to consider that the Session Authentication Agent is a separate program that has to be installed in each user's machines, and that it is a Windows-Only program. Furthermore, the last available version is from NG Feature Pack 1 and there's no NGX version (yet).

> **WARNING**
>
> The firewall will try to authenticate all sessions that fall under a Session Authentication rule. If you configure a rule for authenticating any service to any destination, you might end up authenticating every DNS query and NBT broadcast sent, overloading the firewall authentication mechanism and network. Limit the number of services that use session authentication.

Configuring Session Authentication in the Rulebase

To allow session authentication, create a new rule. In the source field, select **Add User Access**, and then add the user groups that will be able to authenticate, and optionally restrict the location from where those groups can connect. Then, add the appropriate destination to that rule (if you want to authenticate all traffic to the Internet, leave it as **Any**), select which services you'll authenticate (try not to use **Any**), select **SessionAuth** as the Action, and add the appropriate Track, Time, and Comment configurations, as in Figure 9.27.

Figure 9.27 Configuring Session Authentication in the Rulebase

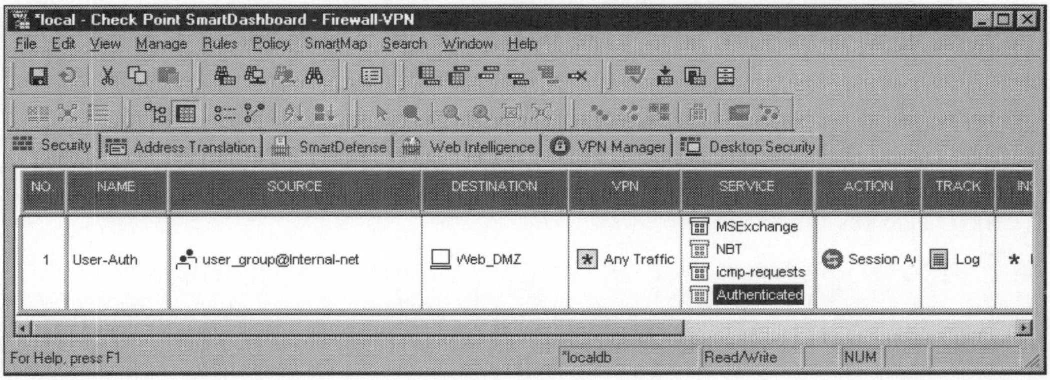

Let's take a look at the **Action** column of the Session Authentication Rule. Right-click on the field and select **Edit Properties**, as in Figure 9.28.

Figure 9.28 Properties of the Session Authentication Action

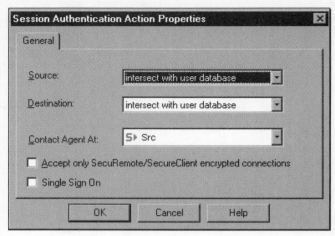

SessionAuth | Edit Properties | General | Source

Source is used to control whether the **Restrict To** location in the source of the rule has to intersect the configured location of the user in the database, or if it can ignore the location. Select **Ignore** to override the user database.

SessionAuth | Edit Properties | General | Destination

Destination is similar to Source, in which you can choose to ignore the user database so that if a user has a configured destination location, and that location does not intersect the destination of the rule, the authentication will still take place.

SessionAuth | Edit Properties | General | Contact Agent At

The Session Authentication Agent doesn't have to be installed in the machine that wants to access restricted resource (the source of the connection). You can define the location that Check Point NGX will query to authenticate a connection. The options are **Src** (the source of the connection), **Dst** (the destination of the connection), or you can select a specific host or gateway configured in the object tree. You would be able to configure this so that a supervisor grants access to specific resources, or for authenticating X Windows connections, or when a user wants to authenticate incoming connections.

SessionAuth | Edit Properties | General | Accept Only SecuRemote/ SecureClient Encrypted Connections

If you select this option, only users connecting via a remote access VPN will be able to authenticate.

SessionAuth | Edit Properties | General | Single Sign-On

Selecting this option will restrict authentication to UserAuthority and UserAuthority SecureAgent.

Configuring Session Authentication Encryption

One of the advantages of Session Authentication is that you can configure the Session Authentication Agent to communicate using SSL, to prevent password sniffing. You may change the **snauth_protocol** setting from the **Policy | Global Properties | SmartDashboard Customization | Configure | FireWall-1 | Authentication | Session Authentication** dialog box, as shown in Figure 9.29:

- **None** (or blank) No encryption of the authentication will be performed.

- **SSL** SSL will be active on all Session Authentication Agents. If you have an old agent you will not be able to authenticate.

- **SSL + None** SSL will be active on all Session Authentication Agents, but if you have an old agent you will be able to authenticate without encryption.

Figure 9.29 Changing the Session Authentication Protocol

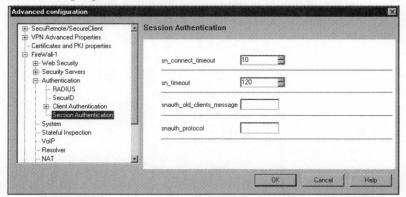

The Session Authentication Agent

The Agent is needed to use Session Authentication. It's a small 2MB program that installs without requiring a reboot. Since it is not included in the Check Point NGX CDs, you will have to download it from the Check Point User Center (usercenter.checkpoint.com) NG FP1 downloads section, as in Figure 9.30, or get it from a Check Point NG or Check Point NG with Application Intelligence CD.

Figure 9.30 Downloading the Session Authentication Agent

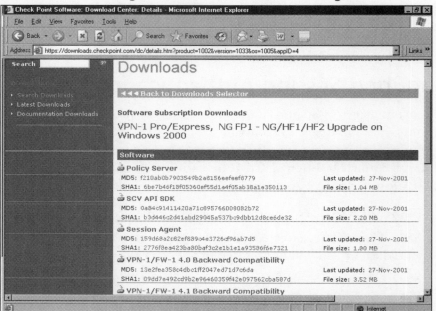

Once installed, the Session Authentication Agent will show up in the Windows Taskbar Notification Area as a blue circle with yellow and green arrows (see Figure 9.31), and open port 261 for listening to authentication requests from firewalls. If a request is received, the user automatically will see a Check Point prompt for username and password, making it easy for a novice user to understand what's going on.

Figure 9.31 The Session Authentication Agent Icon

If you double-click on the agent icon, you can modify its configuration via three sections.

Configuration | Passwords | Ask for Password

You can configure three behaviors for the Agent, as shown in Figure 9.32:

- **Every Request** Passwords will not be cached, and every request will need to be authenticated. Very secure, but also very cumbersome.

- **Once per session** Passwords will be cached the first time the user enters it. No reauthentication will be needed until the users logs out of the Windows session.

- **After X minutes of inactivity** Passwords will be cached the first time the user enters it. Reauthentication will be needed after the agent doesn't authenticate connections for the amount of minutes entered.

Figure 9.32 Configuring the Session Authentication Agent Passwords

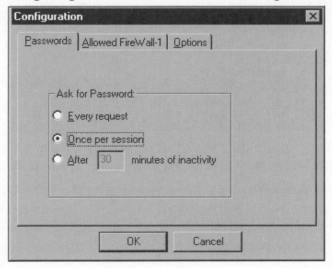

Configuration | Allowed FireWall-1 | Allow Authentication Request From

You can configure the Agent to accept requests from Any IP Address, or specify up to three IPs that the agent will respond to requests, as in Figure 9.33.

> **TIP**
>
> By limiting the requests, you can prevent a rogue firewall or program from contacting agents and receiving usernames and passwords.

Figure 9.33 Configuring the Session Authentication Agent Allowed FireWall-1

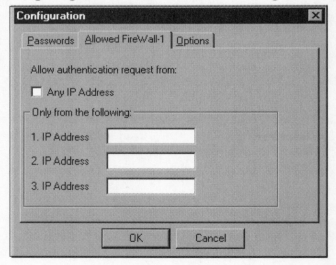

Configuration | Allowed FireWall-1 | Options

Here you can configure whether to Allow Clear Passwords or not. Uncheck Allow Clear Passwords to ensure SSL encryption is used, if you've configured the protocol for it. You can also configure whether the agent should resolve addresses with DNS (see Figure 9.34).

Figure 9.34 Configuring the Session Authentication Agent Options

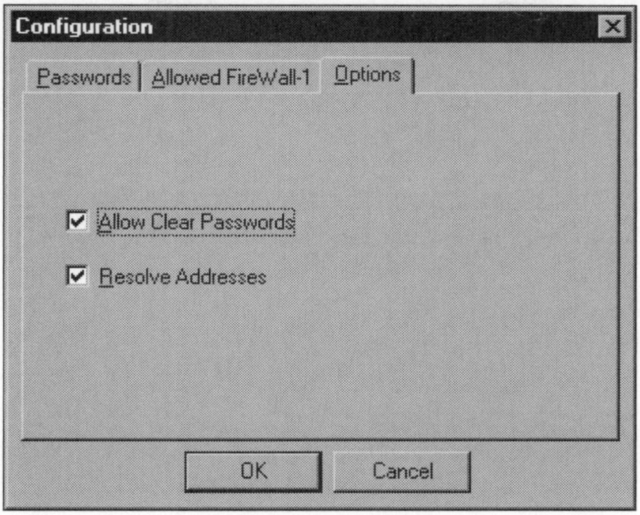

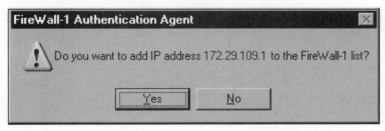

Interacting with Session Authentication

When you authenticate with Session Authentication, the user will be shown up to
three prompts to authenticate a connection.

First, if it is the first time a particular firewall is requesting Session
Authentication, the Session Authentication Agent will ask the user for permission to
send authentication to that firewall, as in Figure 9.35. If accepted, it will also add the
firewall's IP to the list of gateways from which it will accept requests.

Figure 9.35 Accepting Session Authentication Requests

Second, the Agent will ask for the username. It will display the name of the firewall making the request, the destination of the connection, and the service
requested, as in Figure 9.36.

Figure 9.36 Entering the Username for Session Authentication

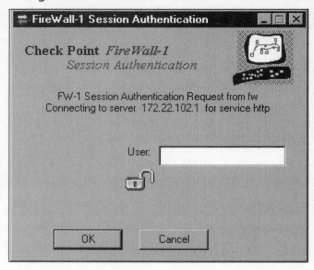

Finally, the user will enter the password and can then be granted access to the desired resource, as in Figure 9.37.

Figure 9.37 Entering the Password for Session Authentication

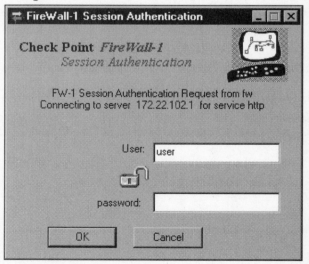

In the SmartView Tracker, you can see an authentication entry with the FW1_snauth protocol, and following that, the actual session. For every session, you will see an authentication entry above it, as in Figure 9.38.

Figure 9.38 Session Authentication in the SmartView Tracker

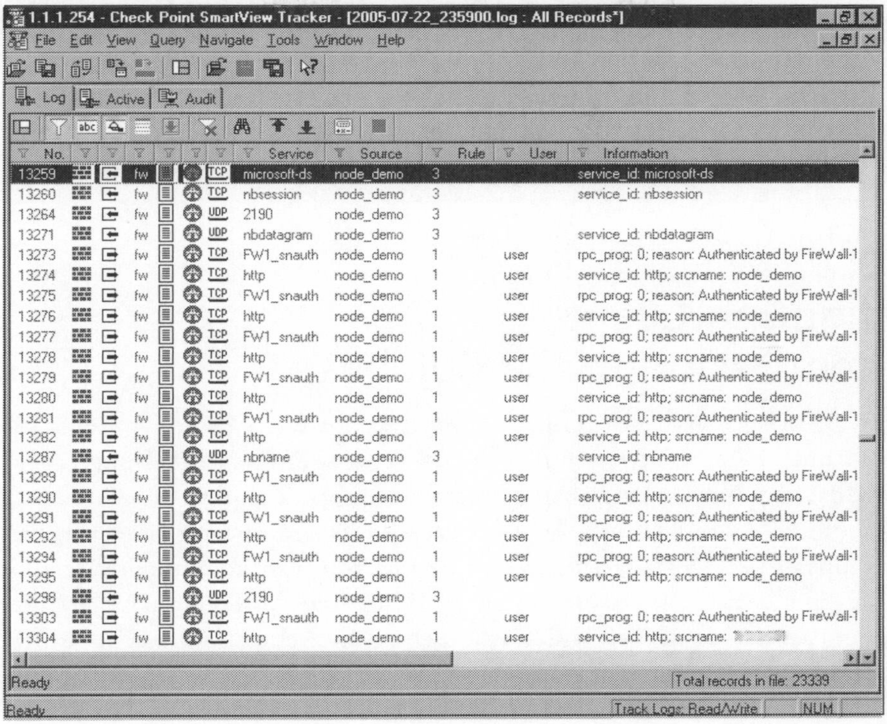

Client Authentication

Client Authentication is a versatile authentication method that can be used for most of your needs. Unlike User authentication, in which a connection is being authenticated, here you authenticate a machine or an IP (which the firewall considers the client). Client authentication is not transparent, which means that the connection has to be directed to the firewall so that it can ask for the specific authentication. Some of the benefits of client authentication are that any service can be authenticated, and that the authentication can last for a specific period of time or number of sessions (by default, five sessions in 30 minutes). Once a user achieves client authentication, traffic can flow freely with little intervention. Since the firewall doesn't have to interpret or modify the passing connections, is it faster than user or session authentication and doesn't intervene in the HTTP traffic passing through the gateway.

> **WARNING**
>
> Client Authentication has some security disadvantages. In a multiuser environment (i.e., Citrix or Terminal Services), all requests originate from the same IP and will be given the same access. Also, if the user doesn't sign off, other users that log at that machine will have permissions as the previously authenticated user until the authorization expires.

Configuring Client Authentication in the Rulebase

To allow client authentication, create a new rule above any rule that would block ports 900 and 259 to the firewall (usually the Stealth Rule). In the source field, select **Add User Access**, and then add the user group that will be able to authenticate, and optionally restrict to a location, where that group can connect from. Then, add the appropriate **Destination** to that rule (if you want to authenticate all traffic to the Internet, leave it as **Any)**, select which **Services** you'll authenticate (here you can use any service at all), select **Client Auth** as the Action, and add appropriate **Track**, **Time**, and **Comment** configurations, as in Figure 9.39.

Figure 9.39 Configuring Client Authentication in the Rulebase

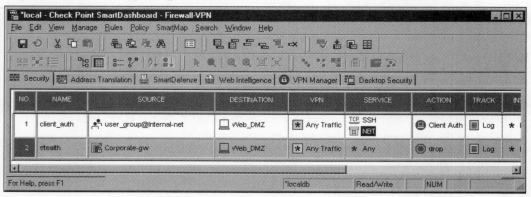

Let's take a look at the Action column of the Client Authentication Rule. There are many different behaviors that you have to select according to your desired policy. Once you select **Client Auth** as the Action, right-click on the field and select **Edit Properties**, and you will see the Client Authentication Action Properties window, as in Figure 9.40.

Figure 9.40 Configuring Client Authentication Action Properties

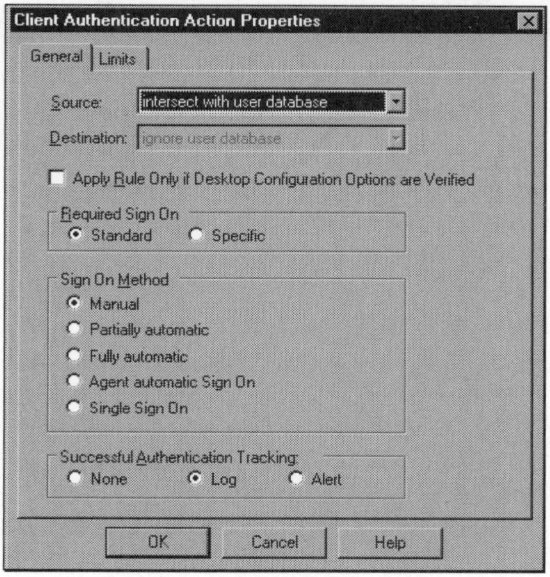

ClientAuth | Edit Properties | General | Source

As in other authentication actions, **Source** is used to control whether the source of the rule has to intersect the configured **Location** of the user, or if it takes precedence. Select **Ignore** if you want to override the location configured for the user.

ClientAuth | Edit Properties | General | Destination

Client Authentication cannot determine the final destination of a connection, since users are authenticating directly to the firewall. Therefore, the destination field is grayed out and cannot be selected.

ClientAuth | Edit Properties | General | Apply Rule Only If Desktop Configuration Options Are Verified

Checking this box will allow the client to access resources granted in the rule, once the user authenticates, only if they are using Check Point SecureClient and the Secure Configuration Verification (SCV) has succeeded.

ClientAuth | Edit Properties | General | Required Sign-On

If you select **Standard Sign-On**, users will be able to access all resources permitted in the rule at which they authenticated. If you select **Specific Sign-On**, users will have to explicitly specify, through a form or a sequence of prompts, the services and destinations allowed for the client. Specific Sign-On is useful for a kiosk machine, where an administrator can authorize access to certain sites or services only, without interacting with the firewall administrator.

ClientAuth | Edit Properties | General | Sign-On Method

The **Sign-On** method is one of the most important settings when using Client Authentication. Be sure to know how each method works to be able to select the most appropriate to your environment.

Manual Sign-On

Manual Sign-On method activates two ports on the Firewall Gateway for receipt of the authentication. They are port 900 using HTTP, and port 259 using Telnet (as in Figures 9.46, 9.47, and 9.48). Since users need to access these ports on the Firewall, the Client Authentication rule must be placed above the Stealth Rule (the one that drops all connections to the Firewall module).

This method is nontransparent, meaning that users will know they are first authenticating to a firewall, and then able to access the appropriate resources.

If you want to HTTP to port 900, you can look at Figure 9.41 where you enter the username, then in Figure 9.42 you enter the password, and in Figure 9.43, you select the Sign-On method. If you select Specific Sign-On, you will see Figure 9.44, where you can enter a list of services and destinations to authorize, and in Figure 9.45 the successful authentication screen (both for Specific and Standard Sign-On methods).

Figure 9.41 HTTP Manual Client Authentication—Entering the Username

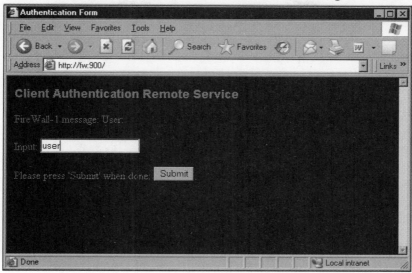

Figure 9.42 HTTP Manual Client Authentication—Entering the Password

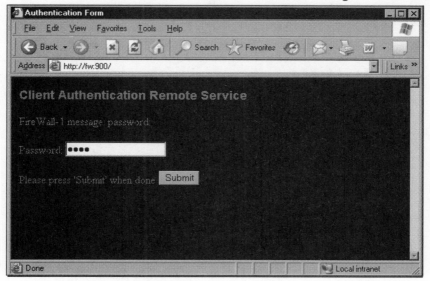

Figure 9.43 HTTP Manual Client Authentication—Selecting the Sign-On

Figure 9.44 HTTP Manual Client Authentication—Specific Sign-On

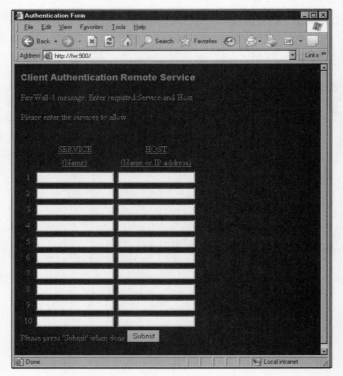

Figure 9.45 HTTP Manual Client Authentication—Successful Sign-On

If you want to Telnet to port 259, Figure 9.46 shows the Standard Sign-On method, and Figure 9.47 shows the Specific Sign-On method.

Figure 9.46 Telnet Manual Client Authentication—Standard Sign-On

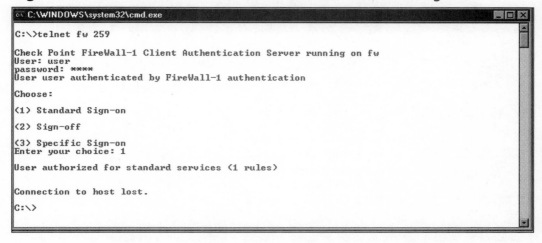

Figure 9.47 Telnet Manual Client Authentication—Specific Sign-On

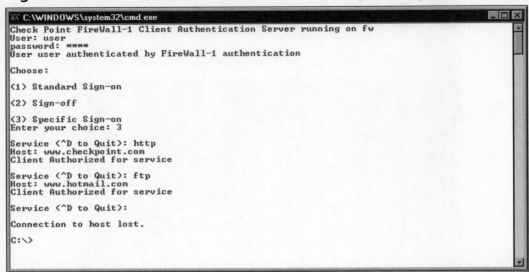

If you want to sign off, Figure 9.48 shows the Telnet client authentication Sign-Off method.

Figure 9.48 Telnet Manual Client Authentication—Sign-Off

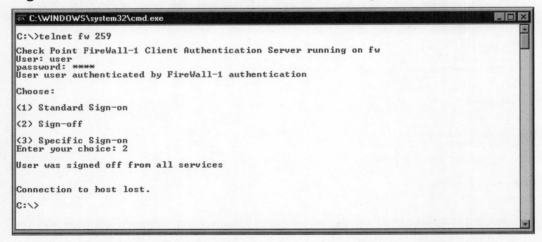

Partially Automatic Sign-On

With Partially Automatic Authentication, if a user tries to access a resource that he or she could authenticate for, using any of the Authenticated services (remember,

HTTP, FTP, Telnet, or RLOGIN), then the firewall will intercept the connection and request authentication from the user, like it would do with User Authentication. Manual Authentication may still be used.

Once the user enters the username and password, the firewall interprets the authentication as it had been manually entered to the firewall as in client authentication. This is extremely useful, since now users will be required to authenticate only once and can use any resource that the rulebase allows them to. Partially Automatic Authentication is one of the most used methods of authentication. One thing to keep in mind is that as with User Authentication, it can be easy for an intruder sniffing the network to decipher usernames and passwords.

Fully Automatic Sign-On

With Fully Automatic Authentication, you further extend the ways the firewall can request authentication from the user. If an Authenticated service is used, the firewall intercepts the traffic and requests authentication as in User Authentication. For other services, it will try to invoke Session Authentication to authenticate the user at the connecting machine. Manual Authentication may still be used.

Agent Automatic Sign-On

With Agent Automatic Authentication, the firewall will try to authenticate connections using only the Session Authentication Agent at the connecting machine. Manual Authentication may still be used.

Single Sign-On

If you select Single-Sign On, the firewall will try to contact a User Authority server to query the identity of the user logged in at the station. You need to have a User Authority license, and the User Agent installed at the connecting machine.

General | Successful Authentication Tracking

Here you can select whether you want information or alerts sent to the log when a user successfully authenticates. If you select Alert it will also write the information to the log.

Once you configure the General properties for Client Authentication, you can configure the Limits for Client Authentication sessions. Figure 9.49 shows the tab for configuring these properties.

Figure 9.49 Configuring Client Authentication Limits Properties

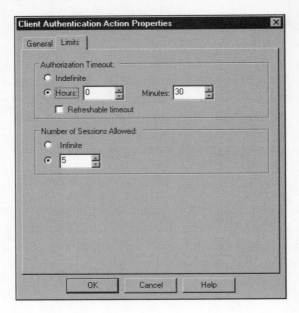

Limits | Authorization Timeout

Here you can select how long the user authorization lasts. Select indefinite to require an explicit sign-off from the user (via HTTP to port 900 or Telnet to port 259) to cancel the authorization (as in Figures 9.41 through 9.48). Select a specific time limit, in hours and minutes, if you want to require reauthentication after a time has lapsed. Select refreshable timeout if you want that as long as the connection is being used, the user will not be required to reauthenticate. This is similar to setting a time for a screen saver to come in—as long as there's activity in the machine, the screen saver doesn't come in. This is useful so that if a user leaves his machine, someone else can't sit down and use it.

Limits | Number of Sessions Allowed

This limits the amount of open connections an authenticated user can make through the firewall. If you're using FTP, Telnet, or RLOGIN connections, you could limit the number of sessions through this property. However, if you're using HTTP connections, you will need to select **Indefinite** sessions because a browser will normally open many sessions when browsing a single page.

Advanced Topics

Client Authentication opens up the functions of authentication to more services and more situations. These additional functions also have additional features to configure, and we look at some of them here.

Check Point Gateway | Authentication

There are some properties that you need to configure and verify per gateway, to fine-tune the authentication experience for your users, as in Figure 9.50.

Figure 9.50 Check Point Gateway | Authentication

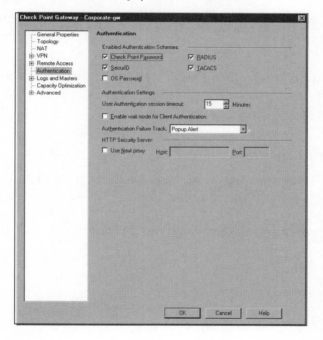

Enabled Authentication Schemes

It is very important to select which authentication schemes the gateway will allow for its users. If a user selects an authentication with a scheme that the gateway does not accept, the user will not be granted access to resources on the Gateway. You can select Check Point Password (previously VPN-1/FireWall-1 Password), SecurID, OS Password, RADIUS, and TACACS.

Authentication Settings

The user can select the following authentication settings:

- **User Authentication session timeout** This setting (by default, 15 minutes) has two behaviors. For FTP and Telnet connections, connections with no activity are terminated after the timeout expires. For HTTP, it applies to the use of one-time passwords (i.e., SecurID tokens). Although the timeout hasn't expired, the server will not request another one-time password for access to a previously authenticated server.

- **Enable Wait mode for Client Authentication** This setting applies to Telnet Client Authentication, where the Telnet session remains open, and when the user closes the session (CTRL-C or some other manner), the authentication expires. If this option is not selected, the user will have to manually sign off or wait for the session timeout.

- **Authentication Failure Track** Here, you can define if a failed authentication will generate an alert, a log, or no activity. We recommend at least logging all failed authentications.

HTTP Security Server

If you use an HTTP Security Server, you can configure an HTTP Proxy Server behind the Security Server. Enter the Host and Port for the proxy server to activate it.

Global Properties | Authentication

There are certain properties that are configured globally for all authentication performed by the Check Point gateways. Appropriately enough, you access them from the **Global Properties | Authentication** tab, as in Figure 9.51.

Figure 9.51 Global Properties | Authentication

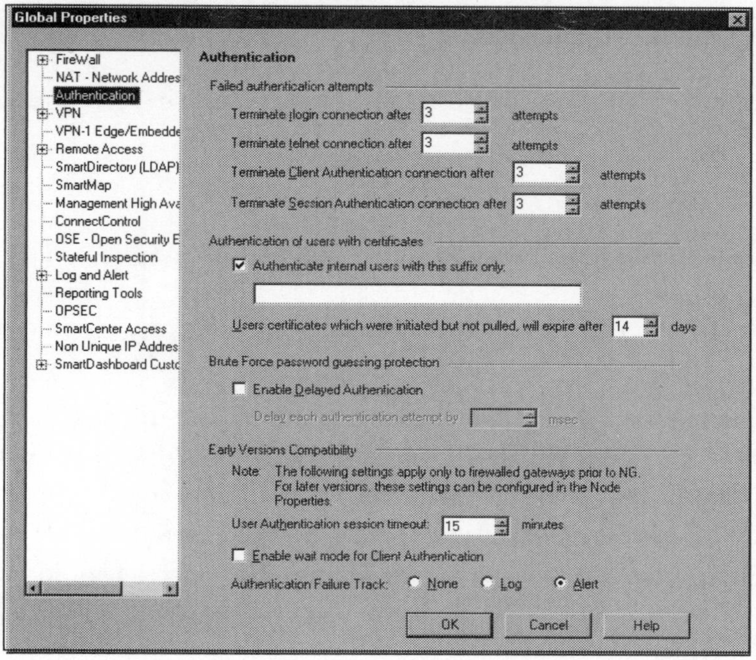

Failed Authentication Attempts

To prevent an intruder from brute-force guessing your passwords, the *Failed Authentication Attempts* setting can be used to terminate connections after a set number of failed attempts (i.e., wrong passwords). You can set a different amount of allowed tries for RLOGIN, Telnet, Client Authentication, and Session Authentication connections.

Authentication of Users with Certificates

For Remote Access VPNs, if you are using VPNs, you can restrict the gateway to accept only users who have a specific suffix in their certificates. Also, if an administrator *initializes* a certificate in the Certificate Authority, you can define how many days users have to pull that certificate before it expires.

Brute-Force Password Guessing Protection

To prevent an intruder from brute-force guessing your passwords, you can enable this protection, which is new for NGX. By setting a specific number of milliseconds to delay each authentication, you can dramatically affect any automatic password guessing system, while a user will barely notice a difference.

Early Version Compatibility

If you are managing gateways prior to NG, the following setting can be applied globally. For NG or later gateways, these settings are set per gateway. By the way, since there isn't the option to administer pre-NG gateways in NGX, you can probably ignore this section.

Registry Settings

Most of Check Point configuration is done from the SmartDashboard. However, some settings are not available through the SmartDashboard and have to be accessed directly in the Check Point internal registry. There are three ways you can access the registry:

- Some settings are available in the SmartDashboard through the **Policy Menu | Global Properties | SmartDashboard Customization**, which opens a tree of different settings you can change.

- You can use the GuiDBedit program, which is included in the installation folder of the Check Point SmartConsole clients. Its default location is **C:\Program Files\Check Point\SmartConsole\R60\PROGRAM\GuiDBedit.exe**. The program gives you complete access to the registry.

- You can use from the command line (or SecurePlatform's expert mode) the **dbedit** program, which is a text interface to the registry. You will need to know the exact setting you want to access, since it isn't very user-friendly.

Let's look at some of the settings you might need when dealing with Authentication.

New Interface

The default Client Authentication HTTP interface requires four pages for a successful login: the username page, password page, method page, and the optional Specific Sign-On page. If you enable the *hclient_enable_new_interface* setting using the **Policy Menu | Global Properties | SmartDashboard Customization | FireWall-1 | Authentication | Client Authentication | HTTP**, the HTTP interface will combine the username and password pages into one, thus streamlining the user experience, as in Figure 9.52.

Figure 9.52 Client Authentication HTTP New Interface

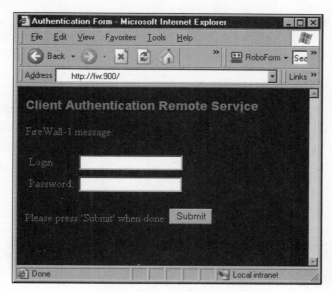

Use Host Header as Destination

If you are using Partially or Fully Automatic Sign-On with HTTP connections, once the connection is authenticated the firewall needs to redirect the original query to the intended destination. It does so by looking at the original URL's IP address, and redirecting the user's browser to that IP. However, if the firewall resolves the destination URL to a nonroutable IP (i.e., the non-NAT'ed IP), or if the Web server is configured to need the Host Header for access (i.e., a Web hosting service that shares one IP with multiple web pages), then the connection will fail. To avoid this, enable the *http_use_host_h_as_dst* setting using the **Policy Menu | Global Properties | SmartDashboard Customization | FireWall-1 | Web Security | HTTP Protocol**.

Opening All Client Authentication Rules

When you begin to create a complex policy with different rules for granting user access to different resources, you need to take into consideration that the default behavior for Client Authentication is to grant access for the rule only where you authenticated. If you need to authenticate once and be granted access by all rules that would permit the user, you have to enable the *automatically_open_ca_rules* setting using the **Policy Menu | Global Properties | SmartDashboard Customization | FireWall-1 | Authentication | Client Authentication** section.

Configuration Files

Besides the configuration of gateway properties, global properties, rules, and registry settings, some configuration files can change the authentication behavior, to include encryption or to present your own look and feel to the user.

Enabling Encrypted Authentication

Since Telnet and HTTP are not encrypted, Client Authentication is inherently less secure than Session Authentication. However, you can configure NGX to enable HTTPS Manual Authentication, which will give you the encryption you want when using the built-in HTTP server at port 900 for authentication. Look in the "Are You Owned?" sidebar for details.

Are You Owned?

Securing Client Authentication

Although Client Authentication is a great tool, flexible and easy to understand, you have to be aware of its security implications. When you enable Client Authentication and place the rule above the stealth rule, you're opening ports 259 and 900 to the firewall. Remember that neither of these services is encrypted, so that you're vulnerable to sniffing attacks. Never allow Client Authentication from **Any** sources, as it's easy for a scanner to detect these ports running on your firewall and try to brute force a username and password combination (use the new NGX **Brute Force Protection** to minimize this).

It's a good idea to change the HTTP server on port 900 to an encrypted HTTPS server, and to disable Telnet authentication to port 259. Edit the *$FWDIR/conf/fwauthd.conf* file and change the line

```
900     fwssd        in.ahclientd     wait      900
```

to

```
900     fwssd        in.ahclientd     wait      900 ssl:defaultCert
```

and eliminate the line

```
259     fwssd        in.aclientd      wait      259
```

You could also change the default 900 and 259 ports to other port numbers, and edit the fw1_clnauth_http and fw1_clnauth_telnet services to reflect the new ports.

Custom Pages

If you will use Client Authentication's HTTP interface, you will probably want to change its appearance and include your company's logo, an unauthorized use warning, and some nice graphics. You can do this by editing the HTML files in the directory *$FWDIR/conf/ahclientd*. Remember to leave the **%** commands intact, as they are used by NGX to insert the information it needs.

Installing the User Database

The Check Point User Database is independent of the SmartDashboard objects and rulebases. When you install a policy (from SmartDashboard, **Policy | Install...**), in fact the SmartDashboard saves the current policy, and installs the policy (containing the objects and rules) and the user database. If you have made changes only to the user database (password changes, created users, changed group membership), you might want to install only the user database, which is a lot faster.

To install the user database, from the SmartDashboard you can select **Policy | Install Database...**, or from the **Manage | Users and Administrators** dialog, click on **Actions...** and then select **Install...** as in Figure 9.53.

Figure 9.53 Using Actions in the Manage Users and Administrator Dialog

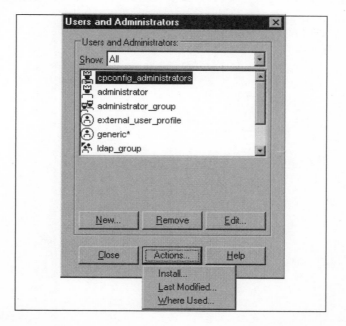

You will see the *Install Database* window, like in Figure 9.54. You can then select **OK** to install the database. If you have more than one gateway or SmartCenter, you will see different objects and select among them.

Figure 9.54 Installing the User Database

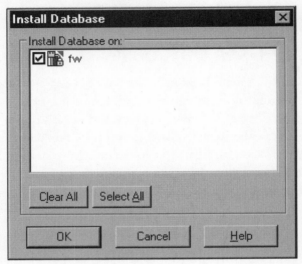

Summary

Many security rulebases do not have the need for individual user rights, and work with Hosts, Gateways, Networks, Groups, Ranges, and Servers. However, both for security and for tracking purposes you might need to integrate authentication with your security policy. You'll be able to identify users' navigation, and grant privileged users access to restricted resources or connections with specific services.

You have a choice of how to recognize a user, accessing external directory servers with RADIUS or TACACS, or using the internal user database. You can integrate with Microsoft Active Directory through the Microsoft Internet Authentication Service, or get the SmartDirectory license for LDAP integration.

You can choose between User, Client, and Session Authentication, depending on your needs and a balance of security, ease-of-use, and flexibility. User authentication is easy to use and transparent, but is not flexible, has no security, and can be cumbersome for accessing external web sites. Client Authentication is flexible and can be secure, but it is not transparent to the user and less secure than other methods. Session Authentication is flexible, secure, and easy to use, but installing the agent on each machine will be something you have to consider.

Check Point NGX gives you many options; you just have to choose which to implement.

Solutions Fast Track

Authentication Overview

☑ With authentication you can grant specific permissions to groups of users who might have different IPs and be moving around different computers.

☑ Users in DHCP environments are suitable for implementing authentication, as well as roaming administrators who need to access special files.

☑ Authentication rules had to be placed carefully, so that a nonauthentication rule does not override the need for a user to authenticate.

Users and Administrators

☑ Several schemes are available to authenticate users, both from the internal database and from external directories like RADIUS, TACACS, LDAP, SecurID.

☑ Administrators are created in the SmartDashboard and assign Permissions Profiles to limit their actions within the configuration applications.

☑ Users are created based on templates, and should be placed in groups to be integrated with the rulebase.

User Authentication

☑ User Authentication is transparent to the user and doesn't require configuration of client machines.

☑ Only the four Authenticated services—HTTP, FTP, Telnet, and RLOGIN—can work with User Authentication.

☑ User-authenticated HTTP access to the Internet will require users to authenticate multiple times for a single Web page.

Session Authentication

☑ Session Authentication can authenticate each session from the client, and it can have encryption enabled for security.

☑ Session Authentication requires a Session Authentication Agent installed in the authorizing machine.

☑ The Session Authentication Agent can be configured to respond only to certain firewalls and with encryption.

Client Authentication

☑ Client Authentication works with any defined service available.

☑ Manual Authentication is performed by an HTTP connection to the port 900 or Telnet to port 259.

☑ Other sign-on methods integrate User, Session, and SSO Authentication into Client Authentication.

Frequently Asked Questions

The following Frequently Asked Questions, answered by the authors of this book, are designed to both measure your understanding of the concepts presented in this chapter and to assist you with real-life implementation of these concepts. To have your questions about this chapter answered by the author, browse to **www.syngress.com/solutions** and click on the **"Ask the Author"** form.

Q: How can I enter a single user in a rule instead of a group?

A: You can enter only groups in a rule. However, you can create a group that contains only one user.

Q: Can I use Check Point NGX as a Web proxy?

A: Yes, you can. However, NGX does not store in memory frequently accessed pages, so the connections will not be accelerated. These connections will use the HTTP Security Server for additional protection, and you need to enable the http_connection_method_proxy property using dbedit or GUIDBedit

Q: Which authentication should I use?

A: For HTTP intranet access, try User Authentication. For accessing the Internet, try encrypted Manual Client Authentication. Try redirecting nonallowed traffic to the Client Authentication page using a resource.

Q: We came back from our New Year's celebration and no one could authenticate to the firewall. What can I do?

A: Check the expiration date of the users.

Q: I would like to give external access to an internal Web site. What authentication method should I use?

A: I would recommend user authentication, since you have a controlled environment (your Web site) and you should authenticate every session, for increased security.

Q: When trying User Authentication, users received the error "FW-1 (password) Reason FW-1 Rule." The rulebase is configured, the user is configured, and the traffic should be accepted.

A: Edit the properties of the **User Auth** action, and make sure the HTTP property is set to **All Servers.**

Q: Is there a limit to the numbers of users available in the internal Check Point database?

A: There is no set limit for the Check Point user database. However, if you have a large number of users, integrating with an external user directory will be easier to manage.

Q: A user cannot authenticate with his password, after he recently changed it. In the SmartView Tracker is, there an error regarding a URL worm?

A: HTTP Passwords are obscured when transmitted, and the new obscured password could have a pattern similar to a known URL worm, and could be blocked by Web Intelligence's General HTTP Worm Catcher feature. You can either remove the pattern being enforced, or (new for NGX) configure the General HTTP Worm Catcher to apply only to selected Web servers.

Q: In a thin client environment (Citrix, Terminal Services), which authentication method should I use?

A: In a thin client environment you should configure User Authentication. Both client and session authentication will not be able to authenticate a specific user's connection.

Q: Is there a Session Authentication Agent for non-Windows systems?

A: There is no Check Point-provided nor supported Session Authentication Agent for non-Windows systems. However, you can find an agent written in Perl on the user-supported sites like www.cpug.org.

Q: Is there a way to show users a message when they need to first use Client Authentication, or to redirect them to the authentication page?

A: You can create a URI resource that will match all pages, and has a Replacement URI pointing to the authentication page or the message page.

Create a rule among the last in the rulebase, with the HTTP service using the created resource and a drop action.

Q: A user cannot authenticate when connected from Network X, only when connected from Network Y. Other users cannot authenticate at all. What should I check?

A: Verify each users' location properties. Remember that there needs to be an overlap of the location defined in the user properties and the location (source or destination) defined in the rulebase. Try to edit the Action properties to ignore the user database, to see if that is the source of the problem.

Chapter 10

Content Security and OPSEC

Solutions in this chapter:

- OPSEC

- Security Servers

- CVP

- UFP

- MDQ

- Secure Internal Communication

☑ Summary

☑ Solutions Fast Track

☑ Frequently Asked Questions

Introduction

In this chapter you will learn how Check Point FireWall-1 can integrate with third-party products. Check Point does content security by pushing traffic through built-in application layer gateways. Also known as proxies, these engines allow you to actually scan and modify the data portion of TCP-based traffic.

Check Point FireWall-1 has the ability to redirect traffic to a third-party appliance for antivirus scanning. Check Point also has a product that performs antivirus scanning inside of the firewall product. Check Point certifies third-party solutions with the OPSEC (Open Platform for Security) Alliance. OPSEC-compliant antivirus scanners use the CVP (Content Vectoring Protocol) to communicate with FireWall-1. There are several interfaces available to OPSEC vendors to communicate with Check Point products.

We will cover all five proxies available to us in FireWall-1; each has unique options that allow you to further secure network environments. We will also cover internal Check Point communication and how certificates are used to secure the security products.

OPSEC

OPSEC (Open Platform for Security) represents Check Point's efforts to allow third-party companies to produce Check Point integrated solutions. The OPSEC Alliance is a collection of security vendors that have been OPSEC Certified by Check Point Software. There are hundreds of vendors that develop OPSEC-compliant software. A list of these products is available on the OPSEC Alliance Web site, www.opsec.com.

Check Point has made an API (Application Programming Interface) available for these companies to use to communicate with Check Point's product line. The SDK (Software Development Kit) requires knowledge of the C programming language. The SDK contains software to integrate with the following interfaces:

- **CVP** The Content Vectoring Protocol allows antivirus solutions to talk to FireWall-1.
- **UFP** The URI Filtering Protocol allows Web filtering to integrate.
- **LEA** The Log Export API enables you to export log files to third-party log servers.
- **ELA** The Event Logging API allows Check Point to receive logs from third-party software.

- **SAM** The Suspicious Activity Monitor enables you to integrate intrusion detection systems.

- **CPMI** The Check Point Management Interface gives a third-party device access to the Check Point management utilities. For example, this would allow a device to read the object database.

- **AMON** The Application Monitor allows a third-party device to tell Check Point its status. This will allow the product to show up in the SmartView Status monitoring application.

- **UAA** The User Authority Agent allows Check Point to integrate into Microsoft environments.

- **SAA** The Secure Authentication API allows for integration into authentication systems.

- **SCV** The Secure Client Verification API allows SecureClient to talk to third-party software on remote VPN clients to ensure end-user compliance.

NOTE

The CVP, UFP, and ELA protocols are by far the most popular Check Point APIs used by OPSEC vendors. Each of these protocols uses a different port number and requires SIC (Secure Internal Communication) established with the host in order to work.

Custom Check Point Communication

The protocols for "talking" to Check Point are well documented, and the API is available from www.opsec.com. Sometimes it may be necessary to code your own tool to get the functionality you desire. There are several different ways to authenticate to the firewall using OPSEC communication. NGX supports five different legacy methods of Check Point communication, so even services that talk to the older 4.1 or 4.0 Check Point protocols usually work fine.

In older versions of Check Point software, the interface for talking to FireWall-1 uses the older OMI (Object Management Interface) protocol. Though it is not recommended, OPSEC traffic can be sent clear text without any encryption at all.

Partnership

Any vendor of security-related products can sign up for the OPSEC Alliance at www.opsec.com. Access to OPSEC resources is free after you sign up. There is a small fee for certification for OPSEC compliance.

Antivirus

Check Point FireWall-1 has the capability of doing antivirus scanning using CVP. This protocol allows Check Point to redirect most TCP-based traffic to an antivirus scanner and returns cleaned data. Check Point also has a product with built-in antivirus functionality called Check Point Express CI. This virus scanner uses Computer Associate's antivirus engine and is meant to add functionality to firewalls in organizations with 25 to 500 employees.

Web Filtering

Web filtering is performed using UFP. There are several solutions available to curb excess Web site surfing. Check Point has the ability to take a text file of URLs and block access to them without using a UFP server, although it is not recommended to have over 50 entries in the list.

OPSEC Applications

When using an OPSEC-compliant solution on the firewall, an OPSEC Application object must be used. You can create one by clicking Manage → Servers and OPSEC Applications, then clicking New… → OPSEC Application… You can also click the fourth tab in the Objects Tree on the left, and right-click OPSEC Application and click New → OPSEC Application.

A Node object should be created beforehand so it can be selected in the Host box. There is a New… box you can click to create one while you are creating your OPSEC Application object (see Figure 10.1). There are predefined Vendors that select the Entities for you on the bottom. You can always leave the Vendor on User defined and select your own Server and Client Entities.

Figure 10.1 OPSEC Application Properties

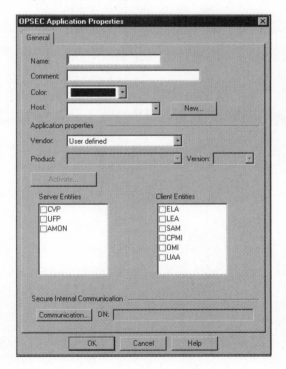

Security Servers

The application layer gateways on Check Point FireWall-1 are referred to as Security Servers. These Security Servers run as separate processes on the firewall. Configuration is done through the SmartDashboard GUI. To use an antivirus scanning engine, or any product that scans layer 7 data, the data must first go through one of these Security Servers. Each Security Server has unique features based on functions in the protocol.

WARNING

Keep in mind that Security Servers take additional resources to run. Traffic that has to go through a Security Server will be slower than traffic that does not.

Figure 10.2 shows a resource used in the policy. To use a resource, right–click the service field and click Add With Resource…. When a resource is used in a rule, no other services can be in the same rule.

Figure 10.2 SmartDashboard Resources

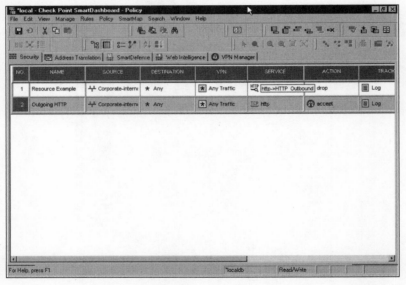

TIP

Using Security Servers also gives you additional benefits from the Application Intelligence functionality of FireWall-1. Some types of signatures can be used without using a Resource. When using a Resource, you have the ability to use several more signatures to stop worms and viruses from spreading!

URI

The URI (Uniform Resource Identifier) Security Server is used for HTTP-based traffic. To create a URI Resource you can click Manage → Resources, then click New… → URI…, or click the third tab in the Objects Tree window on the left and right-click Resources and click New… → URI.

Tools & Traps…

Reverse Proxy

It is possible to use the URI Security Server as a Reverse Proxy. Most of the time the URI Security Server is used to control Web-based traffic destined to computers inside your internal network. Used as a Reverse Proxy, Check Point can filter traffic coming into a Web site through the firewall. A single IP address can proxy to several servers on the back end and the user will never know they are accessing multiple resources from the browser.

    This also increases the security of your Web servers since clients are not making direct connections to the Web servers from the Internet. It is important to note that unlike traditional proxy servers, Check Point proxies do not cache Web traffic.

The default settings are shown in Figure 10.3. When Optimize URL logging is selected, all the other features of the resource are disabled. This is used to simply log the URL's (Uniform Resource Locator) your users are going to. Enforce URI capabilities gives you the most options. This allows you to do content inspection in the Security Server and send the traffic to a CVP or UFP server. Enhance UFP performance is used when all you want to do is send the URL to a server for Web filtering.

Figure 10.3 The URI Resource

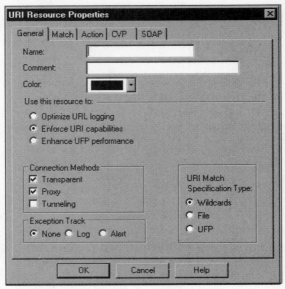

The URI Match Specification Type windows allow you to select the method you use in order to choose what URIs trigger this resource. Wildcards will allow you to type a string to look for. File allows you to import a file of strings to look for. We recommended that this file contain fewer than 50 strings. It can quickly become unmanageable! Selecting UFP allows you to send the URL to a UFP scanner for Web filtering.

The Match tab changes based on whether you pick Wildcard, File, or UFP in the first tab. Figure 10.4 is the result when Wildcard is chosen. By default it applies the resource to any URL.

Figure 10.4 Result from Selecting the URI Resource's Wildcard Option

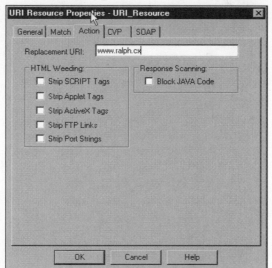

The Action tab allows you to perform HTML Weeding, which is striping selected data out of the content of the packets. A replacement URL can be chosen here to automatically send users to when they violate policies. You can also have the Security Server block Java code.

The CVP tab allows us to select an antivirus server for scanning. We'll discuss CVP in more detail later in this chapter.

SOAP (Simple Object Access Protocol) is an XML–based Web protocol for transferring data. The last tab gives you the ability to block or accept specific SOAP traffic (see Figure 10.5). Tracking options are available as well.

Figure 10.5 Blocking SOAP Traffic with the URI Resource

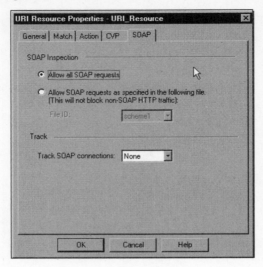

SMTP

The SMTP (Simple Mail Transfer Protocol) Resource is one of the most common proxies used on FireWall-1. When using this Resource you can modify and block e-mail.

As you can tell, the options in the SMTP Resource are quite a bit different from the URI Resource. The Mail Delivery Server setting is optional and allows you to enter a mail host to forward mail to (see Figure 10.6).

Figure 10.6 The SMTP Resource

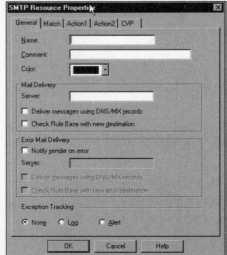

The Match tab allows you to specify which Senders and Recipients can be in the e-mail. Typically, two Resources are created, one for incoming e-mail and one for outgoing e-mail. You can specify a domain name in one of these boxes to make sure only e-mail with certain Senders or Recipients are passing in a certain direction (see Figure 10.7). You can use wildcard notation (i.e. *@domain.com) for specifying domains.

Figure 10.7 The SMTP Resource's Match Tab

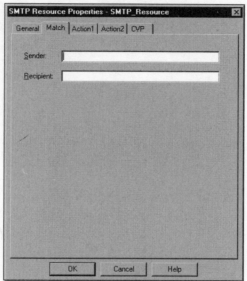

The Action1 tab allows for selective rewriting of SMTP headers. This is not used very often, but is a good way to hide to the outside world what type of e-mail clients are sending mail from the inside of your network (see Figure 10.8).

Figure 10.8 The SMTP Resource's Action1 Tab

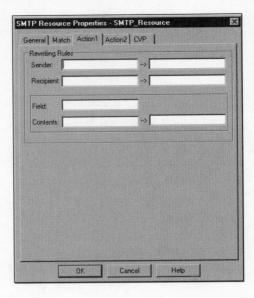

The Action2 tab allows for stripping of certain attachments and e-mail sizes. You can also strip out script content using the Weeding box at the bottom. The CVP tab allows for selection of the CVP server and associated options (see Figure 10.9).

Figure 10.9 The SMTP Resource's Action2 Tab

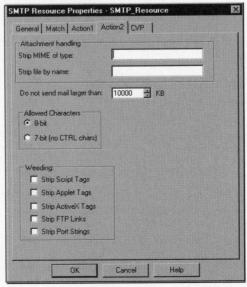

FTP

The FTP Security Server is not used very much, but has a few cool features. The one drawback to the FTP Security Server is that when you use it, downloads or uploads of files trickle down very slowly to the client while the firewall buffers the entire file, scans it, then pushes down the file in its entirety to the client. The users of the network should be informed of this behavior so they do not think the download is not working.

As you can see in Figure 10.10, the FTP Resource does not have too many options. Typically, this resource is used only if you want to send FTP traffic to a CVP server for antivirus scanning.

Figure 10.10 The FTP Resource

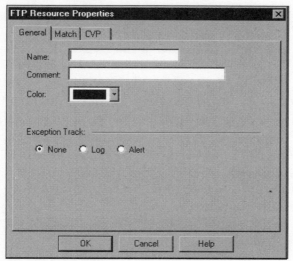

Using the screen shown in Figure 10.11, you can block GET or PUT FTP methods. This is an easy way to disallow uploading or downloading of files via FTP in a certain direction.

Figure 10.11 Blocking GET and PUT Methods with FTP Resource

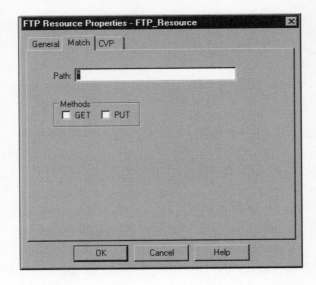

TCP

The TCP Resource is used only to send generic TCP traffic to a UFP or CVP server. This is useful if you want to apply content inspection to protocols other than the supported TCP protocols (see Figure 10.12). To enable a service to use a TCP resource, you need to edit the service, go to the Advanced settings, and select **Enable for TCP resource**.

Figure 10.12 The TCP Resource

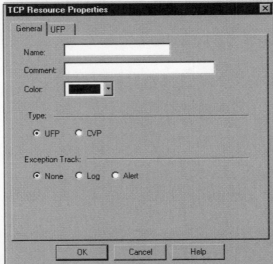

NOTE

When using a TCP Resource with UFP, only the IP address is sent to the UFP server.

CIFS

The CIFS (Common Internet File System) Resource is used to proxy Microsoft networking traffic. Using this resource can ensure unwanted network paths and printer shares are allowed through the firewall.

This Resource also can block registry access. Keep in mind that your traffic has to go through the firewall for this Resource to take effect (see Figure 10.13). For the CIFS resource to work with Microsoft shares, you need to allow the IPC$ (Inter-Process Communication) share to each server.

Figure 10.13 The CIFS Resource

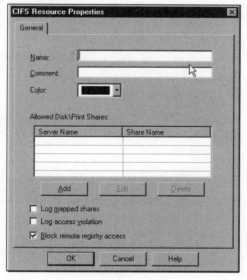

CVP

The Content Vectoring Protocol is how Check Point sends data to a third-party server for content inspection. Check Point uses TCP port 18181 to send data to the CVP server. The CVP server scans the data and sends the data back to the firewall on TCP port 18181. Check Point recommends that CVP servers be placed on a separate segment of the network directly connected to the firewall for best performance. If an extra interface is not available, then the CVP server should be placed in the DMZ.

> **TIP**
>
> Take into account how much traffic will be going to the CVP server. If it is a large amount of traffic, a dedicated interface is a must.

Resource Creation

In order to use CVP for TCP traffic, a Resource of some type must be created. Every resource, with the exception of CIFS, has the ability to use the CVP protocol.

Figure 10.14 shows the CVP tab in the URI Resource object. An OPSEC application needs to be created first that has the CVP protocol box checked in it. When you select the drop-down menu next to CVP Server, it will list all the CVP server and CVP groups. When CVP servers are placed into a CVP group, they can be load balanced or chained.

Figure 10.14 The URI Resource's CVP Tab

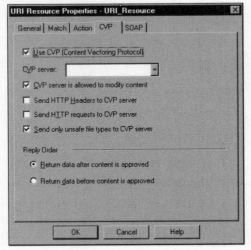

UFP

A UFP server allows you to send the URI of Web pages to a server that contains a list of Web sites and tells FireWall-1 which category the URI belongs to. Check

Point uses TCP port 18182 to send data to the UFP server. There are products that contain lists of millions of Web sites placed into categories. Once the UFP tells FireWall-1 the URI's category, FireWall-1 can use resources to decide whether to block access to those sites or allow it so that users can be restricted to only those categories. In essence, the UFP server is a category look-up tool for FireWall-1.

When an OPSEC Application object is created for a UFP server, the categories can be downloaded to the firewall by clicking Get Dictionary…. (see Figure 10.15).

Figure 10.15 Creating an OPSEC Application Object for a UFP Server

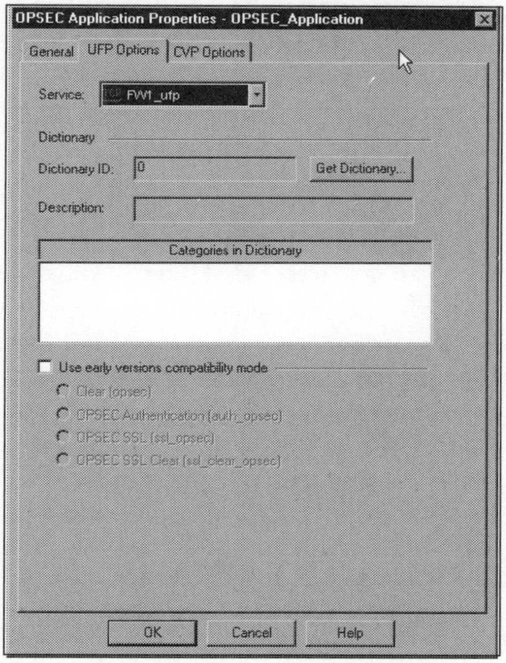

Resource Creation

To use UFP in a Resource, Enhance UFP performance can be checked or the URI Match Specification Type can be set to UFP. The UFP server can be selected on the Match tab along with the Categories that this Resource should match on. UFP Groups can also be created to load balance UFP traffic.

MDQ

The MDQ (Mail Dequeuer) runs as a process on FireWall-1. MDQ handles the spooling of e-mail for the SMTP Security Server. The process will show up as mdq on any FireWall-1 platform. MDQ Enqueuer accepts inbound e-mail and places it into the $FWDIR/spool directory. MDQ then sends a copy of that e-mail to a CVP server if the firewall policy calls for it. Then the MDQ Dequeuer sends the e-mail outbound. The terms inbound and outbound relate to the firewall and the policy, regardless of the direction of the e-mail.

> **NOTE**
>
> The SMTP Security Server can run as a proxy and in transparent mode. Transparent mode can be nice since it does not require changes to the e-mail environment. The e-mail server does not even know it is there!

How to Debug

At times the MDQ process can get overloaded. The command **fw mdq** will restart the MDQ process and start filtering e-mail again. A **cprestart** will also restart the MDQ process. It is possible a malformed e-mail may hang the process. If this happens, the e-mail should be tracked down in the $FWDIR/spool directory, moved out of that directory, and **fw mdq** should be run to restart the MDQ process. Every e-mail is in a separate file and this directory can be emptied while the firewall is stopped if MDQ is not working to make it work again.

Secure Internal Communication

SIC (Secure Internal Communication) refers to the technology that controls internal Check Point communication. When the Check Point Management Server is installed, Check Point creates a Certificate Authority. All internal Check Point traffic is encrypted with these certificates using PKI (public key infrastructure). The Check Point Management Server holds the master certificate, and every Check Point product has one certificate cut from the master certificate.

When creating Check Point objects and OPSEC Application objects, you'll see a SIC Communication box at the bottom of the object window. When the software is installed, a one-time password is required. When the object is created on the Check Point SmartDashboard, this one-time password is used to encrypt the certificate while it is being installed on the device. Once the certificate is downloaded, all future traffic is encrypted using this certificate.

WARNING

Do not rename the Check Point Management Server without first consulting with your Check Point vendor or Check Point support. The Management Server's master certificate is tied to the name of the server, and changing this setting may break Check Point communication!

Notes from the Underground...

Protect Check Point Communication

Internal Check Point communication normally is encrypted with internal certificates. This is very secure when used properly. Beware of third-party devices that use clear OPSEC communication. If a product is not encrypting the data going to Check Point, then it may be possible to inject an attack into the communication.

Check Point may drop support for clear OPSEC completely someday soon. In this day and age it may by too risky even to allow products to talk to the firewall in the clear. If at all possible, never Telnet to a Check Point firewall.

Summary

In this chapter we learned about the ability of third-party products to communicate with Check Point products. Check Point has a vendor alliance called OPSEC. This program certifies third-party products for use with Check Point. There are several application programming interfaces that Check Point has made available for communication with the Check Point product suite.

We learned about the Security Servers and the ability for Check Point to modify layer 7 traffic. Traffic can be send to an antivirus server using the CVP protocol or a Web filtering server using the UFP protocol. We also learned about the MDQ process and how the SMTP Security Service works on FireWall-1.

Check Point NG introduced SIC (Secure Internal Communication), which encrypts internal Check Point communication with certificates.

Solutions Fast Track

OPSEC

☑ OPSEC stands for Open Platform for Security and is a program for vendors to write code that integrates with Check Point products.

☑ OPSEC protocols include CVP, UFP, AMON, ELA, LEA, SAM, CPMI, SAM, UAA, SAA, and SCV.

Security Servers

☑ Check Point's Security Servers are application layer gateways (proxies) that run as separate processes on FireWall-1.

☑ There are five Security Servers: URI, SMTP, FTP, TCP, and CIFS.

☑ Using a Security Server allows Check Point to do modification of layer 7 data.

CVP

☑ CVP stands for Content Vectoring Protocol and is used to send traffic to an external server for antivirus scanning and content modification.

☑ CVP used TCP port 18181 by default.

☑ In order to use CVP, a Node object for the CVP server needs to be created, an OPSEC Application object referencing the Node object, a Resource object referencing the OPSEC Application, and a rule in the policy referencing the Resource object.

UFP

☑ UFP stands for URI Filtering Protocol and is used to send Web site addresses to an external server for Web filtering.

☑ UFP uses TCP port 18182 by default.

☑ In order to use CVP, a Node object for the UFP server needs to be created, an OPSEC Application object referencing the Node object, a Resource object referencing the OPSEC Application, and a rule in the policy referencing the Resource object.

MDQ

☑ The MDQ process runs on FireWall-1 and runs the SMTP Security Server.

☑ The commands **fw mdq** or **cprestart** will restart the MDQ process.

☑ E-mail is spooled in the $FWDIR/spool directory for processing.

Secure Internal Communication

☑ Secure Internal Communication refers to internal Check Point communication between different Check Point products and integrated third-party devices.

☑ SIC uses certificates to encrypt data.

☑ The Check Point Management Server is the Certificate Authority that controls the certificates used in the Check Point product suite.

Frequently Asked Questions

The following Frequently Asked Questions, answered by the authors of this book, are designed to both measure your understanding of the concepts presented in this chapter and to assist you with real-life implementation of these concepts. To have your questions about this chapter answered by the author, browse to **www.syngress.com/solutions** and click on the **"Ask the Author"** form.

Q: What does OPSEC stand for?

A: OPSEC stands for Open Platform for Security. OPSEC is a program run by Check Point in order to certify vendors that create solutions that integrate with Check Point products.

Q: What are the five Security Servers supported by Check Point FireWall-1?

A: They are URI for HTTP-based traffic, SMTP for e-mail traffic, FTP for file transfers, TCP for generic TCP-based protocols, and CIFS for Microsoft networking traffic. These security servers run as separate processes on the Check Point FireWall-1 product.

Q: What port does CVP run on?

A: The Content Vectoring Protocol runs on TCP port 18181. Third-party content scanning products create a Secure Internal Communication (SIC) relationship with the Check Point firewall and use the CVP port to communicate to the firewall.

Q: What port does UFP run on?

A: The URI Filtering Protocol runs on TCP port 18182. Third-party Web filtering products create a Secure Internal Communication (SIC) relationship with the Check Point firewall and use the UFP port to communicate to the firewall.

Q: What process on the firewall handles the SMTP Security Server?

A: The process that runs on the firewall is called the Mail Dequeuer (MDQ). This process runs on the firewall and collects incoming e-mail, spools e-mail in the $FWDIR/spool directory, sends it to the CVP server if specified, and sends the e-mail to the outgoing e-mail server.

Q: What does Check Point use to secure internal communication, passwords or certificates?

A: The Check Point product line uses Secure Internal Communication (SIC) to communicate with each other. Certificates are used to secure this communication. A one-time password is used to transfer the initial certificate from the Check Point Management Server to the integrated product.

Q: How would a firewall administrator integrate an antivirus scanning product into a Check Point environment?

A: A Node object would be created to represent the antivirus scanner. Next an OPSEC Application object would be created for the antivirus server using the Node object as a reference. A Resource would be created that specifies what type of traffic would be redirected to the antivirus server. A rule in the policy would need to be created using the Resource that actually sends specific traffic to the antivirus server.

Chapter 11

VPN

Solutions in this chapter:

- **Encryption Overview**
- **Simplified versus Traditional VPN Configuration**
- **Route-Based VPNs**
- **Tunnel Management and Debugging**

☑ **Summary**

☑ **Solutions Fast Track**

☑ **Frequently Asked Questions**

Introduction

The emergence of the Internet has allowed the increasing growth of companies that are using it as a backbone to connect remote offices, partners, and remote clients. The Internet is a public network, in that no single entity owns the Internet. When you send data through the Internet, you have no way of knowing who owns the devices that the traffic is passing through, or who may be able to view that data. Because of this, virtual private networks (VPN) were developed. A VPN provides a means of encrypting your data such that only other authorized systems can decrypt it. Because of this, VPNs allow you to maintain the confidentiality and integrity of your data across an inherently insecure medium.

This chapter will focus on configuring site-to-site VPNs and the different design considerations that are involved. Refer to Chapter 12 for more information on remote clients, and remote client VPNs. This chapter describes many new features that will be discussed and demonstrated so that you may easily set up a VPN between two Check Points or even another vendor's device, such as a Cisco PIX firewall. We will start by explaining some key VPN-related concepts and then explain and demonstrate the different methods for setting up a Check Point VPN and configuring your rulebase in order to complete your VPN solution. We will also explain troubleshooting steps you can take when working with VPNs.

Encryption Overview

Encryption is the process of turning something that is normally readable (plaintext) into something unreadable (ciphertext). The reverse process, decryption, will turn the ciphertext back into plaintext. In practice, encryption is done by applying a mathematical formula to the plaintext. There are many types of encryption formulas or algorithms, and some are more effective at keeping the plaintext secure than others. Some forms of encryption are intended to provide data confidentiality; others also have measures to provide data integrity as well. Before discussing Check Point's specific VPN implementation, we'll review some encryption basics.

One form of simple encryption is a substitution cipher, where one character of the plaintext is replaced with another character. The classic example of this is where a is 1, b is 2, c is 3, and so on. Thus the plaintext "checkpoint" becomes "03080503111615091420" as ciphertext. Although this may seem secure, it would take a typical computer less time to try every single letter, number, and punctuation mark substitution for each character of the ciphertext, than it would for you to type the ciphertext in the first place. Because of this, most modern forms of encryption rely on the use of a *key*. The encryption key is much like a physical key, in that you need it to encrypt or decrypt the ciphertext.

Symmetric and Asymmetric Encryption

A key is used to both encrypt (lock) and decrypt (unlock) the plaintext and ciphertext, respectively. When the two keys are the same, this is *symmetric* encryption. In this system, the security of the entire encryption process relies on keeping the key a secret. If anyone learns the key, they will be able to decrypt the ciphertext and read the original message. Because the recipient needs to have the key to decrypt the message, you must have a secure way of transferring the secret key to the recipient before he or she will be able to decrypt the ciphertext.

In addition to the logistics of getting your secret key to your intended recipient, if you have two different recipients you want to send encrypted messages to, but you don't want either of them to be able to read messages intended for the other, you would need to use two different keys. This doesn't sound too bad, but imagine if you were in a midsize company of 200 users. For each user to have a secret key for use with every other user would require 19,000 unique keys. In a company with more users the number would only get even more unmanageable.

With asymmetric encryption the sender and receiver don't need to have the same key. Instead they each have a different, but *mathematically related* key. This method greatly reduces the number of keys that are needed. Each person then needs only two keys, a *public* key and a *private* key. The public key is publicly known and can be distributed freely. When senders encrypt something with their private key, the public key can be used (by anybody) to decrypt it. This has the added benefit that you know the message was encrypted by the intended person or else the public key would fail to decrypt the message. When you send something to someone, you would use their public key to encrypt the message and only the intended recipient with the proper private key could decrypt the message.

Given the advantages of asymmetric encryption, you might wonder why anybody would ever use symmetric encryption. Primarily, it's a matter of speed. The additional computations needed to use asymmetric encryption generally make it far slower than using a symmetric algorithm. When you are sending large volumes of data, such as in a computer network, where encryption and decryption are done frequently, a hybrid approach typically is adopted. This usually involves the asymmetric encryption of a symmetric key. In this way the secret symmetric key can be encrypted and distributed securely. This symmetric key is then used for future bulk data transfers.

Certificate Authorities

Given the importance of exchanging keys securely, the questions arises of how you can be sure that the (public) key you are exchanging really belongs to the person or organization you think it does. A *certificate authority's* (CA) sole function is to provide a trusted way of obtaining public keys. When you are dealing with public keys outside your organization, typically you would need to rely on a trusted third party as your CA, such as VeriSign. For key distribution between internal devices and systems, you can act as your own CA, since you trust yourself to provide legitimate public keys. This enables you to use asymmetric encryption protocols internally without having to register and pay for each certificate to be used with each key.

Exchanging Keys

As you can see, reliable encryption depends on the secure distribution of encryption keys. Managing the distribution in a secure and reliable way is handled through a key exchange protocol. Although there are multiple key exchange protocols available, Internet Key Exchange (IKE), is one of the most widely deployed key exchange mechanisms. IKE is an industry standard (RFC 2409) that can be implemented on many different platforms to provide key management functionality. IKE functionality includes establishing a security association (SA), which is a set of parameters that are used to encrypt and decrypt information between two devices. The SA will include things such as what encryption algorithm to use, how to endure data integrity (a hash algorithm), and how to renew keys.

Tunnel Mode versus Transport Mode

There are primarily two ways to encrypt IP-based traffic. One is *tunnel mode*, which takes the entire IP packet, and encrypts it, and then encapsulates this encrypted packet in a new header. The other is called *transport mode*, which encrypts only the data portion of the packet, and leaves the headers relatively intact. An advantage of tunnel mode is that it encrypts the entire original header, meaning that even the original IP addresses cannot be seen without decrypting the packet. This provides a higher degree of privacy than transport mode, which leaves the source and destination IP addresses and other header information unencrypted. On the other hand, because tunnel mode is encrypting the original packet in it's entirety, and adding a new header, it is increasing the packet size of every single packet.

Encryption Algorithms

Once you have decided that encryption is needed, and determined whether symmetric or asymmetric encryption would be more suitable, you need to choose an encryption algorithm to use. There are a large number of different encryption algorithms available. Check Point NGX supports the following encryption algorithms:

- Digital Encryption Standard (DES)

- Triple Digital Encryption Standard (3DES)

- Advanced Encryption Standard – 128 bit key (AES-128)

- Advanced Encryption Standard – 256 bit key (AES-256)

- CAST Encryption

DES may be adequate for some encryption needs, but as processing power has increased, cracking DES by *brute forcing* the key (guessing every possible key combination) is becoming increasingly feasible. In July 1998 DES was cracked in three days by a specially built computer costing around $250,000. Only six months later in January 1999, DES was again cracked by a distributed network of 100,000 Internet computers in 22 minutes. For this reason, DES is no longer considered adequate encryption for important data. 3DES is cryptographically stronger, and currently remains the minimum recommended encryption strength to be used.

Hashing Algorithms

Once you have encrypted a piece of data, you need some way to ensure that is had not been tampered with. A hash algorithm is a mathematical formula that takes a given string of input, and generates as output a unique string of a fixed size (a message digest). The computation is reproducible, meaning that the hash will be the same for the same input each time. If you change the input, the message digest will change as well. If you were to generate a message digest for the entire novel *War and Peace* and then changed a single character anywhere in it, the next message digest that you generate would be different from the first. The hash function is *not* reversible. This means that if you have the message digest, there should be no way to derive the original message that was used to produce it.

The practical use for a hash function (in a VPN) is to ensure data integrity. If you generate a hash of a given message before sending it, and the recipient then generates the same hash from the message they received, then you know that they received exactly what you sent. When you combine the message digest with an encryption algorithm, you can ensure both data integrity and confidentiality. Check Point NGX supports the following hash algorithms for VPNs:

- MD5
- Secure Hash Algorithm Version1 (SHA1)

A message digest also can be used to ensure the identity of the sender of the message. To do this, the sender encrypts the message digest using his or her private key. The recipient of the message can use the sender's public key to decrypt the message digest. The recipient then recalculates the message digest to ensure that it matches the one the sender provided. Assuming they match, the recipient knows that the message was unchanged, and that it was sent by right person. The process of encrypting the message digest to verify the identity of the sender and the integrity of the message is called a digital signature.

Public Key Infrastructure

As you can see there is a complicated interdependency between all these systems to make modern encryption work securely. If any one of these elements are compromised the entire communication stream is at risk for being intercepted. All these various systems and components work together to get the job done. The entire infrastructure that is used to provide secure public keys distribution and support digital signatures is referred to as a *public key infrastructure* (PKI).

Simplified versus Traditional VPN Configuration

In Check Point's VPN-1 there are two primary ways to configure your VPN between sites. One is the *traditional* way, which requires you to explicitly configure the access rules that specify what traffic should be encrypted. This method is more complex but allows for a high degree of control over exactly what gets encrypted. The other, *simplified* approach, allows you to simply specify what devices should have their communications encrypted, and the needed rules will be created automatically. This makes setting up a VPN between a branch office and the main office pretty painless. You can specify which method to use by going to **Policy | Global Properties | VPN**, as shown in Figure 11.1.

Figure 11.1 VPN Configuration Method Selection

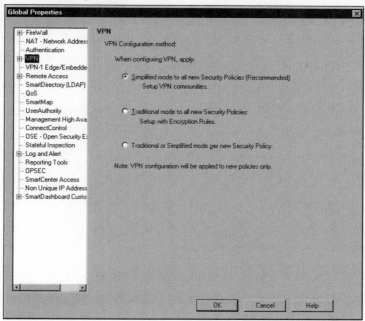

The following VPN examples will be configured between two Check Point Enterprise/Pro NGX devices. The devices should be able to communicate with each other and your secure internal communications (SIC) should be working properly.

Using the Simplified Configuration Method

Note that some of the features of Check Point's FW-1 and VPN-1 are available to you only if you use the simplified approach for VPN configuration. Generally, if you do not have a need for creating complicated and very granular encryption rules, the simplified method will be much easier to use. Because you can change methods only by creating and applying an entirely new policy, the decision of which method to use should be made with some caution. To configure a VPN using the simplified approach, follow these basic steps:

1. Enable the VPN product on the gateways.

2. Configure the VPN Domain.

3. Configure the VPN Community (Star of Mesh).

4. Install the policy.

VPN Communities

The first concept to understand when dealing with the simplified approach is the concept of VPN Communities. A VPN community is essentially a centralized object containing all the configuration settings needed for establishing an SA between devices. Members of a VPN community can be single machines, or entire sites. The community is merely a collection of objects who share the same encryption settings so that they can establish VPNs between them. By placing all these settings in a single community object, all the devices that need to use those setting in order to establish a VPN tunnel can be made members of the community. This method is not only simpler than manually configuring each of the individual gateways, but it reduces the chance of an error being made when entering the settings over and over.

There are two types of VPN communities you can create. One is the meshed, which simply stated, allows encrypted communication to occur between all gateways in the community. The meshed community usually will be the best one to use unless you have specific requirements to use the other type, the star community, which does not allow encrypted communication directly between the satellites in the star.

Meshed VPN Communities

A meshed VPN community is the simplest to configure and would be most appropriate in many cases. A meshed configuration would be adequate if you have multiple offices that all need to share data and communicate with each other across the public Internet. In this scenario, the communications are fairly distributed and all the offices need to communicate with each other to access various services that each site might hold.

The first step to establish a VPN tunnel is to go into the properties of both gateway devices and ensure that the **General Properties** sheet shows **VPN** as an enabled product. If it is not, you will need to select it and click **OK**. You may get an alert dialog box informing you that an internal CA certificate will be created and the IKE properties set. Click **OK** again. The property window for that device should close when the process is completed.

TIP

You can quickly verify that you are using simplified mode by inspecting the tabs across the top of the SmartDashboard. When in simplified mode there will be a SmartDashboard tab for VPN Communities. If there is no tab, your current policy is using the traditional configuration method.

You must then configure each network object to ensure it has the proper VPN Domain configured. You can do this by viewing the object's properties and clicking **Topology** on the left side of the window. The default will be for all IP addresses behind the gateway to be a part of the same VPN domain. You can click the Show **VPN Domain button** and the objects will be highlighted in the SmartMap pane. This makes it easier to graphically see which devices are configured as part of the same VPN domain.

You must now define the VPN community itself. You can do this by going to the network objects tree and selecting the **VPN Communities** tab. Right-click **Site to Site**, and select **New Site to Site | Meshed** as seen in Figure 11.2. You can also do this without the network objects tree by right-clicking in an empty area in the **VPN Manager** tab and selecting **New Community | Meshed**.

Figure 11.2 Creating a New VPN Community

From the following window you will configure the properties of the VPN community, as shown in Figure 11.3. In the **General** section, choose a descriptive name for the community. You can optionally select **Accept all encrypted traffic**, which means that any traffic between the endpoints will be encrypted. This option has some security implications, as you will not be able to specify which traffic to allow and disallow with security rules. Generally, you will want to leave this option unchecked and create rules in the security rulebase that specify the community in the VPN column.

Then highlight **Participating Gateways** in the left pane. Click **Add** and select your two or more gateway end points and click **OK**. The **VPN Properties** section will allow you to specify the encryption and hashing algorithms to use for key exchange and the primary data encryption.

Figure 11.3 Meshed Community Properties

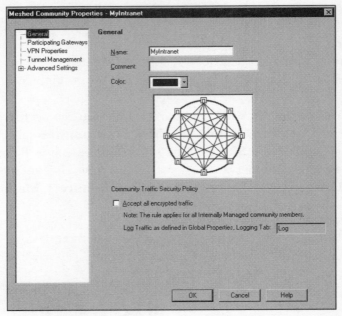

The next section is **Tunnel Management** (see Figure 11.4). When selected, these properties allow greater control over when a VPN tunnel is created. The **Set permanent tunnels** option will create the VPN tunnel and then leave it open even when there is no data to be sent across it. Because there is overhead in creating and tearing down tunnels, using permanent tunnels can improve performance, especially between sites with frequent need to send encrypted data. A remote office, who needs to get all their Internet access and file server access from the corporate office, would be a good candidate for configuring the tunnels to be permanent. If, on the other hand, the remote site only rarely had a need to send encrypted data back to the corporate office, leaving it unchecked would allow the tunnel to be created only when needed, freeing resources on the gateway the rest of the time.

Enabling route injection will cause the firewall to modify its routing table when the tunnels are unavailable. This option is only of value if the gateway device is using a dynamic routing protocol, so that it can propagate the routing changes to other devices. There are also options to log tunnel creation and tunnel failure. These options can be set for each community, or globally set for all communities under **Policy | Global Properties | Log and Alert | Community Default Rule**. The last option on this screen is for VPN Tunnel Sharing. This determines how many VPN tunnels to create between devices. Depending on the devices you have at either end, you may need any one of the three options.

Figure 11.4 Tunnel Management

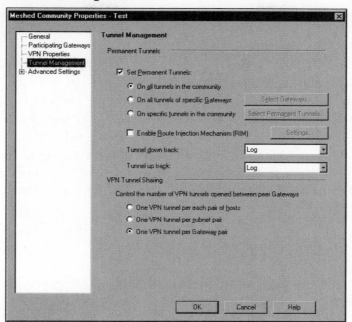

Once this is done, click **OK**. Using the simplified VPN configuration will cause the community to create a rule that encrypts the traffic. If you selected **Accept all encrypted traffic**, a new rule is also created to allow the encrypted traffic. If you didn't choose **Accept all encrypted traffic** you will need to create a rule in the rulebase to allow the traffic. The key here is that the simplified approach will create the rule to encrypt the traffic, but it still must be allowed on the gateway. To view the encryption rules select **View | VPN Rules**. If you selected **Accept all encrypted traffic**, you can view the rule that option creates by clicking **Created by community** at the top of the rulebase. You can also verify that there are no errors by checking the VPN section of the SmartView Tracker. A successful tunnel will have periodic encrypt and decrypt entries with a service of tunnel_test.

If you expand the **Advanced Settings** tab, you can select Excluded Services, Shared Secret, Advanced VPN Properties, and Wire Mode to fine-tune the VPN Community encryption. In **Excluded Services**, you can **Add** services that will not be encrypted within the VPN community. This could be useful, for example, to have troubleshooting access to remote gateways.

In **Shared Secret**, you can enable **Use only Shared Secret for all External members.** Gateways controlled by the same SmartCenter will always authenticate themselves with the certificate the ICA issued them. For Externally Managed

Gateways or Interoperable Devices (i.e. non–Check Point gateways that participate in a VPN), you can enter a Shared Secret (an agreed–upon password) for establishing a VPN with your gateways. You will need to select each external member, click on **Edit…** and enter the Shared Secret, which should be as complex as you can make it.

In **Advanced VPN Properties**, you can select the Diffie-Hellman group to use in Phase 1, the lifetime for Phase 1 (by default 1440 minutes or 1 day), and whether to use Aggressive Mode or not. For Phase 2, you can select whether to use Perfect Forward Secrecy (and which Diffie-Hellman group to use), the lifetime for Phase 2 (by default 3600 seconds or 1 hour), and whether to support a IP compression. You can also click on **Reset All VPN Properties** to reset all settings to their default. Finally, in this tab is the option **Disable NAT inside the VPN community.** With this option, all Automatic and Manual NAT rules will not be applied to traffic going through the VPN community. This is important and useful so that communication between branch offices uses the real IP address and not public IPs.

Star VPN Communities

Using the star-based communities is also referred to as *VPN Routing*, because the VPNs themselves can be made to route through a central hub gateway or group of gateways. In this way you can enforce a policy that requires all encrypted traffic to be inspected at a central office. For example you might want all the encrypted traffic for branch offices to be routed through the central office, where it is decrypted, inspected for malicious code, and then encrypted and sent to another branch office.

Configuring a star VPN community is similar to how you configured the meshed community, with only a couple of differences. You can create the new community by right-clicking in an empty area in the **VPN Manager** tab and selecting **New Community | Star**. You will see a window like the one shown in Figure 11.5. You will need to give the community a descriptive name, as before. If you want the access rule to allow the encrypted traffic to be created automatically, check **Accept all encrypted traffic**.

Figure 11.5 Star Community Properties

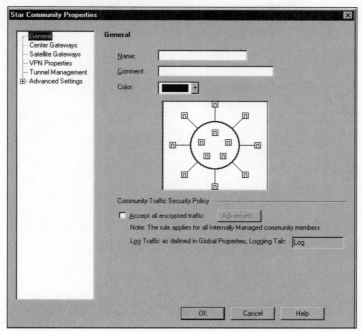

Now by clicking **Center Gateways** in the left-hand pane, you can add any gateway you wish to be at the center of the star here and click **OK**. If your organization is large enough to have several gateways at the central site, you can check the box titled **Mesh Center Gateways**. If this box is not checked, the central gateways of the star will not be able to encrypt traffic between themselves. If you have only a single central gateway there is no impact for checking this box.

Next, click **Satellite Gateways** in the left pane. From this window, you will add any satellite gateways you wish. Remember, the satellite gateways will not be able to communicate via encrypted tunnels directly between themselves. The next step is to click **VPN Properties** in the left pane and set the parameters for encryption that all community members will use. After this is done, click **Tunnel Management** in the left-hand pane where you can specify how many tunnels to bring up in the same fashion as the meshed community.

If you click the **Advanced Setting** in the left pane, and then select **VPN Routing**, you will be presented with a properties screen as shown in Figure 11.6.

Figure 11.6 VPN Routing Settings

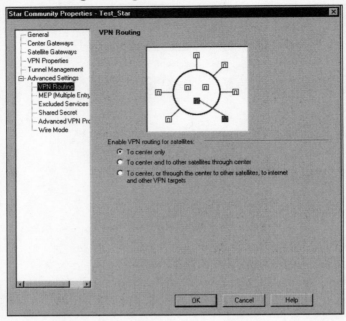

This is where the *VPN routing* aspect of a star VPN community comes into play. Although only three options are presented, they have a significant impact on how traffic is routed between the satellites and the hubs. The meaning of the options is summarized as follows:

- **To Center only** Strictly speaking, this option does not use any VPN Routing, since only encrypted traffic between the central hub and the satellites go through the VPN tunnel.

- **To Center and through to other satellites through center** All *encrypted* traffic passes through the hub(s), even traffic between satellites.

- **To center, or through the center to other satellites, to Internet and other VPN targets** *All traffic,* encrypted or unencrypted, must pass through the central hub(s).

Multiple Entry Point (MEP)

Multiple entry point (MEP) is a function that allows you to configure more than one gateway to act as the hub for a star VPN community. The advantage of this is that you can provide redundancy for your VPN termination from the satellite sites.

In order to configure MEP, go into the properties for your star VPN community and click **Central Gateway** in the left pane. Add one or more central gateways that you wish to provide redundancy for each other. Then click **Advanced Settings** to expand it, and select **MEP (Multiple Entry Points)**. The MEP property screen is shown in Figure 11.7.

Figure 11.7 Configuring MEP

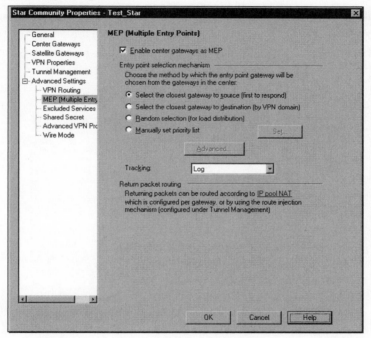

Once you have enabled MEP by checking the box Enable center gateways as MEP, you are given a few options as to how the entry point is chosen. The specifics on those options are as follows:

- **Select the closest gateway to source** With this option the first gateway to respond to a Check Point *proprietary* reliable data protocol (RDP) packet from the satellite in question becomes the gateway for that satellite.

- **Select the closest gateway to destination** With this option the gateway selected is the domain gateway whose IP belongs to the same VPN domain as the destination IP address for the VPN tunnel.

- **Random Selection** The terminating gateway will be chosen randomly. This serves to provide load balancing across the MEP group.

- **Manually set priority list** This option allows you to choose a first, second, and third priority gateway to be used and set any exceptions. This option might be useful if you had a high end firewall with another less robust machine acting as secondary, allowing you to configure the high end machine as the primary.

Installing the Policy

Once you have configured your policy in SmartDashboard you must install it. Click **Policy | Install**. You will be presented with a window that allows you to choose which devices to install the policy on, as shown in Figure 11.8. In this case you would select the hub gateway(s) and any satellite gateways and click **OK**.

Figure 11.8 Installing a Policy

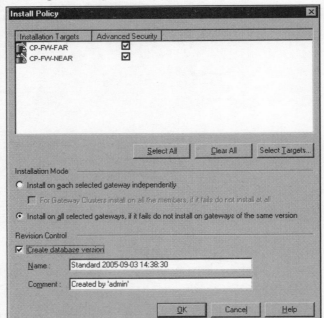

There are only a few options on this screen. One is the installation mode. Selecting **Install on all selected gateways, if it fails do not install on gateways of the same version** is recommended. This will ensure that if there is a problem, you don't end up with some gateways using the new policy and others using the old policy, possibly resulting in an inoperable state. Click **OK**. When the install is completed you will see a window indicating that the install was successful. If there were any problems you will be able to view any errors or warnings associated with the installation process by clicking **Show Errors**.

Configuring a VPN with a Cisco PIX

At this point we have walked through configuring a simplified VPN with both a star and a mesh VPN community between two Check Point Enterprise/Pro NGX gateways. We will now show how to configure a mesh community with one endpoint of the VPN being a Cisco PIX 501 firewall. Even though the Cisco PIX will not be able to pull the VPN settings from the VPN Community, there could still be value in setting up the VPN with the simplified approach over the traditional approach. By using a community, additional Check Point gateways can still take advantage of the community settings, and the automatically generated rulebase will provide the needed connectivity to the PIX. You must still configure all the VPN settings on the PIX manually for the VPN tunnel to work.

The following example assumes you already have IP connectivity between the Cisco PIX firewall and the Check Point Enterprise/Pro NGX gateway. On the PIX enter the following commands while in privileged mode, followed by a carriage return, to configure the VPN tunnel.

```
configure terminal
access-list 101 permit ip 192.168.3.0 255.255.255.0 any
```

Access list 101 will be used to specify what traffic should be encrypted, in this case all traffic *from* 192.168.3.0.

```
access-list nonat permit ip 192.168.3.0 255.255.255.0 any
nat (inside) 0 access-list nonat
```

The named access list `nonat` is used to specify what traffic *not* to NAT, in this case any traffic from 192.168.3.0.

```
sysopt connection permit-ipsec
```

This tells the PIX to accept all IPSEC authenticated traffic. This setting is similar in function to the Accept all encrypted traffic setting on the Check Point device.

```
crypto ipsec transform-set rtptac esp-3des esp-md5-hmac
```

This configures the IPSEC encryption settings. The VPN community on the Check Point gateway will need to have identical settings for the VPN tunnel to work.

```
crypto map checkpointmap 10 ipsec-isakmp
crypto map checkpointmap 10 match address 101
crypto map checkpointmap 10 set peer 192.168.2.1
crypto map checkpointmap 10 set transform-set rtptac
```

This set of commands defines the cryptomap named `checkpointmap` to be used with peer 192.168.2.1.

```
crypto map checkpointmap interface outside
isakmp enable outside
```

These commands apply the cryptomap to the outside interface of the PIX.

```
isakmp key syngress address 192.168.2.1 netmask 255.255.255.255
```

This uses the shared secret key `syngress` for IKE authentication with peer 192.168.2.1.

```
isakmp policy 1 authentication pre-share
isakmp policy 1 encryption 3des
isakmp policy 1 hash md5
isakmp policy 1 group 2
isakmp policy 1 lifetime 86400
```

These settings define the ISAKMP policy for the PIX; again, these setting must match the VPN community settings. One this is done, you are ready to create the corresponding VPN community on the Check Point gateway. Right-click anywhere in the SmartMap area and select **New Network Object | Interoperable Devices**. On this screen, fill out a name, and the externally facing IP address. You will then need to click **Topology** on the left and manually enter the interface information for the PIX.

You will need to create a VPN community as we did earlier, either a mesh or a star, with the appropriate encryption settings. While viewing the VPN community settings, click **Advanced Settings | Shared Secret** and click to enable **Use only shared secret for all external members**. Then, with the new PIX gateway, click **Edit** and enter the shared secret syngress and click **OK** twice to close the properties. Install the policy.

At this point encryption between the two gateways should be working. You will need to test by sending traffic to destinations behind the PIX gateway. If you try to generate test traffic with a destination IP of the PIX itself it might fail, while traffic destined to an IP behind the PIX is working properly.

Tools & Traps…

Reading Logs

Remember as you read the SmartView Tracker logs to try and see what traffic is or is not working properly, to consider the source of your information. When you have two Check Point devices at each end of the tunnel, you will see an encrypt and a decrypt log entry for each session. When one of the gateway devices is a PIX you will not see any feedback from the PIX in your SmartView Tracker logs. You will need to connect to the PIX itself to troubleshoot any connectivity issues.

You can access some PIX statistical information related to VPNs by using any of the following commands. The debug commands will show information on the console as the encryption process occurs. This allows you to see and troubleshoot the encryption process as it occurs. The **show** commands will display the current settings that are in working memory.

```
#debug crypto isakmp
#debug crypto ipsec
#show access-list
#show crypto ipsec security-association
#show crypto isakmp
```

Using the Traditional VPN Configuration Method

In some cases you might want more granularity over the encryption process. For example, to save on CPU cycles you might choose to encrypt only a particular traffic flow and leave the rest of the traffic unencrypted between locations. In this case, you can use the traditional method. Select the traditional method by going to **Policy | Global Properties | VPN**, as shown previously in Figure 11.1, and select **Traditional**. If you already have the policy defined as simplified, you must create a new policy (**File | New**) to use the traditional method. The basic steps of traditional VPN configuration are as follows:

1. Enable the VPN product on the gateways.

2. Configure the VPN Domain.

3. Configure the Traditional Mode Configuration properties on each gateway object.

4. Create the encrypt rule in the rulebase.

5. Install the policy.

The primary difference between the two approaches is that instead of the gateway deriving all of its encryption settings from the VPN community it belongs to, they are specified in the properties of each gateway object. View the gateway object's property pages as before, and ensure that **VPN** is an activated product. Now select **VPN** on the left pane, and click **Traditional Mode Configuration,** as shown in Figure 11.9.

Figure 11.9 Traditional Mode VPN Configuration

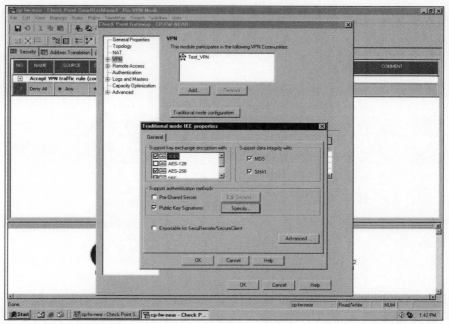

You must then manually configure the types of encryption to be used for key exchange and which hash algorithm to use for data integrity. You must also specify which authentication methods to use. Once this is completed, you must create a rule that specifies what traffic to encrypt. From within the **Security** tab, select **Add rule above current**. The rulebase gives you a high degree of control over what types of traffic you want to encrypt. If you want to encrypt all traffic between the two gateways, you create a group and add both gateway endpoints to the group. Once this is done modify the new rule and change both the source and destination to the new group you just created. Change the action to **encrypt**, and change the track to **Log**. Your rule should look like rule number 1 in Figure 11.10.

Figure 11.10 Traditional Mode Encrypt Rule

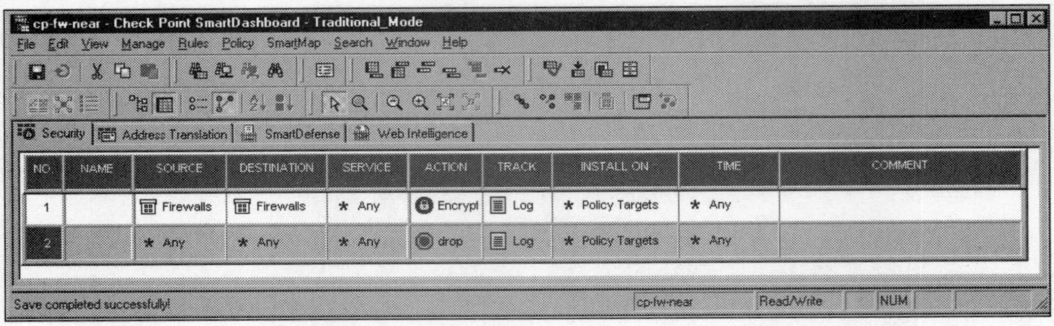

VPN Directional Matching

VPN Directional Match is an option you can enable that allows you to control when traffic should be encrypted, not only based on its source and destination within different VPN communities. This would allow you to specify that all traffic from a particular VPN community to any other community be encrypted, but traffic flowing from other communities into that community doesn't need to be. You can enable directional matching by going to **Policy | Global Properties | VPN | Advanced** and checking the box **Enable VPN directional match in VPN column**.

> **NOTE**
>
> The VPN Directional Match feature is supported only on IPSO, Linux, SecurePlatform, and SecurePlatform Pro.

Once it is enabled, when you right-click on the VPN column and select Edit, you are provided a new window, with some additional options for encryption as seen in Figure 11.11. You can choose to encrypt traffic in both directions (the default behavior) or only in one direction. If you select **Match traffic in this direction only** and click **Add**, you are able to then select the source and destination community objects for the rule to match against.

Figure 11.11 VPN Directional Match

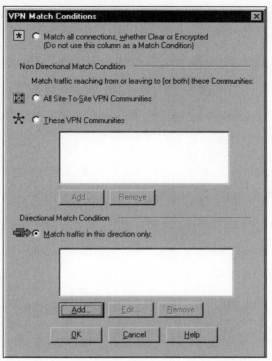

Route-Based VPNs

Route-based VPNs are a mechanism whereby the VPN gateway can participate in and understand routing protocols and use that information to dynamically work around network failures. Before getting too deep into how this is done, it's worth discussing a little bit about what a *routing* protocol is.

Routing Protocols

When an IP packet is sent out across a network, routers have to make decisions about which interface to use to send the packet on its way. A router in this instance can be almost any network device, as long as it is connected to more than one network and it makes decisions as to which interface to send the traffic through. The router makes these decisions based on entries in a routing table. In a simple network this routing table is generally created by manually entering the routes or building automatically based on the network interface configuration. Once entered these manual routes don't change. If a link goes down, the router simply continues attempting to send the traffic out the interface indicated in its routing table. This means until the problem is fixed, traffic won't be able to reach its intended destination.

With a dynamic routing protocol, a router can learn about links to different networks and share that information with other routers. The learning process can be from a manually entered route, or because it heard about it from another router. In this way, if a link goes down, the router closest to the fault can inform the other routers and if there is an alternate path, they can adapt and route traffic through the alternate path so that it reaches its destination. Of course this is somewhat of a simplification as routing protocols can be very complex, with entire books dedicated to a single routing protocol and its use.

Routing protocols are not to be confused with *routable* protocols. A routing protocol is the specific protocol used by a router to learn and share information about routes. A routable protocol is a protocol that can be redirected based on the router's information. IP for example is a routable protocol, whereas BGP or OSPF are routing protocols.

Configuring VTIs

When using route-based VPNs you must configure a VPN tunnel interface (VTI) on the gateway. This *virtual* interface is configured and managed at the OS level. The decision to encrypt traffic is then made by the OS based on which interface the traffic is routed through, instead of being made based on parameters set within some other software running on the machine in question. For this to function, the gateway itself needs to participate in and understand a dynamic routing protocol. Thus, route-based VPNs allow the gateways to dynamically reroute the VPN traffic based on topology changes, much like a router would reroute IP traffic based on topology changes.

NOTE

Route-based VPNs are supported only on SecurePlatform and Nokia IPSO 3.9. Route-based VPNs can be implemented only between two gateways within the same VPN community, using the simplified VPN configuration method.

Both SecurePlatform and Nokia IPSO support route-based VPNs using open shortest path first (OSPF), but only SecurePlatform supports route-based VPNs using border gateway protocol (BGP4). The dynamic routing protocol is implemented via the GateD software. Also, when configuring the VTI, it can be configured as an unnumbered interface (Nokia IPSO 3.9 only) or a numbered interface. If the VTI is configured as an unnumbered interface, the source IP address of the encrypted traffic will be that of the physical interface.

Configuring VTI Example

We will now walk through an example where we configure VTI on a SecurePlatform Pro NGX machine. For the example, our two gateways can see each other and communicate, and SIC is working properly. We have already set up a meshed VPN community and encryption is working properly between the two gateways.

Start by configuring the virtual interface. You can access the commands to configure a virtual interface by going into the VPN shell by typing the following followed by a carriage return or pressing Enter:

```
vpn shell
```

The vpn shell is used to configure various setting related to VPNs. Once in the shell you can add a *numbered* VTI by entering the following command, filling in the appropriate IP addresses for your environment:

```
>/interface/add/numbered <local IP> <peer IP> <peer name> <interface name>
```

Specifying an interface name is optional; in our example we entered the following:

```
>/interface/add/numbered 192.168.2.90 192.168.2.1 CP-FW-NEAR
Interface 'vt-CP-FW-NEAR' was added successfully to the system
```

You can then use the ifconfig command to verify the interface configuration. The output should show the newly added interface in the list of interfaces. The next step is to enable the routing protocol. You enable a routing protocol, in this case OSPF by entering the following commands:

```
>router
>enable
#configure terminal
(config)#router ospf 1
(config-router-ospf)#router-id 192.168.2.90
(config-router-ospf)#redistribute kernal
(config-router-ospf)#network 192.168.2.1 0.0.0.0 area 0.0.0.0
(config-router-ospf)# network 192.168.2.90 0.0.0.0 area 0.0.0.0
(config-router-ospf)#exit
(config)#exit
#write memory
```

Then enter the following command to verify that the changes were saved and applied sucessfully.

```
#show ip ospf interface
```

You will then need to complete the configuration by enabling OSPF on all SecurePlatform or Nokia ISPO gateways in this VPN domain.

Tunnel Management and Debugging

Although Check Point makes setting up VPN tunnels relatively simple, there will be times when you need to troubleshoot a VPN tunnel that isn't working properly. In these cases you will need to use your understanding of the encryption process, and the tools available to you, to make some informed decisions about what the problem is. In the next section, we will discuss some of the most useful troubleshooting tools that are provided.

Using SmartView Tracker

The built-in logging facility, SmartView Tracker, will be your primary source of information concerning the health and status of your gateways and VPNs. The SmartView Tracker comes with some preconfigured log queries. If you are consolidating and viewing a lot of logs from several different devices the logs can be a little overwhelming to sort through. The left-hand pane is where you can select some predefined queries. By going to **Log Queries | Predefined | VPN** you can restrict the view to only those entries related to tunnel creation and maintenance.

If you find you still have too many VPN entries to sort through effectively, you can filter the display even further. Do this by clicking a column at the top. For example if we wanted to see only VPN logs between two particular gateways, we would right-click the top of the **VPN Peer Gateway** column and select **Edit Filter**. We are then presented with a list of objects in the left-hand pane of the window. Select the two you would like to view and click **Add**. This moves them to the right-hand pane, as seen in Figure 11.12. When you are done click **OK**. The

SmartView Tracker VPN query will now show only the VPN logs between the two

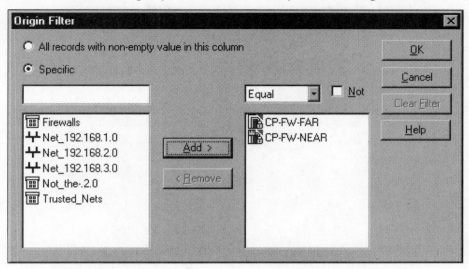

devices you selected.

Figure 11.12 Filtering Logs in SmartView Tracker

Check Point makes administration of the firewalls and VPNs easier by including some automatically generated rules in the security rulebase. If you go to **View | Implied Rules** you can see the rules that Check Point has created automatically. If you are using the simplified VPN configuration method, you can also enable the display of the automatically created VPN rules on the same menu. You'll notice all these automatic rules are set not to generate log entries. You cannot click on the **Track** column and edit these rules directly; instead, if you want to see log entries for the implied rules go to **Policy | Global Properties** and check the box at the bottom, **Log Implied Rules**. Depending on your configuration this may generate a lot of log entries so it is recommended to use this only if you are troubleshooting an issue or if the load on the gateways is minimal.

The Global Properties also has some additional settings you can enable by clicking **Log and Alert** in the left pane. This will display the screen shown in

Figure 11.13. The first three settings relate specifically to VPN logging. They should

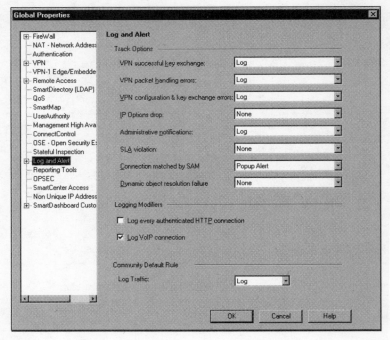

be set to **Log** by default; however, you may want to make certain they are checked if you are not seeing all the log entries you should be.

Figure 11.13 Log and Alert Options in Global Properties

Using cpstat

Cpstat is another tool you can use to see the current status of the gateways. Cpstat is a command line tool without a GUI interface. To run it you can simply go to a command prompt and type **cpstat**. If you type it with no other parameters, you get the following help screen as output.

```
C:\WINNT>cpstat


Usage: cpstat [-p port][-f flavour][-o polling [-c count] [-e period]] [-d]
application_flag


-p Port number of the AMON server.
   Default is the standard AMON port (18192).
```

```
-f The flavour of the output (as appears in the configuration file).
   Default is to use the first flavour found in the configuration file.

-o Polling interval (seconds) specifies the pace of the results.
   Default is 0, meaning the results are shown only once.

-c Specifying how many times the results are shown.
   Default is 0, meaning the results are repeatedly shown.

-e Period interval (seconds) specifies the interval over which
   "statistical" oids are computed. Ignored for regular oids.

-d Debug mode

Available application_flags:

------------------------------------------------------------
|Flag          |Flavours                                    |
------------------------------------------------------------
|asm           |default, WS                                 |
------------------------------------------------------------
|fw            |default, interfaces, policy, perf, hmem, kmem, |
|              |inspect, cookies, chains, fragments, totals,   |
|              |ufp, http, ftp, telnet, rlogin, smtp, sync, all|
------------------------------------------------------------
|fg            |all                                         |
------------------------------------------------------------
|os            |default, ifconfig, routing, memory,         |
|              |old_memory, cpu, disk, perf, multi_cpu,     |
|              |multi_disk, all, average_cpu, average_memory, |
|              |statistics                                  |
------------------------------------------------------------
|persistency |product, TableConfig, SourceConfig          |
------------------------------------------------------------
|polsrv        |default, all                                |
------------------------------------------------------------
|vpn           |default, product, IKE, ipsec, traffic,      |
|              |compression, accelerator, nic, statistics,  |
|              |watermarks, all                             |
```

Although the cpstat can provide a wealth of information, for purposes of troubleshooting VPNs we are most concerned with the VPN application flag. By specifying the VPN application flag, you are telling cpstat that you want to see only VPN-related information. If you don't specify a "flavor" the default will be to output all the VPN-related information. The Flavor flag allows you to further specify what subset of information you want to see. The following example shows some of the output related to IKE negotiation:

```
cpstat -d vpn -f IKE <ENTER>
<content ommitted>
IKE current SAs:                                    1
IKE current SAs initiated by me:                    0
IKE current SAs initiated by peer:                  1
IKE max concurrent SAs:                             2
IKE max concurrent SAs initiated by me:             1
IKE max concurrent SAs initiated by peer:           1
IKE total SAs:                                      4
IKE total SAs initiated by me:                      2
IKE total SAs initiated by peer:                    2
IKE total SA attempts:                              1
IKE total SA attempts initiated by me:              0
IKE total SA attempts initiated by peer:            1
IKE current ongoing SA negotiations:                0
IKE max concurrent SA negotiations:                 1
IKE no response from peer (initiator errors): 0
IKE total failures (initiator errors):        0
IKE total failures (responder errors):        0
IKE total failures (initiator + responder):   0
<content ommitted>
```

NOTE

The application and flavour flags are case sensitive, so in the preceding example, cpstat –d vpn –f IKE would produce the desired output, and cpstat –d vpn –f ike would result in an error.

Summary

At this point you should have a basic understanding of encryption principles and their application. Confidentiality of data is ensured through encryption, and the security of that encryption is dependent on the quality of the encryption algorithm used. Certificates issued by a trusted third-party certificate authority are attached to public encryption keys to validate who the owner of a given public key is. Message integrity and authentication are ensured through the use of digital signatures and certificate authorities. And the entire process of distributing keys securely is handled by key exchange protocols such as IKE.

All these things together are used to make secure communication across insecure media possible. If any one component is implemented improperly the entire process becomes vulnerable to compromise. The largest symmetric key won't be of any value if it's easily obtainable by unauthorized parties. The best encryption algorithm does no good if you can't validate to whom you are speaking. In short, the entire infrastructure and every component must be implemented with care and planning for it to provide the security that was intended.

Given the fact that such a high level of planning is required for a successful VPN implementation, we have included a functionality matrix to help locate what VPN features are compatible with which platforms in Table 11.1.

Table 11.1 Feature Support Matrix

	Nokia IPSO	Linux	SecurePlatform	Windows
Simplified VPN Star Community	VPN Routing MEP Route-based VPN (OSPF) Unnumbered VTI Numbered VTI VPN Directional Match	VPN Routing MEP – – VPN Directional Match	VPN Routing MEP Route-based VPN (OSPF) Route-based VPN (BGP) Numbered VTI VPN Directional Match	VPN Routing MEP – – – –
Simplified VPN Mesh Community	Route-based VPN (OSPF) Unnumbered VTI Numbered VTI VPN Directional Match	– – VPN Directional Match	Route-based VPN (OSPF) Route-based VPN (BGP) Numbered VTI VPN Directional Match	– – –

Solutions Fast Track

Encryption Overview

☑ Symmetric encryption means both the passwords used to encrypt and decrypt are the same; asymmetric encryption means the two passwords are different.

☑ Tunnel mode encryption encrypts the entire packet, and rewrites a new header, thus hiding the original IP address; transport mode encryption encrypts only the data portion of the packet.

☑ Encryption algorithms vary in strength and quality.

☑ Hash algorithms use a variable length string as input, and create a unique fixed length string as output.

☑ Certificate authorities are trusted entities used to validate the owner of a given public key.

Simplified versus Traditional VPN Configuration

☑ Meshed VPN communities allow encryption between any of their members.

☑ Star communities can be used to control the flow of VPN tunnels such that they must pass through specific central hub gateways.

☑ Multiple entry point is a star community feature to provide high availability and load balancing for hub gateways.

☑ Encryption rules are used in the rulebase in traditional VPN configurations to specify what traffic should be encrypted.

Route-Based VPNs

☑ Dynamic Routing protocols are used to dynamically communicate topology changes to other devices so that traffic can be routed most efficiently.

- ☑ Virtual Tunnel Interfaces are used to enable Nokia IPSO and SecurePlatform devices to participate in routing decisions by using a dynamic routing protocol.

Tunnel Management and Debugging

- ☑ SmartView Tracker is the utility for centrally viewing logs generated by Check Point products.
- ☑ Cpstat is a command–line utility to viewing FW-1 and VPN-1 configuration settings and status.

Frequently Asked Questions

The following Frequently Asked Questions, answered by the authors of this book, are designed to both measure your understanding of the concepts presented in this chapter and to assist you with real-life implementation of these concepts. To have your questions about this chapter answered by the author, browse to **www.syngress.com/solutions** and click on the **"Ask the Author"** form.

Q: If I create a mesh VPN community and then later decide I want to use a star, can I convert them somehow or can I mix the two types?

A: If you need to convert between a mesh and star you will need to create a new community of the desired type and add the gateways as members. You can mix and match the two community types and a given gateway can par–ticipate in more than one community.

Q: If I am using the simplified mode for VPN configuration and want to change to traditional mode, can I?

A: You can, but you will have to create an entirely new policy and specify tradi–tional mode at the time of policy creation. You will then need to recreate all your objects within the new policy. A *unsupported* utility to export and import objects in SmartCenter is Object Filler and Object Dumper. These are not supported by Check Point and come with no warranty whatsoever, but this tool is widely used (http://www.phoneboy.com/bin/view.pl/FAQs/ObjectFiller).

Q: If I am using the traditional mode VPN configuration and decide I want to use the simplified mode will I have to create a new policy?

A: No, you won't. Traditional mode policies *can* be converted by going to **Policy | Convert To | Simplified VPN**. There is no conversion option if you are going from simplified to traditional mode.

Q: Which encryption algorithm should I use for my VPN?

A: Generally speaking, you should use the strongest algorithm your hardware can support while maintaining acceptable response times. 3DES is considered the minimum standard to secure data of any importance. Remember, not all vendors will support all algorithms. For example, Cisco PIX currently supports only DES and 3DES so you couldn't use AES-128 or AES-256 for a VPN using a PIX.

Q: Can I use create a VPN tunnel between my Check Point VPN-1 and <insert product name here>?

A: Check Point's VPN-1 product has been certified by the ICSA (www.icsalabs.com/icsa/icsahome.php) to be IPSec compliant. This means that it *should* work with any other device that complies with the IPSec standards. For details on configuring your specific product, refer to Check Point's Web site and the Web site for your other product. A lot of helpful information can be found from the FireWall-1/VPN-1 FAQ page at www.cpug.org/forums, which isn't affiliated with Check Point in any way.

Q: Can I send the SmartView Tracker logs to a syslog server?

A: Not easily as there is no built in syslog support. You can work around this in several ways. You can view the raw logs in the log directory ($FWDIR/log) and export them to other utilities for analysis or syslog logging. You should familiarize yourself with the *fw log* command options as well.

Chapter 12

SecuRemote, SecureClient, and Integrity

Solutions in this chapter:

- SecuRemote
- SecureClient
- Office Mode
- Secure Configuration Verification
- Integrity

☑ Summary

☑ Solutions Fast Track

☑ Frequently Asked Questions

Introduction

The two most common cries of corporate management through the late 1990s and early 2000s were, "We must be secure" and "We must be flexible." In order to be flexible, a workforce must be mobile and adaptive to change. In essence, the workforce has to be fluid. The nature of security inherently places restrictions on the workforce. Either they can no longer access every file on a given share drive, or need to call a help desk because they can't remember the password for a particular server. Every one of these incidents creates a lag in time, where productivity seems to slow down or stop. Fluidity changes to solidity, and it's the fault of security… or at least that's how it's perceived.

This chapter is dedicated to the increasing number of employees that are either working comfortably at home or just simply away from the office, who need corporate access as if working locally. Since 1996, SecuRemote has been the primary VPN client from Check Point, made freely available, providing your firewall has proper VPN licensing. In 2001, Check Point released SecureClient, which provides additional and increased security over its little brother. SecureClient has the ability to receive a desktop policy from a VPN-1/Firewall-1 Policy Server. This increased security requires a SecureClient license, which is licensed by the number of users that can download a policy from your gateway.

In late 2003, Check Point focused the direction of their corporate strategy, increasing development on internal and web security. The new strategy boldly reflects their new approach to security: perimeter, internal and Web security. In early 2004, Check Point purchased Zone Labs, makers of the popular freeware desktop firewall ZoneAlarm, and brilliantly incorporated the enterprise version of ZoneAlarm, Integrity, with SecureClient to create Integrity SecureClient. Integrity is a desktop firewall that incorporates real-time protection against malicious code and is centrally manageable. In this chapter, we will discuss setup and configuration of these products to gain the highest level of client protection that Check Point offers its customers.

SecuRemote

SecuRemote is Check Point's VPN-1 Client product. It is an agent that sits on the client machine, providing encrypted secure access to a company's private network. It has been a mainstay of the security industry, as Check Point was one of the first companies to market an easy-to-use graphical user interface (GUI) VPN client. SecuRemote utilizes the IKE (ISAKMP) key exchange protocol to establish an encrypted tunnel between the desktop machine and the VPN-1 Firewall gateway.

This allows the desktop to be connected to any Internet connection, and still allow the user to securely access a company's internal network resources, such as e-mail or internal web applications.

> **NOTE**
>
> Internet connectivity to build a VPN tunnel can be tricky. Most corporations and some Internet Service Providers (ISPs) block IPSec protocols (50 & 51) and port 500 via egress firewall filtering. This is sometimes used as an additional security mechanism to ensure the company or ISP can monitor the traffic leaving their private network. A strong argument can be made that blocking encrypted VPN tunnels ensures that corporate proprietary or classified data is not leaving the private network in an unknown or uncontrolled manner. In situations such as this, it is important to identify the acceptable use policy of said entity, and determine if you are allowed to utilize VPN tunneling technology. If restrictions have been placed on your ability to build a VPN tunnel and obtaining access to your private network is critical to your mission or goal, contact the ISP's or corporation's Information Security department and request a waiver. Additionally, you may need to provide written justification for allowing an encrypted VPN tunnel to your company's private network.

What's New with SecuRemote in NGX?

Some of the more interesting additions to SecuRemote in NGX are:

- **NAT-T Support** SecuRemote now supports the industry-standard Network Address Translation (NAT) Traversal. This is an improved way to handle NAT on VPN gateways.

- **Office Mode** The address assigned by office mode can now be utilized to access other gateways within the private network.

- **Multiple Entry Point (MEP)** With MEP configured, SecuRemote can now take advantage of a centrally managed connection profile providing a backup gateway, without needing to make a MEP decision.

- **General Connectivity** The encryption domain of the gateway can now be defined differently for site-to-site VPN, and for remote access VPN.

Standard Client

The standard SecuRemote client provides a GUI interface, allowing users to easily set up VPN connectivity to multiple sites residing in different encryption domains. An encryption domain is determined by the IP address of the destination you are attempting to access. For instance, if you are currently located at 10.10.10.10, and the resources you are attempting to reach are located at your company's private network, with an IP address of 192.168.100.120, the encryption domain for your company's private network might be 192.168.100.0/24 (given your company uses the entire subnet). This means any traffic destined for an IP address between 192.168.100.1 and 192.168.100.254 would be routed through your encrypted VPN tunnel to your company's private network. If you then added an additional site, giving it an encryption domain of 192.168.168.0/24, any resource you attempted to reach with an IP Address within the 192.168.168.0 subnet would be routed through a different encryption tunnel to reach that resource.

This flexibility allows users to connect to different locations to gain the specific access they require without having multiple remote access clients installed. Users should begin by installing the SecuRemote client after downloading it from Check Point's Web site, www.checkpoint.com, or obtaining a prepackaged version of the software that has already been configured using the SecureClient Packaging Tool, available with the Smart Center Management Suite.

TIP

An extremely easy way to distribute SecuRemote or SecureClient to your user community is to take advantage of Check Point's SecureClient Packaging Tool. It is a handy package builder that allows administrators to configure a SecuRemote or SecureClient installation package that contains all important site and installation options they require. The tool is versatile, allowing the administrator to show the installing user as much or as little information about the client install as they like.

Particularly useful features of the Packaging Tool include a silent install that doesn't prompt the user for any additional information, choosing whether or not to force the installing user to reboot after installation, or even the ability to disallow the user from disabling SecuRemote or SecureClient. In any environment where the general user community's comfort level with technology can vary greatly, the SecureClient Packaging Tool can be a life saver during any deployment.

Basic Remote Access

There are two main steps in setting up secure VPN connections to your private network. First, the Check Point VPN-1/Firewall-1 gateway must be configured to accept the incoming connection. The encryption domain must be defined, users must be created, and a Security Policy must be written to allow user connectivity to the gateway in order to access the private network. Depending on the size of your network, and the resources available to you, it may be a smart move to utilize an authentication mechanism such as RADIUS to authenticate your user community. Check Point supports multiple authentication methodologies, such as RADIUS, SecureID, TACACS, LDAP, Check Point Password, and Certificate Based Authentication via the internal Check Point CA, or a Check Point OPSEC partner CA product. This will save time defining hundreds or thousands of users in Check Point's Smart Console, and it is likely that even small to medium companies will have some type of user database available for authentication purposes. In large scale environments, it is necessary to explore user management and authentication outside of the Check Point Management Console. Check Point supports multiple authentication methodologies, such as RADIUS, SecureID, TACACS, LDAP, Check Point Password, and Certificate Based Authentication. Certificate Based Authentication is supported via the internal Check Point Certificate Authority (CA), or through a Check Point OPSEC Partner's CA product (such as Entrust). In this chapter, we will describe setting up authentication based on Check Point username and password authentication.

> **NOTE**
>
> Although RADIUS, TACACS, and LDAP support mostly username and password authentication, that may not be secure enough for your environment. Authentication is the most important issue when setting up any type of remote access capability. It is also frequently the biggest obstacle. In order to allow any access to your private network, you must be reasonably certain that you are granting access only to those who should have access. It is possible for anyone to download Check Point's SecuRemote product, add your VPN-1 gateway as a site, and attempt to access your private network posing as one of your legitimate users.
>
> Username and password is typically the weakest form of authentication because in some situations, they can be easily inferred or guessed. The most secure of these methods is Certificate Based Authentication, providing the user with a certificate that must be presented to the VPN-1 gateway to gain access to the private network. RSA SecureID is another increased form of security in which the user is given a physical- or software-based token that generates a seemingly random number that must be typed in to access the private network. In both cases, the user must present an object to gain access to the private network, which decreases the opportunity of an attacker gaining unauthorized access. Instead of using inference, or research to gain access to your private network, the attacker must then acquire one of the physical SecureID tokens, or break into and steal the legitimate user's certificate or SecureID software—both of which require significantly greater skill than utilizing password cracking techniques.

Next, the SecuRemote client must be installed and configured on the end user's machine with the correct site information for the VPN-1 gateway. The user then enters his or her credentials (username and password) and connects to the VPN-1 gateway. SecuRemote downloads the necessary information to build an encrypted tunnel to the VPN-1 gateway and the user can then access resources located within the company's private network.

Defining the Connection Policy

In this section, we will explain rule generation and policy definition of setting up SecuRemote/SecureClient Remote access. We will set up a simple policy that allows a predefined group of SecuRemote users access to the private corporate network. If you are not familiar with SmartDashboard, and how to create objects and users, refer to Chapter 5.

First, log in to SmartDashboard (see Figure 12.1).

Figure 12.1 Logging in to SmartDashboard

Identify where the new rule should belong in the security rule set and then right-click on the rule below where you want your new Remote access Rule. Select **Add Rule Above** (see Figure 12.2).

Figure 12.2 The Security Rule Set

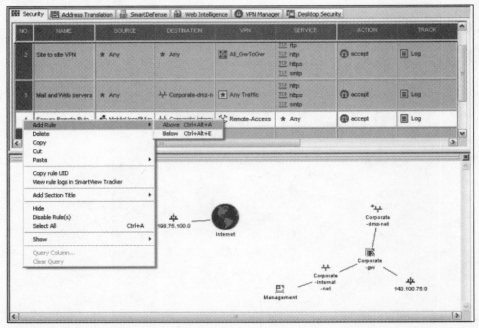

Double-click on the name field of the rule you just created, and type a brief descriptive name for this rule. For this example, the rule will be called new SecuRemote rule (see Figure 12.3).

Figure 12.3 Selecting the New SecuRemote Rule

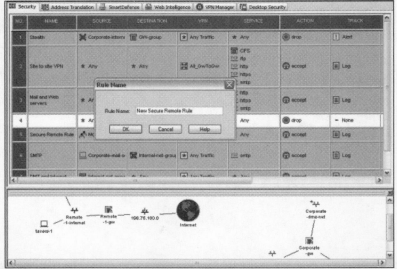

Next, right-click on the Source field of your "New SecuRemote Rule" and select **Add User Access.** This will bring up a new window that allows you to choose which groups can use this rule to connect to the VPN gateway. Select the MobileUser group and click **Edit** (see Figure 12.4).

Figure 12.4 Assigning User Access to the VPN Gateway

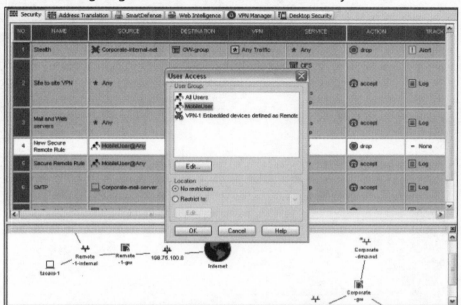

Another new window will open, giving you the ability to chose which users should be in the group MobileUser. Select the appropriate users and click **OK** (see Figure 12.5). At this point you can also define restrictions on from where this user group can access this rule. For example, this rule may be for internal users to access a protected network. You wouldn't want them to be able to access this network from anywhere, so you can restrict access based on the location from where they are attempting to connect. For the purpose of this example, we will allow this group of users to access the corporate network from any location. Leave the No restriction radio button selected, and click **OK**.

Figure 12.5 Choosing Users for the MobileUser Group

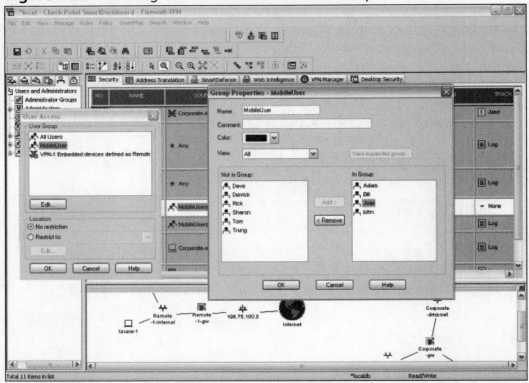

Next, right-click on the destination segment of your rule and select **Add** (see Figure 12.6).

Figure 12.6 Selecting Add from the Destination Segment of a Rule

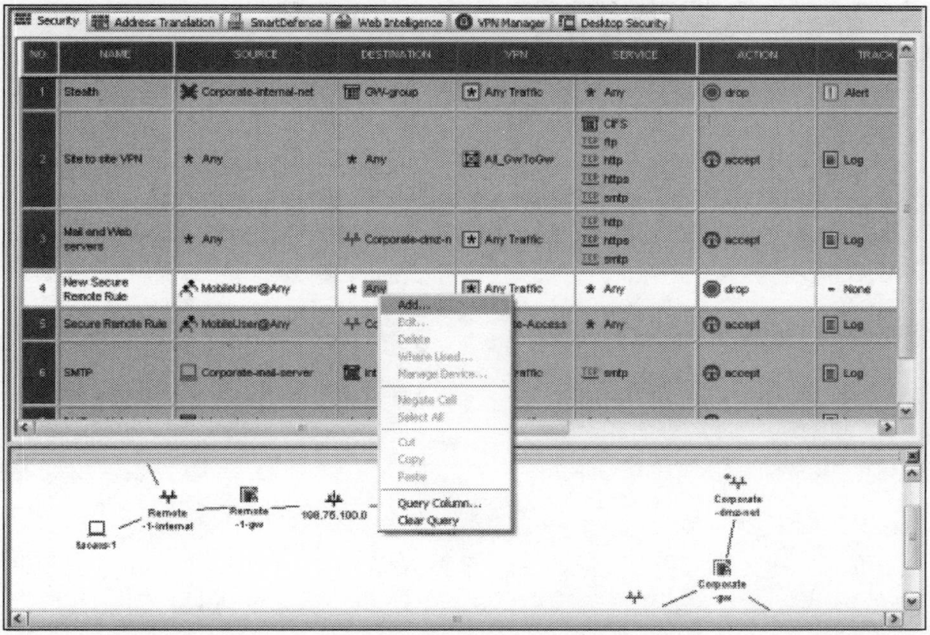

A new window will open and give you the ability to select the destination to which you want the user group to be allowed access. You can create a new network object, or select a previously created network object. Select the Corporate-internal-net and click **OK**. The point of this exercise is to allow a group of users to access the corporate private network from anywhere in the world (see Figure 12.7).

Figure 12.7 Selecting Destinations for MobileUser Group Users

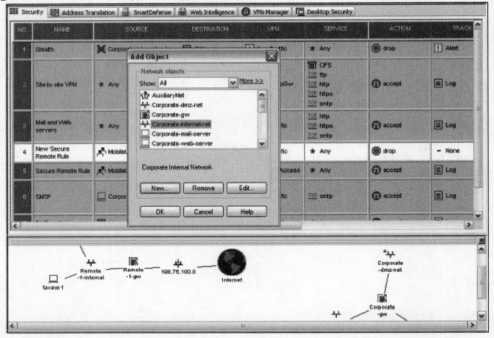

Next, select the VPN field in your current rule and right-click **Any Traffic** (see Figure 12.8). We are going to stipulate that this rule is a Remote Access VPN Rule.

Figure 12.8 Selecting the VPN Field

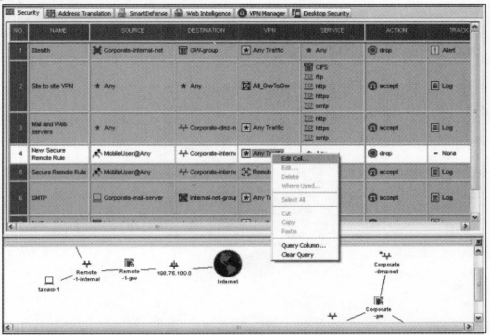

Once the new window opens, select the third option down, Only accept connections encrypted in specific VPN Communities (see Figure 12.9). This selection provides for connections from one of two options, either Site-to-Site connections between hosts in the VPN domain of Site-to-Site communities, or connections in specific VPN communities selected, in this case the Remote Access VPN community.

Figure 12.9 Selecting Connectivity Options

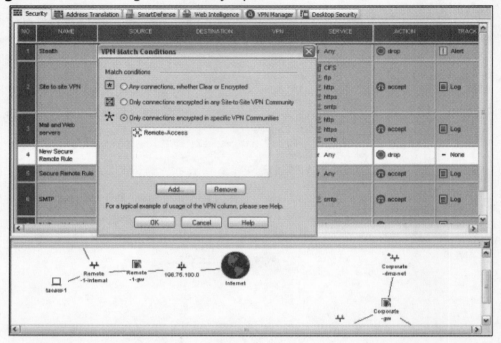

Click **Add** to add the VPN community to the rule, and select the Remote Access community. Click **OK** (see Figure 12.10).

Figure 12.10 Adding the VPN Community to a Rule

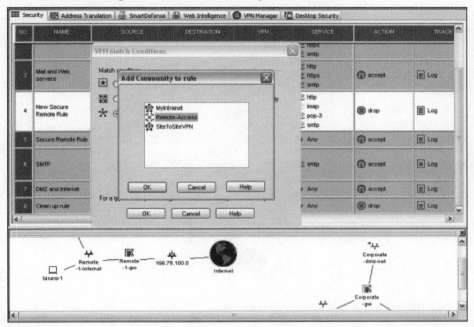

Now, click the VPN field, selecting the new Remote Access icon, and click **Edit** (see Figure 12.11).

Figure 12.11 Selecting Remote Access

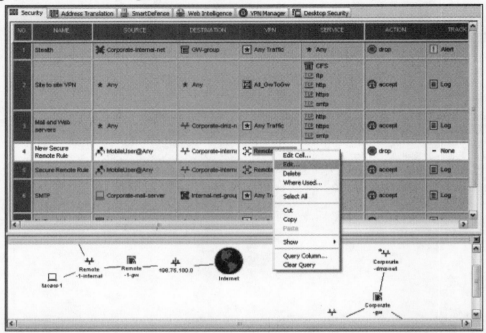

Now, select the second option down on the left, Participating Gateways (see Figure 12.12).

Figure 12.12 Selecting the Participating Gateways Option

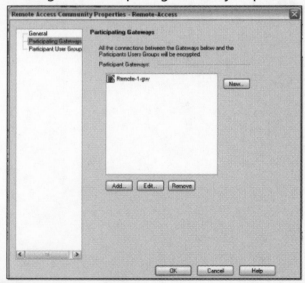

It may already have your VPN gateway listed, but if it doesn't, click **Add** and select the VPN gateway you want your users to connect to for access to the corporate network (see Figure 12.13). Click **OK** to select the participating gateway, and click **OK** again to close the edit community window.

Figure 12.13 Selecting the VPN Gateway

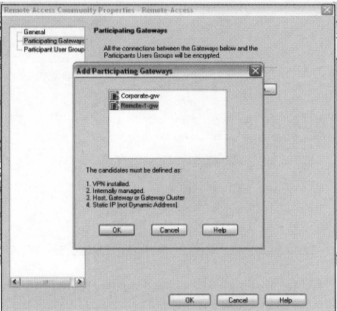

Next, right-click the **Any** icon under the services field of your rule and select **Add**. Here, you can select the services you want to allow your remote users the ability to use while connected to the corporate network via Remote Access (see Figure 12.14). For this example, we will use HTTP, SMTP, POP3, and IMAP4. This will allow users to browse Web pages on the internal network, as well as send and receive e-mail.

NOTE

You can select as many services as you would like to let your Mobile User group use when connected to the VPN gateway. You can also select multiple services at one time using the CTRL key.

Figure 12.14 Selecting Services for MobileUser Group Users

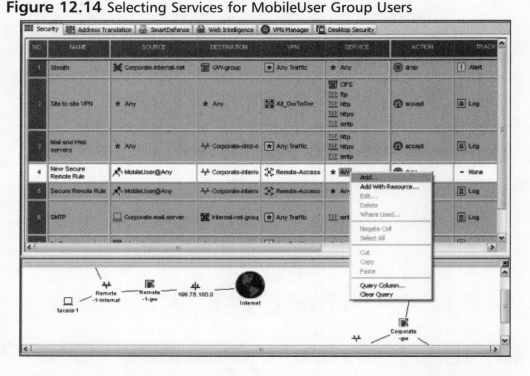

Once the Add Object window has popped up, select the HTTP, SMTP, POP3, and IMAP services, and click **OK** (see Figure 12.15).

Figure 12.15 Selecting Services

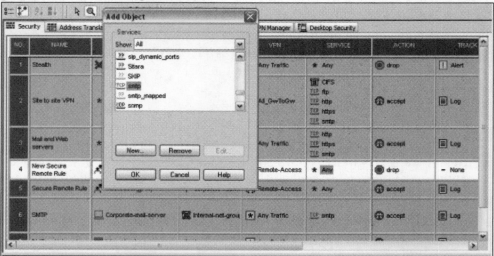

Now, we must provide an action when this rule is matched for access to the network. Right-click on the action field in the rule, and select Accept to allow SecuRemote Access (see Figure 12.16).

Figure 12.16 Allowing SecuRemote Access

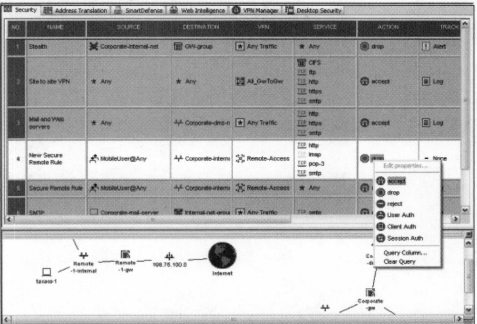

Another important field in each rule is the Track field (see Figure 12.17). The Track field provides a mechanism for maintaining information about the rule when it is matched. When a packet arrives that matches the rule we have created for Remote Access, the VPN gateway can alert, log, or begin another action defined by the VPN gateway administrator. Tracking provides the VPN gateway Administrators with the ability to troubleshoot connectivity issues, as well as obtain immediate notification information to be alerted when certain rules are matched, such as malicious traffic. In this example, we will log this rule, in order to be able to troubleshoot connectivity issues should they arise.

Figure 12.17 The Track Field

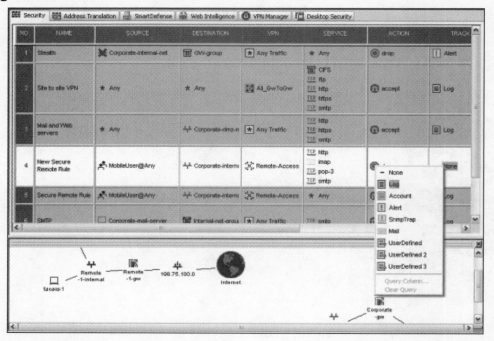

After selecting the appropriate tracking options, you must select the location to install this policy (see Figure 12.18). For this VPN example, the rule should be installed on the VPN gateways. Right-click on the **Install** field of your rule, select **Add**, and then select **Gateways**. In addition, you can also create a time object that can stipulate between what times your users can connect to your corporate network. We will be allowing our users access at all times, so you can leave this field unchanged.

Figure 12.18 Selecting the Location for Tracking Options

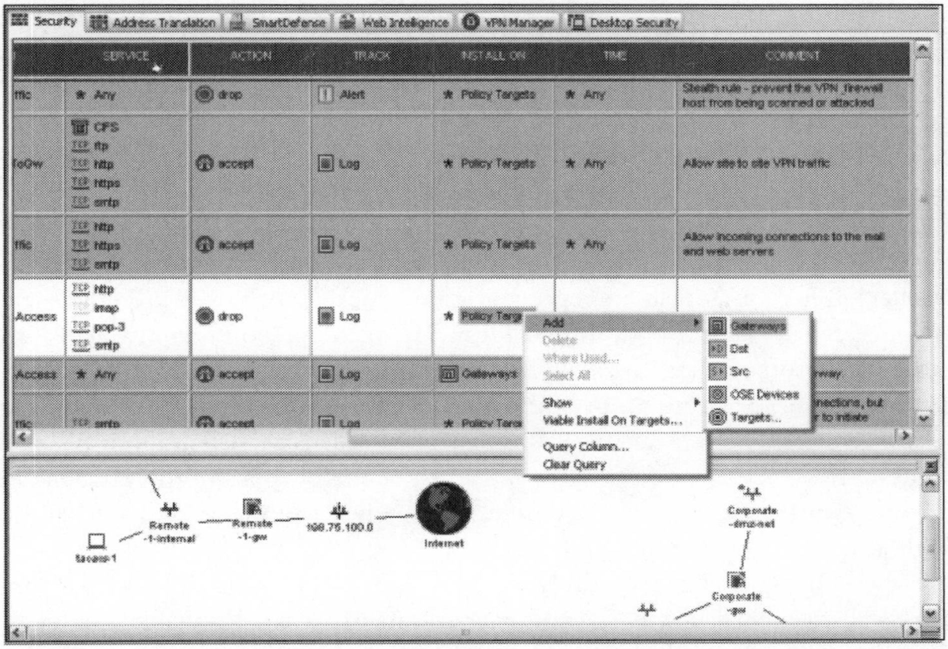

Finally, you can add a more descriptive comment to your rule, so you can quickly know exactly what it is doing (see Figure 12.19). This is especially valuable for other administrators, as it is easy to track who made what changes to the VPN gateway policy, if they are keeping good comments.

Figure 12.19 Adding Comments to a Rule

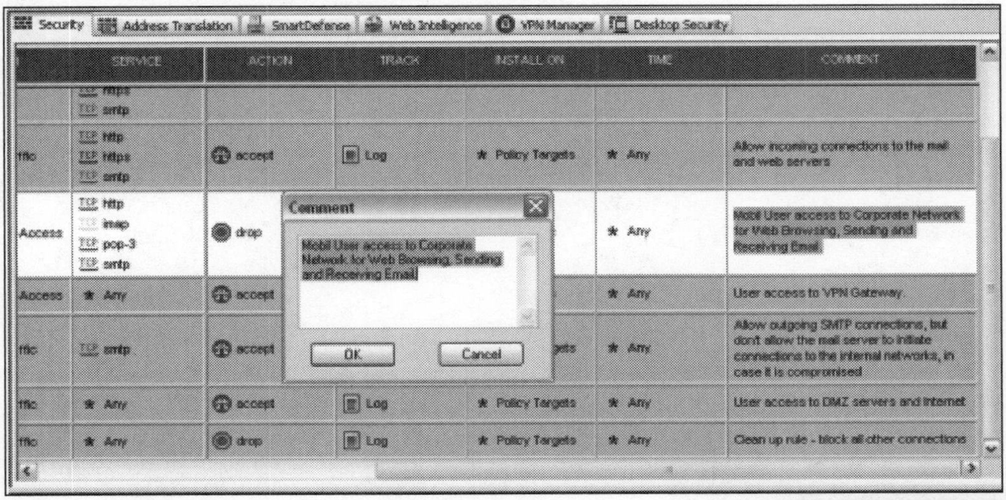

Once the final step has been completed, your rule is ready to be installed on the VPN gateway. Go to **Policy | Install**. This will push your new policy out to the gateway, and the gateway should then be able to accept incoming SecuRemote connections from the users listed in the Mobile User group.

SecuRemote Installation and Configuration on Microsoft Windows

To begin the SecuRemote Installation, download the SecuRemote executable from www.checkpoint.com, or obtain a preconfigured package of the SecuRemote client from your Security Administrator. The advantage of the preconfigured version is exactly what it sounds like. Normally, the preconfigured version is already configured with the corporate site information and specific options direct from your security administrator. The standard SecuRemote client needs a small amount of manual configuration to connect to the VPN gateway. For the purpose of this chapter, we will assume a preconfigured SecuRemote package is not available, and we will walk through a manual installation of SecuRemote. From http://www.checkpoint.com/techsupport/eula_sr.html, you can download a configurable installation package (which you have to unzip), or an executable .exe or .msi file. You can also download files for Mac OS X, Red Hat Linux, or Pocket PC. After downloading, run the setup file to begin installation. You will be greeted with the SecuRemote installation welcome screen.

After the installation welcome screen, you will have to agree to Check Point's End User License Agreement (EULA). Click **Yes** to accept Check Point's EULA and proceed with the installation (see Figure 12.20).

Figure 12.20 Check Point's EULA

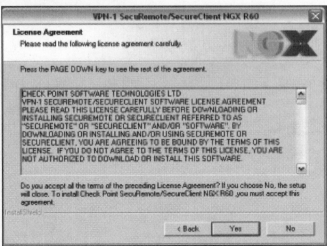

The SecuRemote/SecureClient installation wizard will prompt you for an installation location (see Figure 12.21). It is advisable to keep the default installation path, as it will decrease the time spent searching for configuration and log files during troubleshooting.

Figure 12.21 Choosing a Destination Location

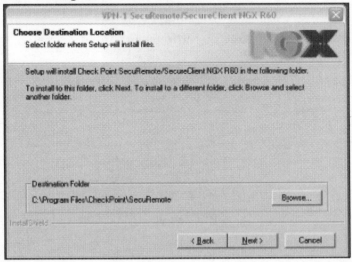

SecuRemote will then display an installation progress bar (see Figure 12.22). Once the progress bar reaches 100%, the installer will prompt you to install

SecuRemote or SecureClient. Select **SecuRemote** and Click **Next** to continue the installation.

Figure 12.22 The Installation Progress Bar

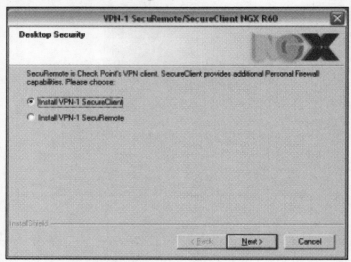

The SecuRemeote/SecureClient installer will then make some changes to the Windows Registry, and install the SecuRemote/SecureClient kernel (see Figure 12.23).

Figure 12.23 Installing the SecuRemote/SecureClient Kernel

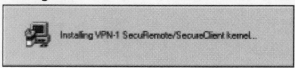

You will be prompted to reboot the machine when the install is completed. Select **Finish**, and the installer will reboot your machine for you (see Figure 12.24).

Figure 12.24 Rebooting the Machine

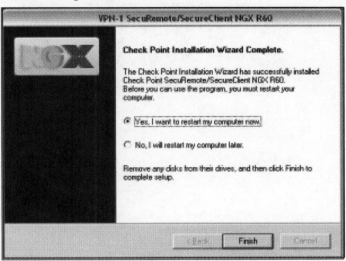

After the machine is rebooted, a new icon will be visible in the machine's system tray. The SecuRemote icon looks like a golden key with a red letter X above it (see Figure 12.25). In order to connect to the VPN gateway and build the encrypted tunnel necessary to access resources on the private corporate network, you need to first create a new site and configure it using the IP Address of the VPN gateway.

Figure 12.25 The SecuRemote Icon

Right-click on the SecuRemote icon to display the SecuRemote menu (see Figure 12.26). Click the **Settings** menu item.

Figure 12.26 Displaying the SecuRemote Menu

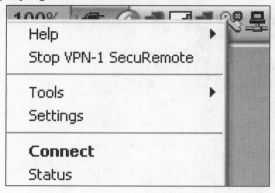

This opens the Settings dialog box. Click the button on the right labeled **New**. This will bring up the Site Wizard (see Figure 12.27).

Figure 12.27 The SecuRemote Settings Dialog Box

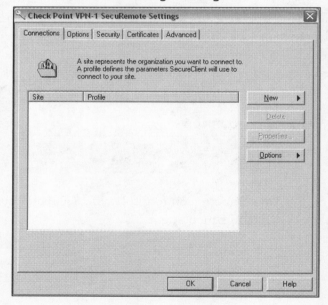

Type the IP Address/DNS name and a Display name of the VPN gateway you are trying to establish a VPN tunnel with and click **Next** (see Figure 12.28).

Figure 12.28 The Site Wizard

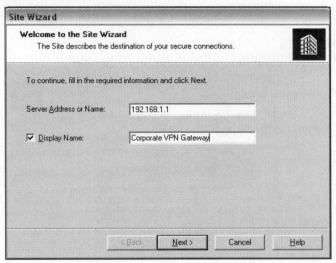

Select the Authentication method (see Figure 12.29). This must be configured correctly according to the settings on the VPN gateway. For this example, select **Username** and **Password** and click **Next**.

Figure 12.29 Selecting the Authentication Method

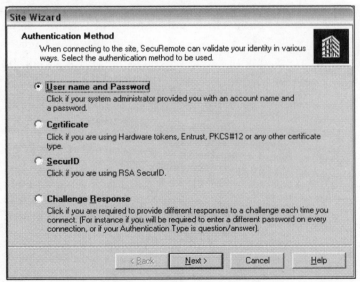

Type the username and password that was provided by your security administrator and click **Next** (see Figure 12.30).

Figure 12.30 Adding User Details to the Site Wizard

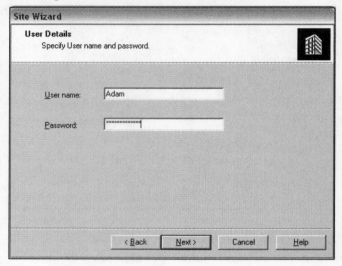

SecuRemote will then attempt to connect to the VPN gateway (see Figure 12.32). It will first check if you want to attempt a Standard or Advanced connection. Standard utilizes the normal method of IKE negotiation. If you experience issues when attempting a Standard connection with your VPN gateway, clicking **Advanced** will perform IKE over TCP. This solves most connectivity problems due to ISPs and other network administrators blocking the protocols and ports necessary for standard IKE.

Figure 12.31 Downloading Topology and Site Data from the VPN Gateway

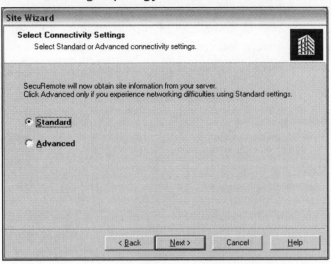

SecuRemote will attempt to validate the VPN gateway (see Figure 12.32). In some secure environments, the security administrator will provide the VPN gateway's internal Certificate Authority's certificate fingerprint. SecuRemote will present the certificate that it obtained from the VPN gateway and ask you to validate it against the information provided by your security administrator. Verify that the Common Name (CN) and Organization (O) are correct, and click **Next**.

Figure 12.32 Validating the VPN Gateway

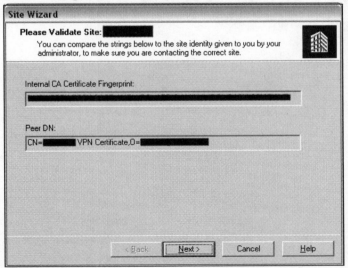

After clicking **Next**, SecuRemote will connect to the VPN gateway, download the necessary information to form encrypted connections, and display a Site Created Successfully dialog box (see Figure 12.33). Congratulations, your site has been created and you can now form a secure encrypted connection to your corporate VPN gateway.

Figure 12.33 Successful Creation of a Site

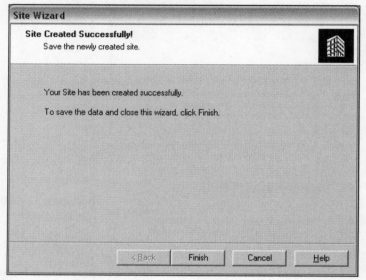

Connecting to the VPN-1 Gateway

To connect to the gateway, double-click the SecuRemote icon located on the task bar (see Figure 12.34).

Figure 12.34 Connecting to the Gateway

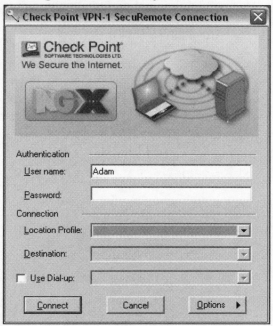

This will bring up the connection dialog box. Enter your username and password, and click **Connect** (see Figure 12.35).

Figure 12.35 The Connection Dialog Box

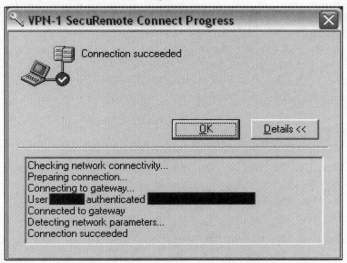

SecuRemote will open a new dialog box, and if you click the Details button, it will display the details of the connection that is being attempted. After the encrypted tunnel is built, SecuRemote will notify you that the connection has been established, and you can securely begin communicating with the private corporate network.

It is important to keep in mind that SecuRemote is able to provide only Remote Access connectivity. It contains no desktop security enhancements, and is not able to accept a Desktop Security policy to secure the desktop from attack. SecureClient, which is installed in the exact same manner, except you need to select Install SecureClient when prompted, provides the added benefits of enhanced desktop security and a centralized point to manage the Desktop Security policy.

Notes from the Underground…

The Beauty of userc.c

"After hacking into this guy's computer, I found myself rooting around looking for credit card numbers and other valuable information when I came across this little file in the SecuRemote directory. This simple flat file is full of valuable information about this guy's company, what the network topology is like, IP Addresses of other firewalls and network entry points, and what the access method is. This one file gives me plenty of information to launch a dedicated attack and attempt to infiltrate this guy's company network.

"It's funny, most security dudes that are familiar with Check Point know to encrypt this file. Looks like this group of security guys ain't the sharpest knife in the drawer…their loss = my gain!"

To avoid having this happen to you, you can edit the userc.c file and change the :encrypt_db setting to **True**. You can also create a package from the SecureClient Packaging Tool that has this setting preconfigured.

SecureClient

Whereas SecuRemote provides the user with the ability to access the company's resources from remote locations, SecureClient allows for increased desktop security. As a corporation, it is important to ensure that your traveling workforce has the ability to access and transfer information to and from the company's private network. However, once information has been downloaded to a user's laptop or remote machine, the data is vulnerable to attack. Also, if a user's machine is compromised, the entire corporate private network could be vulnerable to malicious code such as worms, viruses, or even an attacker looking for proprietary information.

Check Point looks to solve this vulnerability with SecureClient, a centrally managed desktop firewall bundled with the SecuRemote VPN client. Upon connecting to the VPN-1 gateway, SecureClient downloads the most recent, applicable Desktop Security policy and enforces it on the end user's machine. SecureClient sits at the kernel level, inspecting all network traffic to and from the machine to protect the end user from malicious traffic and attacks.

The Desktop Security policy is similar to the FireWall-1 security policy. Rules are created for inbound and outbound access, and events can be logged or ignored. The Check Point administrator defines the Desktop Security policy from the SmartConsole administration center. The policy is then pushed out to all SecureClients once they update their site information.

SecureClient also adds some connectivity options to SecuRemote. SecureClient supports Office Mode, so that a virtual interface adapter on the remote machine can receive a virtual IP, Visitor Mode, so that the encrypted communication is tunneled over a single port, usually 443 (HTTPS), and Route All Traffic Through Gateway, so that when a VPN tunnel is active, all communications from the remote machine, include to the Internet, are routed first through the VPN gateway.

What's New in SC NGX?

SecureClient supports all new features incorporated in SecuRemote. Additionally, new features of NGX that apply to SecureClient are:

- **Policy Expiration** When connected, SecureClient will now attempt to update the policy in exactly half the specified interval expire_time. If SecureClient is unable to download the most recent policy, it will not revert to the default policy.

- **RADIUS** Policy enforcement on the desktop now allows for RADIUS groups.

Installing SecureClient on Microsoft Windows

In the previous section, we stepped through the process of installing SecuRemote. The installation process for SecureClient and even the installation package are identical to that of SecuRemote, provided earlier. The only difference is to select SecureClient instead of SecuRemote when you install the package. Because the Desktop Security policy is generated and maintained on the Policy Server, the configuration of

SecureClient is also almost identical to that of SecuRemote. There are only two small differences that are obvious during configuration. First, upon the first successful connection to your newly created site, SecureClient will download the Desktop Security policy and begin enforcing it. Second, once the Desktop Security policy is loaded and enforced, a small blue lock becomes visible over the SecureClient icon on the taskbar to notify you that you are currently being protected.

Policy Server

The Policy Server for SecureClient is the overarching component that allows for centralized administration of the entire SecureClient deployment. It typically is incorporated with the VPN-1 gateway that SecureClient is configured to connect to. It provides SecureClient with network topology information as well as the Desktop Security policy. You can access the Desktop Security policy from the SmartDashboard Desktop Security tab.

Inherently, SecureClient seeks to obtain its Desktop Security policy from the Policy Server. In previous versions of Check Point's software, it was not possible to separate the Policy Server from the VPN-1 gateway SecureClient was connecting to. In NGX however, it is now possible to have a dedicated server supply the Desktop Security policy using a special parameter in the SecureClient Profile. In order to do so, perform the following: First, **Add** the separate Policy Server to the profile. Second, change the database entry use_profile_ps_configuration to **True** via the dbedit tool. When you attempt a connection to the VPN-1 gateway, it will direct SecureClient to the Policy Server to download the applicable Desktop Security policy.

Desktop Security Policies

One of the major arguments in paying for SecureClient licensing over utilizing SecuRemote is the ability to secure individual machines with Desktop Security policies. Desktop Security policies are similar to the policies that protect Check Point's perimeter suite of products, like Firewall-1/VPN-1. They provide security administrators with a familiar interface that can be used to create rules that protect their end user community. Desktop Security policies are essentially rules that can be defined by Source, Destination, Desktop, Service, and Action. They allow security administrators the ability to approve or deny traffic based on any combination of components: port, network, or service. For instance, if a new worm began spreading across the Internet, it would be possible for a security administrator to proactively update the Desktop Security policy and restrict access to the service or port that is vulnerable on every desktop in their environment that was currently utilizing SecureClient. Once the Desktop Security policy has been downloaded, it remains on the computer, protecting it from attacks when it is in both connected and disconnected states. Desktop Security policies are defined in two parts: an inbound policy, where connections originate from external sources attempting to reach the desktop; and an outbound policy, referring to connections originating from the desktop and attempting to reach external resources.

Configuring Desktop Security Policies

In this example, we will provide a step-by-step configuration of a Desktop Security policy that will allow users the rights to perform the following actions:

- Browse the Internet and access DNS information.
- Send and Receive e-mail from the corporate e-mail server through the VPN tunnel.
- Allow IT Personnel to access Corporate Network Resources via SSH and SFTP through the VPN tunnel.
- Utilize Instant Messaging Applications for Instant Messaging.
- Allow incoming SNMP traffic from corporate SNMP servers.

We will begin by launching the SmartDashboard (see Figure 12.36).

Figure 12.36 The SmartDashboard Welcome Screen

Once you have logged in, continue by clicking the **Desktop Security** tab in the right window.

The Desktop Security policy should now be visible in the right window. Right-click the existing outbound rule and select **Add Rule | Below**. Repeat the last step to add four more rules to the outbound policy.

It's important to differentiate among user groups. When a Desktop policy contains the All Users group, the policy is applied both when the VPN tunnel is active and when it is not. The All Users rules are applied from the moment the machine receives a policy from the Policy Server. When a rule contains a specific group (IT_group, for example), then the rule is active only when a user in that group establishes a VPN tunnel to the gateway. This allows you to have a stricter set of rules when the VPN connection is active.

NOTE

Mobile VPN users may be granted access to corporate resources based on a completely different set of access controls (due to their inherently insecure nature), compared to users sitting behind a Corporate Firewall-1 gateway. Users who are inside the corporate network are protected by border firewalls and typically are granted greater flexibility when accessing internal corporate resources. Mobile VPN users could be connecting to the Corporate VPN-1 gateway from anywhere in the world, through safe or possibly hostile infrastructure. Generating a strict Desktop Security policy to ensure security for your Mobile VPN and internal user base is a security best practice; it is important to look beyond the perimeter to secure a corporate infrastructure.

Create the rules shown in Table 12.1 in the outbound portion of the Desktop Security policy.

Table 12.1 Outbound Policy Rules

Rule Number	Desktop	Destination	Service	Action	Track	Comment
2	All Users @ Any	Any	HTTP HTTPS DNS	Accept	Log	Allow all users to browse Internet and corporate network.
3	All Users @ Any	Corporate-mail	SMTP IMAP POP-3	Encrypt	Log	Allow all users to connect to the corporate mail server to send/receive e-mail.
4	IT_Users @ Any	Corporate-Int.	SSH SSHv2	Encrypt	Log	Allow all users to access internal corporate resources via SSH and SSHv2 (including SFTP).
5	All Users @ Any	Any	Messenger_Apps	Accept	Log	Allow all users to access instant messenger applications for work collaboration.
6	All Users @ Any	Any	Any	Block	Log	Log all attempted activity from users attempting to establish connections outbound that is not expressly allowed above.

The Encrypt action allows only traffic that is encrypted through the VPN tunnel. This way you can be sure the traffic is not sent in the clear, which could be intercepted.

The **Outbound Rules** section should look like the screen in Figure 12.37 when you are finished.

Figure 12.37 Outbound Policy Rules

Outbound Rules						
NO.	DESKTOP	DESTINATION	SERVICE	ACTION	TRACK	COMMENT
4	All Users@Any	Corporate-gw	IKE	Accept	Log	Allow all Users to access corporate gateway to download desktop security policy.
5	All Users@Any	Any	TCP http / dns / TCP https	Encrypt	Log	Allow all Users to Browse Internet and corporate network.
6	All Users@Any	Corporate-mail-serve	TCP smtp / TCP pop-3 / imap	Encrypt	Log	Allow all Users to connect to the corporate Mail Server for sending/receiving email.
7	IT_Users@Any	Corporate-internal-ne	TCP ssh / TCP ssh_version_2	Accept	Log	Allow all Users to access internal corporate resources via SSH and SSHv2 (including SFTP).
8	All Users@Any	Any	Messenger_Ap	Accept	Log	Allow all users to access Instant Messenger applications for work collaboration.
9	All Users@Any	Any	Any	Block	Log	Log all attempted activity from Users attempting to establish connections outbound that is not expressly allowed above.

These rules grant permissions based on users, destination, and service. The comments in each rule are descriptive and explain the reason they appear in the policy. The outbound policy allows all users to accomplish specific tasks like Web browsing, sending e-mail, and utilizing Instant Messaging for collaboration. The final rule of the outbound policy stipulates that if a user attempts to access a resource other than those listed, the traffic will be blocked. This type of egress filtering typically is used for multiple reasons. First, it keeps the user community focused on their particular task or job duties by decreasing the actions that the user can perform. Second, it decreases the opportunity for an employee to access sensitive corporate information and transmit it to a third party without generating a noticeable amount of tracking information. Last, it decreases the likelihood of a worm or virus running wild on the corporate network, because the desktop machines that are secured with SecureClient will not accept incoming connections from other machines unless expressly allowed by the Desktop Security policy.

Once the outbound rules have been created, we will continue with securing the desktop by creating the inbound portion of our Desktop Security policy. Inbound rules will secure our users from outside attacks, but also allow important corporate services to initiate connections to them for monitoring and patch management.

Right-click on **rule number 1**, and select **Add Rule | Below**. Repeat this step so that three rules are visible under the inbound policy. Begin by creating the rules shown in Table 12.2.

Table 12.2 Inbound Policy Rules

Rule Number	Desktop	Destination	Service	Action	Track	Comment
1	Corporate-AV-Mgmt Corporate-Patch-Mgmt	All Users @ Any	Patch-update AV-Def-update	Encrypt	Log	Allow AntiVirus and Patch management servers to connect to all user machines.
2	Corporate-Enterp-mgmt	All Users @ Any	SNMP SNMP-read SNMP-RO	Accept	Log	Allow corporate enterprise management servers to gather system information on all user machines.
3	Any	All Users @ Any	Any	Block	-	Deny all other connections originating from external sources.

The inbound policy should look like the screen shown in Figure 12.38.

Figure 12.38 Inbound Policy Rules

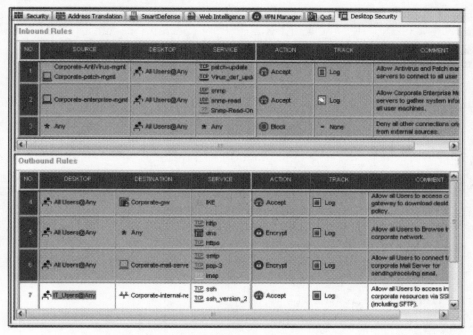

This Inbound policy will allow network administrators and information security engineers to force patch and anti-virus updates to all desktop machines. It is also going to allow auditors the ability to gather system specific information from each desktop via the Simple Network Management Protocol (SNMP). If traffic attempting initial connections to the desktop do not meet the previously mentioned requirements, it will not be accepted. Once the new inbound rules have been added, the rule numbers for the existing outbound rules will have been incremented (based upon the number of rules you added to the inbound policy. This is because SecureClient understands the policy as a rule set, and applies traffic to the policy in order. When the traffic reaches a rule that it applies to, SecureClient takes the action specified in the rule.

It is important to keep in mind that the connections we are discussing when creating policy rules are stateful. In essence, this means that while Check Point monitors each and every single bit of communication occurring between your computer and the remote system, it applies only the initial connection to the rules on the Desktop Security policy. When an incoming or outgoing connection is attempted, the SecureClient (sitting at the kernel level) determines which rule the attempted connection applies to and places the information about the traffic and the corresponding rule into a state table. When replies come from the desktop, or from a remote computer in response to that initial connection that had been accepted, SecureClient verifies that the traffic is related by checking it against the information in the state table, and allows it to pass into or out of the desktop.

For example, when you attempt to access a Web page on the Internet, a request is made by your computer to the computer that hosts the Web page. The computer hosting the Web page answers back with data, and your computer in turn responds, continuing a "conversation" with the computer hosting the Web page until the Web page is fully transferred to your computer. If it were necessary to have a rule for all individual traffic, it would be a configuration nightmare as well as infeasible to secure due to the sheer amounts of traffic and time required.

Once the Desktop Security policy has been Verified and Installed, the preceding rules will allow users who are currently running SecureClient, and have downloaded the Desktop Security policy, to perform the actions listed earlier (Internet browsing, e-mail, ssh). Traffic that is not accepted in the policy will match the last rule and be blocked.

Disabling the Security Policy

It may be necessary in special circumstances where SecureClient is enforcing a Desktop Security policy that is inhibiting the user community to disable the security policy. In any case where SecureClient is impeding users from a critical task, or important mission objective, the Desktop Security policy can be temporarily disabled. In order to disable the Desktop Security policy, locate the SecureClient icon on the system tray, and select it with a left mouse click.

This will open the SecureClient menu. Select **Tools | Disable Security Policy** (see Figure 12.39).

Figure 12.39 SecureClient Icon Menu

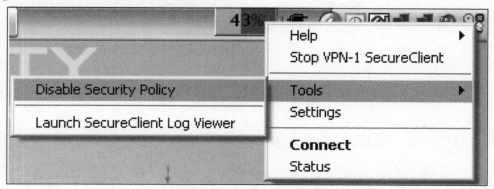

SecureClient will prompt the user to make sure they wish to disable the Desktop Security policy (see Figure 12.40). It also reminds the user that the computer is no longer protected by the SecureClient firewall. Click **Yes**, and the dialogue box will close. If you now move your mouse over the SecureClient icon in the system tray, a small notification box will open, letting you know if SecureClient is currently connected to a VPN-1 gateway, and that the Security Policy is currently disabled.

Figure 12.40 SecureClient Verify Disable Policy Dialog

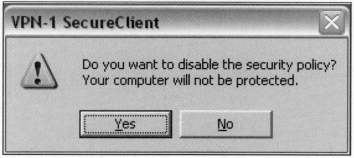

It is a best practice for users to complete whatever actions are necessary and quickly reenable the Desktop Security policy. The policy can be enabled by selecting the same menu items. This will bring the computer back into a protected mode.

Secure Configuration Verification

Secure Configuration Verification (SCV) additionally provides the security administrator with the capability to verify if machines internal to the private network or attempting to remotely access the private network are compliant with the corporate security policy. SCV works by utilizing built-in checks to SecureClient to check for security updates, operating system versions, running processes, and even browser settings. If a machine is found to be out of compliance, their access to the private network can be revoked, and they are notified of their machine's discrepancies with the Corporate Security policy. Once the machine is brought back into a complaint state, they are again granted access to the private network. Secure Configuration Verification is discussed in greater depth later in this chapter.

Office Mode

After installing, configuring, and attempting to use SecuRemote or SecureClient, it is common for a specific concern to be quickly identified. For some unforeseen reason, the client is not able to communicate with any host inside the private network, and in some cases can't even establish a connection to the VPN-1 gateway. It doesn't take long for a security administrator to realize that an IP Address conflict has occurred between the user's home and the corporate networks, typically because both networks are using the same nonpublic address space. It is very common for an organization to utilize nonpublic address space behind a Network Address Translation (NAT) router or firewall in order to save money on purchasing publicly routable address space for all hosts on their network.

This is both fiscally responsible, as well as a security best practice. First, it is very difficult to obtain, and is expensive for small and medium sized businesses to use publicly routable IP address space for each and every computer that will open connections to the Internet. Second, using NAT can provide added security as it decreases the ability of an attacker to get into your network from a remote location. It also leaves less information about your network's topology out on the Internet for anyone to research. In essence, your company's network is less attractive to the average attacker because it takes an advanced skill set to gain remote access to a nonpublic address space. Using NAT, the vectors of attack have been greatly reduced. A good rule of thumb for securing your network is to keep anyone outside your organization from knowing too much about your network, its layout, or security controls. In fact, the less they know the better.

When a VPN user behind a NAT router or firewall with a nonpublic, reserved IP address (within networks such as 192.168.0.0/16, 172.16.0.0/12, or 10.0.0.0/8) attempts to connect to another network that already has a host with the same IP address, IP address conflicts occur, and traffic is not routed appropriately. This conflict is easily understood in today's world of broadband service providers. Most home users are behind broadband cable or DSL modems that obtain the IP address via Dynamic Host Configuration Protocol (DHCP). Most broadband users then connect some type of router to the broadband modem, and use NAT to connect multiple computers to a single connection with a single public IP address.

Another common problem that occurs with VPN users connecting into a private network is the network engineers or security administrators utilizing access control lists (ACLs) on the routers to help secure parts of the network. When ACLs are used, typically they are defined with only internal address space in mind. Obviously, with a mobile workforce, it would be technically infeasible to attempt to add new rules to the ACLs every time a user connected to the private network from a different IP address.

Why Office Mode?

Office Mode allows security administrators to overcome the ACL and IP address conflict problems by assigning every SecureClient an IP address for use while it is connected to the private network. Office mode works like this: Let's say, for example, a user attempts to connect to your corporate VPN gateway. The IP address of the remote user's computer is 192.168.1.10, which coincidently is the IP address of your company's internal e-mail server. Without office mode, all response traffic to the remote users requests would either be dropped, or misrouted to the e-mail server, which wouldn't recognize the traffic, and so would drop it. If, however, office mode is enabled, SecureClient enters a special configuration mode during the initial phase of IKE, and requests an IP address from the VPN gateway. This new IP address is then assigned to a virtual network adapter, which is then used to send traffic to the corporate internal network. Office Mode is available only on SecureClient.

Client IP Pool

Check Point's VPN-1 gateway provides many different options for assigning IP addresses for Office mode SecureClient configurations. Different conditions are better suited to different methods of assigning IP addresses. Check Point supports IP address assignment via a configuration file that resides on the VPN-1 gateway, and assigns IPs per individual user, RADIUS server, IP pools based on preassigned network blocks or DHCP server.

IP pools are defined as a range of addresses that are given to SecureClients requesting access to the private network while in Office mode. You can also assign domain names or WINS information along with IP addresses to make communication with remote users easier. Check Point VPN-1 can be configured to assign IP addresses to all SecureClient users or to a given group of users.

Configuring Office Mode with IP Pools

The simplest way to assign Office mode addresses is using a manual IP pool. The range of addresses assigned to SecureClient users has to be a range that is not used within your corporation. Moreover, there should be a static route on internal routers that directs the IP pools to the VPN gateway, especially if there is a chance that asymmetric routing could direct traffic to those addresses elsewhere. In a Cluster environment, each cluster member needs to have a different IP pool defined.

Configuring the VPN-1 Gateway for Office Mode

Configuring Office mode can be done quickly and easily with a simple configuration change to both the VPN-1 gateway and SecureClient. Start by launching the Smart Dashboard Policy Editor, and selecting the **Network Objects** tab in the left window. In order to configure Office mode with IP pools, we need to create a network object that will serve as the list of IP addresses reserved for SecureClient users. Right-click **Network Objects** and select **New | Network**. This will open a Network Properties window where you can enter the network information for the IP pool (see Figure 12.41). For this example, we are going to use one of the subnets in the reserved nonpublic class C address space 192.168.0.0. Be sure to enter **192.168.2.0** as the network address, and **255.255.255.0** as the net mask. This means when users connect to the VPN-1 gateway while in Office mode, they will obtain an address for use on the internal private network between **192.168.2.0** and **192.168.2.254**. Click **OK** to continue.

Figure 12.41 Creating an Office Mode IP Pool Network Object

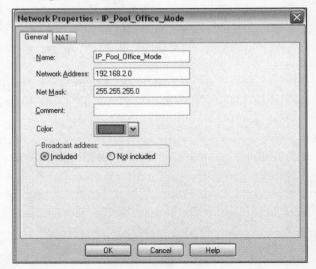

Once the IP pool network object has been created, right-click on the
VPN-1 gateway on which you wish to enable Office mode, and select **Edit** (see
Figure 12.42).

Figure 12.42 Office Mode Default Page

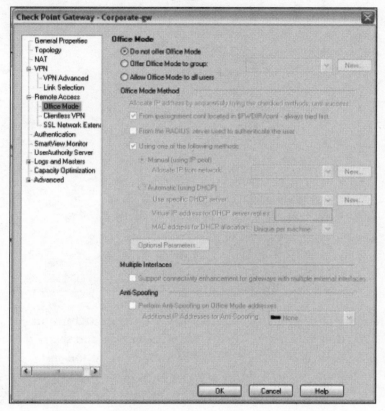

This will open the properties window for the VPN-1 gateway you selected.
Expand the **Remote Access** selection and click **Office Mode**. Select the option
Allow Office Mode to all users (see Figure 12.43).

Figure 12.43 Office Mode Gateway Configuration

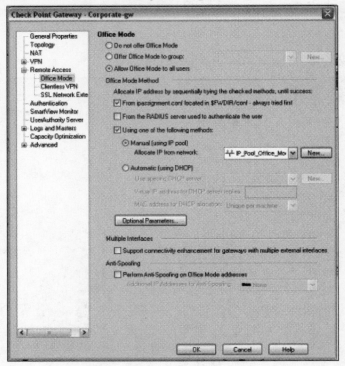

Click the radio button next to the Manual option, located just underneath the Office Mode Method heading. Click the drop-down box, and select the network that was created for IP pools. Click **OK** to continue. Verify and install the policy onto the VPN-1 gateway. The VPN-1 gateway is now read to provide users who are utilizing Office mode IP addresses that can be routed on the internal private network.

TIP

It is a common practice to use a Many-to-One Network Address Translation (NAT) on incoming VPN connections so that the packets are easily routed internally. Usually the VPN-1 gateway's internal IP address is used in this case to facilitate easy traffic routing. This can cause major problems when attempting to track a remote VPN user, especially if the user is in Hub mode and all outbound traffic is being routed through your Enterprise firewall. In this case, when you are attempting to track a specific VPN user, the IP address of all VPN users are displayed as the internal interface of the VPN-1 gateway. This makes things extremely difficult, to say the least, as you need to then attempt to trace the logs on the VPN-1 gateway, and match up the time to determine the original IP address of the user you wish to track. A good configuration tip when utilizing Office mode and IP pools is to provide a group of nonpublic address space that can be assigned to SecureClient users. This will allow you the ability to easily track each user that connects to the VPN-1 gateway, and you have the option of utilizing NAT if you then chose to use Hub mode and force all of the client's traffic to traverse your private network.

Configuring SecureClient for Office Mode

Begin by right-clicking the **SecureClient** icon in the system tray. Select **Settings** and the **Connections** tab and the Settings window will open (see Figure 12.44).

Figure 12.44 SecureClient Connection Settings

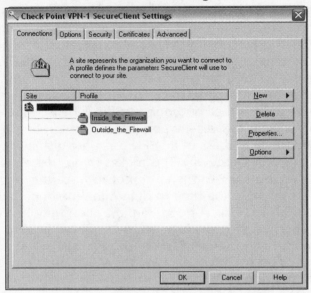

Select the profile for which you wish to enable Office mode and click **Properties**. When the Profile Properties dialog box appears, select the **Advanced** tab (see Figure 12.45).

Figure 12.45 SecureClient Profile Properties

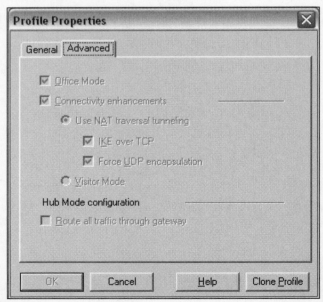

Under the **Advanced** tab, you can select **Office Mode** along with other useful options for SecureClient. Once you have checked the box for Office mode, continue by clicking **OK**.

SecureClient is now configured to connect to a VPN-1 gateway utilizing Office mode.

Secure Configuration Verification (SCV)

Even the least technically savvy know they need to be secure, and that it's important to the company to protect proprietary data. This, however, doesn't stop anyone from writing their password down on a sticky note and placing it under their keyboard. Security most commonly is met with fearsome apprehension; anyone who has attempted to restrict users to being less than administrators on their corporate machines knows exactly what I am talking about. Mostly, this is because security administrators sometimes lose sight of the purpose of the company in order to secure it. I know I have.

In the wake of more prolific worms and viruses, such as Code Red/Nimda, Blaster/Lovsan, and Nachi/Welchia, security administrators were pulling their hair out trying to fight mobile users from infecting the entire private network with these bandwidth crippling worms. Most security administrators knew to combat these viruses and worms by blocking the ports they utilized at the perimeter. In effect, the viruses or worms shouldn't be able to infect the private network because they couldn't get through the firewalls to the vulnerable machines. Unfortunately, it was then made painfully obvious how soft the underbelly of the private network was. In the end, it didn't take a critical firewall vulnerability to allow Distributed Denial of Service (DDoS) attacks to bring networks to their knees. It was as simple as an authorized user returning to work from telecommuting.

Worms like Blaster/Lovsan and Nachi/Welchia were blocked at the perimeter, however remote access (whether dial-in or VPN) and traveling users returning to the office introduced and spread the bulk of worm and virus infections. Some security administrators even denied all remote access initially in order to protect the network, and slowly allowed small pools of users connectivity to the private network in order to identify infected machines and have them cleaned and inoculated. This was an extremely expensive lesson for two reasons. First, many security professionals wasted hundreds, and in some cases, thousands of hours getting networks back up and machines secure. Second, the loss of employee productivity was incredible. Millions of dollars were lost because employees couldn't perform the simplest of business functions.

Check Point heard the screams of the security community and answered with Secure Configuration Verification (SCV). SCV gives the security administrator the ability to verify if a machine is compliant with the corporate security policy prior to granting access to the private network. SCV works on machines that exist inside the private network as well as machines attempting to form VPN tunnels into the private network from other locations. In order to take advantage of SCV, you must have a fully licensed copy of Check Point's SecureClient to enforce the corporate security policy.

WARNING

Even though Secure Configuration Verification (SCV) is an extremely useful option to assist in securing your network, it may not be the most feasible deployment option for your environment. Some major consideration should be put into policy development prior to deployment. Check Point admits that if your environment consists of users that have administrative privileges, it may not be conducive to check for certain parameters in order to verify a secure configuration. Users with administrative privileges can inadvertently modify their machine's configuration and cause the system to fail the SCV check. Depending on the security policy, this may disable remote access connectivity to the private network.

This can cause a dramatic increase in help desk traffic, as more users will need assistance troubleshooting remote access connectivity issues. This will also cause a decrease in productivity, as users who fail the configuration check will be unable to get work done. If you choose to use SCV, be sure to spend considerable time deciding what configuration checks are appropriate. You don't have to check for every parameter on the system, only valid risks to your environment. With too much security, anything can become useless. Find a balance that works for your situation

---

What's New with Secure Configuration Verification (SCV) in NGX?

Some of the more interesting additions to Secure Configuration Verification in NGX are:

- Exceptions: It is now possible with the release of NGX to specify hosts or services that are allowed access to the private network even if the SCV check fails.

- OS Monitor is now able to recognize Windows 2003 server.

- SCV does not support SecuRemote, however it is now possible to allow SecuRemote clients access to the private network even if SCV checks are enabled. To enable this feature, find the parameter scv_allow_sr_clients in the userc.c file, and set the value to **true**.

- The following registry keys can now be checked with Registry Monitor: HKey_Local_Machine, HKey_Current_User, and HKey_User.

Configuring the Policy Server to Enable Secure Configuration Verification (SCV)

In order to enable Secure Configuration Verification (SCV), it is necessary to modify some minor settings in the Global Properties menu of your Firewall-1/VPN-1 gateway policy server. Specifically, login to SmartDashboard, and select **Policy | Global Properties** from the menu bar. Once the Global Properties dialog box is open, expand the left menu for **Remote Access** and select **Secure Configuration Verification**. The window will look like the screen in Figure 12.46.

Figure 12.46 The Secure Configuration Verification Global Properties

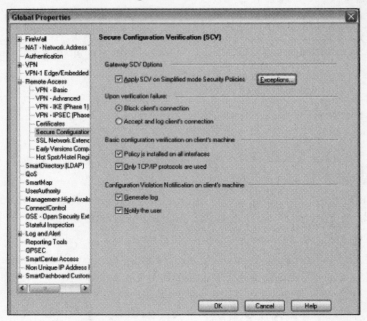

Ensure the first check box (Apply SCV for Simplified mode Security Policies) is selected and click **OK**.

In addition to making the aforementioned change, a policy file named local.scv, located in the Firewall Configuration Directory ($FWDIR/conf), must be configured to use the provided checks correctly to verify clients are within compliance.

Secure Configuration Verification (SCV) Checks Available

SecureClient NGX comes with SCV installed, and some SCV checks are predefined and ready for use:

- **Process Monitor** Checks if a process is running or not.

- **Version Checker** Checks the current version of SecureClient.

- **Group Monitor** Checks if the user currently logged on to the machine running SecureClient is a member of a Domain User Group.

- **OS Monitor** Verifies the version of the Operating System that is currently running, what service packs the OS is at, and the configuration of the screen saver.

- **HotFix Monitor** Verifies that certain Microsoft Security patches are installed.

- **Browser Monitor** Checks the current version of Internet Explorer, as well as its configuration and settings information.

Check Point OPSEC Vendor SCV Checks

Some Check Point OPSEC partners have developed their own SCV checks, such as Okena and PestPatrol. An updated list of OPSEC Partners and their service offerings is available at www.ospec.com.

Other Third-Party Checks

OPSWAT (www.opswat.com) has developed SCV checks for HfNetCheck and Norton AV. OPSWAT is also willing to write customized SCV checks. They can be contacted at their Web site.

Create Your Own Checks

In order to create SCV checks, you must utilize the SCV Software Developers Kit (SDK), available at www.opsec.com.

Integrity

Integrity is an interesting addition to the Check Point family of products. Originally, SecureClient was Check Point's desktop firewall, and aside from desktop security policies, was important from the perspective of centralized administration. Although SecureClient provides SecuRemote with the added connectivity options and the benefits of a rule-based desktop firewall policy and Secure Configuration Verification (SCV), Integrity goes further to secure the user's desktop. Integrity is a corporate desktop firewall, much like Zone Lab's ZoneAlarm. In fact, a common user would be hard pressed to find many differences between ZoneAlarm Pro and Check Point's initial offering of Integrity. In fact, many of the logos and icons that are used in the Integrity program still bear the label "Zone Labs." However, for security professionals, the differences between the two programs immediately stand out.

Integrity actually monitors the inbound/outbound traffic on multiple levels. It allows for rules similar to those found in the policy of the SecureClient desktop firewall, but also inspects each program that attempts to access the network, and prompts the user to ensure that this traffic should be allowed. It functions in the same way for incoming traffic to the desktop, prompting the user to ensure it is safe and should be granted access. This is important because the current state of information security does little to protect against malicious code and ad-ware that use typically open ports as vectors of attack. Newer attacks, and arguably the most dangerous ones, include DNS redirects, which send users that are browsing the Internet to phony Web sites that download malicious code to their computers. Most commonly, this includes ad-ware, Trojan horses, and key logging software. Since HTTP traffic typically is allowed outbound on both the perimeter and desktop firewalls, the traffic is never under too much scrutiny because it's compliant with the policy. Attackers have learned to use this type of attack in interesting new ways, and it causes the information security field to spend more and invest more time in defending against it.

Another major difference that will save security administrators time and effort will be the centralized administration via the Integrity Server. Check Point's Integrity Client is a complex program that allows for multiple configuration settings and centralized administration through an Integrity Advanced Server. Due to space limitations, it is not feasible to walk through and explain the server configuration or even all possible client configuration options that are available in this chapter. This chapter will then serve as an introduction to the Integrity Client, and some of the features it allows security administrators to use in securing the end user desktop environment.

The Integrity Server allows the security administrator the ability to centrally configure access policies, expert rules, program access defaults, privacy restrictions, predefined zone information and many other new functions. The security administrator even has the ability to determine the level of involvement that end users are able to have with the Integrity Client. For instance, upon deployment of the Integrity Client, a security department must decide whether to roll out the Integrity Agent, which is a silent version of the client that doesn't prompt the user for any actions; or the Integrity Flex Client, which gives the user privileges to allow or deny traffic, privacy controls, expert rules, or change other configuration options. Aside from different names, these two versions of the Integrity client provide completely different deployment solutions that can be tailored to the specific environment they will be used in. Depending on the deployment and resources of the corporate environment, it may behoove the security staff to roll out Integrity as a standalone product with no centralized administration. In that situation, Check Point makes available Integrity Desktop, which is the Flex version of the client without the centralized administration option.

History of Integrity

Following Check Point's acquisition of Zone Labs, they began to make additions and changes to ZoneAlarm that would allow for more flexibility in enterprise environments. Zone Labs was the original creator of ZoneAlarm, which was arguably one of the best personal desktop firewalls freely available for the Microsoft Windows environment. ZoneAlarm had a great reputation for being a robust, free, desktop firewall that was intuitive and easy to understand and use for most nontechnical end users. When any traffic was detected, the ZoneAlarm client provided the end user with allow/deny options, but also created MD5 checksum values for each program that requested Internet access. If the program's checksum value changed, ZoneAlarm knew that could mean the program could be a malicious Trojan, and again prompted the user on what action to take. In essence, Check Point's new Integrity Client is ZoneAlarm with more advances in rule and policy governance of the desktop. It also incorporates centralized management, which allows easier integration with large-scale deployments for enterprise and government customers.

Integrity Client Installation

Installing Integrity is as simple as running a standard windows executable. The installation process is the same for the Integrity Flex, Integrity Agent, and Integrity Desktop clients. In this example, we will focus on the Installation and Configuration of Integrity Flex without configuring the integration with the Integrity Advanced Server.

Begin by downloading the Integrity Flex Client. Double-click the installer executable to begin installation (see Figure 12.47).

Figure 12.47 Integrity Flex License Agreement

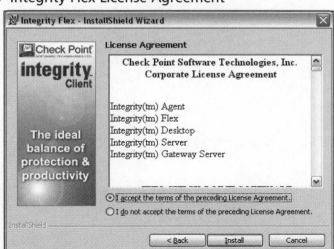

The Installer program will ask you to agree to Check Point's End User License Agreement. Select the radio button next to "I accept the terms of the preceding license agreement" and click **Install**.

The Integrity Flex installer will then prompt the user to approve the default installation location or enter a new location. Accept the default location and click **Next** (see Figure 12.48).

Figure 12.48 Integrity Flex Installation Location

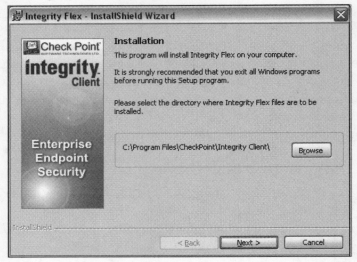

The Integrity Installer will now begin installing the client on the desktop machine (see Figure 12.49).

Figure 12.49 Integrity Flex Installation Progress

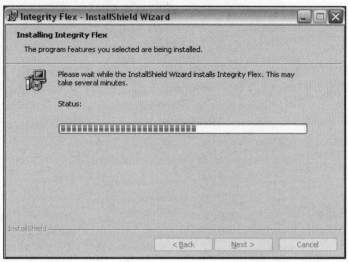

After the installation is completed, Integrity will prompt the user to reboot the system to fully complete the installation and begin using Integrity. Click **Yes** to restart the system.

After the system is rebooted, Integrity Flex will be available to protect the desktop (see Figure 12.50).

Figure 12.50 Integrity Flex Reboot Dialog

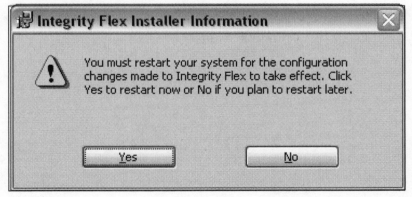

Integrity Client Configuration

After rebooting the system and attempting to launch Integrity, it will walk through a brief configuration wizard, and when it is completed, it is strongly recommended that anyone using Integrity use the tutorial for an in-depth explanation of how the Integrity Client works to secure the desktop.

Integrity Clientless Security

In some circumstances or environments, it may not be feasible or possible to install an Integrity client on every desktop machine to assist in securing end users from attacks. Check Point has provided a plug-in that creates a secure Integrity Browser, entering the user into a secure session during Web browsing. This browser is accessible when a user connects to the SSL Network Extender, both in a VPN-1 Pro gateway and in a Connectra gateway. It actively scans the desktop machine for malicious code, key loggers, spyware, and Trojan programs before it allows a user to provide information to a Web site. Integrity Clientless Security is configured and deployed without the hassle of touching each desktop computer. It also allows the administrator to easily select and search the desktop for malicious elements he is concerned with. Integrity Clientless Security incorporates privacy protection, adware protection, and advanced protection from malicious code such as Trojan horses. It also protects any passwords, cookies, or attachments in e-mail messages that are used during the secure session. Integrity Clientless Security also provides a mechanism for administrators to deploy the Integrity Client automatically.

Summary

In this chapter, we explained the history and usefulness behind Check Point's SecuRemote, SecureClient, and Integrity products. One take-away that was presented consistently throughout the chapter is the interoperability of the products, and the security provided to the remote user and private network user community by proper configuration and maintenance of the clients and policies that secure the user community. Though there will always be obstacles to building a remote access infrastructure and securing it, we have tried to provide information that will assist in working around those issues, such as Office mode and Secure Configuration Verification.

It is also important to understand that although SecuRemote provides Remote Access security for mobile users, it protects only the information being sent through the encrypted tunnel. SecureClient and Integrity have the ability to protect the desktop and user community regardless of their physical location. They secure the desktop, ensuring data is secure while resting on the computer as well as in transit to the corporate private network. SecureClient also provides Secure Configuration Verification, which checks to ensure that users connecting to your private network meet certain configuration specifications to obtain access, such as being on a Windows XP machine with Service Pack 2, specific Hotfix patches installed, and browsers configured to disable javascript.

As SecureClient builds on SecuRemote, providing the functionality of a desktop firewall, it only allows the administrator to block entire services, sites, or networks. Most of the time, malicious code such as ad-ware and Trojan horses find their way onto end-user computers through seemingly normal traffic that is allowed by the SecureClient and even the perimeter firewall. Integrity builds on the functionality of SecureClient, proving additional security mechanisms to protect the user from attacks that utilize typically open ports or services as vectors. It creates a hash of any program that attempts to connect to the network, and if that hash value changes, it notifies the user that something is wrong.

All three clients serve an important role in enabling users to be secure and flexible. While utilizing Check Point's desktop clients, the end user can continue to travel, provide valuable productivity, and ensure that company proprietary or privacy information remains safe. It's a marriage of fluidity and security for the company on the move.

Solutions Fast Track

SecuRemote

☑ SecuRemote is Check Point's VPN client that uses IKE to establish an encrypted tunnel for mobile or remote users to securely communicate with a private network's VPN gateway.

☑ To utilize SecuRemote, a VPN-1 gateway and Policy Server must be installed and configured to accept connections for secure communication. A desktop connection policy must also be created to allow access for remote users to the private network.

☑ SecuRemote is strictly a Remote Access client, providing users secure access to private network resources.

SecureClient

☑ SecureClient adds to the SecuRemote client the ability to download and enforce a Desktop Security policy, consisting of access rules for traffic to and from the desktop.

☑ Desktop Security policies are defined and configured in the Smart Dashboard Policy Server. It is possible to disable the security policy on the SecureClient if it contradicts an important mission or task that must be completed.

☑ SecureClient also allows for Secure Configuration Verification, which allows security administrators the ability to test a end user's computer configuration against a policy to ensure they are secure, and can be granted access to the private network and its resources.

Office Mode

☑ Office mode is a configuration option that allows remote users who have the same IP address as another host on the private network, to communicate with the private network via a virtual adapter that is assigned a new IP address from the VPN-1 gateway.

☑ Office mode incorporates IP pools that can be defined and configured on the VPN-1 gateway, or through a RADIUS server to assign IP addresses to SecureClient.

☑ Office mode must be enabled on both the Policy Server as well as the SecureClient.

Secure Configuration Verification

☑ SCV allows security administrators to perform specialized checks on remote computers who use SecureClient, and are attempting to access private network resources. If the computer is out of compliance with the defined policy, access to the private network is denied.

☑ Check Point has provided some predefined checks that can be configured to check for policy compliance. The policy that is enforced by SCV is located in the $FWDIR/conf directory, and is named local.scv.

☑ Additional checks can be created by either using the SCV Software Developers Kit (SDK), or contracting out to a Check Point OPSEC partner that provides SCV code writing services.

Integrity

☑ Integrity is the product of Check Point's Zone Labs acquisition, providing a highly configurable desktop firewall client that provides e-mail, privacy, and malicious code protection.

☑ Integrity is available in three different clients, each serving a different deployment scheme depending on the user environment. Integrity Agent is a silent client that provides for centralized administration with no end-user interaction. The Integrity Flex client allows the end user to have a greater role in the security of their desktop. Finally, Integrity Desktop is a standalone version of the Integrity Flex Client, without the centralized administration.

☑ Integrity Clientless Security provides a robust defense against malicious Trojan code, privacy intrusions, ad-ware and other attacks without the need for a bulky desktop client.

Frequently Asked Questions

The following Frequently Asked Questions, answered by the authors of this book, are designed to both measure your understanding of the concepts presented in this chapter and to assist you with real-life implementation of these concepts. To have your questions about this chapter answered by the author, browse to **www.syngress.com/solutions** and click on the **"Ask the Author"** form.

Q: Why can't I get SecuRemote to work from my home computer?

A: In some situations, the IKE key exchange can be hindered by ISPs or network firewalls. If users are experiencing difficulties with connecting to the VPN-1 gateway, try having them use **IKE over TCP** and **Force UDP encapsulation**. This wraps the packet in UDP, allowing it to pass through most networks that may be blocking the IKE protocols.

Q: I can connect to my VPN-1 gateway, but I can't seem to reach any resources inside my private network. Any suggestions?

A: The user may be experiencing a routing error due to an IP address conflict. Try having them enable Office mode on the SecuRemote client. This will provide their computer with a temporary virtual address to communicate with resources on the private network.

Q: I need to transfer a file to another computer for a presentation, and I can't seem to connect to it. I even have tried disconnecting my SecureClient from the VPN-1 gateway, but I still can't send the file. What am I doing wrong?

A: Typically, users will attempt to disconnect from the VPN-1 gateway to get around the Desktop Security policy. This will not stop SecureClient from enforcing the Desktop Security policy, as it is continually in effect once it is downloaded, and remains valid. The user should disable the Desktop Security policy. This will allow the user to perform actions that were previously disallowed by the policy, like transferring files. The user should enable the Desktop Security policy once the necessary action has been completed.

Q: When I put my SecureClient in Office mode, I can't seem to access the Internet. Why?

A: Some security administrators create IP pools to provide SecureClient users with internally routable IP address while they are trying to access internal resources. If the end user has their SecureClient in Hub mode, all locations they attempt to access will be routed through the private network and out the Perimeter Gateway firewall. In this case, the security administrator may have assigned an IP pool of nonpublic address space, or blocked the specific address in the IP pool from leaving the private network. Having the end user disable Hub mode typically solves this problem.

Chapter 13

SmartUpdate

Solutions in this chapter:

- **License Management**
- **Package Management**
- **Administration**
- **Upgrade Examples**

☑ **Summary**

☑ **Solutions Fast Track**

☑ **Frequently Asked Questions**

Introduction

In this chapter we will examine the functionality of SmartUpdate as a SmartConsole client in your Check Point environment. This client is designed to simplify the administrative tasks of software and license management. The firewall administrator has a single tool for viewing the list of software and licenses for all modules managed by a specific SmartCenter Server. The license and package repositories are data stores where software packages and licenses can be distributed to the managed modules.

Centralized and local licenses can be attached or removed from modules as necessary regardless of the complexity of your environment. Upgrades and patches for Check Point and OPSEC certified applications can be remotely distributed to various modules. Additionally IPSO and SecurePlatform operating systems can be upgraded using SmartUpdate.

In NGX there are new features available in SmartUpdate. Upgrades can be performed to a version earlier than the current SmartCenter version. Upgrading SmartPlatform includes options for reverting to specific images. Packages can be distributed to remote devices prior to performing the actual upgrade. The last notable feature addition is the ability to generate a CPInfo file for a specific module. There are minor column changes in the License Management and License Repository tables.

SmartUpdate Licensing

Using this tool to upgrade the software or operating system does require specific licensing for your SmartCenter Server and is based upon the number of managed devices. The value of having a centralized location to manage patching and upgrading increases with the size and complexity of your environment. Using this tool to view current software versions, licensing management, and CPInfo file creation does not require the additional license.

SmartUpdate Views/Screens

There are two main views in SmartUpdate: Package Management and License Management. Switching between these two views is done by selecting the Packages or Licenses tabs below the toolbar. The Package Management view lists the Operating System (including version) and Installed Packages (including vendor and major and minor package versions) on managed modules. The information in this window is populated by selecting **Packages | Get Data from All**. Package information for a specific module is retrieved by selecting the module and then selecting **Packages | Get Gateway Data**.

The License Management view lists all licenses attached to managed modules. The information in this window is populated by selecting **Licenses | Get all Licenses**. License information for a specific module is retrieved by selecting the module, then selecting **Licenses | Get Licenses**.

There are three additional windows that can be toggled on/off using the menu options or toolbar buttons: the Package Repository, License Repository, and Operation Status. All three of these windows can be closed by clicking the X in the upper-left corner of the window. The Package Repository lists the various software packages available for installation or distribution to all managed modules. There are no packages in the repository by default and you must add packages. Viewing this window is toggled on/off using the menu selecting **Packages | View Repository** or with the Package Repository button in the toolbar.

The License Repository lists all licenses installed on the SmartCenter Server regardless of the type (local or central) or attachment status. The SmartCenter license(s) is in the repository by default. Populating the License Management view will automatically add licenses to the repository. Viewing this window is toggled on/off using the menu selecting **Licenses | View Repository** or with the License Repository button in the toolbar.

The Operation Status window lists all the operations performed or in progress during the current session of SmartUpdate. A successful operation is indicated with a green check mark, an unsuccessful operation with a red X, and operations that are cancelled or that contain errors are indicated with a yellow exclamation mark. Details for a specific operation are displayed by double-clicking on a particular operation or by right-clicking an operation and selecting **Status**. Running operations are indicated by a blue hourglass. Running operations can be stopped by right-clicking an operation and selecting **Stop Operation**. Completed operations can be removed from this window using the menu selecting **Operations | Clear all Completed**, or right-clicking an operation and selecting **Clear**. The main menu options and the toolbar buttons are pictured in Figures 13.1 and 13.2.

Figure 13.1 SmartUpdate Primary Menus

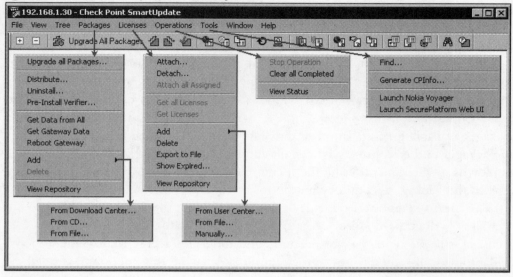

Figure 13.2 SmartUpdate Toolbar

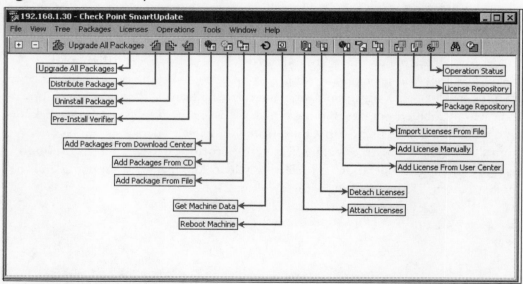

NGX Differences

The NGX License Management view has only minor changes from NG. The Check Point Gateways column is renamed to Machines. The name change is notable because not every module listed is a Check Point Gateway. Other systems under the administrative control of the primary SmartCenter Server are displayed as well; for example, a secondary SmartCenter Server or a Log server. The type column has been removed and there are two new columns, Version and State. The new columns in the License Repository screen are State and Upgrade Status. This information is linked to the need to upgrade licensing to NGX licenses.

License Management

Centralized licensing introduced in Check Point NG simplifies licensing administration in your environment. Centralized licenses are generated using the IP address of your SmartCenter Server, added to the license repository, and are attached/detached as desired to managed modules. Local licenses are generated using the IP address of a specific module. The benefit of centralized licenses is that an administrator does not need to generate new licenses when changing the IP address on a module.

License Repository

There are three ways to add licenses to the repository using the SmartUpdate Client. The choices are from the User Center, from a file, or manually. From the menu bar select **Licenses | Add** then select from one of the choices, **From User Center**, **From File** or **Manually**. An alternative method to reach the Add menu is to right-click in the License Repository area of the screen and select **Add**.

The **From User Center** option opens a web browser window to the Check Point User Center. Log in using your credentials and proceed to the appropriate products screen for the license you wish to download. Check next to the license you wish to add and select **Get** for that particular row or the **Get License** link from the top of the products list.

The **From File** option opens a window prompting you to specify the actual license file on the local computer where you are running the SmartUpdate client. License files automatically are attached to confirmation e-mail when generating or changing parameters. These files are available from the User Center at any time.

TIP

When you generate a license in the User Center you will receive a confirmation e-mail with the applicable license attached as – CPLicenseFile.lic. This same filename is also the default when you download a license file directly from the User Center. Make sure to modify the filename or directory when downloading or extracting a license file from e-mail so you do not overwrite an existing file. Licenses in the License Repository can be exported to a single or multiple files. Select one or more licenses followed by **Licenses | Export to File**.

The **Manually** option opens a window where you will need to type the specific parameters of the license (see Figure 13.3). The fields are Name, IP Address, Expiration Date, Features, Signature Key, and Certificate Key. This information is available in the Registration Confirmation e-mail from the User Center. You can copy the **cplic** command from the body of the e-mail message and use the Paste License button on the page to populate the required fields.

Figure 13.3 Manually Adding a License

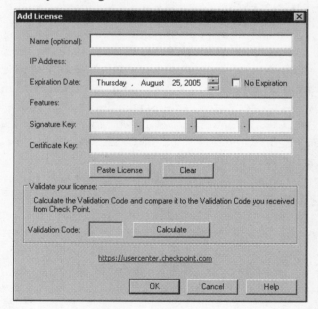

Attaching Licenses

Once central licenses are added to the license repository they must be attached to a specific module. Local licenses added into the repository are attached automatically to the module configured with the IP address contained in the license. There are multiple ways to attach or detach a license from the module. The simplest way to attach a license to a module is to drag and drop a specific license from the License Repository onto a specific module in the License Management view. From the menu select **Licenses | Attach...** or the Attach Licenses button in the toolbar, and this will open a window listing all the applicable modules to which a license can be attached. Select the specific module then click **Next** to open a window of the available unattached licenses. Select the specific license(s) then click **Finish**. If the Attach option or button cannot be selected, then you have no unattached licenses available.

The other two options are shortcuts to the process that we just described. In the License Management window right-click the module to which you want to attach a license and select **Attach Licenses**. This will open a window listing the available unattached licenses. Select the specific license(s) and click **Attach**. In the License Repository window right-click on the individual license or select multiple licenses using the CTRL button, then right-click and select **Attach**. This will open a window listing all the applicable modules to which the license(s) can be attached. Select the specific module and click **Attach**.

Detaching Licenses

The process for detaching licenses is similar to the attachment process, but there are a few notable differences. Detaching any local license from a module automatically deletes the license from the repository. From the menu select **Licenses | Detach...** or the Detach Licenses button in the toolbar to open a window listing all the possible modules from which a license can be detached. The remaining steps are similar to the attachment process. The differences are with detaching from the License Management and License Repository windows.

In the License Management window a right-click on a particular gateway lists **Detach All Licenses**. This will detach all licenses from the module. A confirmation window opens, including a warning message advising that local licenses are deleted from the repository when detached from a module. Right-click a specific license attached to this module for the **Detach License** option to remove that particular license. In the License Repository window, right-click the individual license or select multiple licenses using CTRL, then right-click and select **Detach**. If you should select multiple licenses that are not all attached to the same module, the **Detach** option is grayed out and cannot be selected. If you select a local license in the License Repository and select **Detach**, the confirmation window contains the message that local licenses are deleted from the repository when detached.

Deleting Licenses

Expired and unnecessary licenses can be removed from the License Repository. This includes licenses from old versions, licenses linked to old addresses, and evaluation licenses that are expired. A license must be unattached from a module before deletion. The two methods to delete licenses require selecting one or more licenses in the License Repository screen. Select **License | Delete** from the menu or right-click on the licenses and select **Delete**.

NOTE

A prerequisite to utilize SmartUpdate functionality is to establish SIC (Secure Internal Communication) between the SmartCenter Server and the managed modules. The default implied rules allow the administrative communications necessary. If you disable the implied rules make sure that the predefined services CPD (Check Point Daemon) and FW1_CPRID (Check Point Remote Installation) are opened from the SmartCenter Server to modules.

Package Management

One of the more tedious tasks as a firewall administrator is staying current with software and hot-fixes throughout the environment. Manually transferring files and performing upgrades on individual machines will tax available resources. SmartUpdate is the centralized tool designed to minimize the time and energy necessary to keep your environment up to date. Packages are added to the Package Repository then pushed to modules at your discretion. The process of upgrading Nokia and SecurePlatform firewalls is covered in the last section of this chapter.

Package Repository

Before any package is pushed out to modules, it must be added to the Package Repository using one of three methods. The available methods are **From Download Center**, **From CD**, or **From File**. Select the option from the menu

Packages | Add or use the associated button in the toolbar. Another method of accessing the **Add** menu is to right-click in the Package Repository window. The procedure for adding packages is dependent on the method you select.

The **From Download Center** opens a license agreement the first time this option is used; accept the license agreement to continue. Enter the appropriate User Center credentials to authenticate access to the Download Center. A window titled Get Packages From Download Center opens, listing the available downloads. Select the desired package(s) and click the Download button (see Figure 13.4).

Figure 13.4 Get Packages from Download Center Window

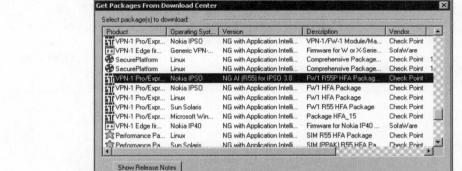

> **NOTE**
>
> There are no NGX packages currently available in the Download Center. NGX packages must be added to the repository using one of the NGX CDs in the media kit. IPSO packages are not available on CD2 even though they are listed using the **From CD** option. The IPSO VPN-1 Pro/Express package must be downloaded from the Download Center and added using the **From File** method. The IPSO wrapper download is not a valid SmartUpdate package.

The **From CD** option will open a Browse for CD drive window. Select the appropriate drive, click **OK**, and another window opens listing available packages. Select the package(s) to add to the repository and click **OK**. The **From File** method will open an Add Package window. Browse to the appropriate directory and select the file(s) and select **Open**. Packages can be deleted from the repository by highlighting the package you wish to delete then select **Packages | Delete** from the menu. Alternatively you can simply right-click on a package and select **Delete**.

TIP

Adding packages using SmartUpdate from a GUI client involves transferring the file from the client to the SmartCenter Server. This process can be expedited running SmartUpdate directly on the SmartCenter Server where possible. The packages are transferred internally to the repository directory.

Installing/Distributing Packages

There are two methods for installing/upgrading packages to managed modules. The first is to use the Upgrade All Packages option to bring all modules up to the version of software running on the Smart Center Server. This option is available from the menu by selecting **Packages | Upgrade All Packages** or the Upgrade All Packages button in the toolbar. This option examines all the managed modules and verifies that all necessary packages are in the repository. If the packages are not in the repository you will be prompted to add the missing packages. There is a verification process that will review compatibility, dependencies, and disk space requirements for the intended upgrades. The operation will fail if there are verification issues; review the operation status for specific errors.

The verify function can be performed independently prior to performing any upgrade. This option is available from the menu by selecting **Packages | Pre-Install Verifier** or the Pre-Install Verifier button in the toolbar. This is not a requirement but provides the opportunity to discover and resolve potential problems.

The other method is to use the Distribute functionality. This option is available from the menu by selecting **Packages | Distribute** or the Distribute Packages button in the toolbar. This option is for performing specific package upgrades on specific modules. Upgrading to a version below the current SmartCenter version, applying hot-fixes, and upgrading IPSO versions requires using the Distribute method. The first time you initiate the Distribute function a warning will appear stating the Upgrade All Packages option is the preferred method for upgrading NG machines. The reason for this is to avoid version incompatibility on a module.

The Distribute function contains three different actions while working with packages. Packages can be distributed and installed, distributed only, or installed at a later time. The distribution-only option may be used prior to using the Upgrade All option to save resources.

Administration

The License and Package Repositories are stored on the SmartCenter Server. The License Repository directory is $FWDIR\conf\ on either platform. The default Package Repository directory is defined by the $SUROOT environment variable. The default values are C:\SUroot for Windows and /var/suroot for UNIX. Use the cppkg setroot (new directory) command to change the directory defined for the $SUROOT environment variable. Reboot the SmartCenter Server after issuing this command.

Command Line

For those who prefer a command line over using a GUI, there are three main commands for license and package management. The **cplic** command performs various license functions applicable for modules and the SmartCenter Server. This command performs license distribution and License Repository functions. The **cppkg** command performs various functions with the Package Repository. The **cprinstall** command performs the package distribution functions.

! **W**ARNING

There are command-line options for performing a significant amount of the functionality provided by all the SmartConsole tools. There are commands for performing tasks not specifically available in the SmartConsole tools. Familiarize yourself with command-line tools before choosing CLI (command-line interface) as your primary management method. Review release notes and Check Point reference guides to learn of version differences.

CPInfo

The CPInfo function generates a text file of configuration information for a managed module. Check Point and operating system parameters contained in this file are necessary when working with technical support. Use SmartUpdate to create this file locally on your client workstation. Pre-NGX versions require local generation of CPInfo files. The tool includes the ability to name the output using a service request number if desired.

   Generate a CPInfo file by selecting a specific module, then select **Tools | Generate CPInfo**. A window opens to specify a location and file naming options (see Figure 13.5). Specify additional options for including log files and windows registry information if desired and click OK. The progress is tracked in the Operation Status view.

Figure 13.5 The Generate CPInfo Window

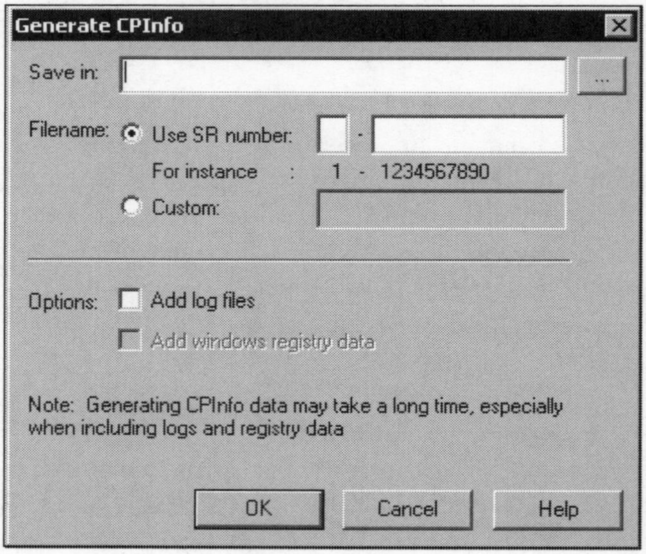

Upgrade Examples

The following upgrade examples are intended to apply the information learned in this chapter to perform upgrades on Nokia and SecurePlatform firewalls. The first walkthrough upgrades a Nokia IP330 from IPSO 3.8 Build 33 running NG-AI HFA-R55P-05 to IPSO Version 3.9 Build 35 running NGX. The second walkthrough upgrades a SecurePlatform running NG-AI R55 with HFA-12 to NGX.

Nokia Upgrade

A Nokia IP330 is configured as a firewall with the latest NG–AI hot-fix applied. A new VPN-1 Pro/Express Gateway object is created in SmartDashboard. SIC is initialized and NG and NGX licenses are attached to the module. The starting point for the upgrade is illustrated in Figure 13.6. The necessary IPSO 3.9 and NGX software are downloaded to the SmartUpdate client before beginning the actual upgrade.

Figure 13.6 The Package Management View Nokia Pre-Upgrade

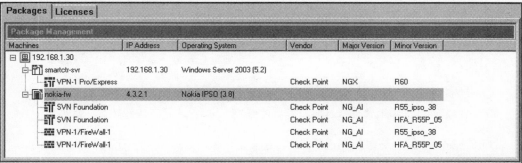

The next step is to add the necessary packages to the Package Repository using the Add Package From File option. Figures 13.7 and 13.8 illustrate the screens used to add the IPSO and Check Point NGX software to the repository.

Figure 13.7 Add Package—IPSO

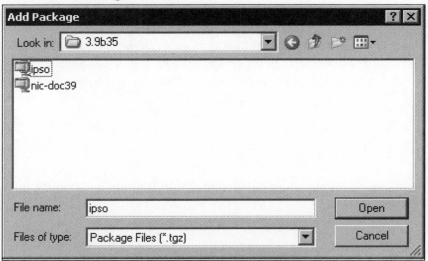

Figure 13.8 Add Package—NGX VPN-1 Pro

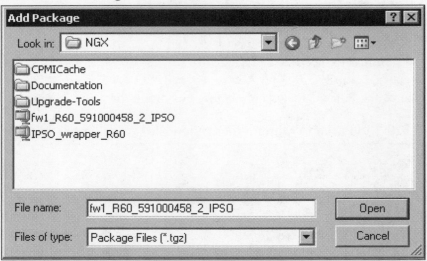

The packages are successfully added to the repository as illustrated in Figure 13.9.

Figure 13.9 Package Repository for Nokia Upgrade

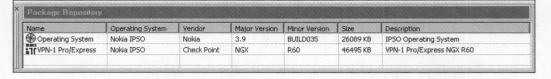

There are two main steps to upgrade the Nokia firewall. The first step is to use Distribute Package to upgrade the operating system. Right–click the Operating System package, and select **Distribute** to open the window shown in Figure 13.10.

Figure 13.10 Distribute Package—IPSO Operating System

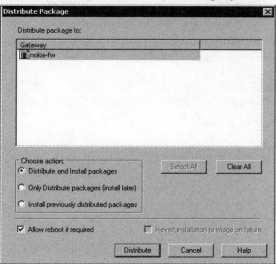

Select the Distribute and Install Packages option, check Allow reboot if required, and click **Distribute**. The process of this operation is shown in Figure 13.11.

Figure 13.11 Operation Status IPSO Distribution

Status	Time
Operation started	Aug 27, 2005 12:47:10
Checking cprid connection...	Aug 27, 2005 12:48:31
Verified	Aug 27, 2005 12:48:32
Getting data...	Aug 27, 2005 12:48:33
Operation completed successfully	Aug 27, 2005 12:48:45
Updating machine information...	Aug 27, 2005 12:48:45
Update successfully completed	Aug 27, 2005 12:48:47
Checking available disk space...	Aug 27, 2005 12:48:47
Verified	Aug 27, 2005 12:48:47
Checking compatibility with installed packages...	Aug 27, 2005 12:48:47
'Operating System' is compatible with installed packages	Aug 27, 2005 12:49:02
Checking if the 'Operating System' package already resides on ...	Aug 27, 2005 12:49:02
The 'Operating System' package was not found	Aug 27, 2005 12:49:04
Transferring file, 100% complete	Aug 27, 2005 12:54:31
'Operating System' was successfully transferred	Aug 27, 2005 12:54:31
Installing 'Operating System' (may take some time)	Aug 27, 2005 12:54:31
'Operating System' installation completed	Aug 27, 2005 12:56:06
Initiating reboot...	Aug 27, 2005 12:56:06
Trying to reestablish connection...	Aug 27, 2005 12:58:47
Reboot completed successfully	Aug 27, 2005 12:59:50
Checking cprid connection...	Aug 27, 2005 12:59:50
Verified	Aug 27, 2005 12:59:51
Getting data...	Aug 27, 2005 12:59:54
Operation completed successfully	Aug 27, 2005 12:59:58
Updating machine information...	Aug 27, 2005 12:59:58
Update successfully completed	Aug 27, 2005 13:00:00
Checking installation status	Aug 27, 2005 13:00:00
Package 'Operating System' was installed successfully	Aug 27, 2005 13:00:00
Install operation completed successfully	Aug 27, 2005 13:00:02

The Package Management view of the nokia-fw object is updated automatically, as shown in Figure 13.12.

Figure 13.12 The Package Management Post IPSO Upgrade

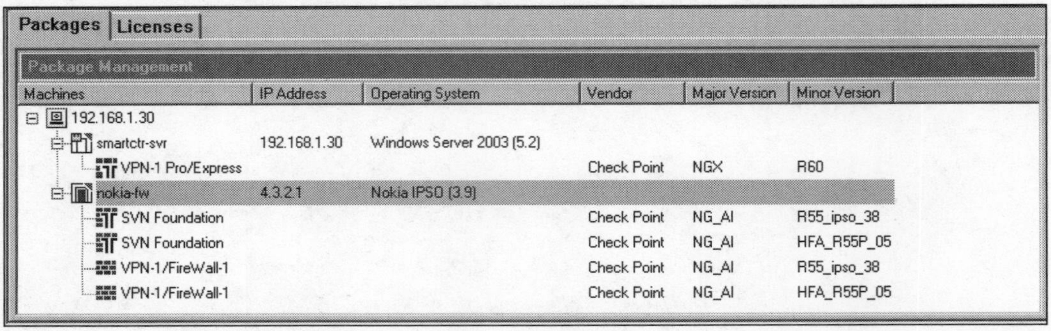

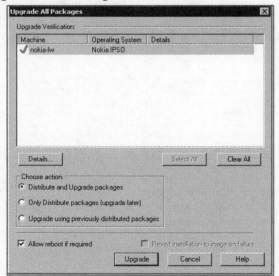

During the IPSO upgrade the boot manager is upgraded automatically, the NG-AI software stays enabled, and the Nokia automatically boots to the new image. If the upgrade is done manually on the Nokia you need to specify the –k flag to keep the existing packages enabled. Press the Upgrade All Packages toolbar button to open the Upgrade All Packages window shown in Figure 13.13.

Figure 13.13 Upgrade All Packages Window Nokia

Select the Distribute and Upgrade Packages option, check Allow reboot if required, and click **Upgrade**. The process of this operation is shown in Figure 13.14.

Figure 13.14 Operation Status Upgrade All Packages Nokia

Status	Time
Operation started	Aug 27, 2005 13:01:05
Checking cprid connection...	Aug 27, 2005 13:01:05
Verified	Aug 27, 2005 13:01:06
Getting data...	Aug 27, 2005 13:01:08
Operation completed successfully	Aug 27, 2005 13:01:14
Updating machine information...	Aug 27, 2005 13:01:14
Update successfully completed	Aug 27, 2005 13:01:15
Checking available disk space...	Aug 27, 2005 13:01:15
Verified	Aug 27, 2005 13:01:16
Checking compatibility with installed packages...	Aug 27, 2005 13:01:16
'VPN-1 Pro/Express' is compatible with installed packages	Aug 27, 2005 13:01:23
Checking if the 'VPN-1 Pro/Express' package already resides o...	Aug 27, 2005 13:01:23
The 'VPN-1 Pro/Express' package was not found	Aug 27, 2005 13:01:26
Transferring file, 100% complete	Aug 27, 2005 13:02:08
'VPN-1 Pro/Express' was successfully transferred	Aug 27, 2005 13:02:08
Upgrading the cprid process...	Aug 27, 2005 13:02:27
Installing 'VPN-1 Pro/Express' (may take some time)	Aug 27, 2005 13:02:38
Check Point VPN-1 Pro/Express NGX R60 installation complet...	Aug 27, 2005 13:10:56
Compiling policy 'Standard' for nokia-fw	Aug 27, 2005 13:10:56
Policy 'Standard' compiled successfully for nokia-fw	Aug 27, 2005 13:11:04
Initiating reboot...	Aug 27, 2005 13:11:04
Trying to reestablish connection...	Aug 27, 2005 13:13:45
Reboot completed successfully	Aug 27, 2005 13:14:57
Checking cprid connection...	Aug 27, 2005 13:14:57
Verified	Aug 27, 2005 13:14:58
Getting data...	Aug 27, 2005 13:15:00
Operation completed successfully	Aug 27, 2005 13:15:04
Updating machine information...	Aug 27, 2005 13:15:04
Update successfully completed	Aug 27, 2005 13:15:05
Checking installation status	Aug 27, 2005 13:15:05
Package 'VPN-1 Pro/Express' was installed successfully	Aug 27, 2005 13:15:05
✓ Install operation completed successfully	Aug 27, 2005 13:15:07

The Package Management view of the nokia–fw object is updated automatically, as shown in Figure 13.15.

Figure 13.15 Package Management Post NGX Upgrade Nokia

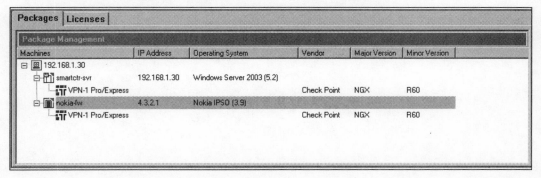

Packages	Licenses

Package Management					
Machines	IP Address	Operating System	Vendor	Major Version	Minor Version
⊟ 🖳 192.168.1.30					
⊟ smartctr-svr	192.168.1.30	Windows Server 2003 (5.2)			
VPN-1 Pro/Express			Check Point	NGX	R60
⊟ nokia-fw	4.3.2.1	Nokia IPSO (3.9)			
VPN-1 Pro/Express			Check Point	NGX	R60

The Nokia is fully functional as an NGX VPN-1 gateway. The nokia-fw object general tab is modified automatically to reflect the current version.

SecurePlatform Upgrade

An IBM e305 server is configured as a SecurePlatform firewall with NG-AI HFA-12. A new VPN-1 Pro/Express Gateway object is created in SmartDashboard. SIC is initialized and NG and NGX licenses are attached to the module. The starting point for the upgrade is illustrated in Figure 13.16.

Figure 13.16 The Package Management View SecurePlatform Pre-Upgrade

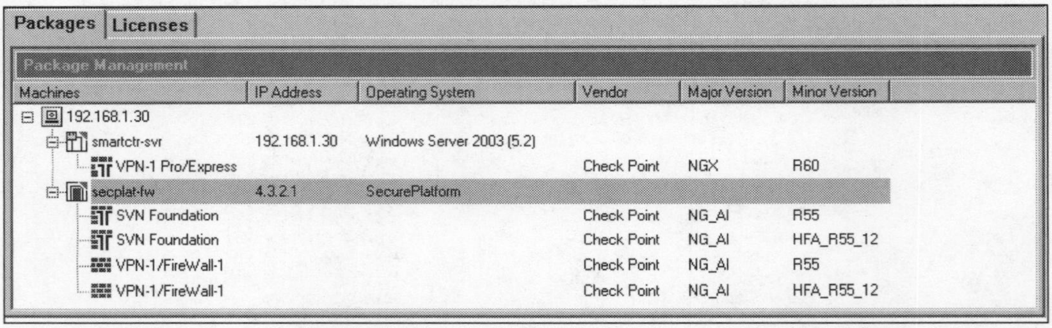

Machines	IP Address	Operating System	Vendor	Major Version	Minor Version
⊟ 🖥 192.168.1.30					
⊟ 📠 smartctr-svr	192.168.1.30	Windows Server 2003 (5.2)			
🔐 VPN-1 Pro/Express			Check Point	NGX	R60
⊟ 📠 secplat-fw	4.3.2.1	SecurePlatform			
🔐 SVN Foundation			Check Point	NG_AI	R55
🔐 SVN Foundation			Check Point	NG_AI	HFA_R55_12
🔳 VPN-1/FireWall-1			Check Point	NG_AI	R55
🔳 VPN-1/FireWall-1			Check Point	NG_AI	HFA_R55_12

The next step is to add the SecurePlatform NGX to the Package Repository using the Add Package From CD option. Insert NGX CD1 containing the SmartUpdate client and click the Add Package From CD button in the toolbar to open a browse window. Select the appropriate drive and the packages are listed as displayed in Figure 13.17.

Figure 13.17 Adding SecurePlatform from CD

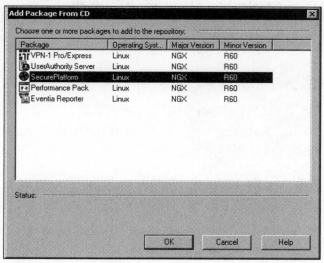

Select the SecurePlatform package and click **OK**. The status area of this window informs you the package is processing (see Figure 13.18); this takes a few minutes before the package begins the transfer to the SmartCenter Server.

Figure 13.18 Package Processing Status

The package takes a few more minutes to transfer after processing. Figure 13.19 illustrates the SecurePlatform package in the repository. The size of the file indicates why this takes a little while.

Figure 13.19 Package Repository for SecurePlatform Upgrade

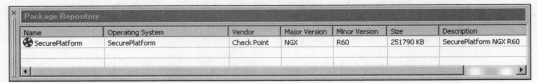

The SecurePlatform package contains both the operating system and VPN-1 software and requires only a single upgrade. Select the Upgrade All Packages toolbar button to open the Upgrade All Packages window in Figure 13.20.

Figure 13.20 Upgrade All Packages Window SecurePlatform

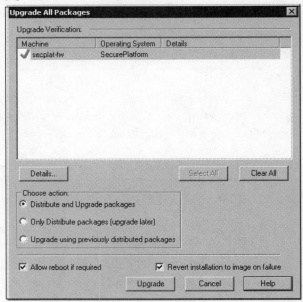

Select the Distribute and Upgrade Packages option, check Allow reboot if required, and click **Upgrade**. The process of this operation is shown in Figure 13.21.

Figure 13.21 Operation Status Upgrade All Packages SecurePlatform

Status	Time
Operation started	Aug 28, 2005 16:20:41
Checking cprid connection...	Aug 28, 2005 16:20:42
Verified	Aug 28, 2005 16:20:42
Getting data...	Aug 28, 2005 16:20:44
Operation completed successfully	Aug 28, 2005 16:20:46
Updating machine information...	Aug 28, 2005 16:20:46
Update successfully completed	Aug 28, 2005 16:20:47
Checking available disk space...	Aug 28, 2005 16:20:47
Verified	Aug 28, 2005 16:20:48
Checking compatibility with installed packages...	Aug 28, 2005 16:20:48
'SecurePlatform' is compatible with installed packages	Aug 28, 2005 16:20:53
Checking available disk space...	Aug 28, 2005 16:20:53
Operation completed successfully	Aug 28, 2005 16:21:02
Creating image snapshot. This process may take some time...	Aug 28, 2005 16:21:02
Image snapshot created successfully	Aug 28, 2005 16:22:15
Checking if the 'SecurePlatform' package already resides on m...	Aug 28, 2005 16:22:15
The 'SecurePlatform' package was not found	Aug 28, 2005 16:22:17
Transferring file, 100% complete	Aug 28, 2005 16:23:03
'SecurePlatform' was successfully transferred	Aug 28, 2005 16:23:03
Installing 'SecurePlatform' (may take some time)	Aug 28, 2005 16:23:03
Upgrading the operating system.	Aug 28, 2005 16:26:17
Please wait while the upgrade process completes.	Aug 28, 2005 16:26:17
Installation finished successfully	Aug 28, 2005 16:26:17
'SecurePlatform' installation completed	Aug 28, 2005 16:26:17
Compiling policy 'Standard' for secplat-fw	Aug 28, 2005 16:26:17
Policy 'Standard' compiled successfully for secplat-fw	Aug 28, 2005 16:26:23
Initiating reboot...	Aug 28, 2005 16:26:24
Trying to reestablish connection...	Aug 28, 2005 16:29:05
Reboot completed successfully	Aug 28, 2005 16:29:06
Checking cprid connection...	Aug 28, 2005 16:29:06
Verified	Aug 28, 2005 16:29:07
Getting data...	Aug 28, 2005 16:29:08
Operation completed successfully	Aug 28, 2005 16:29:10
Updating machine information...	Aug 28, 2005 16:29:10
Update successfully completed	Aug 28, 2005 16:29:11
Checking installation status	Aug 28, 2005 16:29:11
Package 'SecurePlatform' was installed successfully	Aug 28, 2005 16:29:11
✓ Install operation completed successfully	Aug 28, 2005 16:29:12

The Package Management view of the secplat-fw object is updated automatically, as shown in Figure 13.22.

Figure 13.22 Package Management Post NGX Upgrade SecurePlatform

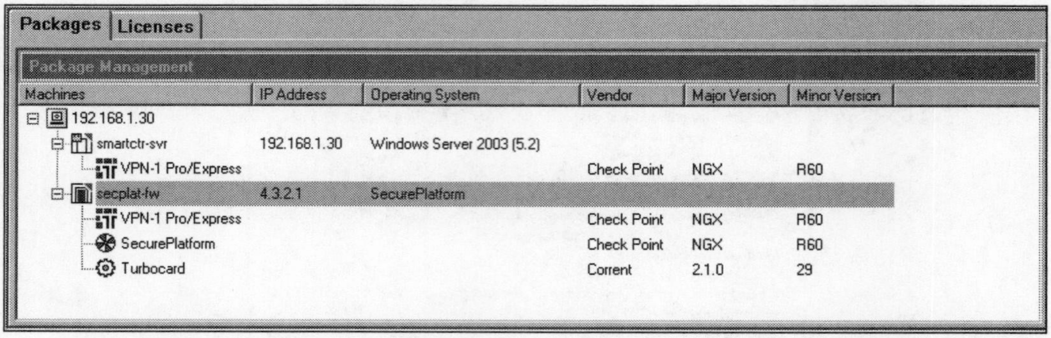

Machines	IP Address	Operating System	Vendor	Major Version	Minor Version
⊟ 🖥 192.168.1.30					
⊟ 📠 smartctr-svr	192.168.1.30	Windows Server 2003 (5.2)			
┊ ⋯📠 VPN-1 Pro/Express			Check Point	NGX	R60
⊟ 📠 secplat-fw	4.3.2.1	SecurePlatform			
┊ ⋯📠 VPN-1 Pro/Express			Check Point	NGX	R60
┊ ⋯✹ SecurePlatform			Check Point	NGX	R60
⋯⚙ Turbocard			Corrent	2.1.0	29

Packages | Licenses

Package Management

The SecurePlatform module is fully functional as an NGX VPN-1 gateway. The secplat-fw object general tab is modified automatically to reflect the current version. There are some new features in SecurePlatform NGX that are covered in the next chapter. You should familiarize yourself with these changes before performing the upgrade.

Summary

SmartUpdate is the SmartConsole tool designed to easily manage licenses and packages across your Check Point environment. The ability to manage licenses, view product and operating system versions, and generate CPInfo files is available without any additional licensing. The size of your environment is the primary factor in deciding to purchase the additional SmartUpdate license required to install/distribute packages, patches, or operating systems.

The need to upgrade existing NG licenses to NGX will have many administrators using this tool. Using the license tools to add and distribute licenses is a quick and easy task. All the SmartConsole tools are designed to simplify the management tasks for your Check Point environment. Behind these GUI tools are the command lines that execute the various operations. Choose the management interface that you feel is most comfortable.

Solutions Fast Track

License Management

- The License Repository contains all the licenses for modules under the administrative control of the SmartCenter Server.

- Centralized licenses provide greater flexibility for administrators to attach and detach licenses as necessary.

- Local licenses are maintained in the repository only when attached to modules.

- Expired and unnecessary licenses are easily removed from the environment.

Package Management

- Current operating system and package versions visible in a single screen.

- The Package Repository contains packages for performing installations and upgrades.

- Package distribution and installation are controlled from the SmartCenter Server.

Administration

- Licenses and Packages are stored locally on the SmartCenter Server.

- Command-line options exist for GUI functionality.

- CPInfo files for troubleshooting can be generated for remote modules.

Upgrade Examples

- Nokia firewalls can be upgraded in two operations: upgrading IPSO then VPN-1 Pro.

- SecurePlatform firewalls can be upgraded in a single operation.

Frequently Asked Questions

The following Frequently Asked Questions, answered by the authors of this book, are designed to both measure your understanding of the concepts presented in this chapter and to assist you with real-life implementation of these concepts. To have your questions about this chapter answered by the author, browse to **www.syngress.com/solutions** and click on the **"Ask the Author"** form.

Q: What functionality of SmartUpdate requires additional licensing?

A: Package installation/distribution requires SmartUpdate licensing. Specific license requirements are based on the number of managed modules. License management and CPInfo functionality do not require additional licensing.

Q: Do I need to upgrade module licenses before upgrading the packages?

A: Although not required it is recommended that upgraded licenses should be attached to modules prior to upgrading to ensure proper operation.

Q: What is the validation code used for?

A: The validation code is a hash value based on the specific license parameters. When the required fields are added manually, you can generate the validation code based on the entered information. If it does not match the code provided from Check Point, one of the fields is not completed properly.

Q: How important is the name field for a license?

A: Functionally there is no importance. Modifying the name from the default (feature code, date, time) to something readable eliminates needing to know feature strings.

Q: Do I have to close SmartDashboard to retrieve module package information in SmartUpdate?

A: No, the database locking issues are resolved in NGX.

Q: Do I need to save a license file after adding it to the repository?

A: No, you can extract individual licenses to a single file or extract all licenses to a single file using the Export to File feature.

Q: Can I download NGX packages from the Download Center?

A: Not currently. You must use the CDs in the NGX media kit or download the IPSO version from the download center.

Chapter 14

SecurePlatform

Solutions in this chapter:

- **Installation**
- **Web User Interface**
- **Command-Line Configuration**
- **CPShell**
- **Expert Mode**
- **Dynamic Routing**

☑ **Summary**

☑ **Solutions Fast Track**

☑ **Frequently Asked Questions**

Introduction

Check Point has been doing all its research and development on SecurePlatform with other operating systems being done later. SPLAT (SecurePlatform) has been taking over the market since its arrival with Check Point Next Generation Feature Pack 2. We will take a tour of SecurePlatform with the different operating system capabilities and the Check Point supported add-ons to SPLAT. A lot of emphasis has been put on SPLAT by Check Point and many other operating systems have been replaced by an Intel-based system to run SPLAT as their underlying OS to run VPN-1 Pro.

In version NGX, Check Point offers SecurePlatform Pro, which extends the functionality and performance of this operating system.

With the popularity of appliance devices in the market, and the cost-effectiveness of utilizing Intel-based hardware instead of more expensive, proprietary hardware, Check Point is offering more flexible and cost-effective solutions by continuing to develop the SecurePlatform Operating System.

Installation

The installation of SecurePlatform is designed to be a very easy process. In this section, we will cover the installation process and the configuration of SecurePlatform using both the Web user interface (WUI) and the command-line tool sysconfig.

Bootable CD

To install SecurePlatform using the CD-ROM-based installation, simply power on your machine with the SecurePlatform CD-ROM in the drive. The SecurePlatform installation program automatically starts. When the welcome screen appears, press **Enter**. The installation program boots and loads the necessary drivers for the hardware it detects.

After the SecurePlatform installation program is finished booting, you are presented with a few options. In most cases, unless you know you need to install additional drivers, you can choose **OK** to continue.

The next screen asks you which version you wish to install. The options are SecurePlatform or SecurePlatform Pro. Unless your infrastructure requires advanced routing options such as OSPF or BGP, most users should choose SecurePlatform. The advanced routing options of SecurePlatform Pro will be covered later in this chapter.

The next screen asks for some localization information. Choose the proper information to match your hardware. The next step asks which Ethernet device to configure. The default is the first NIC the system recognizes. In most cases, you will want to have the primary interface (and the IP address the hostname is tied to) be the external address—especially for VPNs. However, at this point, the address you specify here is just for you to get the system on the network after you have rebooted. Note: This system must be accessed from the same subnet because no default route or static routes are in effect at this point. This also stops people who are not on the local network from attacking the system before it is configured.

The next screen asks if you wish to enable https server for server configuration. If you would like to secure your https server, or if you plan to use the Remote Access features of VPN-1, you can change the default port used to communicate with SecurePlatform.

You are prompted to confirm the formatting of the hard drive, and then the installation program begins copying the SecurePlatform files. After this step is completed, you are prompted to reboot the machine.

Tools & Traps…

Hardware Considerations

Before you even buy the hardware for your SecurePlatform system, it is very important to check the hardware compatibility guide available from Check Point. Although the SecurePlatform software can run on any x86 hardware, Check Point supports, and includes drivers for, only a limited number of hardware platforms. You can find a listing of supported platforms at http://www.checkpoint.com/products/supported_platforms/secureplatform.html.

Bootable Floppy and Network Installation

You can also install SecurePlatform from a floppy disk or the network if your machine does not have a CD-ROM drive. You can transfer the necessary images from an FTP, HTTP, or NFS server.

Copy the contents of the "SecurePlatform" directory on the CD to a UNIX-based server. Next, you must create the bootable floppy disk. To do so, you need a blank, formatted floppy and a Windows PC. Insert the floppy into your drive. Open the CD in Windows Explorer, and navigate to the SecurePlatform/images directory.

Click and drag the bootnet.img file over the cprawrite icon. This will walk you through the process of creating the bootable floppy disk.

After the floppy disk is made, insert it into your SecurePlatform machine and power on. The SecurePlatform installation program starts automatically. When the welcome screen appears, press **Enter**. The installation program boots and loads the necessary drivers for the hardware it detects.

After the SecurePlatform installation program is finished booting, it prompts you for the type of network server you wish to install from. Select the desired network installation methods, select **OK**, and press **Enter**. Next, the Interface Selection menu is displayed. Select the network interface card that is connected to the network where the network server resides, select **OK**, and then press **Enter**. The Configure TCP/IP menu is displayed. Specify the IP settings for this machine, select **OK**, and then press **Enter**.

Depending on which install method you chose, a window appears asking for the parameters of the connection (for example, the URL for an HTTP installation). Enter the session details, select **OK**, and then press **Enter**. The installation program reads the distribution files from the network and displays the Welcome screen. From this point, the installation is the same as a CD-ROM-based installation.

If your machine does not have a CD-ROM or a floppy disk drive, you can use alternative methods for installation. Refer to the appendix entitled "Installation on Computers without Floppy or CD-ROM Drives" in the "*SecurePlatform/SecurePlatform Pro User Guide,*" available from the Check Point Web site.

Web User Interface

The preferred method of configuring SecurePlatform is via the Web user interface (WUI). This section describes the initial configuration steps for the SecurePlatform device. For NGX, the WUI has been totally redesigned. In order to use the WUI, you must have Internet Explorer (Version 5.5 or higher) or Netscape (Version 7.1 or higher) installed on your administration workstation.

OS Configuration

To configure SecurePlatform with the WUI, open your Web browser and connect to https://<*IP address you used during installation*>. This brings you to the license agreement shown in Figure 14.1. Click **I Accept** to continue.

Figure 14.1 The SecurePlatform License Agreement

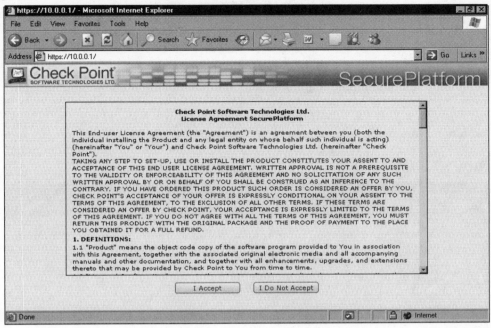

You must now log in. The first time you log in, use the default username (admin) and password (admin), as shown in Figure 14.2.

Figure 14.2 The SecurePlatform Login Screen

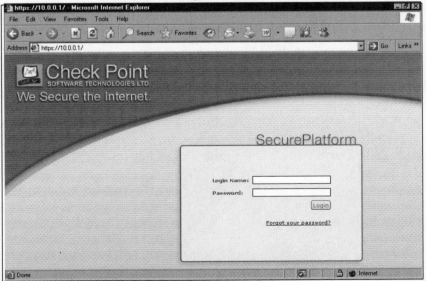

The installation requires you to change the password to a new one, as shown in Figure 14.3. Type a new password into the appropriate box, verify it in the next box, and click **Apply** to save your new password.

The new password must be between 6 and 32 characters in length and cannot be a word found in the dictionary (for example, "password").

You can click the **Token** button to save a small file you can use to authenticate to the box if you forget the password. You should put the file on a diskette and store it in a safe place. This token can be used to reset the password and log on the WUI. Click **Save** and **Login** to continue.

Figure 14.3 Changing the Default SecurePlatform Password

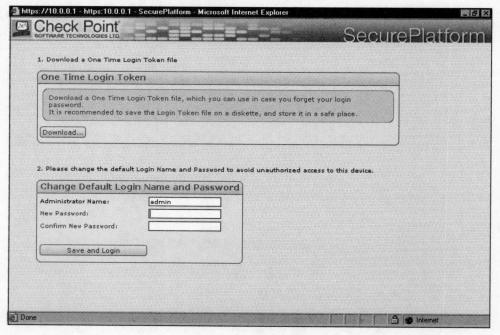

You are then presented with the first time configuration wizard. The welcome screen is shown in Figure 14.4. Click **Next** to continue. You may also click **Quit** to configure SecurePlatform without using the wizard.

Figure 14.4 The SecurePlatform Configuration Wizard

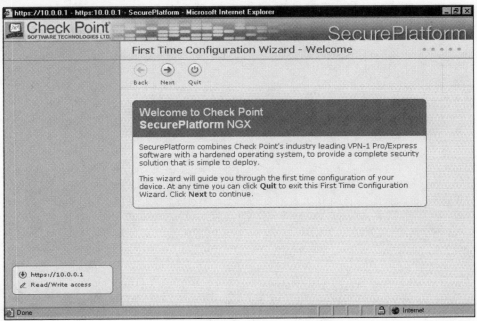

Next, you are presented with the Network Connections page. On this page you can modify, add, or delete Ethernet devices. You can also adjust the IP address and subnet properties of each device. You can also set each interface to use DHCP if necessary. You should configure all your interfaces on this screen. Clicking the interface name enables you to enter an IP address and netmask for the interface, as shown in Figure 14.5. If you happen to modify the interface you are connected through, you will be required to log on again and restart the wizard.

Figure 14.5 SecurePlatform Network Configuration

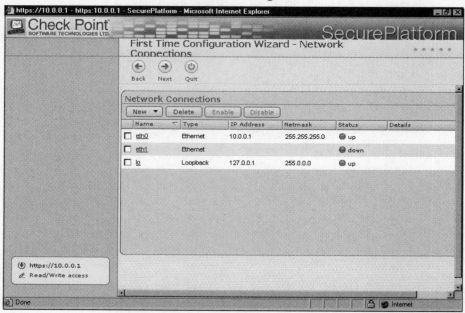

The next screen enables you to adjust the routing table (see Figure 14.6). You can add a new static route or default route. Make any necessary changes, and then click **Next** to continue.

Figure 14.6 SecurePlatform Routing Table

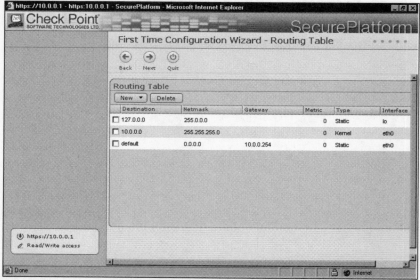

The next screen enables you to enter DNS Server information (see Figure 14.7). Add up to three DNS Servers, then and click **Next** to continue.

> **TIP**
>
> Proper DNS configuration is extremely important. There are many functions on the firewall that depend on proper DNS resolution. Also, only use trusted DNS Servers for your firewall. This will prevent attacks such as DNS Poisoning.

Figure 14.7 SecurePlatform DNS Servers

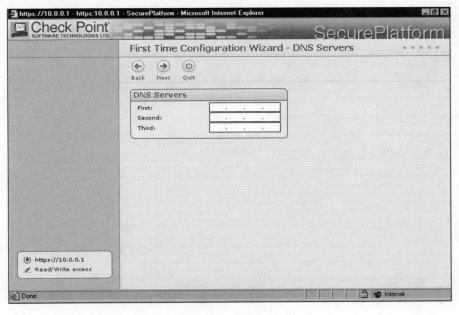

Now you can modify the hostname, the domain name, and primary interface for your machine. You should also make sure you set the hostname and domain correctly (see Figure 14.8). This is especially important if you are going to install a management station, because of the InternalCA and CRL lookups. The Check Point software relies on certificates to verify the authenticity of the various components. If Check Point modules cannot authenticate each other properly, communications between the modules will not work. Set the primary interface correctly. This should be the interface that the hostname resolves to through DNS. Click **Next** to continue.

Figure 14.8 SecurePlatform Host and Domain Name

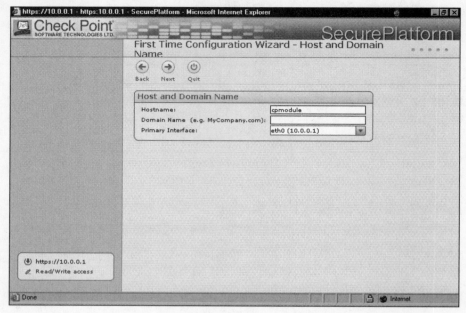

Next, you are prompted to set the date and time for the SecurePlatform machine (see Figure 14.9). You can enter the information manually or use the Network Time Protocol (NTP) for automatic configuration. Enter the correct information, then and click **Apply** to set. Click **Next** to continue.

NOTE

Network Time Protocol is important on all devices in your infrastructure. If the clocks on your devices are not in sync, it makes log correlation and incident tracking extremely difficult.

Figure 14.9 SecurePlatform Device Date and Time Setup

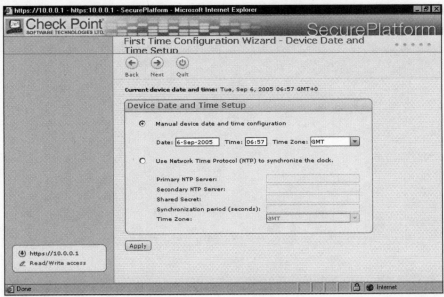

The Web and SSH Clients screen enables you to limit connections to SecurePlatform (see Figure 14.10). The default is to allow connections from any host. It is recommended that you allow connections only from administrative workstations or networks. Click **Add** to enter either a hostname or IP address, or you can choose to enter a network. After entering Web and SSH Clients, click **Next**.

Figure 14.10 SecurePlatform Web and SSH Clients

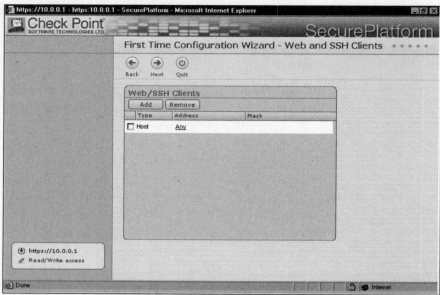

The next portion of the wizard asks which installation options you wish to configure (see Figure 14.11). Depending on which license you have purchased, choose either the Enterprise/Pro or the Express option. Click **Next**.

Figure 14.11 SecurePlatform Installation Options

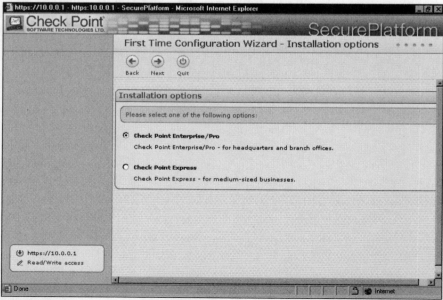

You are then prompted to choose which products you wish to install (see Figure 14.12). At a minimum, you are required to choose VPN-1 Pro if this device will be used as a gateway, or SmartCenter if the device will be used as a management server. You can also choose to install both products on the same machine. Choose the proper options, and then click **Next**.

Figure 14.12 SecurePlatform Products

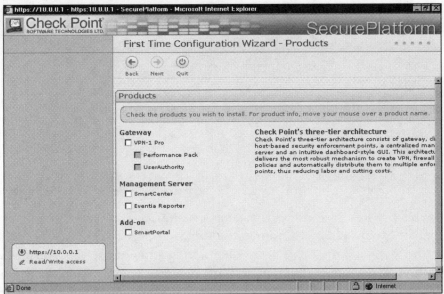

If you chose VPN-1 Pro (the enforcement module), you are prompted to define the gateway type (see Figure 14.13). If this device will be a member of a cluster or uses DHCP for IP Addressing, choose the correct options. Otherwise, you can skip this step.

Figure 14.13 SecurePlatform Gateway Type

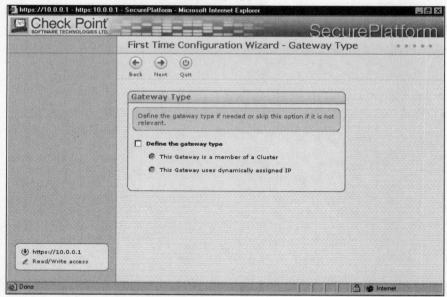

If you choose not to install a management station, you are asked to set the activation key for Secure Internal Communication (SIC), as shown in Figure 14.14. This is a one-time password used only for authenticating a module to the management station. After they have authenticated each other, a new digital certificate will be generated for the module; this certificate is used to secure all communications between the module and the management station.

Figure 14.14 SecurePlatform Secure Internal Communications Setup

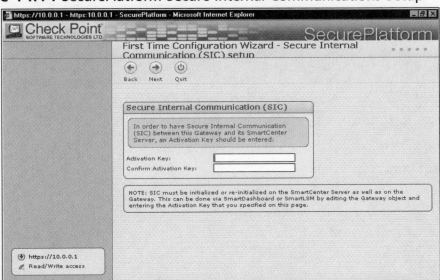

If you chose to install a management server on the Products page, you are prompted to decide if the machine will act as a Primary SmartCenter, a Secondary SmartCenter, or a Log Server (see Figure 14.15). If this is the first SmartCenter you are installing, choose Primary SmartCenter. Secondary SmartCenters or Log Servers require additional licensing. Choose the proper option, and then click **Next** to continue.

Figure 14.15 SecurePlatform SmartCenter Setup

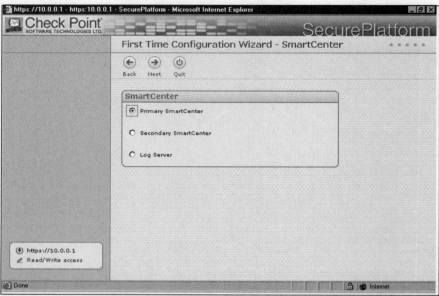

After setting the SmartCenter type, you are prompted to add GUI Clients (see Figure 14.16). GUI Clients are a set of IP Addresses or Networks that are permitted to connect to the SmartCenter Server using the Check Point SMART Clients. You must enter at least one GUI Client before continuing. Click **Add**, and then enter the host, IP address, or network you wish to allow to connect. Click **Apply**, and then click **Next** on the GUI Clients screen to continue.

Figure 14.16 SecurePlatform GUI Clients Setup

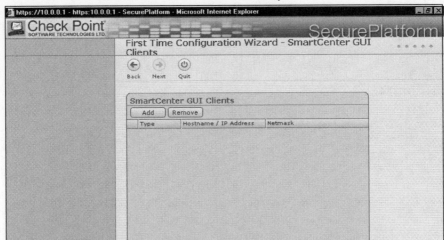

The next step is to define SmartCenter Administrators (see Figure 14.17). These accounts are used to log on the SmartCenter with the SMART Clients and are different from the SecurePlatform admin account. You must define an Administrator during this step, and you can only add one during the setup wizard. You can add more administrators later via the SmartDashboard GUI.

The administrator account defined during initial configuration has full administrative power over the Check Point installation. In previous versions, you could define multiple administrators through the cpconfig utility. In NGX, only one administrator can be defined. If you wish to add more accounts, you must use SmartDashboard.

Included in NGX is the new utility cp_admin_convert utility, which enables you to convert the administrative accounts defined in cpconfig to administrators in SmartDashboard.

Figure 14.17 SecurePlatform Administrators Setup

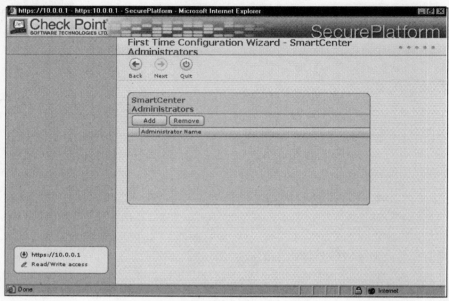

After completing all the wizard steps, you are presented with a summary screen. If you are satisfied with the configuration, click **Finish**. You are prompted to confirm the start of the configuration process. After the wizard finished the configuration, the wizard automatically reboots the machine. When the reboot is complete, click **OK**. You are taken to the Device Status Screen. At this point, installation and initial configuration is complete.

Command-Line Configuration

Although the preferred initial configuration method is the WUI wizard, you can access the command line the same way you installed the system—via a serial connection or via the console with a keyboard and mouse. If you choose to use a serial connection, you should set your terminal program to 9600 baud, 8 data bits, no parity, and 1 stop bit. You can change this setting in /etc/grub.conf later.

If the machine that you are installing on has more than one serial port, the SecurePlatform installer uses the first available serial port.

If you are using a keyboard and mouse, you can open multiple sessions to SecurePlatform by using the keyboard combinations of ALT-F1 through ALT-F4. This enables you to perform multiple tasks and switch back and forth between these tasks.

In addition, you can access the SecurePlatform system via *ssh* if you so choose. Once logged in, you must change your password to a strong password. Doing so will drop you into the Check Point restricted shell (CPShell). This is much like a router in that you have only a few commands to choose from. You can enter **?** to get a listing of available commands. From there, the easiest way to configure the system is to use the *sysconfig* utility.

> ◤ **W**ARNING
>
> For users who are familiar with the Linux operating system, it might seem easier or more efficient to configure the SecurePlatform manually via the file system. It is very important to utilize the tools supplied by Check Point to configure the operating system, because the Check Point tools may alter more configuration files than is apparent.

Sysconfig

The *sysconfig* utility is a text-based, menu-driven system used to configure the SecurePlatform operating system, as shown here:

```
Choose a configuration item ('e' to exit):
-------------------------------------------------------------
1) Host name                   7) DHCP Server Configuration
2) Domain name                 8) DHCP Relay Configuration
3) Domain name servers         9) Export Setup
4) Time and Date              10) Products Installation
5) Network Connections        11) Products Configuration
6) Routing
-------------------------------------------------------------
(Note: configuration changes are automatically saved)
Your choice:
```

Set the Hostname

The first step in configuring SecurePlatform is to configure the Host name. We will configure the hostname by selecting **1, Host name**. The next thing we will do is choose a hostname and tie the hostname to the appropriate address.

```
Choose an action ('e' to exit):
-----------------------------------------------------------------
1) Set host name
2) Show host name
-----------------------------------------------------------------
(Note: configuration changes are automatically saved)
Your choice: 1
```

If this is a firewall object, you should assign the hostname to the external address. If this is set as an internal (non-external) address of the firewall or an address other than the one in the General Properties page of the object in the SmartDashboard GUI, it can cause issues with establishing a VPN connection.

```
Enter host name: splatngx
Enter IP of the interface to be associated with
this host name (leave empty for automatic assignment): 10.0.0.1

The host name is set.


Press Enter to continue...
```

This returns you to the menu shown in the preceding section. Select **e** to go to the main menu and continue to the next section.

Set the Domain Name

Next, you will set the default domain name the system will use. In this case, you will use example.com. First choose to set the domain name and then enter your chosen domain:

```
Choose an action ('e' to exit):
-----------------------------------------------------------------
1) Set domain name
2) Show domain name
-----------------------------------------------------------------
(Note: configuration changes are automatically saved)
Your choice: 1
Enter domain name: example.com

The domain name is set.


Press Enter to continue...
```

Set the DNS Servers

Many functions of the firewall may require a DNS lookup of an IP address or name. You should define a domain name server (or better yet, multiple DNS servers) to ensure proper resolution. You can choose the **Add** option multiple times to add multiple servers. Again, select **e** to return to the main menu when you are finished adding DNS Servers:

```
Choose a DNS configuration item ('e' to exit):
-----------------------------------------------------------------
1) Add new domain name server         3) Show configured domain name
servers
2) Remove domain name server
-----------------------------------------------------------------
(Note: configuration changes are automatically saved)
Your choice: 1
Enter IP address of the domain name server to add: 10.0.0.254
```

Set the Time and Date

As described previously, in the Web User Interface section, setting the correct date and time is essential because of the extensive use of digital certificates used to secure communications between Check Point devices. First, you need to set the time zone, as shown here:

```
Choose a time and date configuration item ('e' to exit):
-----------------------------------------------------------------
1) Set time zone           3) Set local time
2) Set date                4) Show date and time settings
-----------------------------------------------------------------
(Note: configuration changes are automatically saved)
Your choice: 1

Identify a location so that time zone rules can be set correctly.
Select a continent or ocean.
 1) Africa
 2) Americas
 3) Antarctica
 4) Arctic Ocean
 5) Asia
 6) Atlantic Ocean
```

7) Australia

8) Europe

9) Indian Ocean

10) Pacific Ocean

11) none - I want to specify the time zone using GMT<+|->N format.

12) cancel - I want to quit without changing the time zone.

#? 2

Select a country.

1) Anguilla	18) Ecuador	35) Paraguay
2) Antigua & Barbuda	19) El Salvador	36) Peru
3) Argentina	20) French Guiana	37) Puerto Rico
4) Aruba	21) Greenland	38) St Kitts & Nevis
5) Bahamas	22) Grenada	39) St Lucia
6) Barbados	23) Guadeloupe	40) St Pierre & Miquelon
7) Belize	24) Guatemala	41) St Vincent
8) Bolivia	25) Guyana	42) Suriname
9) Brazil	26) Haiti	43) Trinidad & Tobago
10) Canada	27) Honduras	44) Turks & Caicos Is
11) Cayman Islands	28) Jamaica	45) United States
12) Chile	29) Martinique	46) Uruguay
13) Colombia	30) Mexico	47) Venezuela
14) Costa Rica	31) Montserrat	48) Virgin Islands (UK)
15) Cuba	32) Netherlands Antilles	49) Virgin Islands (US)
16) Dominica	33) Nicaragua	50) cancel
17) Dominican Republic	34) Panama	

#? 45

Select one of the following time zone regions.

1) Eastern Time

2) Eastern Time - Michigan - most locations

3) Eastern Time - Kentucky - Louisville area

4) Eastern Time - Kentucky - Wayne County

5) Eastern Standard Time - Indiana - most locations

6) Eastern Standard Time - Indiana - Crawford County

7) Eastern Standard Time - Indiana - Starke County

8) Eastern Standard Time - Indiana - Switzerland County

9) Central Time

10) Central Time - Michigan - Wisconsin border

11) Central Time - North Dakota - Oliver County

12) Mountain Time

```
13) Mountain Time - south Idaho & east Oregon
14) Mountain Time - Navajo
15) Mountain Standard Time - Arizona
16) Pacific Time
17) Alaska Time
18) Alaska Time - Alaska panhandle
19) Alaska Time - Alaska panhandle neck
20) Alaska Time - west Alaska
21) Aleutian Islands
22) Hawaii
23) cancel
#? 1


The following information has been given:

        United States
        Eastern Time


Therefore TZ='America/New_York' will be used.
Is the above information OK?
1) Yes
2) No
3) Cancel
#? 1
Updating time zone succeeded.

Time zone is set.
```

Next, you need to select **2** to set the date. Make sure to use numeric representations and the correct format when setting the date:

```
Enter date in format MM-DD-YYYY: 01-01-2005
Date is set.
```

And finally, select **3** to set the time (24-hour format), and then select **e** to return to the main menu.

```
Enter time in format HH:MM: 12:00
Time is set.
```

Configuring Interfaces

The next thing to do is configure all the interfaces to the correct addresses. For simplicity, it is easiest to get all the operating-system-level parameters configured and checked before working with the firewall software, like so:

```
Choose a network connections configuration item ('e' to exit):
-----------------------------------------------------------------
1) Add new connection          4) Select management connection
2) Configure connection        5) Show connection configuration
3) Remove connection
-----------------------------------------------------------------
(Note: configuration changes are automatically saved)
Your choice: 2
```

Next, you are presented with a list of interfaces that are known on the system. If you do not see the correct number of interfaces, you should make sure all your interfaces are supported and defined in /etc/modules.conf. Note that a card with multiple interfaces only shows up once for the first interface in /etc/modules.conf. (We explain how to get access to the file system in the Expert Mode section.) Here is a sample list of interfaces:

```
Choose a connection to configure ('e' to exit):
-----------------------------------------------------------------
1) eth0
2) eth1
-----------------------------------------------------------------
(Note: configuration changes are automatically saved)
Your choice:
```

You are now presented with options to set the IP as well as set up the system for having a dynamic (DHCP assigned) IP address.

```
Choose eth0 item to configure ('e' to exit):
-----------------------------------------------------------------
1) Change IP settings          3) Remove IP from interface
2) Change MTU settings         4) Change from static to dynamic IP
-----------------------------------------------------------------
(Note: configuration changes are automatically saved)
Your choice:
```

If you are configuring an interface for having a dynamic IP address, selecting option 4 seems to do nothing, but look carefully—it will change the word *dynamic* to *static* when it is configured to be DHCP assigned. In addition, when you're in the "Choose a network configuration item" menu, selecting **Show Interfaces** will show the interface as "not configured," even though it is configured to receive a DHCP-assigned IP address. This concept is shown here:

```
eth1 has a dynamic IP configuration
```

Configuring Routing

After we have configured all our interfaces, we need to configure the routing. This is option 2 from the first menu:

```
Choose a routing configuration item ('e' to exit):
--------------------------------------------------------------
1) Add new network route      4) Delete route
2) Add new host route         5) Show routing configuration
3) Add default gateway
--------------------------------------------------------------
(Note: configuration changes are automatically saved)
Your choice:
```

At a minimum, you should add a default route for the device. To add a network or host route, you need to know the IP address (or network and netmask in the case of a network route) as well as the gateway IP address and the interface from which you will be routing the traffic. Selecting option 5 shows the result of a *netstat –rn* from the command line. Configurations here also make changes to the /etc/sysconfig/cpnetstart file. Select option **e** to continue to the main menu.

Completing the Installation

The final thing that is required is to run option 10, Products Configuration, which is essentially *cpconfig*. This will run you through a list of questions related to the products you have selected to install and the part they play in your security infrastructure.

CPShell

When you log on SecurePlatform through the command-line interface via *ssh* or a serial connection, you will be presented with an application-specific configuration interface. This interface is much narrower in scope than a standard UNIX shell. The list of available commands is shown here:

```
? for list of commands
sysconfig for system and products configuration
```

```
[cpmodule]# ?
Commands are:
?                    - Print list of available commands
LSMcli               - SmartLSM command line
LSMenabler           - Enable SmartLSM
SDSUtil              - Software Distribution Server utility
about                - Print about info
addarp               - Add permanent ARP table entries
adduser              - Add new user
arp                  - Display/manipulate the arp table
audit                - Display/edit commands entered in shell
backup               - Backup configuration
checkuserlock        - Check if user is locked
cp_conf              - Check Point system configuration utility
cpadmin              - Control system administration portal
cpca                 - Run Check Point Internal CA
cpca_client          - Manage/configure Check Point Internal CA
cpca_create          - Create new Check Point Internal CA database
cpca_dbutil          - Print/convert Check Point Internal CA database
cpconfig             - Check Point software configuration utility
cphaprob             - Defines critical process of High Availability
cphastart            - Enables the High Availability feature on the machine
cphastop             - Disables the High Availability feature on the machine
cpinfo               - Show Check Point diagnostics information
cplic                - Add/Remove Check Point licenses
cpshared_ver         - Show SVN Foundation version
cpstart              - Start Check Point products installed
cpstat               - Show Check Point statistics info
cpstop               - Stop Check Point products installed
date                 - Set/show date
delarp               - Remove permanent ARP table entries
deluser              - Remove existing user
diag                 - Send system diagnostics information
dns                  - Add/remove/show domain name resolving servers
domainname           - Set/show domain name
eth_set              - Control ethernet interface speed/duplex settings
etmstart             - Starts FloodGate-1
etmstop              - Stops FloodGate-1
```

```
exit              - Switch to standard mode/Logout
expert            - Switch to expert mode
fgate             - FloodGate-1 commands
fips             - Turns on/off FIPS mode
fw                - VPN-1/FireWall-1 commands
fwm               - FW-1/VPN-1 management utility
help              - Print list of available commands
hostname          - Set/show host name
hosts             - Add/remove/show local hosts/IP mappings
idle              - Set/show auto logout time in minutes
ifconfig         - Configure/store network interfaces
lockout           - Configure lockout parameters
log               - Log rotation control
netstat           - Show network statistics
ntp               - Configure ntp and start synchronization client
ntpstart          - Start NTP clock synchronization client
ntpstat           - Show NTP clock synchronization client state
ntpstop           - Stop NTP clock synchronization client
passwd            - Change password
patch             - Install/Upgrade utility
ping              - Ping a host
pro               - Enable/Disable SecurePlatform Pro
reboot            - Reboot gateway
restore           - Restore configuration
revert            - Revert to saved Snapshot Image
rmdstart          - Start SmartView Reporter
rmdstop           - Stop SmartView Reporter
route             - Configure/store routing tables
rtm               - SmartView Monitor commands
rtmstart          - Start SmartView Monitor
rtmstop           - Stop SmartView Monitor
rtmtopsvc         - SmartView Monitor of Top Services
scroll            - Allow scrolling the output of various commands
showusers         - List SecurePlatform administrators
shutdown          - Shut down gateway
snapshot          - Create Snapshot Image
snmp              - Configure SNMP daemon
sysconfig        - Configure your SecurePlatform Gateway
syslog_servers    - Add/remove/show external syslog servers
```

```
time                  - Set/show time
timezone              - Set/show the time zone
top                   - Show the most active system processes
traceroute            - Trace the route to a host
unlockuser            - Unlock user
ups                   - Configure Smart UPS monitoring
vconfig             - Configure Virtual LANs
ver                   - Print SecurePlatform version
vpn                   - Control VPN
webui                 - Configure web UI
```

Expert Mode

Expert Mode is used for advanced configuration of the SecurePlatform device and access to the SecurePlatform file system. To access Expert Mode, type **expert** on the cpshell command line. SecurePlatform then prompts you for the Expert Mode password. The first time you enter Expert Mode, use the same password you set for the admin account during initial setup. Then, the system requires you to change the Expert Mode password.

```
[cpmodule]# expert
Enter current password:

This is the first time you enter the expert mode.
Expert password must be changed.

Enter new expert password:
Enter new expert password (again):

You are in expert mode now.


[Expert@cpmodule]#
```

You know you are in Expert Mode by the change in the command prompt. When in Expert Mode, Expert@ will precede the hostname. Once logged into Expert Mode, you have full bash shell access to the file system with root-equivalent privileges.

Expert Mode is the only mode that enables you to transfer files to and from SecurePlatform. You can use File Transfer Protocol (FTP) or Secure Copy (SCP). If

you wish to use SCP, you must define users permitted to transfer files from
SecurePlatform by editing the /etc/scpusers file.

> ## WARNING
>
> Logging on SecurePlatform in Expert Mode is the equivalent of root
> access on a UNIX or Linux host. You can cause irreparable damage to the
> system. Only use Expert Mode when absolutely necessary, and only give
> authorized users access to the Expert Mode command shell.

Patch Add

Periodically, you might need to add or update packages. You can add packages from
either SmartUpdate or from the SecurePlatform command line. SmartUpdate is definitely the easiest way to upgrade, but if you have a management station running
SecurePlatform or do not have a SmartUpdate license (which is included with a
SmartCenter Pro license), you will be required to upgrade from the command line.

You should always read the release notes before upgrading. You can upgrade by
using a CD, a TFTP server, an SCP server, or files that you have copied over to the
SecurePlatform machine. The syntax for patch add is straightforward:

```
[Expert@cpmodule]# patch add
Usage: patch add tftp <ip> <patch_name>
       patch add scp <ip> <username> <remote_filename> [password]
       patch add cd [<patch_name>]
       patch add <full_patch_path>
       patch log
[Expert@cpmodule]#
```

For example, to install a patch from a CD:

```
[Expert@cpmodule]# patch add cd
Choose a patch to install:

1) SecurePlatform NGX R60 Upgrade Package (CPspupgrade_R60.tgz)
2) Exit

Your choice:
 1
```

```
Calculating the MD5 checksum of the package.
The MD5 checksum is: 6a0b5bc83987830d571f8a2e0549e9f5
Is that right (Y/N)? y
Extracting /mnt/cdrom/SecurePlatform/patch/CPspupgrade_R60.tgz package ..
Start Upgrading ..
```

Backup, Scheduled Backup, and Restore

Another common pair of utilities is backup and restore, for obvious reasons. Backup enables you to create a backup of the system configuration files and save them locally or send them to a TFTP or SCP server. All backups are stored in the /var/CPbackup/backups directory.

```
[Expert@cpmodule]# backup ?
usage:
backup   [-h] [-d] [-l]   [--purge DAYS] [--sched [on hh:mm <-m DayOfMonth> |
<-w DaysOfWeek>] | off] [--tftp <ServerIP> [-path <Path>] [<Filename>]]
                [--scp <ServerIP> <Username> <Password> [-path <Path>]
[<Filename>]]
                [--file [-path <Path>] [<Filename>]]


where:
        -d                              Show debug messages
        -l, --logs                      Back up log files
        -h, --help                      Show this help information
        -t, --tftp                      Transfer backup package to TFTP
server
        -s, --scp                       Transfer backup package to SCP
server
        -f, --file                      Specify local backup package filename
        -e, --sched                     Configure scheduled backup operation
        -p, --purge                     Purge local backup packages older
than DAYS
[Expert@cpmodule]#
```

For example, to back up your system and send it to a TFTP server, you would issue the following command:

```
[Expert@cpmodule]# backup --tftp 10.0.0.254
Are you sure you want to proceed? y
```

```
Creating backup package...
Done
Transferring the backup package...
Done
```

You can also schedule backup to run at regular intervals. For example, to schedule backups to run at midnight every Sunday, you would run the following command:

```
[Expert@cpmodule]# backup --sched on 00:00 -w sunday
```

To cancel a previously scheduled backup, you can execute the following command:

```
[Expert@cpmodule]# backup --sched off
```

Restore enables you to rebuild a system quickly after it is on the network. Like backup, you can restore a backup from a local file, a TFTP server, or an SCP server.

```
[Expert@cpmodule]# restore ?
usage:
restore         [-h] [-d]  [[--tftp <ServerIP> <Filename>] |
                [--scp <ServerIP> <Username> <Password> <Filename>] |
                [--file <Filename>]]


where:
        -d                              Show debug messages
        -h, --help                      Show this help information
        -t, --tftp                      Transfer backup package from TFTP
server
        -s, --scp                       Transfer backup package from SCP
server
        -f, --file                      Specify local backup package filename
[Expert@cpmodule]#
```

Using restore without any command-line switches presents you with a menu which will walk you through the restore process. For example, to restore from a local backup:

```
[Expert@cpmodule]# restore

Choose one of the following:
```

```
------------------------------------------------------------------
[L]      Restore local backup package
[T]      Restore backup package from TFTP server
[S]      Restore backup package from SCP server
[R]      Remove local backup package
[Q]      Quit
------------------------------------------------------------------
Your choice:  L


Choose backup package to restore:
------------------------------------------------------------------
[1]      backup_cpmodule_21_9_2005_09_47.tgz
[2]      backup_cpmodule_21_9_2005_09_44.tgz
[Q]      Quit
------------------------------------------------------------------
Your choice: 1


All information will be restored.
------------------------------------------------------------------


Choose one of the following:
------------------------------------------------------------------
[C]      Continue.
[M]      Modify which information to restore.
[Q]      Quit.
------------------------------------------------------------------
Your choice: C
```

Snapshot, Revert, and Snapshot Image Management

The snapshot utility enables you to create a full image of your SecurePlatform machine. After a snapshot is created, the Snapshot Image Management option is available at boot time.

To create a snapshot of your system, run the *snapshot* command:

```
[Expert@cpmodule]# snapshot


Choose one of the following:
------------------------------------------------------------------
[L]      Create new local Snapshot Image
```

```
[T]       Create new Snapshot Image on TFTP server
[S]       Create new Snapshot Image on SCP server
[R]       Remove local Snapshot Image
[Q]       Quit
-----------------------------------------------------------------
Your choice: T
Enter the TFTP server IP/host name:10.0.0.254
Enter new Snapshot Image filename or [Quit]: snapshot_21_9_2005_10_35
Are you sure you want to proceed? y

Creating the Snapshot Image. This can take up to 20 minutes...
Note that all Check Point products will be stopped
and re-started after the snapshot completes.
Done
Transferring the Snapshot Image...
Done
[Expert@cpmodule]#
```

The *revert* utility enables you to replace the current system state to a snapshot you created earlier. To revert to a snapshot (in this example, we will retrieve the snapshot from a local snapshot), run the *revert* command:

```
[Expert@cpmodule]# revert

Choose one of the following:
-----------------------------------------------------------------
[L]       Revert to local Snapshot Image
[T]       Revert to Snapshot Image from TFTP server
[S]       Revert to Snapshot Image from SCP server
[R]       Remove local Snapshot Image
[Q]       Quit
-----------------------------------------------------------------
Your choice: l

Revert to:
-----------------------------------------------------------------
[1]       snapshot_21_9_2005_10_35.tgz
[Q]       Quit
-----------------------------------------------------------------
```

```
Your choice: 1
```

```
Do you want to save Snapshot Image before revert? n
Reverting to a saved Snapshot Image. This can take up to 25 minutes...
```

After the *revert* command is complete, the system is rebooted.

You can reboot the SecurePlatform machine and choose the *Snapshot Image Management* option from the boot screen. You will be prompted for the expert password, and you can then revert to a snapshot saved on a TFTP or SCP server.

Dynamic Routing

One of the new features in the NGX version of SecurePlatform is the addition of SecurePlatform Pro. Before NGX, support for dynamic routing protocols and multicast protocols was unavailable and a different platform was required to utilize these features. In order to take advantage of SecurePlatform Pro, you must purchase an additional license.

The following Unicast protocols are supported under SecurePlatform Pro: RIP-1, RIP-2, OSPF, and BGP. The following Multicast protocols are supported under SecurePlatform Pro: PIM-DM, PIM-SM, and IGMP.

This section covers the configuration of dynamic routing and multicast protocols within the SecurePlatform Pro platform. Configuration can be accomplished only through the command-line tool *sysconfig*.

Accessing the Router

To configure dynamic routing on SecurePlatform, you must be logged on the machine with administrative privileges. After you are logged on, you can access the router interface by typing the command **router** from either the cpshell or expert command lines.

After you enter the router command line, you can type **?** to see what commands are available to you.

```
[cpmodule]# router
localhost>
  enable          Enter privileged mode
  help            Learn about context-sensitive help
  history         Show command history
  logout          Close the session
  no              Turn off a command
```

```
quit                Close the session
router-context      connect to GateD
show                Show internal values
terminal            Set terminal state
vrf-connect         connect to GateD by VRF
localhost>
```

The first step in configuring the router is to enter the privileged mode. This can be accomplished by entering **enable** on the command line. Notice that the command prompt changes to the privileged mode prompt.

```
localhost>enable
localhost#
```

TIP

Most commands used in the router command shell can be shortened as long as they can be distinguished from other commands. For example, "enable" can be shortened to "en" and "configure terminal" can be shortened to "conf t."

Again, you can use **?** to see what options are available.

```
localhost#
    clear           clear state
    configure       configure router state
    disable         Leave privileged mode
    help            Learn about context-sensitive help
    history         Show command history
    no              Turn off a command
    quit            Close the session
    router-context  connect to GateD
    show            Show internal values
    terminal        Set terminal state
    vrf-connect     connect to GateD by VRF
    write           Write gated configuration
localhost#
```

Next you must enter the configure router state by entering "configure terminal" at the privileged prompt.

```
localhost#configure terminal
localhost(config)#
  access-list      Configure an access list
  dampen-flap      Route flap damping
  end              Exit configuration mode
  exit             Exit configuration mode
  help             Learn about context-sensitive help
  interface        Enter interface mode
  ip               ip commands
  ipip-tunnel      Configure IP-IP encapsulation tunnel
  kernel           Configure Kernel Statement
  log              Configure CLI logging
  martian          Configure Martians
  no               Turn off a command
  route-map        Configure a route-map
  router           Enter router mode
  scan-interval    Configure interface scan interval
  set              Set various values
  show             Show information
  smux             Configure SMUX
  terminal         Set terminal state
  trace            Configure tracing
```

You can perform most of the advanced routing functions by using the **ip** command.

```
localhost(config)#ip
  access-list        Configure an access list
  as-path            ASPATH confgiuration
  community-list     Configure a BGP community list
  community-set      Configure a BGP community set
  dvmrp              Configure DVMRP
  igmp               Configure IGMP
  pim                Configure PIM
  prefix-list        Configure a prefix list
  prefix-tree        Configure a prefix tree
  route               Static route configuration
  router-discovery   Configure Router Discovery server
```

```
router-id          Configure a router-id
routingtable-id    Configure routing table ID
```

You can exit the configure router state by entering **exit.** After you configure the router, and before you exit the privileged mode, make sure you save the configuration by entering the command **write memory**. Otherwise, your configuration will be lost on the next reboot of the machine. The configuration is written to the file /etc/gated.ami.

```
localhost(config)#exit
localhost#write memory
IU0 999 Configuration written to '/etc/gated.ami'
localhost#
```

To exit the router command, type **quit**. This brings you back to the SecurePlatform shell.

For a detailed description of each protocol and examples on how to configure them, see the document entitled "*SecurePlatform Pro & Advanced Routing Command Line Interface,*" available from the Check Point Web site.

Summary

SecurePlatform is a very simple, efficient, fast, and inexpensive platform on which to run Check Point's products. This product enables an administrator to quickly set up a fully supported platform by one vendor, Check Point. SecurePlatform removes the focus and the difficult decisions (as well as a great deal of the cost) from the hardware and puts the focus on the important piece, the software.

You can configure the system two ways: via the WUI or via the command line. The WUI enables you to configure many things, but the most complete way to configure the system is via the command line. A difference between SecurePlatform and a normal Linux distribution is that when you log on the command-line interface, you receive an application-specific configuration and management interface. The CPShell environment enables an administrator to access the commands essential to firewall administration, but it further limits access to the underlying operating system with another separate password. The advanced debugging and troubleshooting mode is referred to as Expert mode.

This chapter also reviewed the new SecurePlatform Pro product that adds support for dynamic routing protocols. Although this version of SecurePlatform means an additional license, it does add functionality that was previously unavailable in SecurePlatform.

Solutions Fast Track

Installation

☑ This installation of SecurePlatform is designed to be a very easy process.

☑ SecurePlatform is installed via a bootable CD-ROM.

☑ The installation gives you the option to install either SecurePlatform or SecurePlatform Pro, which adds functionality.

Web User Interface

☑ In version NGX, the WUI has been totally redesigned.

☑ To access the WUI, you can use the Internet Explorer or Netscape browsers.

☑ When connecting to the WUI for the first time, you are presented with the initial configuration wizard that makes configuring the Operating System a simple process.

Command-Line Configuration

☑ You can access the command-line configuration via ssh or serial connection.

☑ Use the utility sysconfig to configure the Operating System.

☑ The first time sysconfig is run, you will be taken through the initial configuration wizard.

CPShell

☑ CPShell is a protected shell with limited access to the underlying Operating System.

☑ You should use CPShell to perform most of the system configuration.

Expert Mode

☑ Expert Mode enables full access to the Operating System.

☑ Use Expert Mode for advanced configuration.

☑ Use Expert Mode only when necessary.

☑ You can use Expert Mode to perform system maintenance tasks such as backup and restore and to create system snapshots.

Dynamic Routing

☑ SecurePlatform Pro adds support for dynamic routing protocols.

☑ It supports Unicast protocols RIP-1, RIP-2, OSPF, and BGP.

☑ It supports Multicast protocols PIM-DM, PIM-SM, and IGMP.

Frequently Asked Questions

The following Frequently Asked Questions, answered by the authors of this book, are designed to both measure your understanding of the concepts presented in this chapter and to assist you with real-life implementation of these concepts. To have your questions about this chapter answered by the author, browse to **www.syngress.com/solutions** and click on the **"Ask the Author"** form.

Q: Can I use any Intel-based hardware to run SecurePlatform?

A: No. There are only a limited number of hardware platforms supported by Check Point. Because of the hardening of the operating system, Check Point includes drivers for only supported platforms. However, SecurePlatform does include drivers for today's most common devices. You can find a list of supported hardware from Check Point's Web site at: www.checkpoint.com/products/supported_platforms/secureplatform.html.

Q: SecurePlatform doesn't have support for <*insert package name here*>. Can I just add the RPM?

A: Yes. However, Check Point does not support anything that does not come on SecurePlatform. If you install other packages, you might be invalidating the support for the system if it happens to conflict with other packages. Also, some of the libraries needed to run applications may not be available on SecurePlatform.

Q: What Check Point applications does SecurePlatform support?

A: SecurePlatform supports all the main Check Point applications, such as VPN-1 Pro, SmartCenter, and Eventia Reporter. You cannot, however, run the SMART Clients on SecurePlatform.

Q: I installed SecurePlatform, but it doesn't see one or more of my NICs. Can I just add the driver?

A: Yes, you can add the driver, but since it is not officially part of SecurePlatform, it's not necessarily supported by Check Point. In addition, upgrades to the operating system might cause the NIC driver to stop working or create other issues. The best recommendation is to only use supported NICs from common manufacturers. Consult Check Point's Web site, your reseller, or your local Check Point office for information on the currently supported NICs.

Chapter 15

Monitoring Tools

Solutions in this chapter:

- **Installation**
- **Reports**
- **Definitions**
- **Creating Reports**
- **Report Management**
- **Navigating through SmartView Monitor**
- **Gateway Status**
- **Traffic**
- **System Counters**
- **Tunnels and Remote Users**

- ☑ **Summary**
- ☑ **Solutions Fast Track**
- ☑ **Frequently Asked Questions**

Introduction

Check Point has developed a great tool that supplies you with the power to meta-morphose all your raw log data into a more readable format. With options that let you create self-explanatory graphs, Eventia Reporter is great for presentations to senior management. Also, these formats provide you with teaching material in case you need to train other employees or you just want to explain a particular incident to them. In this chapter, we will see what types of native reports are with Eventia Reporter and how you may customize this tool to better accommodate your needs.

In addition, Check Point has enhanced its SmartView Monitor. This chapter demonstrates how to set up SmartView Monitor in a way that will allow you to view all your security components that your SmartCenter manages. It enables the administrator to quickly retrieve the status of each device the SmartCenter Server manages. You will be able to appreciate the many different components for each device or user this tool makes available to you. For instance, SmartView Monitor tracks system information such as disk, memory, and CPU usage for your conve-nience. Moreover, this console displays information regarding the policy you last installed and how many VPN tunnels are active with any associated users. If you recall the SmartView Status console, know that Check Point has removed this and has incorporated it into SmartView Monitor.

Installation

When you initially install your SmartCenter Server, you have the option of installing Eventia Reporter with it. In this manner, you can do all your logging and report generation on one single server. This brings into focus server hardware requirements. If you are planning to write the logs to the SmartCenter Server and also generate reports from these logs, you have to consider performance ramifications.

For starters, your SmartCenter Server should meet the Check Point prescribed minimum server specifications. Other things to consider are most obviously disk space, disk speed, and memory. Since both the SmartCenter logging utility and the Eventia Reporter programs read and write to the disk (a lot), you probably want to max out the speed of your hard drives. Also, you can tweak several memory parame-ters so that the database optimizes memory use. Lastly, you should allocate plenty of disk space for the database. If you don't, you run the risk of running out of room and producing faulty reports, not to mention causing more work for yourself on the back end.

At this point, it is easy to introduce to you the preferred method of installation, the distributed configuration. In this sense, you have your SmartCenter Server that collects log files from your enforcement points. The Eventia Reporter resides on a completely separate server that communicates with your SmartCenter Server via Secure Internal Communications (SIC). In addition, you must install the Eventia Reporter Add-On to the SmartCenter Server. It is important to note that the Add-On is not optional. Proper report generation will not take place unless you have properly installed the correct configuration. In this configuration, you may want to consider which network adapters will provide you superior service as greater transfer rates improve performance within a distributed configuration. This is in addition to the other considerations. Having optimal hardware for any database mining application is critical to timely performance.

Eventia Reporter is compatible with all the standard platforms except Nokia IPSO. However, you can install the Add-On on your Nokia IPSO server running SmartCenter. It goes without saying then, that if your SmartCenter Server is running on Nokia IPSO, you have no choice but to install the distributed configuration. Again, this is not an unfavorable decision. Check Point recommends you choose a distributed installation.

In any case, installing the proper software components to run Eventia Reporter is just as easy as installing SmartCenter or an enforcement point. Of course, the chain of events differs for standalone or distributed installation and for each platform, but the fact remains that you need not have a Harvard degree to install these Check Point products. During the installation process, the GUI will ask you to identify if this is a distributed or standalone installation. Other than this option, the other screens present you with standard installation parameters like license agreement, directory location, and such. In all, the installation process is painless in the least as it loads your gateway with your chosen options.

Gateway

Once you have successfully installed your chosen products onto your server, you will need to define the host within your SmartCenter Server (distributed configuration) and configure the proper options for that host. If you chose distributed installation, you must establish SIC just as with any other Check Point device. In addition, you must define which options are installed on the server by selecting them in the host or gateway properties dialog. Once you have completed the configuration of your Eventia Reporter, simply install the database and your server will begin working as designed.

Now that you have your Eventia Reporter working, you can open the window either directly or indirectly. You can choose to select the **Eventia Reporter** icon from your desktop or applications menu, or choose **Window | Eventia Reporter** from within any of your other Check Point console applications (SmartDashboard, SmartView Tracker, and so on.). If you choose to go directly to Eventia Reporter, then you must supply credentials just as you would logging into SmartDashboard for the first time. As well, you can navigate to any other console via the **Windows** drop-down menu within the Eventia Reporter application.

Licensing

Since Eventia Reporter is a separate product, Check Point requires distinctive licenses for each gateway. Unlike most other licenses within NGX, you must manage licenses through your Eventia Reporter console. You must have a single license per firewall server. However, if you purchase, or already own, an enterprise license, you may extend to an unlimited number of gateways for your single Eventia Reporter Server. If you do not have an enterprise license and you do not have a license for each gateway, you must identify which licenses belong to which firewall server for the reports you wish to develop. In most cases, if you have multiple gateways it may be more effective if you have an enterprise license since it provides increased flexibility not only with reporting, but with all the Check Point products. Also know that if you employ up to five VPN-1 Edge devices, a single license will suffice. However, if your quantity of VPN-1 Edge exceeds this value, then each of the subsequent devices must have a single accompanying license.

To view and manage your licenses, open Eventia Reporter and click **Tools | License Registration….** When this window opens, you will see a similar image as in Figure 15.1.

Figure 15.1 License Registration Window

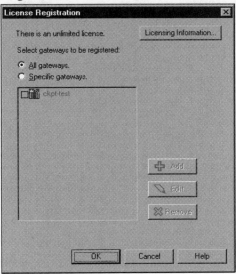

As noted, you see that there is no requirement to identify servers with an unlimited license. If the license associated with this gateway were not unlimited, you would have to register the single (or multiple) license to a particular firewall in the list. Clicking on the **License Information…** button confirms what you have learned here about per-server licensing and VPN-1 Edge product licensing.

Reports

As every professional knows by now, there are numerous reasons why reports are necessary. A few of these reasons may be to educate management, reveal traffic patterns, or to investigate an incident. In any case, Eventia Reporter allows you to mine through a significant amount of data and produce a set of texts, tables, graphs, or charts in order to interpret the results. To do this, Eventia retrieves your logs from your SmartCenter Server (or log server if you have a distributed installation), consolidates them if possible, and stores them into a database table. From this point, you are able to run either existing report templates or create your own custom report to decipher information from the data in the tables.

In this section, you will learn how Eventia prepares data for your reporting needs. In addition, you will get a look at the standard view when you launch Eventia Reporter. Specifically, you'll see the results tab and how you can recall old reports in order to possibly compare them with newer data. Later, you will learn about the intricacies of this interface concentrating on creating and scheduling reports.

Gathering Reporting Data

In the section about installation, you learned that you can have a standalone installation or a distributed installation. In either case, the data flow remains the same with the notable exception of the network presence for the distributed configuration. In this brief description, consider the case where you have deployed a fully distributed configuration throughout your environment. You have a separate enforcement point, SmartCenter Server, and Eventia Reporter Server.

Now that traffic is flowing and all the logging is configured correctly (to go to your SmartCenter Server), you want to run reports against the connection log data. After you install Eventia Reporter and correctly configure and connect (SIC) the server to your SmartCenter Server, the data collection/consolidation process begins.

Start from the instance the log entry makes its way into the firewall log. Then the firewall module sends it on to the SmartCenter Server. Now the Eventia Reporter server pulls it from the SmartCenter Server and sends it through its *Log Consolidator Engine*. This is where the server evaluates the entry against the consolidation policy (more on this later). Once the engine determines how to store the record, it writes it into a table in the *Eventia Reporter Database*. The default table (created during installation) for the database is the *CONNECTIONS* table. All records make their way from the firewall module into this table. At this point you may run reports against the data in the table.

Segregating Report Data

As you will soon learn, there are several ways to modify parameters and generate reports. One of the options you have as an administrator is to store your log data in different tables. It may be the case that you may isolate particular traffic to one table while stuffing all your other traffic into another table. One reason for doing this is to quickly filter through a subset of data. Consider that each time you load records into the database the tables grow. Eventually, there are many records in a single table. Traditionally, the more data you have to search through, the longer the time the report job takes to complete.

So, as you become more advanced, you can create additional consolidator jobs that store the data into different tables. Then, all you need to do is define reports that utilize the new table (not the default CONNECTIONS table) as the source. Minimizing the full scale of search records reduces the execution time and returns results to you in a much more timely manner. There are other ways to optimize your reports for speed, but this way is not entirely difficult and produces the desired results faster than the normal way.

WARNING

Since connection records are stored as they are written, you may run into an issue with DHCP and name resolution. Because of DNS caching, your firewall/SmartCenter may log an entry from one host when it actually came from another host that inherited the same address from the DHCP server. Since the time-to-live (TTL) may not expire at the same time the DHCP lease does, the firewall may not query the address (again) and may record the host incorrectly.

Report Results

When you open the Eventia Reporter for the first time, you see that you have a left and right pane similar to other Check Point console windows. One of the options in the left-hand pane is **Results**. Click this area and you (initially) arrive at an empty right-hand pane. However, once you begin generating reports (with or without data), you will see the results in the right-hand pane, as shown in Figure 15.2.

Figure 15.2 Eventia Reporter Results Window

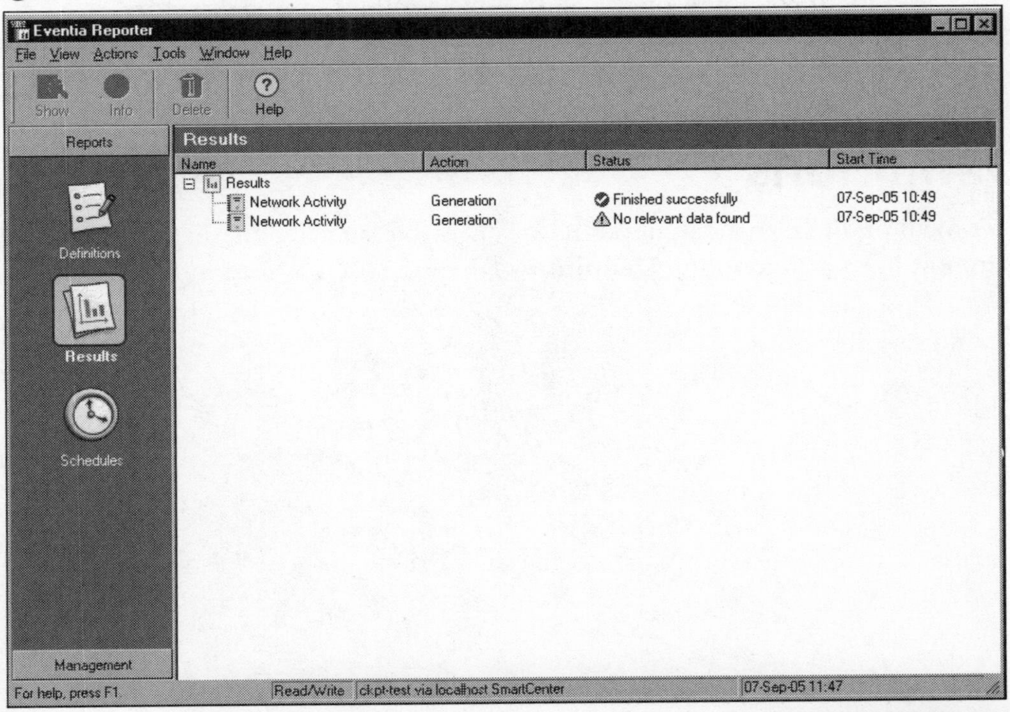

In the right–hand pane of Figure 15.2, you see that the administrator has generated two reports. The first report's status is **Finished successfully**. However, you see that the second report's status reveals that there was **No relevant data found**. In any case, when you execute a report, the results are logged within this window. In addition, you are able to recall the results of these reports and view the data in the specified format (in which you generated the report). This provides a backup of the data in case you have misplaced or removed the original report. To find the location where Eventia stored these reports, you can highlight one of them and click **View | More Information**. You will see in the new window the file location where Eventia stored this particular report. For that matter, all reports are stored in the same location unless otherwise specified. You will see as you generate a report that Eventia Reporter will reveal to you where it will store the report prior to you executing it.

NOTE

All reports are saved in the $RTDIR/Results directory (regardless of the platform) unless you manually change this location. When you generate a specific report definition (Network Activity, Blocked Connections), the results create a directory for that definition (if it doesn't already exist). The process then (for HTML results) creates a folder for each report based on a date/time format and places all the relevant files in this directory.

Definitions

Let's focus on the report definitions now. When you launched the Eventia Reporter, you most likely started in the **Definitions** tab of the GUI as seen in Figure 15.3.

Figure 15.3 Eventia Reporter Definitions

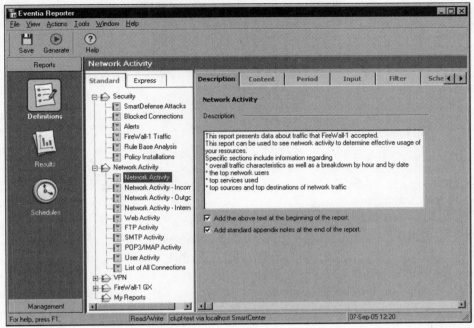

In this figure, you can see that the **Security** and **Network Activity** trees are expanded to reveal their predefined reports. There are two tabs in the left-hand side of the **Network Activity** pane: the **Standard** tab and the **Express** tab (more on this later). The right-hand pane is where you define the parameters for your report. There are several tabs across the top of the pane to switch the context of the parameters. For instance, the **Input** tab lets you define from which firewalls to report, how to report on multiple gateways (individually or summary), and from which table to mine the data for the report. Each tab has its own set of parameters that help you to create a meaningful report.

All the predefined reports (leaves in each tree) represent a set of filters that Check Point provides to you as a general report definition. Similar to the queries in SmartView Tracker, you cannot modify one of these predefined report definitions. Any changes you make and save are written to a new definition under the **My Reports** tree. Also, you are unable to remove any of these definitions. Just as you learned to leverage the queries in the SmartView Tracker, you should also learn to utilize these definitions as a foundation for more specific reports. The only limitation you could possibly run into is storage space as each report writes its own definition file. Just make sure that you use descriptive names for each of your custom reports since you won't want to hunt and peck through them to find the right one.

Standard versus Express

When you look at the two tabs, you see **Standard** and **Express**. What's the difference? Well, basically, it is the data source. Standard reports query the Eventia Reporter Database. This is where the consolidator process stores the records after evaluating your log files. So when you run one of the Standard reports you are essentially mining through the database for your desired results.

On the other hand, Express reports are not mining through the database for results. These reports actually query against data that SmartView Monitor agents collect. As you will learn later, the SmartView Monitor retains system counters and history files for your gateways. When you run an Express report, the system actually executes the query against this set of data as opposed to the Eventia Reporter Database table. Although these reports may not provide a comprehensive outlook, they do provide speedy results.

In both instances, you are able to modify definitions to create a custom set of parameters. However, only in the **Standard** report parameter tabs do you find a **Filter** tab. Together, these two categories encompass a broad range of reports. If you are looking for quick results, then you should go the way of the Express reports. But if you are looking for comprehensive reports, you may be better off mining through the database.

Custom Reports

Just as you were able to create custom reports in SmartView Tracker, you can do likewise with custom reports. Simply utilize one of the existing definitions (predefined or custom), change the parameters, then save the current settings as a new report. Again, all the custom reports you create are stored under the **My Reports** tree in either tab, **Standard** or **Express**. Although the predefined report definitions do provide useful information, they do not provide exactly what you may want from time to time.

For instance, if you are trying to determine whether one of your servers is being used to surf the Internet (against the local policy), then you don't necessarily want to see the whole network activity report. What you want to be able to do is define a set of parameters that filter out everything except this server's traffic. In this sense you will get a better idea of exactly what's going on from that source. When you begin defining custom reports, you will find that the predefined ones don't offer you as much. Check Point understands this, hence, the reason for such great scalability with regard to report definitions.

Creating Reports

The need for reports is obvious. What's even more imperative is that you understand how to generate data that is both relevant and informative. In order to do this, you must have foreknowledge of several items. First and foremost, what are you looking for? Are you seeking a general glimpse of the traffic, or are you searching for specific connections? Second, which data sources are available to you, and which is the best choice for this particular report? Lastly, though not all encompassing, what kind of people constitute the audience for this report? If you know these things, then you are well on your way to creating a meaningful report. Now, let's look at how you can take this knowledge and apply it Eventia Reporter so that you develop your desired result.

Generating a Report

Let's cover what we know. One, you want to see all connections from source address 192.168.69.200. Two, you want to search through the entire database (for today's connections). And finally, this report is for you, so it doesn't have to be pretty, just informative. Now, how do we generate this report? First, bring up the Eventia Reporter window. Then expand the **Network Activity** tree and select the **Network Activity** leaf. Choose the **Period** tab and change the **Relative Time Frame:** option to **Today**. Since we want to search the whole database (CONNECTIONS table) and this is the default setting, move on to the **Filter** tab. Here, place a check in the box next to **Source**. Now click the **Add...** button and enter the IP address 192.168.69.200 in the **IP Address:** field. Then click **Add** and then **Close**. You should now see that the desired source address is now located in the **Match Values:** window. Accept the defaults for the rest of the options, and click the **Generate** button (green circle with arrow in it) on the toolbar to launch your report.

After you run your report, close the window telling you that your request was sent to the server and wait for the next window to pop up. This next window will let you know that your report is ready and ask you if you want to display the result; click **Yes**. This will launch your browser since our report format is HTML, and it will show you something similar to Figure 15.4.

Figure 15.4 Report Results

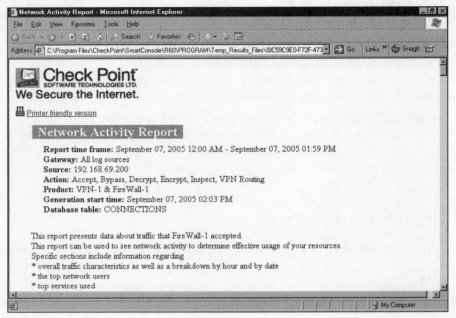

Verify that the source filter is the correct address and that the timeframe for the report is today. If you scroll down through the results, you will see that it reflects the format located on the **Content** tab of our report definition. To save this report, click the **Save** button. There may be a pop-up that explains the inability to save a prede-fined report and asks if you would like to save a new report; click **OK**. Now, write a descriptive name in the **Report Name:** field so that you know what it is when you look at it in the future, then click **Save**. In this example, name the report "Today Src 192.168.69.200" and save it in the **My Reports** tree. When finished, the GUI has now created the report leaf under **My Reports** and placed you in this report.

Though you have numerous other options with regard to what kind of report you generate, how you generate it, and what you do with it when it is finished, you certainly understand the ease with which you can generate a report. Just like all Check Point interfaces, the Eventia Reporter interface reflects a common configura-tion baseline and provides an intuitive format for you.

Creating a Graph

So you've looked over the entire report from the last exercise and wonder about the graphs and tables that Eventia put into our report. Well, you can define which con-tent areas include graphs, charts, or tables for each report. To do this, all you have to do is select your report and click the **Content** tab. Use the report you just saved and select the **Top Network Activity Sources** from the **Section** heading. Now click the **Edit** button and a new windows opens. On the left side, click the **Table/Graphs** option and view the settings on your screen, similar to those in Figure 15.5.

Figure 15.5 Table/Graph Options

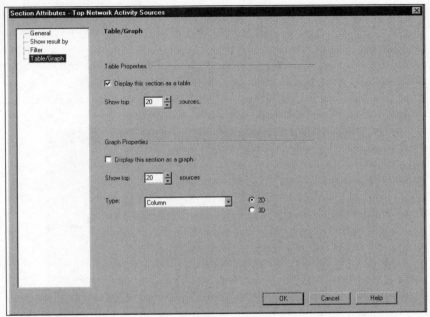

Now you can select which options you like best in order to produce the most helpful report to you and your organization. If you want a graph instead of a table, simply uncheck the **Display this section as a table** option and place a check in the **Display this section as a graph** option. Either way, you have control over how to present the resultant information to yourself, to management, or to your peers. Also, don't forget to save the changes to your report definition if you want to reproduce the same results later.

Scheduling Reports

So you recall that you cannot change predefined report definitions, right? Well, there's an exception to everything, and this is no different. One property that you can change and save to the predefined report definitions is its schedule. Keep in mind that some installations of Eventia Reporter share resources with your SmartCenter Server. In these cases, it is imperative that you not run resource intensive reports while there are more immediate process concerns. For the same reasons that backups are done in the middle of the night, so too can you schedule your reports to run in the middle of the night. Take advantage of low resource utilization and stop waiting on your reports. The reports will be there in the morning, unless something went wrong, of course. Nonetheless, the **Schedule** tab for each definition allows you the flexibility to launch your reports whenever it most pleases you. Even if you have a distributed installation, you may want to stagger your reports so they aren't all running at the same time.

When you open the **Schedule** tab, click the **Add…** button and the **Schedule Properties** window opens, as shown in Figure 15.6.

Figure 15.6 Schedule Properties Window

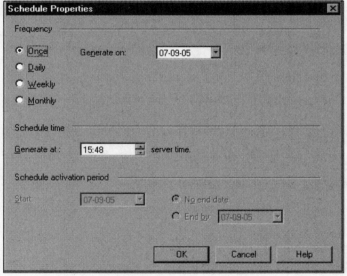

Not only can you schedule a report to run repetitiously (every so often), but you can delay the execution of a report until a later time. Delaying reports is helpful when you have a one-time requirement and cannot afford to steal cycles during the day. Just create the report definition and schedule the job to run during the middle of the night. Of course, if you have other jobs that run at that time, you'll have to plan appropriately to not incur too much overlap. Additionally, you have the option to run reports during a specific time frame.

For instance, let's say that you are launching a new Web site and management has asked for traffic reports for the first two months that the site is operational. Instead of marking your calendar to come back and turn off the report (remove the scheduling), you can simply enable the **Schedule activation period** option and set the **End by:** date to the proper setting. As well, if you have something coming up and want to prepare for the reports, you can delay the activation **Start:** date until the appropriate time.

Report Filters

No surprise here. As you've already witnessed, the Eventia Reporter filters are very similar to filtering found in other Check Point products and consoles. However, by now you certainly understand why this capability exists in each of these technologies. You have the opportunity to store significant amounts of data in log files and database tables. In order to weed through it and find the guts of what you are looking for, you need the ability to filter out all but what you want to see. It is no different for reporting.

Running a report that tells you all the blocked connections from last week may give you a high-level overview. However, targeting one source (IP address, IP address range, or object name) presents you the data you truly want to see. It doesn't matter that one of your remote users forgot to log into the VPN before trying to send out his e-mail. You want to investigate another address that keeps popping up in your e-mail server logs. Creating and applying a filter to a report is a great way to put connections into a historical context. Not only can you view what is currently happening (recently), but also look over a more long-range period to determine if this is a low and slow attack.

Are You 0wned?

Low and Slow

When some attackers target your network or specific hosts for reconnaissance and don't want to set off any alarms, they may try a "low-and-slow" method. This type of recon tries to take advantage of the nature of firewalls and IDS devices. Since most of these devices don't exactly hold on to log data or connection data very long (days/weeks), they may not recognize a network scan spread out over a prolonged period of time. For this reason, correlation databases are valuable. They can not only profile sources (and much more) over an extended period of time but also identify network/host scans that other devices did not detect in real time.

Report Management

The other primary interface that Check Point included in Eventia Reporter is the **Management** tab. You can bring up this tab by selecting **View | Management** or by clicking the **Management** tab in the lower left-hand corner of the **Reports** tab. This window shows a few options to you. First, you see that you are able to modify the consolidation settings. Also, you can modify settings that affect how the database stores data and its physical and logical limitations. Lastly, you can check out the **Activity Queue** and the **Activity Log**. These two options show you what is currently happening, what is going to happen soon, and gives you a recollection of what has happened in the past. In this section, you'll learn a bit more about these options and associated processes. Then, we'll move on to discuss Check Point's SmartView Monitor.

Consolidation Policy

Basically, a consolidation policy is a set of rules that drives the handling of the log data. When the Eventia Reporter retrieves the data from the SmartCenter Server, it evaluates each record against this set of rules (consolidation policy) in order to determine how to store the record in the database. The Check Point default rule set consists of 15 rules, each matching a particular log record type (alerts, message logs, HTTP logs, etc.). Each of these rules then defines how to process each record; either write it to the table as is, or consolidate the log record. If the rule consolidates the log entry, then you must understand that there has to be a time factor associated with the consolidation. As such, the process consolidates all similar records (for this specific rule) during this time limit. Check Point has defined the default time interval to one hour. By the way, there are many references within Check Point's documentation that call your attention to the fact that you should utilize the default consolidation policy. Thus, maybe it is wise for you to stick with the default policy. In the least, it will avoid any problems that may arise because of a faulty policy.

Log Consolidation Process

To provide you more detail about how consolidation occurs, let's take a look at the process from rulebase (consolidation policy) to database (records table). You already know that Eventia evaluates the records against the policy as they come in from SmartCenter. When this happens, the process concentrates on four parts of each record: the destination address, the interface with which the packet came into the firewall, the Rule Name, and the QoS class. If the process finds multiple records with like values for each of these fields, then the process consolidates these *n* records into one database record.

At this point, it would also be nice to know how many records the process consolidated into the one database entry. For this reason, the consolidation record contains a new field containing the number of connections that this one record represents. As you may imagine, there are many records that fit this particular profile and therefore will incur consolidation. This process reduces the amount of space required for the database file while maintaining enough meaningful information to provide for reporting.

Database Maintenance

Looking at the **Database Maintenance** tab in Figure 15.7, you can see that there are several items that should interest you as an administrator.

Figure 15.7 Database Maintenance Window

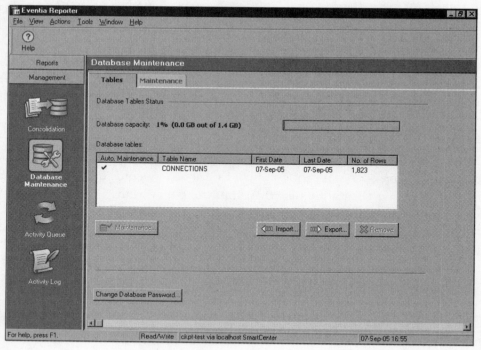

For starters, there is the **Database capacity:** indicator. This value tells you how much space you have allocated for the database file and how much of that space you are currently using. In addition, this tab gives you the ability to import and export tables to and from the database. If you have previously exported data from the database, you can return it into the tables by importing it back in. Lastly, on this page is the **Change Database Password...** button. By executing this action, you change the internal database password for the *RMSERVER* user.

Also, take note of the **Maintenance** tab. Within this tab, you can change the action of the automatic maintenance so that instead of deleting records, the process exports them to a directory. Moreover, you can define the thresholds for cleanup. The default values set by Eventia are **High End** 80% and **Low End** 70%. What this means is that the automatic cleanup will occur when the database is reaches at least 80% capacity. It will clean until it reaches 70%. Again, you are able to modify these values. If you have sufficient disk space, changing the high and low ends may provide you a greater range to search data. However, restricted disk space may cause your needs to change and therefore reduce your high- and low-end variables.

Monitoring Tools • Chapter 15   547

Activity Queue and Log

In the **Activity Queue** tab, you will see a list of pending and current actions. Some of the capabilities Eventia Reporter provides to you here is the ability to cancel an action, or the ability to reorder pending actions. In these two cases, you may be able to better allocate resources for more pressing concerns. Even if you don't want to shuffle the deck, you will still benefit from the data you see here. If, for instance, you just want to verify that scheduled jobs are pending or executing properly, you can visit this tab to do so.

Changing over to the **Activity Log**, you will simply see a record of which processes/reports have completed on your server. If you have reports that have finished successfully, you can right-click the entry and select **Show Report Output** in order to shortcut your way to the actual report data. Again, by right-clicking an entry and selecting **More Information...** you are also able to view the directory location for each specific report. Lastly, you can delete entries that you no longer have a use for by right-clicking an entry and selecting **Delete Action**.

Navigating through SmartView Monitor

To give you a platform for offering a high-level status of your security architecture, Check Point provides to you its SmartView Monitor. As you embark upon managing an entire security environment, as the NGX is, you need a tool that allows you to quickly identify where and how your gateways are using their resources. SmartView Monitor not only tells you about hardware resource utilization, it also presents itself as a one-stop shop to see what's happening with regard to traffic profiles. It doesn't stop there either. You can check out your remote users and see who's doing what and monitor your established VPN tunnels. SmartView Monitor is a resourceful tool that gives you a great insight into many aspects of your gateways' behavior and traffic patterns.

In the remaining sections of this chapter you will acquire an appreciation for the different counters and statistical information that SmartView Monitor dispenses. We'll start by looking at the GUI as a whole, then breaking each component down and relaying the most meaningful aspects of each.

SmartView Monitor Layout

No doubt, SmartView Monitor has many different views to engage, as well as so much information to retain. However, to truly appreciate the usefulness of this tool, you have to open it up and browse around. So let's start there. If you have another Check Point console open, choose **Window | SmartView Monitor**. Otherwise, select the SmartView Monitor from the programs menu. Either way, you should see something similar to Figure 15.8 (with collapsed branches to display each tree).

Figure 15.8 SmartView Monitor Window

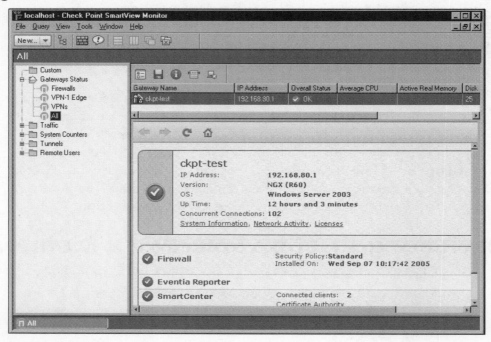

In Figure 15.8 (and on your screen), you see that the overall format is strikingly similar to all the other Check Point graphical interfaces. In general, the GUI displays the menu-driven items in the left-hand pane and shows results and information in the right-hand pane. In total, there are three panes in this view. The first is the left side, which SmartView Monitor calls the *Tree View*. This, as its name implies, is where you choose a view in order to see the results in the other panes. The upper right side view is the *Results View*. In Figure 15.8, the **All** view displays all the devices that your SmartCenter Server manages. In this case, there is only one single firewall server. If you have multiple devices, they will all show up in this area. Since there is only one device, it is highlighted and the *Gateway Details* view in the lower right side displays further details in such a manner that you can click links that lead you to even more information about your device. As you navigate about the page, you'll notice a plethora of information regarding your gateway that is available via one click.

Another great inclusion with SmartView Monitor is the lower window bar. Not that Check Point calls this particular entity that, but it seems to fit and there doesn't seem to be a consensus on a name for it. In any case, each time you introduce a new view, a SmartView Monitor creates a new tab in the lower section of the entire window. In this way, you can switch back and forth between views. We have all been in situations where having access to multiple views is critical. This taskbar seems to satisfy this need in a very exquisite manner. However, if you launch a bunch of views, it may become cumbersome in that there are many tabs along the bottom. Check Point to the rescue yet again! As expected, you can close the views by right-clicking the tab at the bottom and choosing **Close** or **Close All**. However, SmartView Monitor gives you the option to close all the windows except the one you choose. To do this, just right-click on the tab you wish to remain open and select **Close All Except Me**.

TIP

Instead of opening a new view/window each time you need to access information, learn to utilize the browser-like functionality Check Point built into the *Results View* toolbar. You can go back to the previous screen, forward to the screen you came back from, or home to the native screen for the view. In addition, you can click the refresh button to get the most recent statistics or information.

Alerts and Suspicious Activity Rules

As you read about in Chapter 6, SmartView Monitor is where you come to check on your SAM rules. If you are blocking a connection profile, you will find it under **Tools | Suspicious Activity Rules…**. There is no need to rehash what you have already learned, but keep in mind that you do not have to have already invoked any blocking rules in order to view the window. Moreover, you can initiate a blocking rule from within this window. To do so, open the window and click the **Add…** button in the lower left corner. Figure 15.9 shows the set of windows that you can configure.

Figure 15.9 Block Suspicious Activity Settings

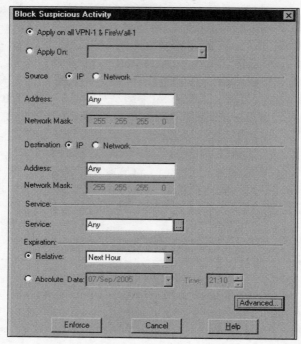

Similar to the way you created the blocking rules through SmartView Tracker, you can do the same here. Note that the options can either be specific or broad ranging. Clicking on the **Advanced...** button gives you options for the action you wish to invoke, how to track the incident, and whether or not to close the connections. Since you've already learned about what blocking accomplishes, we won't cover that again. However, you should know that you have options when it comes to invoking blocking actions. Although it is convenient to block them through SmartView Tracker, you may also enforce restrictions through SmartView Monitor.

As far as alerting goes, we've touched a little on that as well. What we did not touch on is how to define alert thresholds. In SmartView Monitor, you can define global thresholds for your gateway devices. To get there, launch the **Gateway Status | All** view and click the **Thresholds Configuration** toolbar button above the *Results View* pane. This action opens the thresholds setting window as seen in Figure 15.10.

Figure 15.10 Thresholds Settings Window

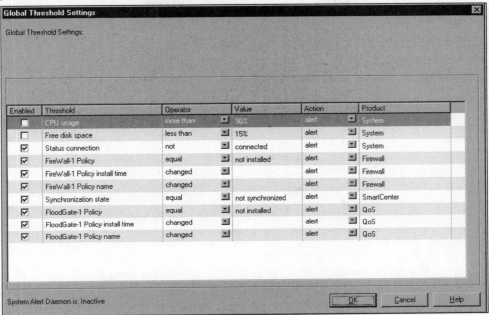

You now know where to configure these settings in order to alert you that something is unusually high or unavailable. Notice in the lower left-hand corner of the window that it states the **System Alert Daemon is: Inactive**. In order to alert for these instances, you must enable this daemon. You can easily do this by clicking **Tools | Start System Alert Daemon**. Once more, the action you wish to invoke is defined through the policy global properties. Since you've already visited the alerts window in Chapter 6, we won't cover those functions again.

Notes from the Underground…

Alerting and Paying Attention

Most administrators set up alerting of some sort and are pleased that it's working. However, a minority actually take the time to properly configure alerting so that events are not drowned among a sea of false positives. When you configure alerting, be certain to not only make sure that it is working, but that you have properly configured all the thresholds so that a "high maintenance" alert does not consume your attention so that a critical alert goes unnoticed. These unattended alerts are often the ones that require the most attention.

Predefined Views

Third verse— same as the first. You cannot modify and save predefined views. What you can do is modify a view and save it under the **Custom** branch of the *Tree View*. Just like all the other customized views, reports, and filters you've created in other tools throughout this book, you do this in order to reduce the resultant set, ultimately reducing the need for a higher amount of unnecessary resource utilization. The same principles apply in SmartView Monitor. Since the predefined views enable all of the most common statistics, you may not need to utilize these on a full time basis. Choose to use them instead as leverage to create a customized view that represents the data you really want to see. Sure, play around with them and become familiar with how different options present material. In the end, though, use customized views more often. If you are at a point where one of your gateways is suffering from high CPU utilization, you may not have the resources to display a predefined view. However, if you have a custom view that shows only specific information, it may use less resources and not be affected by the other resource issues.

Gateway Status

Seemingly the most useful views of all the predefined views are the **Gateway Status** views. As mentioned earlier in this chapter, these views identify devices by their product or group them all together. Choosing one of the devices presents you with other options, and it is up to you to invoke them in order to reveal even more information. As we briefly mentioned already, choosing a device results in information about your devices to populate the *Results View*. In the previous Figure 15.8, you saw that the information told much about the gateway. In fact, SmartView Monitor reported which packages are installed on the device, which versions, the server uptime, the server OS platform, and other informative tidbits about the device. This section goes on to describe the three options available as links in our firewall device window. These links rest just below the **Concurrent Connections** count in the *Results View* from Figure 15.8. Let's explore these options to see what kind of information they reveal.

System Information

When you click the **System Information** link you get more information about the CPU, disk, and memory utilization. These statistics are critical in nature regarding your gateway; specifically, your firewall. If any of these resources become exhausted or consistently run high, you need to consider ramping up in some sense. Either that, or there is a problem with a runaway thread/process. In addition, you could be under some sort of attack that is causing the gateway to consume additional resources. In any event, you need to respond immediately to high utilization whether it's a disk, CPU, or memory.

Network Activity

By clicking the **Network Activity** link you bring up statistics about your gateway's network interface traffic in addition to your routing tables. These traffic counters provide in and out statistics for each interface for dropped, rejected, and accepted packets. What's more, SmartView Monitor shows you how many bytes have traversed each interface. By having quick access to these data, especially the routing tables, you may be able to identify issues more quickly. For instance, if you see an extraordinary amount of dropped packets coming in one interface, there may be a misconfiguration in your network, or worse, it could be some kind of attack. By reviewing the statistics in the SmartView Monitor you can identify this sort of issue without having to delve too deeply into other measures. Of course, if you cannot find any problems here, and in fact, you are having issues, you should then move on to find the source of the problem.

Licenses

Lastly, you can view the licensing associated with each gateway by clicking the **Licenses** link. There isn't anything special about this information other than the fact that you can see what kind of license you have applied to the server and when it expires. Although this is helpful, you should already be familiar with this information because a lapse in licensing can introduce significant issues (DoS comes to mind). If you need to find out or verify this information, this is a good place to look.

Traffic

The traffic views gather information about current connections on your gateway(s). Viewing these statistics will help you understand what is going through your firewall at any given time. Specifically, you can invoke one of these views to identify what abusers are doing on your network. For instance, the **Top P2P Users** view displays which clients are most active with file-sharing applications. In turn, these clients may be sucking up a significant amount of bandwidth. Discovering this information quickly through the SmartView Monitor views is helpful in this instance. There are other views that provide similar data for other items. Further, when you customize each view, it will quickly provide the data you desire to see and present it in an easily readable format.

When you select these views, you can then elect to see the traffic for a specific packet direction (inbound/outbound) and you can also target gateway interfaces. In this way, you can reduce the results to a simple, manageable interpretation of the data. Also, at the bottom of the window you can change the current refresh timer for the view. Either reduce or increase the timer by clicking the appropriate button next to the value.

Another meaningful tool for traffic evaluation is the **Record** tool. If you are testing or know that particular spikes occur in your network at a certain time, you can record a custom view for further investigation. To begin, choose **Traffic | Recording | Record** from the menu. Choose a name for the file that the system creates and your traffic is being recorded. When you are ready to stop, just go back and select **Traffic | Recording | Stop**. Now you can choose to play your recording whenever you have the opportunity to evaluate the results of the view.

TIP

The **Packet Size Distribution** view is a great tool to identify where your large packet transfers occur. Some applications, such as database reporting, often transfer large packets, and this view will help you verify the data flow for such applications. As well, you can possibly identify issues with misconfigurations or attacks. Since you are becoming familiar with your traffic profiles, this tool also provides some guidance to become familiar with volumes passing through interfaces.

Applying Filters

When you invoke one of the **Traffic** views, you can also choose to apply a filter to the monitoring. Since each view is essentially a query, you are able to shape the results to meet your immediate needs. To configure these filters, choose a **Traffic** view and click the **Query Properties** button on the toolbar. After selecting the **Filter** tab from the top, you should now see a window similar to Figure 15.11.

Figure 15.11 Traffic View Query Properties Window

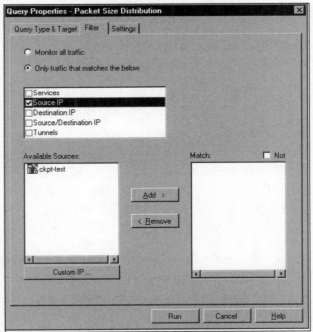

In this particular window, you are filtering the traffic so that it matches a specific **Source IP** address. To choose which address, you may select an object from the **Available Sources:** window or create a new one by clicking the **Custom IP...** and entering the appropriate IP address. The other tabs allow you to configure whether you want to view traffic "real-time" or from a historic perspective. Also, you can set Y-axis properties and the refresh interval for your query.

Creating a Custom View

Similar to the way you have been creating custom queries in SmartView Tracker and custom reports in Eventia Reporter, you can create custom views in SmartView Monitor. Once again, utilize one of the predefined views to begin. Make any necessary changes to narrow down the results to a desirable level and save the new view with a new name. Only this time, to save the view, you must copy the current settings you applied to a predefined view and paste it into the **Custom** branch in the *Tree View* pane. From this point, you are able to modify the name of the view if you wish. Another way to save the current view to a custom view is to click on the disk icon in the toolbar for the *Result View*. When you do this, a window pops up, prompting you for a name for your new view. Since you cannot store them except in the **Custom** branch, select this folder to store your new report.

Exporting Views

Another advantage of SmartView Monitor is that you can export your views to file so that you can take them from one console to the other. Similar to the way that queries are saved on the SmartConsole client, so are views. So in order to have the same views no matter which management client you are on, you must manually copy or export/import them over. This easy task is accomplished by right-clicking one of the reports and choosing export. Choose a filename and directory location and the export file now resides on disk. If you so choose, you may edit the properties manually, but you must first understand the format. Otherwise, just change the settings in the GUI and export the file once you adjust the properties to your liking. SmartView Monitor stores the export files in *C:\Program Files\CheckPoint\SmartConsole\R60\PROGRAM\MonitorData* on the SmartConsole host. Again, these files are simple text files and can be imported back into the original host or another SmartConsole host.

System Counters

Just what you might think, **System Counters** are views that tell you statistics about current or historical resource utilization. These counters are very similar to the network views, except that they deal more with system resources than network traffic. However, these counters do include packet statistics. These counters also present a likeness to others you would normally see for operating systems and other devices.

Just like the **Traffic** views, you are able to tweak the properties for each of these counters. Instead of filtering the data, you just define which counters to apply to a particular view. Figure 15.12 depicts the **Query Properties** windows for the **Firewall History** counter.

Figure 15.12 Query Properties for Firewall History Counter

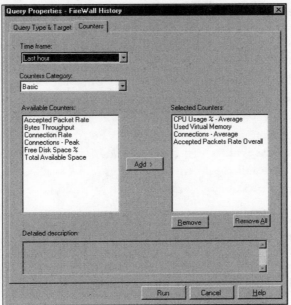

As you can now see, you can configure several items from this one tab. There are several categories for counters as you may have seen in other products. Adding and removing counters to and from the **Selected Counters:** window is just as easy as highlighting a specific value and either adding or removing it by clicking the appropriate button. When you have your properties defined to your satisfaction, click **Run** to invoke your view to the display.

WARNING

> Just as with any process that collects real-time statistics, be careful about resource utilization. Don't invoke a DoS attack against one or more of your servers just so you can monitor it. Other parts of this chapter (and others) have mentioned optimizing your views so that you use only what you need in order to get your desired results. Start small, then grow into a decent view. It is better to get not enough data on the first try rather than crash the server or send utilization (CPU or Memory) into unstable levels.

The Need for Custom Counters

Under the **System Counter** branch you see a handful of views that probably give a lot of meaningful information to you. What you must understand is that some of these reports may give you exactly what you're looking for, but that some of them will not do your curiosity justice. For this reason, you will most likely need to create custom views to track your devices' utilization. Again, you'll have to play around with the properties for each particular counter, but time will help you develop accurate views that skillfully deliver the information you want to know.

This process is no different than, say, implementing a signature-based IDS. When you begin, you have a very loose configuration and as you progress down the line you streamline your signature base so that you are not bogged down with unimportant information. This process will let you configure these views in such a way that the cream (critical statistics) will rise to the top. In this sense, you will not have to drill down into layers of data to discover what ultimately could have lay on the top deck.

Studying History

No, you are not taking a trip back to college (though that isn't such a bad idea). What you can do with counters is reveal usage profiles. When does your gateway seem to work the hardest? What is going on at that particular time that increases usage so much (lunch hour)? Or how about projecting your usage so that you can accurately project scaling. How many times have you wanted to upgrade a server, presented a proposal to management (without scaling statistics), only to hear them deliver the standard answer (no)? Well, if you are able to produce a historical perspective, store the views as files, tie in the coordinating amount of users for that usage, and project solid usage relationships, you may just get that extra server. Facts are hard to dispute. If you present a report showing your growth projections and maximum resource load on your current hardware, your management will be hard-pressed to deny you the new expenditure (if they still deny your request; get a post-dated "I-told-you-so" in writing).

In any event, counters are statistics. Statistics drive predictions and forecasts. Without solid statistics, most plans are semi-worthless. Not to say that experience counts for nothing, but again, facts are difficult to dispute. Utilize the SmartView Monitor tools and develop a solid baseline for statistical forecasting so that you can adequately scale your environment before your users let you know that scaling is now required. It is a significant embarrassment to have to accept the fact that you let something this important slip through your hands. You now have the tools. Learn to use them skillfully and prepare yourself for the road ahead.

Attack Profiles

Ever wonder how many attacks of a certain type are hitting your firewall on a particular day? Rest easy, my friend. SmartView Monitor's counters provide exactly this information. You now have the capability to apply counters (real-time or historical) to any of the attacks defined in both SmartDefense or Web Intelligence. Check Point has made it all too easy to invoke a single counter to relay how many SQL injection attack attempts have come across one of your gateways.

There are so many different attack counters that you can create specific profiles for a group of attacks. Just as you can use historical context to plan for resources, you can study historical context of attacks to prepare your defense. Although all attacks aren't scheduled, you can still normalize the data and make projections about suspected high volumes. Don't underestimate the power of statistics. They can help you build a case for new servers and they can also help you defend your network in a more thorough manner. For instance, what if you determine, through viewing your counters, that most of attack X is coming through one particular gateway? Does that gateway have sufficient resources to withstand the attack? Does the attack vector target availability of the security device? These questions will lead you to make improvements about your security architecture and you will owe it all to (maybe not all) SmartView Monitor. Sure there are other ways to detect such irregularities, but with the statistical data that the views provide, you can prepare for such occurrences before they happen.

Tunnels and Remote Users

With a VPN-1 gateway you have the opportunity to establish a secure connection from one point to another. This encrypted connection represents a point-to-point tunnel. To monitor these tunnels, you can invoke any one of the views in the **Tunnels** tree. These views report collective information about each separate tunnel for all your SmartCenter Managed gateways.

In the same way, you can view the users associated with particular gateways or all the devices your SmartCenter Server manages. These views allow you to administer your current remote user population and decipher how to better meet their needs. With both tunnels and users, you can customize the views to give you just what you want as with the other views. Whereas the others were mostly concentrating on utilization and statistics, these two categories focus on uptime and administration, though both of them also provide you with statistics for the appropriate entity.

VPN Gateway versus Community

Basically, there are two views you can invoke. One of them shows only tunnels involved with a community and the other shows all tunnels for a specific gateway. What's the difference you ask? It's very simple. Communities are groups of gateways that combine to establish tunnels with one another. So on one gateway, you may have multiple communities. Consider four gateways, A, B, C, and D. Further understand that between these gateways, there are two VPN communities. In community 1, A, B, and D are tunneled together (in mesh mode). In community 2, B, C, and D are tunneled together. For this reason, gateway A has one community and one total tunnel. However, gateway D has two communities and two total tunnels. You can certainly understand now that communities establish tunnels between multiple hosts. Gateways define one or more communities in which each participates.

Viewing Users

To see who is logged into your remote VPN, you can easily invoke one of the views under the **Remote Users** branch. This will show you a bunch of information about the user including which gateway he or she is logged into, and from where. Also, you may perform a query for a specific user if you know the username you are looking for. By clicking the **Get User by Name** view, you must enter the distinguished name for your subject. To help out, SmartView Monitor accepts the wildcard character (*) within this query. So if you wanted to find all the people whose usernames begin with "w," click the query and enter *w** in the empty field in the **User DN Filter** window.

Down Tunnels

Since you configure tunnels in order to communicate securely between two end points, you might want to know when any of your tunnels are down. SmartView Monitor has a predefined view just for this purpose. Though some downtime may be scheduled, it is always good to keep tabs on things that say they are down. Also, you can sharpen the properties that you display on each view by modifying the query properties for tunnels. In this manner, you may be able to identify quickly why a tunnel is down (maybe the SA failed). In the best case, this view should have no entries. In the worst case, all your tunnels are down and you most likely have larger issues.

Summary

Check Point really has provided two solid tools that help you to monitor your network architecture as a whole and your individual security devices. Eventia Reporter is a comprehensive database-driven reporting tool that lets you customize and schedule reports so that you are aware of what interests you most. You can install Eventia Reporter on the same server as SmartCenter, or configure it for distributed installation and run it on its own hardware. Either way, you must ensure that you have allocated sufficient disk space, memory, and CPU to run your reports.

With SmartView Monitor, Check Point delivers an extensive collection of reports, views, and counters to help you understand a current profile of your device's utilization and traffic patterns. Moreover, the historical perspective of the counters gives you leverage in order to properly project utilization and plan for appropriate (and timely) scaling. Also don't forget about the alerting and blocking capability you have in SmartView Monitor. Though we brushed over it in this chapter, you should have sufficient understanding of these two offerings from previous chapters.

In all, both of these tools prove considerably useful to any administrator. Being able to run reports, view counters and statistics, and monitor devices is a critical aspect within the scheme of network security. Without these native tools, you would be left to script your own set of tools in order to deliver this data. Even though there are some people out there who can do this, not everyone has the time or the skill to develop such tools. Be grateful that Check Point's NGX solution is so comprehensive.

Solutions Fast Track

Installation

- ☑ Check Point allows you to install Eventia Reporter in either a standalone or distributed configuration. The preferred method is distributed where you apply the Eventia Reporter Add-On piece to your SmartCenter Server.

- ☑ When considering hardware for your Eventia Server, keep in mind that disk reads and writes will dominate. For this reason, you should try to acquire the fastest disk you can. A significant amount of space will aid as well. Eventia Reporter is compatible for all the usual platforms except Nokia IPSO (it can host the Add-On piece).

☑ Because licensing is per server, make sure that you have enough licenses to cover all your firewalls. An enterprise license will suffice as it covers you with an unlimited number of gateways. However, you must attribute individual licenses to a specific firewall within Eventia Reporter.

Reports

☑ Reports allow you to develop data sets that reveal the usage of your firewalls. Check Point's flexible Eventia Reporter gives you numerous options when it comes to generating reports, filtering the data sources, and scheduling reports.

☑ Log entries flow seamlessly from your firewall into the Eventia Reporter Database. In this way, the data is available for reports shortly after your firewall writes the connection to its logs.

☑ As you become familiar with the Eventia Reporter and develop a comfort for modifying the data sources, you can segregate specific data sets into separate tables. By default, all connections go into the same table, but you can create a new process to load data into another table if you so desire.

☑ When you generate a report in Eventia Reporter the results are stored and you can revisit them whenever you wish. You are always able to click a resultant report and recall the data that was generated at run time.

Definitions

☑ As other management interfaces have shown, Check Point provides many predefined reports in order for you to leverage them to produce more concise reports for your organization. Though you cannot change these predefined reports, you can save the changes to a custom report name.

☑ Two types of reports exist in Eventia Reporter, Standard and Express reports. Standard reports mine through the database to retrieve results, whereas Express reports query against historical and counter data that the SmartView Monitor collects. Express reports return results faster since they do not run against the database.

☑ Custom reports allow you to take advantage of the filtering capability within the report definitions. Similar to the way you can filter in the

SmartView Tracker, you can narrow the scope of the results for a report. In this way, you can filter the results to show only what you want to display.

Creating Reports

☑ One of the ways Eventia Reporter displays results is by creating a Web page. This method provides a solid platform for the links and other mechanisms that lead to an easily read format. Other means to generate reports are by e-mail, ftp upload, and custom distribution.

☑ Within each report, you have the option to display the resultant data in plain text, tables, or graphs. Configuration options allow you to use multiple output formats so that you can see different representations of your data.

☑ A flexible report scheduler allows you to optimize your resource utilization. You may not want to run a resource intensive report in the middle of the day, so delaying this job through the scheduler is a terrific option. As well, you can schedule recurring reports to run at the most opportune time for your organization.

Report Management

☑ The consolidation policy that Check Point provides as a default is configured to optimize the data storage into the database. This policy acts as a rule engine that evaluates each record and determines how to write the data into the database.

☑ When the consolidation policy evaluates a record, it can choose to write it to the table as is. If certain characteristics from other records remain the same within a specific time frame, then the engine consolidates the record prior to writing the table entry.

☑ Check Point offers to you the ability to perform maintenance functions for your Eventia Reporter Database. However, they also have a built-in function that automatically applies maintenance procedures to your database in order to keep the file within certain thresholds.

Navigating through SmartView Monitor

☑ The layout of the SmartView Monitor provides a comprehensive view of your resources. Each view displays certain characteristics and allows you to choose other records or expand upon the current resource statistics.

☑ SmartView Monitor provides Suspicious Activity Rules monitoring through its interface. You have the ability to create a blocking rule or just monitor rules you created from the command line, from within SmartView Tracker, or from an earlier session in SmartView Monitor.

☑ Properly configuring alerts within SmartView Monitor can enable quick response in the face of an incident. This incident could be minor, or it could be critical. If you define alert thresholds for resources or other mechanisms to trigger alerts, be sure to follow through with tweaking them to avoid brushing off alerts because of high false positive rates.

Gateway Status

☑ These views display numerous information about your gateway. It tells you which components are installed and which versions are running. In addition, you can display critical system resources by drilling down through some of the interactive links in the standard output.

☑ Network activity statistics allow you, as the administrator, to get a grasp on how much traffic is passing through which interfaces on your hosts. Also, the routing tables can provide to you a quick reference to validate whether traffic is traversing the network properly.

☑ SmartView Monitor makes available other system information, including what license is installed on each gateway and when it expires. Other tools and gadgets are sure to remind you of your soon-to-expire licenses, but this tool presents it in a clear and concise manner.

Traffic

☑ Applying filters to these views is one way to monitor specific connections passing through your gateways. You can choose to see a broad range of connections or narrow the scope of your query so that you are viewing only one particular connection profile.

☑ Saving queries to custom views is a great way to quickly recall a connection profile. Each time you revisit the SmartView Monitor, all you have to do is invoke your saved view instead of configuring a filter for one of the existing views. This reduces the time it takes to retrieve results and also the chance of making subsequent mistakes in the query properties.

☑ The network activity display gives you either real-time information or provides you with a historical perspective of your traffic. Both of these configuration options have different purposes, but you should look into both of them because together they provide a full scope of understanding.

☑ Since views are stored locally on the SmartConsole client machine, Check Point gives you the option to export your view properties to a file so that you can import them into another client machine. In this way, you have the same queries (views) on multiple machines and do not have to rely on one machine to reproduce a certain view.

System Counters

☑ The need for counters is key to managing your resources. Knowing current and historical perspectives of resource utilization is a primary aspect of planning ahead. Without counters, you would simply be unable to provide statistical analysis in order to project usage baselines and scaling milestones.

☑ Comparing current usage to historical trends may help you to identify weaknesses in your architecture. Studying these historical values may seem odd, but when you grasp the possibilities you learn from them, you will truly appreciate what this tool provides to you.

☑ With the Web Intelligence and SmartDefense attack views, you may display counters for a specific threat or multiple threats. This may provide you with verification that you may be under attack. In the least, it will give you some idea of the normal attempts you face and allow you to plan more appropriately if necessary.

Tunnels and Remote Users

☑ These statistics report on tunnels for both communities and gateways. If you want to see only tunnels for a specific community, you can display only this information. Otherwise, you can display all the tunnels associated with a particular gateway. Remember, one gateway can have multiple communities.

☑ Also, you can display the remote users associated with a single gateway or all your SmartCenter managed gateways. Further capability allows you to filter for users based on their distinguished names. If you are unsure of the full username, SmartView Monitor accepts the wildcard character (*) for convenience.

☑ One of the predefined views for tunnels reports the status of down tunnels. This may help you identify why the tunnel is disconnected and lead to quick response and recovery of the tunnel. The view displays (filters for) only inoperable tunnels, so you will not have other data to distract your attention from the service interruption.

Frequently Asked Questions

The following Frequently Asked Questions, answered by the authors of this book, are designed to both measure your understanding of the concepts presented in this chapter and to assist you with real-life implementation of these concepts. To have your questions about this chapter answered by the author, browse to **www.syngress.com/solutions** and click on the **"Ask the Author"** form.

Q: I want to install Eventia Reporter on its own server. How can I do this?

A: Check Point gives you this option to install a distributed configuration for Eventia Reporter. You must install the Add-On product to the SmartCenter Server. When all the products are installed properly, you must configure a Check Point host object for your new reporting server. Make sure you select the proper options for the host and establish SIC from your SmartCenter Server to the reporting server.

Q: I have two licenses for Eventia Reporter, but I have four firewalls. Can I run reports from all these servers?

A: No. Licensing for Eventia is on a per server basis. In the GUI, you must define which licenses are associated with which servers. Up to five VPN-1 Edge appliances can function off of one single license.

Q: I ran a report a couple of weeks ago, but misplaced the files. Is there a way to recover that report?

A: Yes. Remember that the report results are stored on the server as well as wherever else you may store the reports. Just return to the **Results** tab, find the report you are looking for and click the link to launch the report. Also, look in the activity log. You are able to launch reports results from this area as well.

Q: Does all the data that comes into the database go to the same table? What if I want to break it off and start populating a new table?

A: By default, Check Point creates the *CONNECTIONS* table when you install Eventia Reporter. By creating a new consolidation process you can begin populating a new table with data. Since Eventia relies on a database, there are some options available to you regarding how to manage tables and global options for your database file.

Q: There is a report running right now and I need to run another one instead. How can I stop the current report and put my new (important) report next in the queue?

A: If you bring up the Activity Queue you can do both of these tasks in there. First, you need to place your new job so that it is next in the queue. Once you've done this, cancel the job that is currently running. When the job finishes (prematurely), your new job will begin trudging through the database for results.

Q: If the *Consolidation Policy* is similar to a rulebase, why can't I tweak it to do more for me?

A: There really isn't a right answer here. However, Check Point has provided a default policy that best optimizes the data in such a manner as to offer the best set of data to query. Check Point's research efforts have produced this policy based on input from knowledgeable experts as well as from customers. In addition, Check Point strongly recommends that you use the default policy.

Q: I noticed that some traffic is coming through my gateway and I want to kill it. Do I need to open SmartView Tracker to use the Block Intruder function?

A: No. You can configure blocking rules directly from SmartView Monitor. All you have to do is know the parameters of the connection you wish to block. Click **Tools | Suspicious Activity Rules** and then **Add....** Enter your information and then begin blocking the suspicious connections.

Q: I see that the counters are displaying current statistics about my gateway's resources. How can I change this so that I see a historical perspective?

A: When you launch a view, you will see that you can modify the query properties by clicking the button in the toolbar. When you do so, you will see that you can adjust the properties so that you receive more of a historical view instead of a real-time view for your query.

Q: I'm trying to find where a remote user has logged in. Does SmartView Monitor let me find users?

A: Yes. SmartView Monitor provides a filter tool so that you can enter a user's distinguished name (including wildcards) and display information about this user's session. Among the items you will see will be which one of your gateways the user is attached to.

Chapter 16

Enabling Voice-over-IP Traffic

Solutions in this chapter:

- **Why Secure VoIP?**
- **VoIP Security Features**
- **How VoIP Calls Are Made**
- **VoIP NGX-VPN-1 Configuration**
- **VoIP QoS Options**
- **VoIP SmartDefense Options**

☑ **Summary**

☑ **Solutions Fast Track**

☑ **Frequently Asked Questions**

Introduction

The purpose of this chapter is to show, first, the reason why VoIP should be secured and, second, how it is done. The biggest flaw in VoIP is that people get the wrong information about what it is and how it works. When reading books or papers on the Internet, you will see that many different people and organizations have their own opinions on how to secure VoIP. Most people don't think about VoIP in the right way and cite the following reasons for thinking that VoIP is secure with some standard methods:

- I have spent a good deal of capital on new routers, and all the access lists work on them.

- We do have firewalls up in our network.

- The phones are going to be on our internal network only.

- Our engineer has installed QoS on our network.

As you can see by these reasons, most people do not have a full understanding of why and how to secure VoIP traffic on a network. In this chapter we will explain why and how Check Point secures VoIP traffic.

Why Secure VoIP?

The first question most people ask when you broach the subject of security with regards to VoIP is "well, they are just phones; why do they need to be secured?" VoIP is just another set of protocols, like many others that are used on networks today, and so they need to be secured. If they are not secured from each other, they at least need to be secured from other protocols and devices in your network. Network managers usually agree on those points. But it gets much harder to ensure that VoIP is secure, as you will see in this chapter.

When you think of VoIP, you see this new phone sitting on your desk that looks much different from the one that you have now. You see that it runs on the data network and looks as if your computer is plugged into the back of the VoIP phone. Now the network manager has one less line to fix or to monitor in his network; that's great for him. But then you tell him that his network can be taken down if he does not secure the VoIP phone. You tell him a few stories from other reader installs, such as the ones included in this chapter.

Some companies have done VoIP installs in-house and have done everything wrong, from having the voice and the data on the same network. That would mean that they did not set up a separate VLAN on the network for voice or data. There was no protection for either network in case of a security breach. Companies also love to give out VoIP Soft Client to VIPs in the company to use on laptops. What they fail to realize is that they will be used off-net most of the time. How are they going to secure them if they are not in the building?

> **TIP**
>
> If you don't have the internal staff that has the expertise to do the job, always look to a company that *can* do the job. It is much better to pay for someone to make sure your network is secure than to not have a network at all.

The following are reasons why you should secure VoIP:

- It's IP traffic, which like any other, needs to be protected.
- Someone tries to steal calls on the network.
- A hacker could be trying a man-in-the-middle attack.
- A pretender could be trying to use someone else's information to make calls.
- A phone could be trying to flood the system with bad calls.
- Denial-of-service attacks can happen through or with the help of a phone.
- If ports are not set up right to open and close, a hacker could use them after a call.
- A hijacker could be trying to reroute calls.
- Even trusted phones and people can become a liability.
- People can live without a computer for a while, but if they don't have a phone to call someone to say that their computers are down, they are usually not happy.

VoIP Security Features

There are many security features that are specifically meant for VoIP security. In this chapter we look into those security features. Unlike a regular data network where securing IP addresses and ports will work, in the VoIP world it is not that easy. The data network can deal with lost packets or major delays, but you cannot do that in a voice network. The call will end up with broken parts, delay, jitter, or at the worst, the dropped call.

Protocol Management

Today, a VoIP phone may use four different signaling protocols: SIP (Session Initiation Protocol), H.323, MGCP (Media Gateway Control Protocol), and SCCP (Skinny Client Control Protocol). There are also two media protocols: RTP (Real-Time Transport Protocol) and RTCP (Real-Time Control Protocol). Each of these provides a different problem for any firewall because you could have more than one on any call. With an older firewall you would have to open each port in the ranges shown in the next sections to make a VoIP work on your network.

In the following sections we can see how each protocol is used and on what port you would see this on a router or firewall in your network.

H.323

H.323 is a protocol that allows many different communication devices to talk with each other by using a standardized protocol. Here are some examples of communications via the H.323 protocol:

- Unicast GK discovery to UDP port 1718
- Multicast GK discovery to 224.0.1.41 UDP port 1718
- RAS to UDP port 1719
- H.225 (call signaling for hosts) to TCP port 1720
- H.245 (capability exchange) to a negotiation in the range of TCP ports 11000 through 65535

SIP

SIP is a communications protocol that is far easier to learn and use than H.323. It makes reading a sys log much easier because of the way it displays text and addresses. Here are some examples of communicating via SIP:

- SIP uses either the UDP or TCP port for signaling to port 5060.
- The user agent may register with a local server on the startup by sending out a REGISTER request to IP.
- SIP uses address 224.0.1.175 (all SIP servers multicast address sip.mcast.net).

MGCP

Media Gateway Control Protocol provides information and retains information for Media Gateways in the network. It works with H.323 and SIP. Here are some examples of communicating via MGCP:

- MG and CA signaling to UDP port 2427
- MG and CA signaling to MG through UDP port 2427 and CA through UDP port 2727

SCCP

Signaling Connection Control Point is a layer within SS7 that provides connectionless and connection network services on or for Message Transfer Part (MTP). Skinny messages are carried above TCP and use port 2000.

RTP

Real-Time Transport Protocol is an Internet standard and a standard communications protocol that provides real-time data for audio and video communications. RTP audio stream is routed to UDP port 16384 and then through port 32767.

NOTE

RTP port selection is MG specific. Depending on the number of voice ports on the MG, the RTP port range is selected. It does not go as high as 32767, and the range can be as small as 256.

With new advancements in firewalls for VoIP, the ports listed in the previous section and others can be dynamically opened and closed. This happens when the caller makes a call and hangs up a call. Hackers and attackers will be stopped from using the ports that would be normally still open before and after a call. This feature helps make your VoIP a secure one on your network.

Converged Networks

One of the biggest considerations for VoIP is the ROI of running the voice and data on one network drop. This carries even a greater risk of threats from attackers on your network; if they can take one down they will take the other down. Making sure the converged network is secure is vital to any network. Remember that most VoIP PBXes run on a server, just as the ones you have in your data network do.

Since we have servers running in the voice network as PBXes, we need to make sure they are secure from attackers, just as a normal server in a data network is. Failure to do so will result in the following problems:

- Denial-of-service attacks on your PBX, voice mail, video, and conferencing servers

- Trojan horses or viruses on your servers

- Packet-based attacks

- Unsecured soft phones

- War dialing on VoIP network

WARNING

Most people do not understand what a converged network is with regard to VoIP. Make sure you understand this and the security risks listed in this chapter. The risks are many, and knowing how to minimize them will help you when configuring the firewall later in this chapter.

The firewall combats these problems by the use of application intelligence to enforce all policies on the firewall. It looks to make sure the calls coming in and going out conform to all RFC's rules. The use of VoIP domains on the firewall helps in the security of your network by preventing calls going out or coming in from undetermined or unsecured networks.

Voice Quality

Voice quality is the only thing that matters to your end user at the end of the day. Networks must have no more than a 150ms delay one way on voice calls, which Check Point NGX delivers. It ensures that your calls have little or no latency or jitter with Low Latency Queuing (LLQ) and QoS controls.

With LLQ, priority can be given to VoIP over other applications that can withstand the latency. Also the amount of data traffic can be weighted to give VoIP more bandwidth than other applications. It can be weighted in a way that is like many other queuing programs on the market, and LLQ will also provide more control for security professionals.

Working with QoS controls the Differentiated Service (DiffServ) that can be used to prioritize traffic across the LAN and WAN. QoS will also work for minimal delays in the encryption and inspection of the packets for VoIP. Having your firewall work in conjunction with QoS on the network is very necessary; if the two work in opposite ways, you will have problems. Check Point QoS features require the activation of the Floodgate module. This license is included in VPN-1 Pro gateways, and it can be added to VPN-1 Express gateways.

Notes from the Underground...

Passing Muster

No matter how good your data networking engineer says your network is, it is never that good until VoIP can pass across it with no delays. VoIP is a true measure of how good a network is set up for Voice and QoS. Although data can have a few snags once in a while, voice cannot have any. VoIP networks need to be more perfect than even the data engineers thought they could be; if they are not, the VoIP call quality will suffer.

VoIP NAT

Most VoIP professionals will tell you that it is really not a good idea to NAT your VoIP traffic on the network. Some problems that devices used to encounter were external IP addresses, addresses at the network layers, unroutable endpoints, and unroutable traffic behind a NAT Gateway. But with the new NGX Firewall, those problems have been fixed, and you now can NAT VoIP traffic safely and securely across your network.

Check Point offers perimeter NAT security for SIP and H.323. In the next section, we discuss the ways Check Point supports both.

SIP Support

Here are some of the ways that the NGX firewall makes it easier to NAT your VoIP network with SIP:

- Phones and computers can have static NAT or hide NAT in the internal network, external network, or DMZ.

- Incoming calls to hide computers and phones that are behind a gateway using hide NAT are supported.

- SIP-PSTN gateways with hide NAT can have an internal network, external network, or DMZ.

- SIP-PSTN gateways with static NAT can have an internal network, external network, or DMZ.

H.323 Support

Here are some of the ways that the NGX firewall makes it easier to NAT your VoIP network with H.323:

- Gatekeepers can have an external network, internal network, or DMZ using static NAT.

- Gateways/PBXes can have an external network, internal network, or DMZ using static NAT.

- Computers and phones can use static NAT.

- Computers and phones can use hide NAT.

- Incoming calls to hide NAT are supported.

- H.323-PSTN gateways can have static NAT.

- H.323-PSTN gateways can have hide NAT.

How VoIP Calls Are Made

Before you can program or install your firewall you need to understand how a VoIP phone call is made. In the next section we are going to look at the different protocols and how calls are made within each. Each protocol uses different setups and different ports on your network. It will make your job much easier if you understand how a call is set up on the network.

SIP Calls

Figure 16.1 is a simple diagram of how a SIP call is made. To make these more real-world calls, we had these diagrams refer to how a call is made on a Nortel System.

NOTE

The reason we used a Nortel VoIP example is that it was the easiest subject matter to use at the time.

Figure 16.1 Making a SIP Call

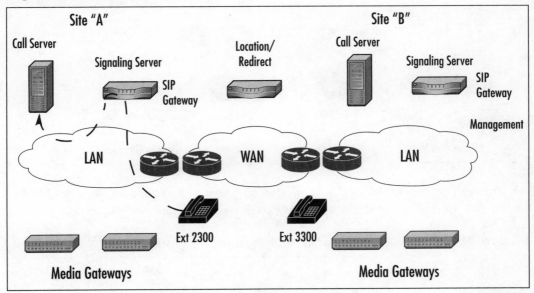

User x2300 (H.323) on site A dials User x3300 on site B. The TPS (Terminal Proxy Server) is notified of the call in progress and digits are dialed (see Figure 16.2).

Figure 16.2 The TPS Dials the Digits for a SIP Call

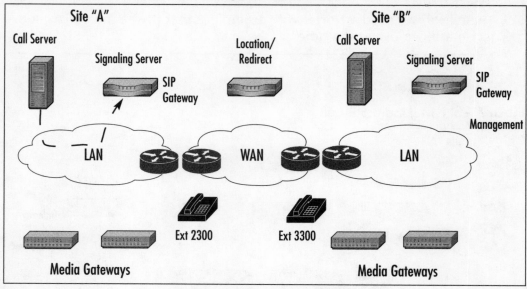

Site A determines that 3300 is at another site, selects the codec list, allocates band-width, and routes the call to the IP network via a virtual trunk (see Figure 16.3).

Figure 16.3 Site A Routes the SIP Call to an IP Network

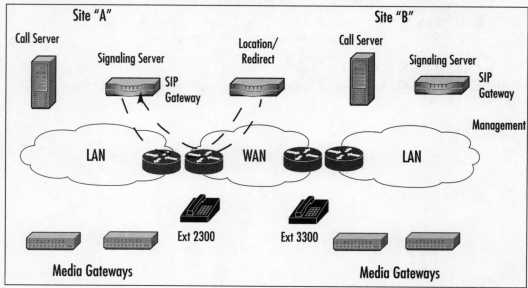

SIP gateway A requests the location redirect server. The location redirect server looks up the number, validates that the endpoint is available (*registered*), and sends the IP address of SIP gateway B to SIP gateway A (*SIP Redirect Message*), as shown in Figure 16.4.

Figure 16.4 A Redirect Message Is Sent from SIP Gateway B to SIP Gateway A

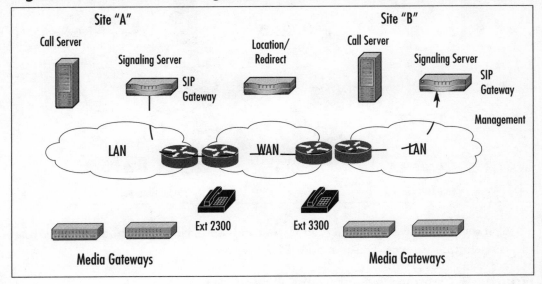

Gateway A sends the setup to gateway B, including DN (see Figure 16.5).

Figure 16.5 The Setup Is Sent from Gateway A to Gateway B

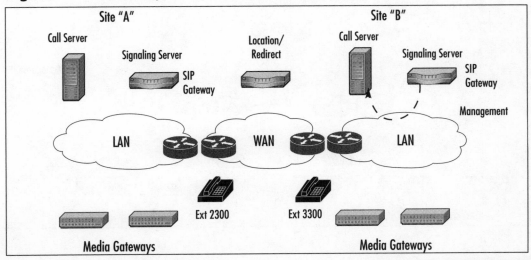

Gateway B sends the call to call server B via a virtual trunk (see Figure 16.6).

Figure 16.6 The Call Is Sent from Gateway B to Call Server B

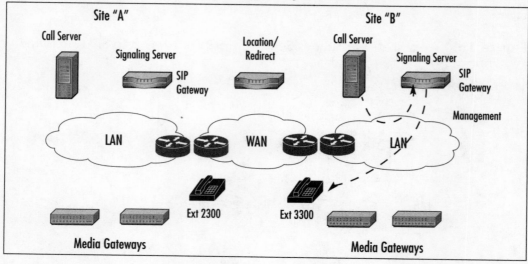

Call server B selects the codec, allocates bandwidth, rings the phone, and sends a message alerting gateway B (see Figure 16.7).

Figure 16.7 An Alert Is Sent from Call Server B to Gateway B

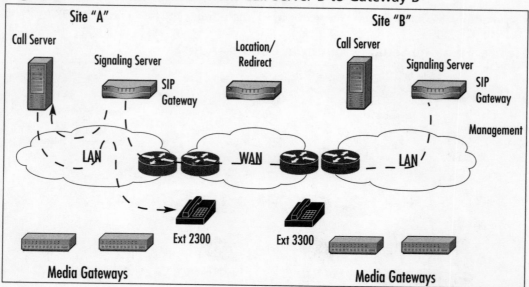

Gateway B sends an alert to gateway A, which sends it to the call server; call server A tells the IP phone to play the ringback tone (see Figure 16.8).

Figure 16.8 The Path of the Call Alert

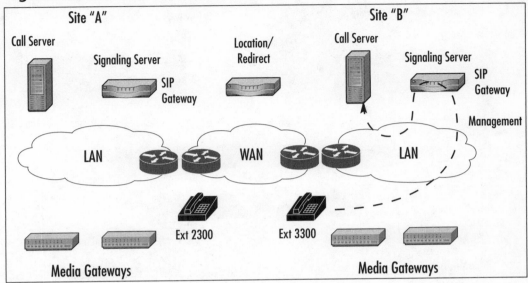

User B (ext. 3300) answers the call (see Figure 16.9).

Figure 16.9 User B Answers the Call

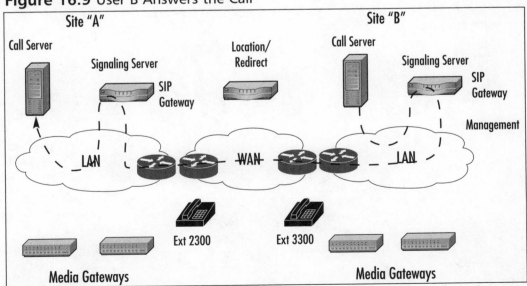

Call server B sends the connect signal to gateway B, which sends SIP connect signaling to Gateway A and call server A (see Figure 16.10).

Figure 16.10 Connect Signaling

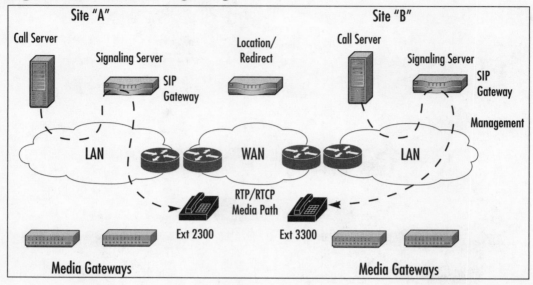

Call servers tell IP phones to start media paths (SIP 2 WAY RTP setup). Figure 16.11 is a simple diagram of how an H.323 call is made on a Nortel system.

Figure 16.11 Making an H.323 Call on a Nortel System

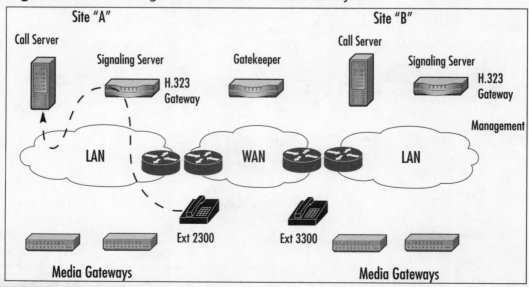

User 2300 on site A dials user 3300 on site B (see Figure 16.12).

Figure 16.12 User 2300 Dials User 3300

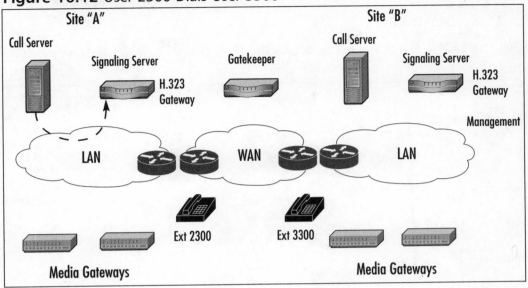

Call server A determines that 3300 is at another site, selects the codec list, allocates bandwidth, and routes the call to an IP network (see Figure 16.13).

Figure 16.13 Call Server A Routes the Call to an IP Network

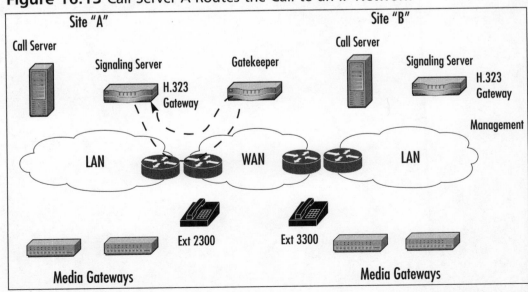

H.323 gateway A requests that the gatekeeper look up DN in the database. The gatekeeper looks up the number, validates that the endpoint is available (*registered*), and sends the IP address of H.323 gateway B to H.323 gateway A (see Figure 16.14).

Figure 16.14 The Gatekeeper Sends the IP Address of H.323 Gateway B to H.323 Gateway A

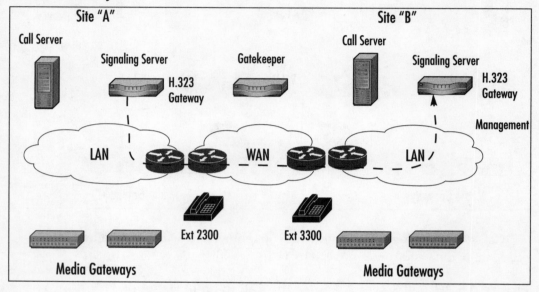

Gateway A sends the setup signal to gateway B, including DN (see Figure 16.15).

Figure 16.15 The Path of the Setup Signal

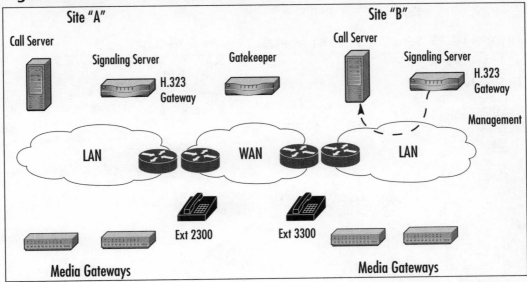

Gateway B sends the call to call server B via a virtual trunk (see Figure 16.16).

Figure 16.16 The Path of the Call from Gateway B to Call Server B

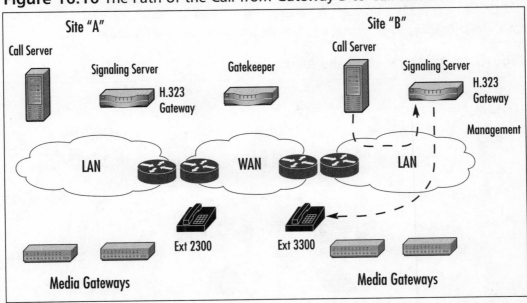

Call server B selects the codec, allocates bandwidth, rings the phone, and sends a message alerting gateway B (see Figure 16.17).

Figure 16.17 Sending an Alert from Call Server B to Gateway B

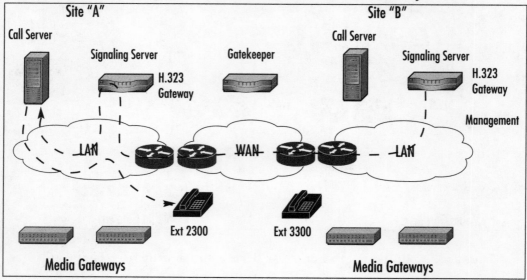

Gateway B sends a message alerting gateway A, which sends it to the call server. Call server A tells the IP phone to play the ringback tone (see Figure 16.18).

Figure 16.18 The Path of the Alert

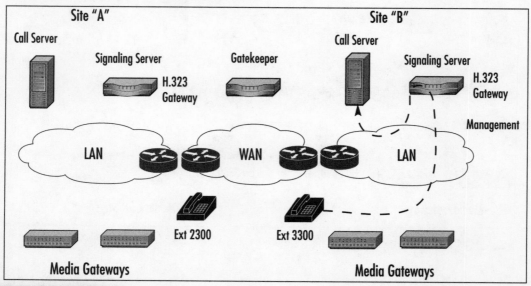

User B (ext.3300) answers the call (see Figure 16.19).

Figure 16.19 User B Answers the Phone

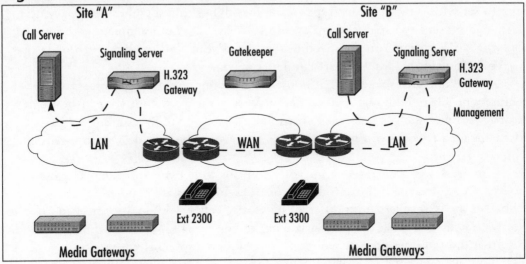

Call server B sends the connect signal to gateway B, which sends H.323 connect signaling to gateway A and call server A (see Figure 16.20).

Figure 16.20 The Path of H.323 Connect Signaling

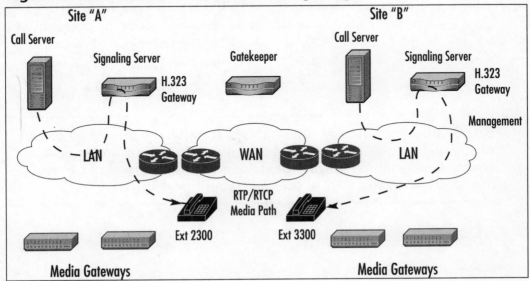

Call servers tell IP phones to start media paths.

VoIP NGX-VPN-1 Configuration

In this section we will look at how to configure your VoIP network and what policies to set within the software. One of the first things to remember before trying to tackle your security issues is to make sure you have all your architecture completed on your VoIP system. You will need to make sure your VoIP network is broken up by VoIP domains before you start configuring your firewall.

A VoIP domain is an area that houses or surrounds a group of phones and equipment. There could be many different VoIP domains within your in-house network for things such as different departments. You also will have different VoIP domains for networks you will connect to that would be outside your firewalls and internal network.

One reason you need to set up VoIP domains to networks outside your own is to make sure that the call handoff is secure. The handoffs are handled by gateways between the two callers from different networks. When you do a secure handoff, the software will verify that the person you are calling is really who you think it is, and also that the call does not get redirected or have any problems with a possible attack.

Now, we are going to look at screenshots from a sample configuration of a VoIP domain. As you can see in Figure 16.21, you can choose different types of VoIP domains. This really depends on what kind of VoIP network you would have. These would be coming from such vendors as Nortel, Cisco, and Avaya, all of which use different signaling methods.

The first type of domain we are going to look at is a SIP domain. In Figure 16.21, you right-clicked with your mouse on the left-hand side of the screen under network objects and then chose VoIP domain SIP proxy. That step took you to a configuration screen in Figure 16.22.

TIP

Before you configure the firewall, it is best to have your VoIP network configured already. Also, if you will be using IP peer networking within your network, setting up your domains ahead of time will cause less confusion when you start to configure your firewall.

Figure 16.21 A SIP Domain

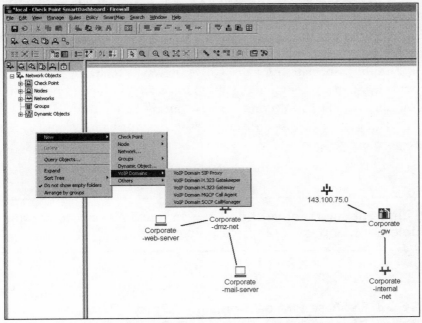

Figure 16.22 VoIP Domain SIP Proxy

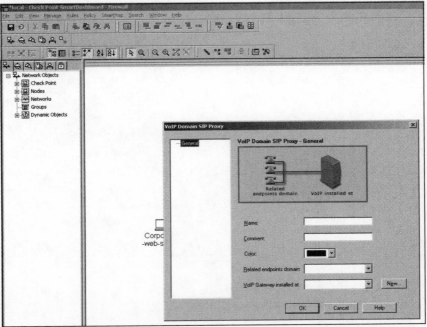

In Figure 16.22 you can see that you have only a few choices within the domain. You will need to provide a name, related domain, and VoIP gateway installed at before you can move on. The comments and the colors are optional. In Figure 16.23 you can see what it will look like in your test case.

In this case the information for the VoIP Gateway was already provided, but if it is not provided or already configured, you will need to configure one for your domain. You may do this by selecting the new button beside the VoIP gateway installed at box. Figure 16.24 is an example of what information you will need to complete your new gateway.

TIP

Use different colors for your domains to make it easier to configure, troubleshoot, and issue on the topology map.

Figure 16.23 Test Case for VoIP Domain SIP Proxy

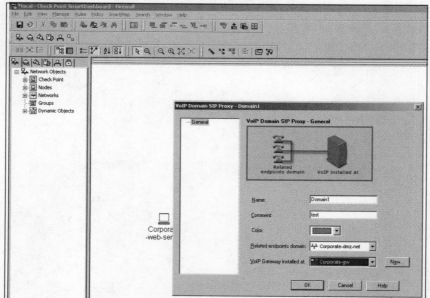

Figure 16.24 General Properties Dialog Box for a New Gateway

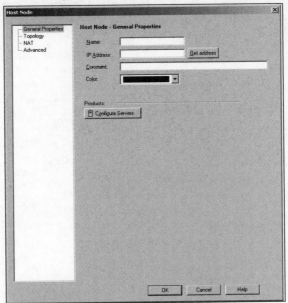

In Figure 16.25 we have filled out a section of the information for the new gateway; on this page you may also click the configure servers. These are going to be more than just VoIP gateways for other solutions. If your gateway is running in your network and has a DNS name, you may input that name and click **Get Address**. If it does not, you will need to fill in the information (see Figure 16.25).

Figure 16.25 Adding General Properties Information for a New Gateway

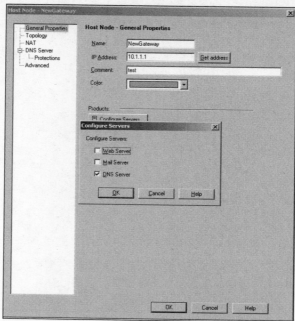

Once the general properties have been filled in, you may move to the topology, which is located on the left side of the box. As you can see in Figure 16.26, the correct interface information will need to be filled in before you move further. Once that information is inputted into the topology, you may move on to NAT feature (see Figure 16.27).

Figure 16.26 Interface Information Required to Create a New Gateway

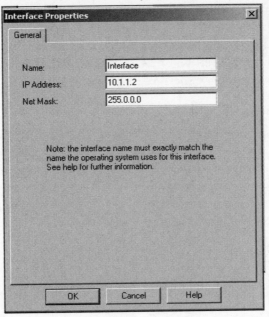

Figure 16.27 Network Address Translation Values

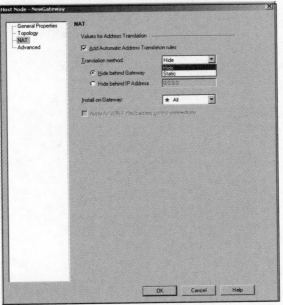

In Figure 16.27 you may choose to turn NAT on or leave if off by default. If you do choose to turn it on, you will have few different options, such as whether your NAT will be a static address or whether you will hide the address. If you decide to hide the address, you can chose to hide it either behind the gateway or behind another IP address. Then you may choose to install this on all gateways or just one that you may choose in the box (see Figure 16.28).

Figure 16.28 Installing NAT

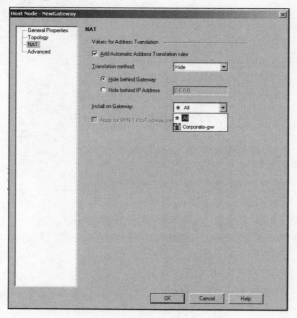

Last, in Figure 16.29 you have an Advanced tab; in this section you may input your SNMP information.

Figure 16.29 An Advanced Tab for Inputting SNMP Information

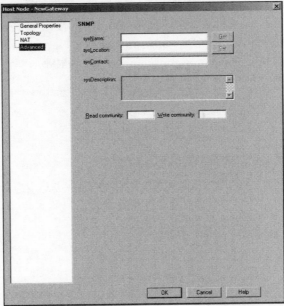

In Figure 16.30 you can see that the information is complete and your new gateway has been added to the topology map.

Figure 16.30 The New Gateway Appears on the Topology Map

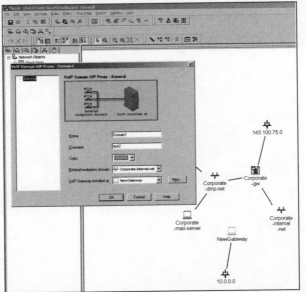

When configuring other VoIP domains such as an H.323 Gatekeeper, H.323 Gateway, MGCP Call Agent, or SCCP Call Manager, the setup for all is similar to SIP. In Figure 16.31 we will look at a gatekeeper setup. The setup for the domain is the same except for the information you can add (see Figure 16.32).

Figure 16.31 A Gatekeeper Setup

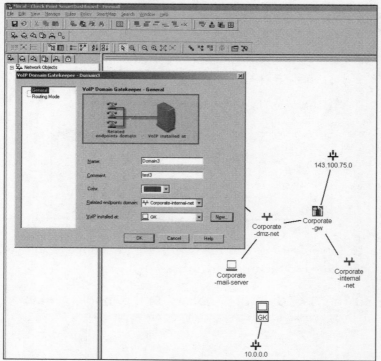

Figure 16.32 The Tab for Inputting Information for a Gatekeeper Setup

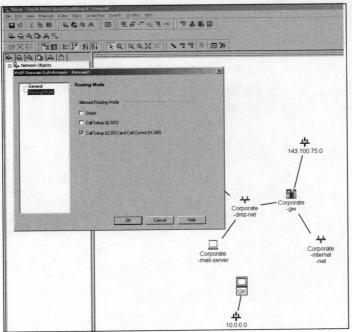

In Figure 16.32 you may choose routing options for your H.323 Gatekeeper. These options will communicate routing modes such as direct, call setup Q.931, or call setup Q.931 and call control H.245. For H.323 Gateways, the routing modes available are call setup Q.931 or call setup Q.931 and call control H.245. You can't configure the routing modes for SIP Proxies, MGCP Call Agents, or SCCP Call Managers. Figures 16.33 and 16.34 show the setup for the MGCP and SCCP, respectively.

Figure 16.33 The Setup for MGCP

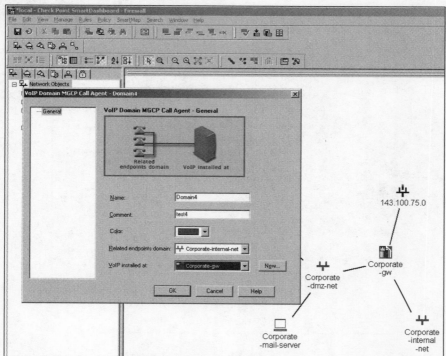

Figure 16.34 The Setup for SCCP

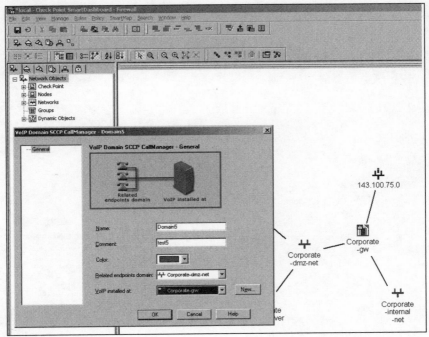

VoIP QoS Options

NGX has the option to configure QoS classes for objects in the domain. In Figure 16.35 you can see that you can choose Best Effort. This would deal with such things as maybe choosing a diffserv as your QoS parameters. Once a type is chosen, the diffserv is automatically filled in for the firewall. Using QoS on the firewall will allow a smooth transition of information that is time sensitive from one host to another.

> **TIP**
>
> If you do not understand QoS, work with your network QoS professional. You could cause more harm than good by setting up the QoS security portion incorrectly.

In Figure 16.36 the choice for your QoS class could also be low latency. These classes can be added with different priorities from 1 to 5.

Figure 16.35 QoS Classes

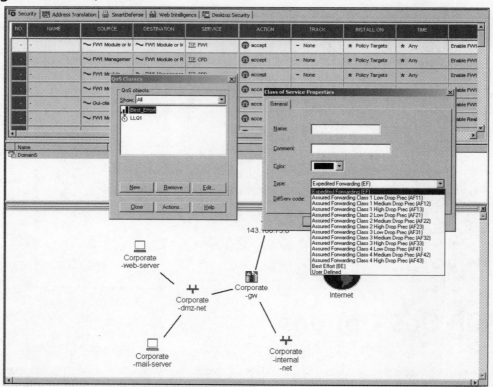

Figure 16.36 Low Latency

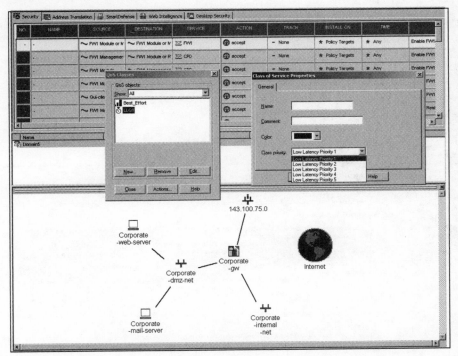

VoIP SmartDefense Options

Within SmartDefense there are many options for VoIP security. In this section we will go over them by signaling protocols. The first one that we will look at will be the tab for just VoIP, as shown in Figure 16.37. There is only one option for this page, and it is recommended that you check this box for VoIP DOS protection.

WARNING

By default these boxes are checked for a reason, which is to protect your network while you are using these different signaling protocols. If you decide to uncheck these boxes and not to use the security that is built into this system, you will leave your network open to attack.

Figure 16.37 The VoIP Tab

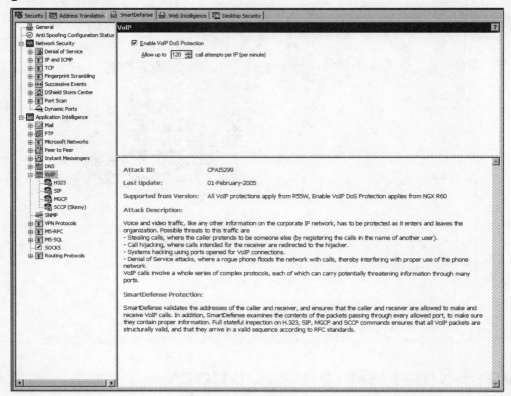

As you can see in the H.323 tab in Figure 16.38, there are six different choices for H.323 security. The recommendation would be to have all these boxes checked to provide your network with the best possible security. In Figure 16.39 eight different boxes are checked for SIP. As with all the signaling tabs, it is recommended to have all boxes checked.

Figure 16.38 The H.323 Tab

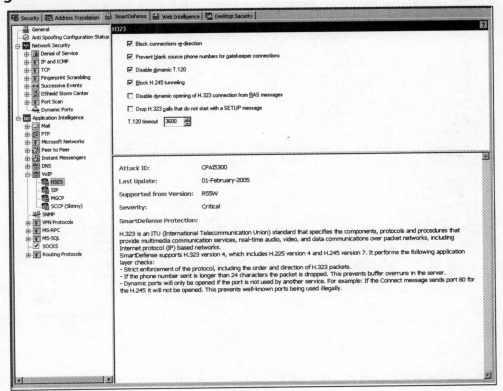

Figure 16.39 The SIP Tab

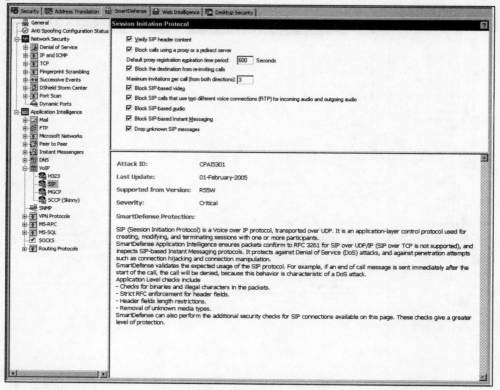

The MGCP tab is set up just a bit different from the others. The security feature for MGCP will block the default commands as you see them on the right, and also allow you to add others on the left (see Figure 16.40).

Figure 16.40 The MGCP Tab

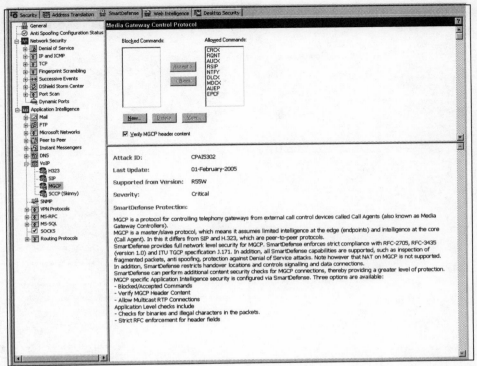

The last signaling protocol that we will look at within the SmartDefense tab is for SCCP. In Figure 16.41 you see that there are only two boxes checked for SCCP, as recommended for all of the signaling protocols.

Figure 16.41 The SCCP Tab

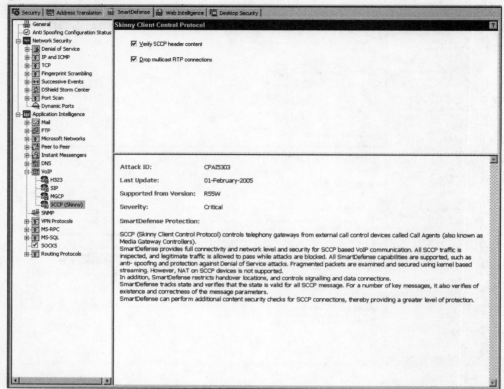

Summary

The NGX firewall provides a reliable and effective way to secure your VoIP network. Allowing the network administrator to configure and secure the VoIP network into domains securely routes all calls to the correct party by verifying the domain and address. The features that have been created in SmartDefense provide the VoIP network with a level of added security to ensure that the network has been locked down from intruders.

Solutions Fast Track

Why Secure VoIP?

- If it runs on your network you need to secure it.

- With converged networks, anyone can plug into a phone and hurt your network.

- A denial-of-service attack will cripple your VoIP faster than a data network.

VoIP Security Features

- One of the main reasons a company goes with VoIP is to put voice and data on the same network. This is the biggest cost savings feature in your ROI and possibly the most unsecured. NGX will allow you to secure your VoIP phone to stop this threat.

- Allowing your network to remain behind a locked door is a good idea; using NAT for VoIP calls has been hard in the past. But with the NGX it has been made simple and easy. You can now use NAT to hide your internal network when going to an outside domain.

- Voice quality is one of the most important features of VoIP; if it is not good, your customers will let you know. Having the correct security will prevent hackers from hurting your voice quality. The NGX firewall will prevent and help your calls be secure from one domain to the other.

How VoIP Calls Are Made

- VoIP calls can be made with different protocols such as SIP and H.323. Both these protocols go through common equipment, but with different names such as call manager and signaling server.

- A call made on a VoIP network does not go through the equipment while the call is in progress. The call is between the two IP phones using RTP and RTCP.

VoIP NGX–VPN-1 Configuration

- Have your network VoIP architecture and routing in place before you start to configure your NGX firewall. If you have your domains set up already and your IP peer networking done, configuring your firewall will be much easier.

- Configuring the correct signaling protocol on your firewall will prevent problems down the road. Just because you have a specific vendor does not mean you are using a signaling protocol that that vendor always uses. Many vendors are getting away from H.323 and using SIP.

- When configuring your VoIP domains, it is good to use different colors for different VoIP domains. Using the topology map facilitates spotting problems or locating where the VoIP domain and related equipment are on the map.

- Remember to configure your security tabs within SmartDefense. This would be for all of your signaling protocols to stop any attacks. These are checked by default, but look to be sure they are all checked.

VoIP QoS Options

- Making sure your QoS security is set up correctly to match your network QoS policy is a must. If these two are not working together, then your traffic will come to a crashing halt.

- The QoS firewall setting allows you to configure different QoS settings for different domains if needed.

- When in doubt about whether you should use different settings other than what you have in your network to prevent network lag, just play it safe and copy the settings from your network.

VoIP SmartDefense Options

- Remember to configure your security tabs within SmartDefense. This would be for all of your signaling protocols to stop any attacks. These are checked by default, but look to be sure they are all checked.

- These options will prevent possible network outages by protecting your network by default from attackers and possible viruses.

- These options should not conflict with any other applications on your network; they are meant to protect, not hinder, your network safety.

Frequently Asked Questions

The following Frequently Asked Questions, answered by the authors of this book, are designed to both measure your understanding of the concepts presented in this chapter and to assist you with real-life implementation of these concepts. To have your questions about this chapter answered by the author, browse to **www.syngress.com/solutions** and click on the **"Ask the Author"** form.

Q: Why do I need a new firewall to use on my VoIP network if I have routers with security features on them now?

A: New firewalls allow the ports used in VoIP to be dynamically opened and closed to ensure security on the VoIP network. Also the level of security for VoIP attacks is addressed within the firewall and each VoIP domain.

Q: Why do I have to configure QoS on my firewall?

A: It is very vital that the QoS policy on the firewall matches that of the network QoS policy. If they do not match, then traffic will not be able to flow from the firewall to the network correctly.

Q: Should I be worried about the extra Ethernet port on a VoIP phone in my network?

A: Yes, you should be worried that it is there; it is an entry point into your network. No matter how much you think a VLAN and a switch will save you in case of a security breach or DOS attack on that port, they will not. You need much more than that to snuff out possible attacks to your network because once attackers get past the switch, the only thing left to protect your network is a firewall.

Q: Do I really have to worry about delay on the network with a VoIP phone?

A: Voice systems do not react well to delay; a data system can cache and resend the data and have no problems. When you get delay on a voice network, you will get jitter and gaps in speech. You will hear bits and pieces of the conversation and not hear every word.

Q: Is one protocol more secure than the others?

A: Not really, and it should not influence a decision on a certain type of VoIP system. It is all in how you set up the system and how it is secured in the network.

Q: If someone is using a soft phone to make a call on the Internet, can they be interfered with by a hacker?

A: Yes, they can, and it is always a good plan for anyone using a company VoIP soft phone to be on a corporate VPN system to protect the voice and data stream from potential hackers.

Q: Should the firewall be the main priority piece of security in my VoIP network?

A: No, the firewall, like other pieces of equipment and policies in place, are just part of an overall corporate security strategy. VoIP security, like regular data security, should fit in and have a place in your network to run correctly.

Index

Symbols

* wildcard character, 560, 568
@ sign, 299

A

abnormal behavior analysis, 201, 207, 231
Accept Outgoing packets originating from
    Gateway option, 109
access control
    configuring, 261
    port translation and, 264
ACLs (access control lists), Office mode
    and, 441–447
activation key, 59, 72
    configuring for SIC, 502
Active Streaming, 208
Active view (SmartView Tracker), 154,
    163–165, 170, 175, 177
Activity Log (Eventia Reporter), 547
Activity Queue tab (Eventia Reporter), 547
Address Resolution Protocol. *See* ARP
Address Translation tab (SmartDashboard),
    102
administrator accounts, 106
    converting definitions for, 505
    creating, 119
Administrator Groups, 280
administrators, 273–292, 332
    defining for SmartCenter, 63, 505
    managing, 273–275, 278–280
    threats and, 191
    unique usernames for, 170
agent automatic authentication, 321
AI. *See* Application Intelligence
alerts, 168–170, 550–552
    defining thresholds for, 550
Allow bidirectional NAT setting (global
    properties), 237, 266
always-on tunnels, 30, 42
antivirus scanning, 340, 397
    FireWall-1 and, 338, 340, 397
Application-Derived State, 9, 17
Application Intelligence (AI), 4, 199–214,
    228

OSI model and, 231
Web Intelligence and, 209
application layer (OSI model), 196, 231
application layer gateways, 4, 7–9, 16
    advantages/disadvantages of, 8
    on FireWall-1. *See* Security Servers
application vulnerability, SmartDefense and,
    25
applications, 106
Apply Rule Only if Desktop Configuration
    Options Are Verified property (client
    authentication), 315
ARP (Address Resolution Protocol),
    248–251, 269
    documenting before upgrading to NGX,
    80
    Merge manual proxy ARP configuration
    setting and, 238
ARP entries, 238, 249, 267, 268
asymmetric encryption, 363
attachment downloads, user authentication
    and, 303
attacks, 42
    system counters and, 559, 565
    types of defended by SmartDefense, 25
Audit Log (SmartPortal), 139
Audit Records pane (SmartView Tracker),
    170
Audit view (SmartView Tracker), 155, 170,
    175, 178, 397
auditing, Eventia Reporter for, 27–29
authenticated services, 293, 320, 332
authentication, 271–335.
    failed, 324, 325
    global properties for, 324
    password, 402
    SecuRemote, 423
    successful, 321
    two-factor, 23
    See also client authentication; session
        authentication; user authentication
authentication banner (default), eliminating,
    301
authentication request message (Check
    Point NGX), changing, 301

N

O

Syngress: *The Definition of a Serious Security Library*

Syn·gress (sin–gres): *noun, sing.* Freedom from risk or danger; safety. See *security*.